AFRICAN STRATEGIES FOR THE NUCLEAR AGE

AMERICAN STRATEGY FOR THE NUCLEAR AGE

AMERICAN STRATEGY
FOR THE
NUCLEAR AGE

Walter F. Hahn and John C. Neff, Editors

Anchor Books
Doubleday & Company, Inc.
Garden City, New York

COVER . DESIGN . BY . PETER . PIENNING
TYPOGRAPHY BY SUSAN SIEN

E
744
H25

WALTER F. HAHN is executive editor of *Orbis*, a quarterly journal of world affairs published by the Foreign Policy Research Institute of the University of Pennsylvania, and a research assistant of the Institute. A graduate of Temple University, where he also received an M.A. degree, he is a frequent contributor to magazines and journals, including the *New Leader* and the *Yale Review*. Mr. Hahn assisted in the preparation of the curriculum for the first National Strategy Seminar for Reserve Officers, held at the National War College in Washington, D.C., 1959.

JOHN C. NEFF, Colonel, United States Army Reserve, is Chief of Staff of the 77th Infantry Division, located in New York City, one of six combat divisions in the Army Reserve. A veteran of five campaigns in the European Theater during World War II, he served in the Intelligence Section of the 83d Infantry Division. A graduate of Kenyon College in 1936, he has published articles, book reviews, and stories in the *New Mexico Quarterly Review*, the *Infantry Journal*, the *Army Information Digest*, the Sunday New York *Times Book Review*, and *Collier's*.

TABLE OF CONTENTS

FOREWORD, *by the Editors*   xvii

PROLOGUE: The Delusion of Appeasement, *by Briga-
    dier General Donald Armstrong, U.S.A. (Ret.)*   xxi

PART ONE—THE MID-CENTURY STAGE

Introduction   1

1. Basic Aims of United States Foreign Policy, *by
    Council on Foreign Relations*   3
    *The Impact of the World Wars—The Postwar Di-
    lemmas—The Cold War—The Configuration of the
    Globe—The Spectrum of Conflict—The Changing
    International Environment—The Role of the United
    States—The Burdens of Leadership*

2. The Protracted Conflict, *by Robert Strausz-Hupé*   16
    *The Systemic Revolution—The Present Paradox—
    The Scavengers of Revolution—The Policies of
    Lenin and Stalin—Containment and the Commu-
    nists' Tactical Shift—A Dialectical Theory of Con-
    flict—Implications of Russia's Technological Leap—
    The Battleground of the "Gray Areas"—Toward an
    Understanding of the Conflict*

3. Can We Survive Technology? *by John von
    Neumann*   32
    *Dangers, Present and Coming—When Reactors
    Grow Up—"Alchemy" and Automation—Controlled
    Climate—The Indifferent Controls—Science, the In-
    divisible—Awful and More Awful*

4. The Diminishing Freedom of Choice, *by Robert
    Strausz-Hupé*   42
    *Means, Timing, and Self-Defense—The Emerging
    One-Way Street of Diplomacy—Postwar Capabili-
    ties—The Shift in the Power Balance—Preventive*

War and Total Conflict—Can We Recapture the Initiative?

PART TWO—COMMUNISM: ITS NATURE, STRENGTHS,
            AND WEAKNESSES

Introduction   53

5. The Ideological Core of Communism, *by Gerhart
    Niemeyer*   55
    *The Ideological Origins of Communism—The Bour-
    geois-Proletarian Polarity—Phases of Historical De-
    velopment—The Basic Legacy of Marx—Lenin's
    Addenda—The Myth of the Revolution—The Role
    of the Party—The Doctrine of the Two Revolutions
    —The Role of the State—The Place of the Soviet
    Union—The Power of Ideology*

6. The Appeals of Communism, *by J. Edgar Hoover*   70
    *Economic Appeals—Sociological Appeals—Politi-
    cal Appeals—Psychological Appeals—A Tarnished
    Image*

7. Whither Soviet Evolution? *by Vladimir Petrov*   75
    *Organization of Soviet Society—Is Democracy Pos-
    sible in Russia?—Government versus Party Controls
    —The Illusion of Freedom in Russia*

8. Communist Vulnerabilities, *by Bertram D. Wolfe*   89
    *The Theoretical Foundation: Marxism—The Su-
    premacy of Politics over Economics—Marxism as
    an "Ism"—The Strategy and Tactics of Leninism—
    The Russian Revolution, Promise and Performance*

PART THREE—COMMUNIST STRATEGY AND TACTICS

Introduction   103

9. The Orchestration of Crisis, *by Colonel William R.
    Kintner, U.S.A.*   105
    *The Strategy of Protracted Conflict—Examples of
    Piecemeal Strategy—Contrasting Concepts of War
    and Peace—The Undesirable Status Quo—The War
    of Attrition—Ethics-in-Reverse Concept of Conflict
    —The Instruments of Terror*

10. The Larger Strategic Vision, *by Alvin J. Cottrell and James E. Dougherty*   117
   The Globe as a Battlefield—The Interchangeability of Military and Political Instruments—The Ebb and Flow of the Revolutionary Tide—Exploiting the Colonial Struggle—Military Conflict for Political Objectives—Soviet Controlled Warfare—The Larger Dimensions of Conflict

11. Communist Psychological Warfare, *by Stefan T. Possony*   129
   The Conditioned Reflex—The Use of Freud's Theories—The Psychoanalytic Interview—Hypnosis and Suggestion—Communism and Religion—Communist Sociological Assumptions—Communist Crowd Psychology

12. Soviet Strategy of Disarmament, *by Thomas W. Wolfe*   139
   Preferred Strategy and Dictates of Reality—Just and Unjust Wars—Avoidance of Frontal Military Encounter—Dual Approach to the Power Struggle—Soviet Proposals of Full and Partial Disarmament—Will Soviet Disarmament Strategy Change?

13. Changes in Soviet Conflict Doctrine, *by Anne M. Jonas*   152
   Khrushchev's Strategic Innovations—The Role of Nuclear Weapons—The Role of Peaceful Revolution—Paralyzing the Will of the West—The Role of War—Initiation of War—The Search for a Strategic Synthesis

PART FOUR—PROBLEMS OF MILITARY STRATEGY

Introduction   169

14. Values, Power, and Strategy, *by Richard B. Foster*
   The Power of Nuclear Weapons and Fundamental Values—Polarity of Power and Formulation of Strategy—Planning and Uncertainty—Relative Advantages in the Balance of Power—Power, Value, and National Resolve—Value Considerations Re-

    *lated to Strategic Problems—Your and My Respon-
    sibility*

15. Strategy on Trial, *by John F. Loosbrock*   188
    *The Margin of Deterrence—Survival and Penetra-
    tion—The Idea of Mutual Invulnerability—Con-
    trolled Peace*

16. The Delicate Balance of Terror, *by Albert
       Wohlstetter*   197
    *The Presumed Automatic Balance—The Quantita-
    tive Nature of the Problem and the Uncertainties—
    The Delicacy of the Balance of Terror—The Uses
    and Risks of Bases Close to the Soviets—Summary*

17. The Nature and Feasibility of War and Deter-
       rence, *by Herman Kahn*   219
    *Damage versus Commitments—Type 1 Deterrence
    (Deterrence against a Direct Attack)—Type 2 De-
    terrence (Deterrence of Extreme Provocation)—
    Type 3 Deterrence (Deterrence of Moderate Prov-
    ocation)*

18. The Lead-Time Problem and Technological
       Waste, *by Ellis Johnson*   238
    *The Cost Factor—The Effect of Lead Times and
    Obsolescence Policy—The Dilemma of the Opti-
    mum—Effect on Military-Economic Competition—
    The Cumbersome Industrial-Military System—How
    Security Regulations Can Increase Lead Time—
    Forgotten Lessons of World War II*

19. Limited War, *by Hanson W. Baldwin*   249
    *What Is "Limited" War?—Can Wars Be Kept from
    Spreading?—The Need for Clear Objectives Clearly
    Defined—Nuclear Bombs Mean Total War—Clean
    and Dirty Bombs—Radioactivity and Small Weap-
    ons—Nuclear War in Europe—Quemoy and the Nu-
    clear Threat—Nuclear Bombing and Asian Opinion
    —Ability to Fight Is Our Best Defense*

20. Needed: A New NATO Shield, *by Alvin J. Cot-
       trell and Walter F. Hahn*   268
    *The Strategic Requirements of the United States
    and Western Europe—The Alternative of Reliance*

on Tactical Nuclear Weapons—The Alternative of
Disengagement—The Alternative of "Nuclearizing"
Our NATO Allies—A Dual Capability

21. Security through Sea Power, *by Commander
Ralph E. Williams, Jr., U.S.N.*   287
*Weapons' Cost—Strategy of the 1950s—The Dan-
ger of a Fortress America Strategy—The Advan-
tages of a Sea-Based Deterrent—A Comprehensive
Military Posture*

22. Unconventional Warfare, *by James D. Atkinson*   301
*Unconventional Warfare as a Modern Phenomenon
—Communist Propaganda—Espionage and Subversion—Economic Warfare—Guerrilla Warfare—Political Warfare—Summary*

23. Disarmament: Illusion and Reality, *by Henry A.
Kissinger*   313
*The Vicious Circle of Armaments—The Technologi-
cal Problems—Inspection and Control—"Preventing" Surprise Attack—The Chimera of an International Authority*

24. The Strategic Role of Civil Defense, *by Rogers
Cannell*   326
*Nonmilitary Protection in Total War—The Cost of
Protection—The Objective of a Civil-Defense Pro-
gram—Civilization Can Recover—Recovery from
Total War*

PART FIVE—PROBLEMS OF ECONOMIC STRATEGY

Introduction   337

25. The Economic Threat of Soviet Imperialism, *by
Lieutenant General Arthur G. Trudeau, U.S.A.*   339
*Steel and Petroleum Production—The Soviet Labor
Force—The Soviet Industrial Surge—Comparative
Trade Positions—Economics as a Controlled Soviet
Weapon—The Gross-National-Product—Debt Ratio
—Increasing Our Growth Rate—Pressing Our Eco-
nomic Advantages*

26. Soviet Economic Growth and United States Policy,
by Howard C. Petersen   351

*Ways in Which Soviet Economic Expansion May
Affect Us—Military Strength—Aid and Trade with
Underdeveloped Countries—Attitudes of Peoples
Throughout the World—Implication for U.S. Policy
—A Competition of Systems, Not of Growth Rates
—Our Untapped Economic Resource*

27. The Stages of Economic Growth, *by Walt W.
      Rostow*   365
      *The Stages in History—The Stages Today—The
      Conditions of Aid—Many Roads to Growth*

28. Military or Economic Aid: Questions of Priority,
      by Arnold Wolfers   375
      *Labels versus Purpose—Short-Run Defense Needs
      —External versus Internal Defense—Stability Aid:
      Military and Economic—Economic-Development
      Aid*

29. Private Enterprise: America's Best Export, *by
      Robert L. Garner*   388
      *The Stakes in the Underdeveloped World—
      The Fallacy of Rapid and Massive Development
      Schemes—The Characteristics of Underdeveloped
      Areas—The Shortcomings of Government Assist-
      ance—The Merits of Private Investment—Some
      Concrete Measures*

30. The Defense We Can Afford, *by James F.
      Brownlee*   398
      *Threats We Face—The Problem of Choice—The
      Health of Our Economy*

PART SIX—RESPONSES TO THE CHALLENGE

Introduction   407

31. The Premises of American Policy, *by Dean G.
      Acheson*   409
      *The Requirement of Western Unity—Selectivity in
      Assistance Programs—The Requirements of Mili-
      tary Security—The Chimera of a "Moral" Solution*

32. A Political Offensive against Communism, *by David Sarnoff*   422
Our Counterstrategy—The Enemy Is Vulnerable—Guidelines for Political Offensive—The Message of Freedom—Toward Cold-War Victory: Organization — Financing — Implementing the Counteroffensive — Propaganda — Communist Targets — Free World Targets—Use of Facilities in Friendly Countries—Passive Resistance—Organized Resistance—Collaboration with Emigrés and Escapees—Planned Defection—Training of Cadres—Diplomacy Is a Weapon

33. What Is to Be Done? *by Frank Rockwell Barnett*   440
The Lead Time of Survival—Students of Strategy — Where Our Opportunities Lie — The Fourth Weapon: Psychopolitical Forces—Citizen Experts in Political Warfare—Proposal: A Dynamic History of the American Experiment—Proposal: A Propaganda-Analysis Newsletter — Proposal: Business Training for Overseas Community Relations—The "Ultimate Weapon"

EDITORS' NOTE

This book is published under the auspices of the Institute for American Strategy, 140 South Dearborn Street, Chicago 3, Illinois. The Institute is a voluntary, tax-exempt, educational entity, organized by private citizens to widen public understanding of U.S. strategic problems in a world threatened by Soviet military, scientific, and industrial might, combined with Communist techniques in propaganda, subversion, insurrection, and economic and psychological warfare. The Institute is nonprofit and nonpartisan. Its directors are eminent educators, businessmen, and retired senior officers. The current chairman of its Executive Committee is Mr. Edwin A. Locke, Jr., President, Union Tank Car Company. Its executive director is Mr. Dan Sullivan, of the Armour Research Foundation of the Illinois Institute of Technology. The Institute organizes the annual National Military-Industrial Conference in Chicago and sponsors Strategy Seminars in various parts of the country.

The Foreign Policy Research Institute of the University of Pennsylvania, under whose direction this book was prepared, was established in February 1955. Its task is to submit fundamental and long-range problems in U.S. foreign policy to disciplined examination by men and women selected on the basis of intellectual achievement and practical experience in international relations. The research product of the Institute is designed to provide imaginative and constructive concepts on vital issues which will confront the United States for many years to come.

The Institute, directed by Dr. Robert Strausz-Hupé, is a nonprofit and tax-exempt organization. It is supported largely by research grants by private foundations to the trustees of the university. The Richardson Foundation, Inc., of Greensboro, North Carolina, and New York, made the initial grant establishing the Institute. Subsequent grants of this and five other foundations have contributed toward the financing of operating costs and special projects. Some research is also conducted under contract with agencies of the U. S. Government.

Three broad areas of research make up the total field of the Institute's activities: the world-wide Communist movement; the systemic revolution in the underdeveloped world; and the Western alliance. The Institute relates its research in each area to the problems of decision making created by the organization of the federal government, the difficulties of operating a peacetime alliance, and the evolution of the pattern of international organizations.

One hundred years ago, national strategy was the exclusive concern of only a few men, all at the top echelons of government. Today, the conflict we are engaged in is total, its strategy is total, it involves every facet of society and is the concern of everyone in the Free World. The fundamental question before mankind today is this: Will the globe be dominated by communism or will it, in its diverse ways, achieve freedom? In brief, the formulation of national strategy has become the urgent concern of everyone.

Today, at the beginning of the second half of the twentieth century, communism has made some notable advances. So far, the Communist leaders have understood better than the leaders of the West the revolutionary character of our times. Only an informed public can and will muster the energy and determination needed to win this global struggle and to master the forces designed to defeat not only freedom but civilization itself.

What is the changed global environment in which we find ourselves today? What is the nature of our enemy—his strengths, weaknesses, strategy and tactics? What is the scope of the military challenges confronting us? What are the economic policies by which we can meet the challenges? Finally, what are some of the specific courses of action which should be taken if we are to win the struggle?

This book attempts to answer these and other questions. It is an outgrowth of the first National Strategy Seminar for Reserve Officers, held at the National War College, Washington, D.C., in July 1959. It contains edited versions of many of the addresses presented there as well as the writings of other authorities which have appeared in various magazines, journals, and books during the past few years. The majority of the contributions are presented in book form for the first time. The editors do not presume to consider this volume of readings definitive. Admittedly there are many other writings which could have been included. But within the space available, the editors have tried to present a comprehensive account of as many aspects of the Free World's struggle against communism as possible.

The Seminar mentioned above was held under the authority of the Joint Chiefs of Staff and was attended by two hundred and eighteen carefully selected reserve officers, representing all branches of the armed services as well as the fifty states and Puerto Rico. Participating organizations were the Institute for American Strategy, the Foreign Policy Research Institute of the University of Pennsylvania, the Reserve Officers Association. The Richardson Foundation, Inc., of New York City, made available the funds needed to develop the curriculum. It was addressed by more than fifty speakers distinguished by their understanding of the many aspects of the conflict between the Communist world and the Free World.

The student body of the Seminar included two governors, three congressmen, seventy educators, and more than forty men in the newspaper, publishing, radio, television, and writing fields. The Seminar was designed to provide a better understanding of the cold war, of the organization, resources, and methods used by the Communists in their drive to dominate the world, and to develop programs for creating the resolute, informed, and vocal public opinion without which the contest cannot be won.

The Seminar provoked a chain reaction of conferences across the country which continues to this day. Two seminars were conducted in New York City—one for officers of the Regular and Reserve forces, another for business and industrial leaders. In April 1960 the Stanford Research Institute, in co-operation with the U. S. Sixth Army, conducted a seminar for 500 reserve officers at Asilomar, California. In Chicago, Cleveland, New Orleans, and Wilmington, Delaware, seminars were held for business, industrial, financial, and educational leaders. Conferences have also been conducted in California, Massachusetts, Texas, and Washington, D.C. Tens of thousands of Americans have thereby become better equipped to understand and to cope with the problems of national strategy.

This volume could not have been prepared without the permission of copyright owners to use their materials. For their generous co-operation the editors are indebted. The editors also wish to thank the staff and associates of the Foreign Policy Research Institute of the University of Pennsylvania for their assistance in the selection and preparation of many of the chapters which follow. Particular debts of gratitude are given to the following: Dr. Robert Strausz-Hupé, director, Dr. William R. Kintner, deputy director, and Drs. Alvin J. Cottrell, James E. Dougherty, and Mr. Robert C. Herber, research assistants of the Foreign Policy Research Institute; Mr. Frank R. Barnett, director of research of the Richardson Foundation, Inc.; Brigadier General Donald Armstrong, U.S.A. (Ret.); Rear Admiral Chester Ward, The Judge Advocate General, Department of the Navy; Inspector William C. Sullivan, the Federal Bureau of Investigation; and officers of the Army, Navy, Air Force, and of the Joint Chiefs of Staff responsible for service information and education programs. The editors are especially grateful for the assistance of these three people in the task of proofreading: Marjorie Barnett, Barbara Mitchell, and Robert E. Maxwell. Finally, the editors thank the directors of the Institute for American Strategy, who authorized the publication of this book, and the Donner Foundation, whose generosity made it possible.

May 2, 1960   WALTER F. HAHN
                                                COLONEL JOHN C. NEFF, U.S.A.R.

PROLOGUE

The Delusion of Appeasement

History's verdict on appeasement is unmistakable: it simply does not pay. It has been tried many times. It has been the refuge of the weaker, less virile, less courageous nation in many a struggle for survival. Inevitably each act of appeasement has made the aggressor stronger and the appeaser relatively weaker. It has usually made war a certainty rather than preserved the peace.

A striking case history of the failure of what must be one of the most abject appeasements on record should be a salutary warning to the Free World today. Moreover, the circumstances of the conflict for mastery of the Mediterranean world twenty-one centuries ago were analogous to the wider world struggle of our own times. Change the names of the protagonists in this sentence from Polybius, the Greek historian in the employ of Rome, and the conclusion must be reached that there is nothing new under the sun: "The Carthaginians were fighting for their own security and the dominion of Africa, and the Romans for the empire of the world."

When our story begins, Rome and Carthage were nearing the end of more than a hundred years of cold and hot warfare. In 149 B.C. the Carthaginians faced a dilemma. Should they "expose their country to war and its terrors, or, not daring to face the attack of the enemy, yield unresistingly to every

Appeared originally as the Foreword to the Summer 1959 issue of World Affairs, *published by the American Peace Society (founded in 1828), Washington, D.C. Reprinted by permission.*

demand"? This same question is being asked in some quarters today. The Carthaginians chose the latter course. What did it profit them to submit to the cynical, ruthless, and arrogant demands of their enemy? They must have known that Cato, like Hitler and the Communist conspiracy, had made no secret of Roman objectives. "Carthage must be destroyed," Cato thundered in the Roman Senate. Let us now examine the valuable assistance the Carthaginians themselves gave the Romans in achieving their own defeat.

The Romans began their negotiations with a demand for 300 children of their noblest families as hostages. If they complied and promised "to obey their orders in other respects, the freedom and autonomy of Carthage would be preserved." So double talk is no new invention, as the event shows. For the Carthaginians complied amid the wailing and lamentations of the bereaved mothers, many of whom, Appian tells us, predicted with rare prescience "that it would profit the city nothing to have delivered up their children."

The next demand came in no time at all. "If you are sincerely desirous of peace, why do you need any arms? Come, surrender to us all your weapons and engines of war, both public and private." Again, the Carthaginians complied, and Appian reports that complete armor for 200,000 men, innumerable javelins, and about 2000 catapults together with the ships of their navy were collected and delivered to the Romans. Then came the ultimatum which was delivered with unparalleled cynicism and arrogance, of which the following excerpt gives only the faintest inkling:

"Bear bravely the remaining command of the Senate. Yield Carthage to us, and betake yourselves where you like within your own territory at a distance of at least ten miles from the sea, for we are resolved to raze your city to the ground." In spite of every effort made by the Carthaginian ambassadors, the Romans refused to soften their ultimatum. When the news reached Carthage there was consternation and a "scene of blind, raving madness." This is not surprising. Carthage, the late dominant sea power, whose livelihood was gained on the waters of the Mediterranean, was ordered to permit the destruction of her city and give up her commerce. In their desperation, the Carthaginians, in spite of having no weapons, declared war, and for three years, with improvised weapons, resisted the siege of their city. The odds were too great, however, and Carthage was finally taken. The comparatively few survivors who did not commit suicide were sold into slavery.

Now, the Romans were, they claimed, peace-loving aggressors. No more than Hitler did they desire war for war's sake. Like all actual or would-be conquerors, before or since, the Romans preferred to get what they wanted without having to fight, and the dove of peace was a convenient symbol for the unwary then as now. And successive demands for concessions and surrender of one thing after another to reduce the will and the ability to fight was one of their most effective tools of aggression.

The Carthage of those days, on one of the world's most magnificent sites, has disappeared completely from the face of the earth. No atomic-bomb attack could obliterate more absolutely any modern city of half a million inhabitants. The epitaph for the city-state of Carthage might well be a warning: "Put not your trust in appeasement."

DONALD ARMSTRONG

Brigadier General, U.S.A. (Ret.), Commandant of the first National Strategy Seminar for Reserve Officers, and former Commandant, Industrial College of the Armed Forces.

PART ONE

THE MID-CENTURY STAGE

INTRODUCTION

In the sweep of the past half century, powerful forces have shattered the retaining walls of the state system and are beating against the last defenses of traditional international society.

One of these forces is the "systemic revolution"—a historic phenomenon which attends the breakdown of an old order and the ensuing quest for a new equilibrium. Another is the technological revolution, which has radically transfigured the globe and broadened the stakes of conflict from "mere" victory or defeat to the survival of civilization itself. In this revolutionary environment, two systems vie for ascendancy. They are locked in a conflict which is protracted in time and ubiquitous in space.

As the late John von Neumann suggests, the velocity of technological change is such that we are literally running out of room. Robert Strausz-Hupé contends that the range of our foreign policy is being similarly constricted. Is it the irony of our times that we are rapidly becoming the helpless prisoners of the very forces which we ourselves set in motion?

1. Basic Aims of United States Foreign Policy

by Council on Foreign Relations

The following chapter is a reproduction of the first portion of a report submitted to the Committee on Foreign Relations, U. S. Senate, by an ad hoc group meeting under the auspices of the Council on Foreign Relations, and published by the U. S. Government Printing Office as Report No. 7, November 25, 1959. The report reflects the group's general thinking but does not represent unanimous agreement on all points. Members participating in the discussion were: Frank Altschul, Hamilton Fish Armstrong, Elliott V. Bell, Adolf A. Berle, Jr., Robert Blum, Robert R. Bowie, Harlan Cleveland, John Cowles, Arthur H. Dean, John Sloan Dickey, Thomas K. Finletter, William C. Foster, W. Averell Harriman, Philip C. Jessup, Joseph E. Johnson, G. A. Lincoln, Henry R. Luce, James A. Perkins, I. I. Rabi, Herman B. Wells, and Henry M. Wriston (chairman).

The Council on Foreign Relations is a nonprofit institution devoted to the study of the problems of foreign policy with emphasis on long-range problems. Through various publications (including the world-renowned quarterly Foreign Affairs) and small off-the-record meetings, it seeks to help members in positions of leadership and others throughout the nation to enlarge their understanding of the problems of U.S. foreign policy.

During the nineteenth century the basic aims of the American nation, which are best expressed in the preamble of the Constitution, were shaped by its geographical position on what had been a virtually empty continent, by its urge for rapid growth, by the nature of its free institutions, and by a sense of destiny and of difference from the Old World. Its foreign policy was directed largely to insuring the nation's ability to grow in freedom and to carry through its expansion to the Pacific. Two historic policies supported that basic purpose: the policy, embodied in the Monroe Doctrine, of preventing non-American powers from establishing themselves in the Western Hemisphere, and the concomitant avoidance of involvement in the alliances and conflicts of the great powers of Europe.

Although insulated by geography and by these policies from the politics and wars of the major powers, the United States was no hermit state. It was a part of the Western world, of the international community of that time. It stood for freedom of the seas, the free exchange of ideas, and freedom for its citizens to trade and to do business abroad without discrimination. It stood for respect for international obligations and the promotion of peace through techniques of negotiation, arbitration, and judicial settlement. It stood also—and this made the United States a revolutionary influence in the world of that time—for the right of all peoples to national and individual freedom, a principle which has remained ever since a salient element of America's attitude toward the world.

Foreign policy in practice, of course, rarely corresponds fully to broad statements of aim and principle, for it must be based also on calculations of national interest in the specific circumstances in which decisions are made and actions taken. American concern for the cause of freedom abroad was an aspiration which colored national attitudes rather than a concrete objective engaging the nation on behalf of popular revolutions all over the world. Nevertheless, the example of America as a working democracy served as a symbol of freedom, and the boldness of its declared position unquestionably exerted a significant moral and even political influence beyond its borders. Thus, when the United States came onto the world stage in the First World War and in the peace settlement rest of the world cannot be indifferent. Political stability has been hard to achieve, as the exercise of self-government proved a more complex task than the attainment of it. The working out of new relationships with the industrial countries has been a particularly difficult process on both sides. Attitudes stemming from the past relationship of dependence did not easily disappear, especially at a time when Communist powers were making strong and not unsuccessful efforts to extend their influence into these areas. Endeavors of the United States to establish a basis of co-operation with the Asian and African nations have been complicated by its association with the former colonial powers, by local conflicts such as the strife over Palestine, and by wide differences of view on the nature of the Communist threat and what to do about it.

Latin America, although outside the main theaters of the cold war, has been beset by political and economic instability and by the problems of adapting its institutions to rapid social change. It is apparent that the attitudes and policies of the United States may be crucial in determining whether the growth and travail of the Latin-American countries will be a controlled revolution taking place without disruption of the inter-American system and the Atlantic community, or whether they will become the scene of uncontrollable unrest and cold-war competition.

The Spectrum of Conflict

The gradual shift from possession of an atomic monopoly toward a position of virtual nuclear parity with the Soviet Union deprived the United States of a significant military advantage. It could no longer regard its massive striking power as so effective a deterrent to aggression or as a guarantee of victory at acceptable cost in the event of the ultimate test of war. The growth of Soviet nuclear power, together with the maintenance of huge conventional forces in the Communist bloc, has compelled the United States and other free nations to be prepared for a wide variety of military moves the Communist powers might make, from the fomenting of civil conflict to the launching of all-out war. Because of the need for a global military posture adequate for deterrence and for the necessary operations if deterrence failed, the United States has had to sustain a peacetime military effort of unprecedented size and cost and has also sought new relationships with a large number of countries based on common efforts for mutual security.

The pace of technological change led to weapons of such destructive power that both the United States and the Soviet Union have had to consider whether the arbitrament of total war could be accepted even as the ultimate means of preserving vital interests and national security. Nuclear weapons and their delivery systems, however, have taken their place beside other weapons within the existing scheme of world politics, which is in essence a conflict between two great blocs over the control or denial of territory, involving on both sides an intricate complex of strategic plans and calculations, fears, warnings, commitments, and considerations of prestige. Thus, while the possession of the means of massive destruction by both sides has produced a situation of mutual deterrence, total war remains a real possibility, whether resulting from a direct military challenge to the territory of one bloc or the other, miscalculation, or a local conflict which could get out of control. The Soviet refusal to accept an adequate system of inspection and control has made it impossible to reach agreement on an international system of arms limitation which would reduce or eliminate these terrible prospects. But the United States can take little comfort in assigning blame for the deadlock to the Soviet Union. The urgency of finding some means to control nuclear weapons and other armaments remains.

The Changing International Environment

In addition to its application to weapons, the march of science and technology is rapidly changing the environment in which all nations live, without necessarily respecting or conforming to the political and other relationships which have grown up over the centuries. The accelerating pace of change has upset traditions, created new demands, encouraged revolutionary ferment. It affects what nations want and what they can or cannot do. Increasingly, their problems have gone far beyond handling as matters of purely national policy. The interdependence and interpenetration of societies require reassessment of what is meant by such terms as "sovereignty" and "nonintervention." Governments find themselves dealing primarily with complex situations, with wide-ranging political and economic forces, not just with relations with other governments. Man's ventures into space call into question existing legal and political concepts. Such problems as are involved in the production and use of the world's resources of energy and raw materials have forced many nations, including the United States, to face new choices on how to work out relations with one another and with existing or new regional groupings, how to modify or expand international economic institutions, and whether to seek the basis of a new world order. Scientific advance, with its promise of plenty, brings not only new problems but great new opportunities.

The Role of the United States

The United States, new to the exercise of vast international responsibilities, has not found it easy to adjust to all these rapidly changing conditions. The fundamental principles of its historic approach to world affairs were surely relevant to the new situation, but its established policies, as well as many of the plans with which it emerged from World War II, were clearly inadequate. Nevertheless, the record of the past fifteen years has been a creditable one. The nation showed that it could adjust constructively to new conditions. At critical points the government took and carried through, with the support of the people, major decisions which were bold in conception and salutary in their effect. Such were the original decisions of 1943–45 to take a leading part in setting up the United Nations, the decisions for aid to Greece and Turkey and for the Marshall Plan in 1947–48, the resistance to Communist aggression in Korea in 1950, and the stand taken in the Suez crisis of 1956.

Many other ground-breaking steps were taken, providing the outlines of a national strategy. At the core of American

policy has been the creation of a common front with lik...
minded nations of the Atlantic world, marked by the establishment and growth of NATO and by the reorganization and
strengthening of the inter-American system. The peace treaty
and security arrangements with Japan provided an anchor of
Free World security in the Far East. The chain of alliances,
regional security organizations, and arrangements for bases—
not all of them of equal importance from the standpoint of
military security and some carrying political liabilities as well
as benefits—was gradually extended to include other countries
threatened by Communist imperialism. The United States, as
the strongest power and the only one participating in all these
alliances, thus became the leader of a world-wide coalition. A
program of military aid has been developed to cement the alliances and to provide strength and self-confidence to the partners. In addition to the alliance system, the United States has
taken the lead in building a wider network of arrangements
for economic and technical assistance to numerous countries
of the Free World (both allies and neutrals), based on mutual
recognition of a common interest in strengthening their independence against outside pressures and in fostering their economic progress.

Concentration on resisting the Communist threat, especially
the military threat, has had its successes. Although Communist
influence has increased in some areas, for all practical purposes the territorial expansion of the Communist world has
been checked since 1949, save for the one breakthrough in
North Vietnam, which received international recognition in
1954. But the demands of the cold war, the need for meeting
successive challenges at this or that point on the periphery of
the Communist empire, have obscured many other demands
which are bound to affect America's interests and role in the
world of the future. They have also tended to divert attention
from the formulation and pursuit of long-term policies, without which we can see no clear outline of our future relations
with other nations, and indeed no successful outcome of the
cold war itself.

The Burdens of Leadership

The record of the postwar period shows abundantly the difficulties and dilemmas which a democracy faces in playing a role of leadership in the contemporary world. A few of the critical issues have been clearly presented, and could be clearly decided. For the most part, the complex forces and situations with which the United States has had to deal require an understanding on the part of government and people and an efficiency in the process of policy-making which we are only beginning to develop. Unlike totalitarian states, the United States has no rigid doctrine, no dreams of empire, no dynamic strategy of expansion by force or subversion. Its concept of a legal international order justifies the use of force to resist aggression but not to engage in it. Concern for the opinion of other free nations and the real risks of war also serve to limit the dynamic nature of the policies the United States can adopt in directly challenging the Communist bloc within the territories it now holds. In that sense American policies have had a defensive character. But clearly the United States could have more dynamic and positive policies in the Free World itself, where it does have more freedom of action and opportunity for leadership.

Here, too, there are real limitations, although they provide no excuse for passivity. World affairs are unpredictable, charged with dilemmas that appear to be, and may in fact be, insoluble in this generation. The United States cannot define for itself a single foreign policy that covers all countries and all contingencies. The choices cannot always be clear and consistent. Policy has to deal with the world as it is and as it evolves. It cannot rest solely on an idea of the world as we would like it to be.

Basically the United States relies on persuasion and consent in order to obtain the co-operation and support of others, and the fact is that nations of the Free World often see the issues in a quite different light from that of the United States: they have their own interests, their own ideas on such matters as the relative importance of the Communist threat and the merits of participation in military alliances. Some of the conflicts within the Free World go deep, and the United States has frequently found that it cannot act decisively in regard to them, especially when it is trying to retain or to win the co-operation and good will of all the contending parties.

Yet the instruments available for the exercise of leadership are considerable. The fact that those nations which seek a balance to Soviet power and security against aggression look to the United States as the nucleus of Free World strength gives this country great influence. Its material wealth and productivity provide economic resources which weigh heavily in relations with other nations. And international leadership based on consent need not mean compromising our fundamental principles and policies. Such leadership makes heavy demands on the leader, but it promises solid and lasting results. It is a matter of finding common ground, for which America's own conduct, both international and domestic, is as important as the persuasiveness of its diplomacy.

When all the factors more or less inherent in the world situation are given their due, it still must be said that the United States has failed to cast its policies adequately for the long term. Part of the explanation may lie in defects in the machinery of policy making, defects which can be corrected. Part may lie in the constitutional division of responsibility for foreign policy between the executive and legislative branches of the government, which, besides requiring a special diplomacy of its own, tends to tie important policies and programs to the procrustean inflexibility of the fiscal year. Yet fundamentally it is a question of attitudes, foresight, and leadership within the American body politic. The traditional division of powers does not preclude co-operation or prevent either branch from taking the initiative in developing such co-operation along new lines of foreign policy. The Senate, in particular, has shown itself on occasions in the past a source of fruitful ideas and approaches. While it should not take on itself the detailed planning and policy functions which lie within the province of the Executive, it can and should play a great part in leadership, especially in the guidance of public opinion, as it has at times of crucial decision: for example, in the Vandenberg Resolution of 1948.

Whatever the reasons, the tendency of the United States up to now has been to treat foreign relations as a series of crises, of moves and countermoves in the cold war, in which the United States has attempted to combine firmness in holding the line against Communist expansion with measures to build up defensive strength in the Free World and with a willingness to negotiate on outstanding issues. This will not be sufficient for the future. The great question is whether the United States can, concurrently, act decisively to meet the succession of threats and challenges from the Communist bloc as they arise and also add new dimensions to its foreign policy by taking measures aimed at the world's other problems and at the longer-term future. Although the past few years have seen many Communist gains, as well as some setbacks, there has been nothing inevitable about it. Present conditions are as favorable to initiatives on the part of free nations as they are to those of the Soviet Union or Communist China. Opportunities to create conditions conducive to the growth of freedom in the world and to the establishment of a durable peace are there. The question is whether the United States will have the will and ability to seize them.

Long-term estimates and planning cannot safely ignore such subjects as the course of developments within the Communist empire over the next ten years, the effects of China's growing power, the kind of relations the United States should aim to achieve with the Soviet Union over the long run, the growth of new international institutions, the future importance of nationalism on both sides of the Iron Curtain, and all the forces near or under the surface today which are likely to change the shape of the world's major problems over the next ten years or so. Constructive planning should guide us not only in meeting the crises of the future but in doing now what we can to shape that future.

2. The Protracted Conflict

by Robert Strausz-Hupé

> *Dr. Strausz-Hupé is recognized as one of the leading writers in the field of geopolitics. Born in Vienna, a banker by profession before he turned to teaching and writing, he is the director of the Foreign Policy Research Institute of the University of Pennsylvania. He has been a consultant to both the United Nations Secretariat and the United States Government and has lectured widely in this country and abroad. He has published many books dealing with geopolitical and strategic problems and has contributed articles to numerous magazines and journals. He is co-author of the book* Protracted Conflict *and is editor of* Orbis, *a quarterly journal of world affairs published by the Foreign Policy Research Institute. Dr. Strausz-Hupé lectured at and was course director of the first National Strategy Seminar for Reserve Officers.*

In the conflict between the United States and the U.S.S.R., two alien systems confront each other. This confrontation takes place in space and in time; the contest is over the domination of the earth—and, now, its outer space—and over the future of human society. It is the climactic phase of the systemic revolution through which the world has been passing ever since 1914. It is thus a struggle of power politics as well as a social contest, a war as well as a revolution.

Adapted from an article, "Protracted Conflict: A New Look at Communist Strategy," Orbis, Spring 1958...

In the language of politics, the term "revolution" stands for a certain kind of historical change: an old order dissolves and a new one emerges; old rulers are replaced by new ones; men feel that the tempo of events is quickening and that, willingly or unwillingly, they are breaking with the past; and the transition is enlivened by more or less spectacular bursts of violence. Indeed, these were the characteristics of the French Revolution and the Russian Revolution, the most familiar examples of "revolution" in modern history. Both these cataclysms lasted for known spans of time; both were national, insofar as they occurred within historical states. It is plausible to say that the two world wars were revolutionary wars. It is easy to identify the milestones of the "Revolution of Our Times." It is more difficult to relate these discrete events—national revolutions and international revolutionary wars—to a general development which, in different ways, occurs in all countries, affects all men, and lasts over an indefinite period of time.

The Systemic Revolution

Cycles of history completed long ago afford us a better insight into the nature of the unfolding world revolution than do the more recent happenings which we call revolutions and which are, in fact, mere tremors, albeit sometimes momentous ones, of a vast and lasting disturbance. Such a vast and lasting disturbance seems to have shaken the ancient world. It started with the Peloponnesian War and reached its climax in the Roman Civil Wars, which pitted first Pompey against Caesar and then Caesar's heirs against one another. The revolution, although its most celebrated stages were Athens and Rome, was not confined to any one city or country. It rolled over the entire Mediterranean region—the universe of the ancients. We may call it a systemic revolution. When it had run its course of four centuries, the state system had changed from one of many city-states into one of a single universal empire. A new order had been established, not only for Rome or Athens, for Italy or Greece, but for all peoples of the Mediterranean region, and even for those peoples who had never known the rule of the city-state. Then again, at the time of the Renaissance and Reformation, Europe was recast. The emergent system of nation-states marked a break with feudalism as radical as that which sundered the universal Roman state from the polis of antiquity.

In each of these systemic revolutions, states fought great wars among one another. These wars between states were also civil wars, for the disturbance of the system spread into all its parts, erasing the distinction between civil and external, national and international. Each of these great upheavals traced a definite pattern of events that baffled the participants although it became meaningful to posterity. The design of the systemic revolution, like that of the business cycle, is woven from the actions of masses of men who neither understand nor desire what they are about to fashion. Design there is, but it is a design that is neither conscious nor rational.

The Present Paradox

This generation faces a bewildering and unprecedented paradox: new and virtually unlimited resources are within our reach, and we stand at the threshold of a new rich and universal civilization; yet the survival of civilization itself has been put in doubt. So terrible is our dilemma and so pressing are the demands of the hour that we incline to mistake each bend of the road for a historic turning point. Unique as is our situation, it is but the latest episode of a long story. No one knows how this story will end and whether the leading characters of the current installment will figure in the next. We can but surmise that destiny has placed us in the midst of a revolutionary epoch, comparable, on a global scale, to those which embraced the passing of the city-state, the "fall" of Rome, and the breakdown of European feudalism. For many decades, historic institutions and their sustaining faiths all over this earth have swayed and broken under the impact of revolutionary forces. The nature of the process is still largely veiled to our eyes, for the complete returns are still not in and our judgment is clouded by passion. We may trace, with some semblance of accuracy, this or that root cause: the truths unlocked and the powers unleashed by the natural sciences; the global spread of industrialization; the rapid growth of populations; and the ever accelerating mobility of men, ideas, and things. Yet the political and social crisis of this century remains as ineffable as the human condition to which it has given rise.

The conflict between the United States and the Soviet Union now holds the center of the historical stage. Yet this confrontation is the mere contemporary expression, the vast powers arrayed in each camp notwithstanding, of pervasive conflict that encompasses all lands, all peoples, and all levels of society. The United States and the Soviet Union are now the leading protagonists; the struggle, which is civil as well as international, cleaves all societies. Hence any effective strategy for waging the ubiquitous protracted conflict must be, by necessity, a revolutionary strategy: to wit, a strategy that puts to its own use the revolutionary forces "on the loose" in politics, economics, culture, science, and technology and denies their exploitation to the enemy. Insofar as Communist strategy has been able to do just that, it has been effective. The Communists have benefited from the errors of their opponents who let themselves be bemused by the Marxist myth of revolution and remained blind to the realities of revolutionary strategy.

The Scavengers of Revolution

Marxist thought is rooted in a concept of dynamic historical change. The Russian Communists, saturated with a dynamic philosophy of history and astride a formidable territorial base of operations, saw what the West did not: that "the august, unchallenged, and tranquil glories of the Victorian age," tarnished by World War I, were to depart forever amid the rising commotion of Asia and Africa.

The West's rapid expansion to all continents challenged gravely the authority of all the world's surviving civilizations. Western society pressed its forms upon all societies; it planted everywhere the seeds of its creativeness—and of its own dissensions. Thus, revolutionary change within the historic West is inextricably linked with the transformation of the non-Western societies. The concurrence of the crisis of the West itself and the impact of Westernization upon the rest of mankind impart irresistible force to the secular and universal, the systemic world revolution.

Far from being revolutionaries in the commonly accepted sense, the Russian Communists have excelled in capturing nascent revolutionary movements launched by others. The Communists have scored their most significant successes wherever an existing "revolutionary situation" offered them opportunities for conspiratorial "boring" from within and military blackmail from without.

The Russian Communists did not create the "revolutionary situation" in Asia; that "situation" had been taking shape for a long time. The Communists, however, were quick to exploit it and "to push what was falling." First hampered by ideological preconceptions, they soon adjusted their sights to political realities: the colonial peoples would forge the political ideas which they had received from the West into instruments for dislodging the Western powers from their imperial holdings. Although the incipient breakdown of the colonial system would be paced by economic and social transformation, the prospect of proletarian revolution held, for the Kremlin, less attraction than the strategic prize: to inflict upon the Western powers, who were, in point of time, the principal opponents of the Soviet Union, heavy losses in political prestige, markets, and raw-material resources and to weaken them through the debilitating effects, military, economic, and moral, of colonial wars of attrition.

The Policies of Lenin and Stalin

Lenin's singular contribution to Communist theory was the conversion of Marxism from an abstract doctrine of conflict between classes into a highly effective instrument of conflict between nations. Lenin projected the class struggle from capitalist society—which Marx had assumed implicitly as being confined by the boundaries of a national state such as nineteenth-century France or England—into world politics. Lenin discerned in the clash of rival imperialisms the swan song of capitalism. By analogy, the competition between capitalists within a state evolves dialectically into a competitive struggle between capitalist states.

The Congress of the Peoples of the East, convened at Baku in 1920, affords a preview of a Communist strategy designed to outflank, so to speak, the capitalist order by carrying the revolution to the colonial empires. At Baku, the Bolshevik leaders met with the national revolutionaries of Asia. The Congress resolved dutifully upon a program for the subversion of the European colonies. The fact that many of the participants played, up until the present, leading roles in Asia's revolutionary movements bespeaks the importance of the Baku Congress. The immediate results of Baku disappointed the Bolsheviks. During the 1920s, one revolutionary attempt after the other ended in failure, partially because the Communists had not allowed sufficient time to prepare the professional core of trained revolutionaries so essential to their method. The Bolsheviks could no longer blink the fact that the resources of Russia were grossly disproportionate to the task of spreading the global revolution and even to the task of keeping communism alive in its first historic abode, namely, in Russia. The eclipse of the ideologists had become a necessity. Stalin assumed the management of Russia and bent the energies of his reluctant countrymen to the establishment of socialism in one country, namely, in their own.

Stalin was no ideological purist. Outside of Russia, the Communist Party was expendable. In Europe, Stalin sanctioned cheerfully such ambiguous devices as the Popular Front and outright alliances with fascism. Outside of Europe, Communist initiative was limited to the oblique and far from generous support of Communist movements that had managed to survive the defeats of the 1920s and the recurrent purges of their respective commands by Stalin. Only in one respect did Stalin prepare the ground for the resumption of the offensive in Asia and Africa: he launched a long-range program for the training of native Communist cadres, to be deployed under more favorable circumstances.

After World War II, Stalin set out to repair the damages caused by German invasion and to modernize the Soviet armed forces. Soviet strategy in the immediate post-World War II period was essentially defensive. Stalin's principal objective was to deter the West from contesting the Soviet gains in eastern Europe and from thwarting, by means of a preventive war, the Soviet Union's gigantic effort to close the military-technological gap. Until Stalin's death, Soviet policy remained relatively inactive throughout the rimlands of Asia, including the Middle East and the Arab world. Although it can be argued that Stalin pursued a positive policy in China, there is strong evidence that Mao Tse-tung often took his own counsel and even proceeded sometimes in opposition to Stalin's wishes.

Containment and the Communists' Tactical Shift

American foreign policy, from the late 1940s onward, was presumably designed to counter the Stalinist policy in Europe. American policy sought to contain what it conceived to be the main thrust of Soviet expansionism directed at central and western Europe. Its principal tools were the Marshall Plan and the Atlantic Alliance. Although the bland doctrine of containment was cast in a global mold, its principal objective was to stop the Russians in Europe.

In January 1954, American policy, by reinforcing the doctrine of containment with the doctrine of "massive retaliation," sought to redress the strategic balance in Europe and signified implicitly the United States' determination to fight for the preservation of the *status quo* in Europe as well as in Korea.

The policy of deterrence forced the Communists to desist from such direct challenges as they had presented in Korea and to devise more subtle modes for the penetration of the "gray areas." Neither John Foster Dulles' "massive retaliation" nor, for that matter, the doctrines of "limited war" advanced by his critics coped adequately with Communist strategy, which now had shifted into new political and paramilitary dimensions. Moreover, the growing nuclear power of the Soviet Union put in doubt the United States' readiness to invoke "massive retaliation" unless confronted by a direct threat to national survival.

The 1955 Geneva summit meeting was made possible, if not unavoidable, by prevailing Western public sentiment—weariness with the exactions of the cold war and a characteristic craving for final and formal settlements—and by mounting disagreements among the Western allies.

The Soviet leaders, although they were fully aware of Western motives and integrated them in their own calculations, prompted the encounter at Geneva because of considerations fundamentally different from those inducing their Western opposites to meet with them at the summit. With the demise of Stalin disappeared a formidable obstacle to liquidating a number of demonstrably unproductive ideological positions. The thesis of capitalist economic crisis could now be put conveniently into storage. The petty feud with Tito had been composed, and the Yugoslav leader's alleged heresy could be turned from an ideological liability into a diplomatic asset. More important still, the long overdue reorganization of the Communist system, blocked by Stalin's personal idiosyncrasies, could now be launched under comparatively favorable conditions. By conceding that "many roads lead to socialism," the Soviets hoped to attract the Afro-Asian neutrals, whom Stalin had neglected and whose aversion to totalitarianism sprang not so much from rooted democratic convictions as from distaste for Stalin's unsophisticated methods. By shifting the international cadres of communism from close-order to open-order drill, by purporting to loosen the reins of Moscow's control over the Communist parties outside Russia, the Khrushchev "collective" sought to check the West's military build-up and occasional psychopolitical stabs at the Soviet empire in eastern Europe.

It is doubtful that the summit meeting at Geneva marked a turning point of history. In the protracted conflict between two vast systems, no single event, be it conference or battle, can be decisive. The real significance of the Geneva meeting seems to lie not so much in the importance of the issues under negotiation as in the insight it afforded into mental states: the Western statesmen, whatever might have been their private reservations, were carried to Geneva on the crest of their peoples' perennial hopes for a settlement with finality and surcease from strife; the Soviets came to establish another position of maneuver in the protracted conflict. The Soviets adroitly avoided, as they always had done before, a showdown with Western strength and shifted their weight, as they always had

done before, to bring it to bear against Western weakness.
The West's key position—NATO—was too strong to be taken
by frontal assault; the Communists moved to outflank it. The
chosen field of maneuver was the area not explicitly covered
by the system of Western alliance treaties. The first probing
thrust, which was launched shortly after the vacuous Geneva
communiqué, was the Czech arms shipment to Egypt. By the
time the numbness induced by Geneva had worn off, the West
saw itself confronted with a phenomenon unprecedented in
modern history: the emergence of Russia as a Middle Eastern
power.

In the West, the summit meeting at Geneva was vested with
a meaning that transcended the reticent phrasing of the decla-
rations issued by the assembled statesmen: the United States
and the Soviet Union, having recognized the catastrophic horrors of thermonuclear war, had reached a *de facto* agreement
to renounce force. If this had been indeed true, a new epoch
of international relations would have opened at Geneva. The
idea that the Soviets now eschewed all violent conflict in favor
of "peaceful" competition was pleasing to the Western mind.
To the Western mind, conflict as a conscious, managed struggle, the goals of which are mutually incompatible, is an unpal-
atable idea, for it does not fit the Western image of modern,
civilized society. By contrast, regulated competition, because
it is impersonal and unconscious in its operation among individual groups bidding for a share of economic goods, is
conducive to economic welfare and, if conducted with pro-
priety, to good feeling. After Geneva, the West construed the
phrase "peaceful, competitive coexistence" in the light of its
own concept of competition, just as in the past it was willing
to accept other samples of Communist semantics, such as "popular democracy," "free elections," "imperialism," and "colonialism," as though they meant the same thing to the Soviets
as they did in Western parlance.

A Dialectical Theory of Conflict

Classic Marxian economics is dead; nowhere is it probably
taken less seriously than in Russia. Yet communism has out-

lived its intellectual sterility as well as its moral bankruptcy. Communism now draws its vigor from a dialectical theory of total conflict of indefinite duration between world political systems.

The salient characteristics of the doctrine of protracted conflict are: the total objective, the carefully controlled methods, and the constant shifting of the battleground, weapons systems, and operational tactics for the purpose of confusing the opponent, keeping him off balance, and wearing down his resistance. The doctrine of protracted conflict prescribes a strategy for annihilating the opponent over a period of time by limited operations, by feints and maneuvers, psychological manipulations, and diverse forms of violence. In Communist theory, various techniques of political warfare and graduated violence are so co-ordinated as to form a spectrum that reaches all the way from the clandestine distribution of subversive literature to the annihilating blow delivered with every weapon available.

We can now see how the Communists have applied this doctrine to the strategic situation confronting them from 1945 to 1957. The problem was to annul the Western democracies' technological and strategic superiority while presenting them with no challenge sufficiently decisive to trigger that type of response which Hitlerian strategy forced upon them. At first, the American atomic monopoly deterred Russia from presenting the United States with a forthright military challenge. Later, even after they had developed their own nuclear power, the Western air-base system, which formed a ring around the Communist heartland, kept them at a strategic disadvantage. Through this period, they confined their military challenges to the indirect and irregular type, employing proxies to do their work.

In June 1950, the troops of the Communist puppet regime of North Korea, striking across the 38th Parallel, put to the test the firmness of American intentions in the Far East. Moscow parried the affirmative American response to that aggression by persuading the Chinese Communist regime to enter the war. Even though the U.S.S.R. supplied arms to the North Korean–Chinese forces, the Russians did not allow themselves to become drawn directly into the war. When, after a year of combat, the Communist forces in Korea were unable to win new ground and the American–South Korean build-up permitted potentially decisive offensive operations, the Russians, far from threatening the West with a general war, suggested, in 1951, that negotiations for a truce be opened.

After the Communists had worn down the West's will to fight in Korea by two years of devious armistice discussions and had blanketed the Free World with their peace propaganda, mounted elaborately and financed largely by the contributions of Western Communists, fellow travelers, and pacifists, the Korean truce signaled a stepping up of the operational pace in Indochina. Here France fought an "old" war, heavily encumbered by ambiguous political and moral issues which militated against any vigorous Western response. The Soviet Union thus embroiled the West in Asian wars waged by its Korean and Chinese as well as its Malayan and Indochinese protégés. Their barefaced connivance notwithstanding, the Soviets dodged the responsibility for the actions of their proxies. In this farce, they were assisted by the legal-mindedness of the Western nations and the political naïveté of many of the "uncommitted" Asians.

Following the Soviet forced march into the realm of thermonuclear power, the Kremlin leadership felt capable of introducing important innovations into its postwar tactics. Initially, the Soviets sought to penetrate contiguous areas. In this endeavor, they depended upon the Sino-Soviet superiority in conventional armies and guerrilla-warfare methods. Now, for the first time in their history, the Soviets were able to "leap over" the Western treaty barriers into the more remote areas to which they had always been denied strategic access. By cannily devising proxy arms deals, the Soviet Union was able to extend its influence to Guatemala, Egypt, Syria, and, through Egypt, to Algeria.

Since 1945, the Communists have succeeded in their efforts to confine, on the whole, the cold war to the "war zone" of the non-Communist world, while keeping the "peace zone," namely the Communist bloc, virtually closed to Western intervention and, incidentally, the ministrations of the United Nations. The West was willing to give a round and take a round. If the West won a round, as in Korea and Jordan, for example, it was in the defense of the *status quo*. When the Communists won a round, as in Czechoslovakia, China, Indochina, and the Middle East, they gained access to ground previously closed to them. At best, the West stood its ground; but the Communists, in winning their rounds, made a net gain. At Geneva, the West accepted, together with the "balance of terror" thesis, the Communist-devised rules of the game, namely, to play it anywhere but in the Communist "peace zone" and to content itself with winning and losing the alternate rounds elsewhere.

Implications of Russia's Technological Leap

The integration, in the early 1950s, of nuclear striking power into the Communist military establishment marked the first significant closing of the gap between the Communist and Western military-technological power. The acquisition of atomic capabilities and delivery systems signaled several important and, for the West, ominous changes in the Communist strategy of protracted conflict. These changes have been not so much in the kinds of techniques used as in the degrees of pressures brought to bear upon the West.

Ever since the Communists had to abandon their hopes for a simultaneous world revolution, they relied primarily on the psychopolitical modes of protracted conflict. Their strategy, in the broadest terms, has been to eschew the massive use of hardware and to produce psychological disturbances within the West, while at the same time keeping the uncommitted nations uncommitted or drawing them into the Communist orbit.

Whatever the pace and intensity of Soviet strategies in a given period, Soviet objectives remain the same. They are, in the short run: first, to force the withdrawal of the West from its strategic footholds, especially from the SAC network of bases; second, to compel the West to divert vital economic and military resources from Europe; third, to take Western pressure and attention off eastern Europe; and fourth, to exacerbate the divergencies within the Atlantic Alliance. The long-run Soviet objectives, too, are the same: namely, to isolate the West, deprive it of its sources of strategic raw materials and markets, and to encircle it via Asia, the Middle East, and Africa, until the West, its economic roots having withered, will fall under its own weight.

The Battleground of the "Gray Areas"

The West is bent upon the crucial problem of its survival in the face of the Communist threat. The West thus offers a ready and profitable target for blackmail. The "backward" peoples' common, albeit naïve, admiration for Communist performance, especially for the Soviets' short cut in industrialization, has been deepened by the Soviets' recent technological triumphs and the West's patent discomfiture. The neutrality of Asian countries such as India, Indonesia, and Egypt tends toward diverse shadings of benevolence toward the Soviets. This brand of neutralism is quick to take offense at any Western initiative—except the West's proffer of gifts "without political strings."

In most of Asia and, to some measure, in most underdeveloped lands, the "forces of history" are not on the side of the West; they favor the Communists. In the short run, at least, Western chances of effecting a decisive improvement in Eastern standards of living are slim. Conceding even the dubious thesis that economic improvement stands in any palpable relationship to the growth of democratic institutions or, for that matter, of any political institutions, it is unlikely that whatever the West manages to accomplish within, let us say, the next twenty or thirty years in assuaging the aspirations of the underdeveloped peoples will alter significantly the power relationship between itself and the Communist bloc. At best, the Communists will not grow stronger; the West will not grow weaker.

The increase of international trade and investment and the more rapid economic growth of Asian and African lands are desirable ends in themselves. As great as are the West's economic and strategic stakes in Africa and Asia, its moral stakes are even more important: the West has accumulated a vast capital of good will among all non-Western peoples. Indeed, in all noncommitted countries large numbers of individuals, including public officials, intellectuals, and members of the professions, are deeply committed to Western values; not a few chafe under the ambiguities of their governments' non-commitment. But hardly anywhere have such pro-Western sentiments sufficed to reverse official policy or, for that matter, the deeper currents of mass hostility.

In the non-Western world, the West's strategy cannot be more than a holding action. There, the task must be to gain time, to avoid fixed commitments, to improvise, and to abstain from action for action's sake. The idea that large-scale and long-range economic aid—a vast program for the development of the underdeveloped countries—can reverse, within the foreseeable future, the verdict of 300 years of history is born of *hubris*. Unseemly pride has led, in the past, many a mighty nation to perdition. It might have been possible after World War I, when the West's power was still unchallenged and the forces of nationalism in Asia were relatively weak, to transform gradually the social and economic order of the underdeveloped lands and to provide an economic basis for stable governments. The very existence of Communist power makes this now impossible. For no matter how much the West is willing and able to invest in the development of the "uncommitted" countries, there will always be a gap between the Western contribution and native expectations. The Communists need only move into this gap, be it even with the most modest resources, in order to divert to themselves whatever credit the recipient peoples might have been willing to accord a foreign giver.

In the area outside of the system of Western treaties of alliance—in the world of ex-colonial peoples and of the colored races—the Communists have learned that they can proceed with impunity and with a minimum of direct or even indirect involvement. Everywhere in this world, powerful forces inimical to the West have been rising. All the Communists need to do is to fan the fire. In most of Asia and Africa, the economic theories of Marx are even more irrelevant than they are in the highly industrialized West; the Leninist theory of imperialism, however, is alive in Communist strategy and, as a doctrine of conflict, marches from victory to victory. In the battle for the "uncommitted" peoples, the West can only expect to hold the ground which it has not as yet lost; it cannot force a decision in the protracted conflict with the Communists.

Toward an Understanding of the Conflict

The West can hope to defeat the Communists only by giving battle on its own chosen terrain. It must carry the battle to the vital sectors of Communist defense. To do that it must learn to counter the strategy of protracted conflict—to manage conflict in space and in time.

The development of proper Western attitudes toward protracted conflict will be immensely difficult. The Communists possess a mentality that is much better suited to protracted and controlled conflict than that of the Western peoples. The West has neither a doctrine of protracted conflict nor an international conspiratorial apparatus for executing it. What is more, we do not want such a doctrine or such a political apparatus, for it would be a tragic piece of irony if the men of the Free World, in trying to combat the Communists, should become like them. Some of our "weaknesses" vis-à-vis the Communists are irremediable: we cannot turn ourselves into a conflict society, nor can we assign to the government and, in the last resort, to the police the discipline of our conscience. It is within these limitations—which are the ramparts of civilized self-restraint—that we are forced to cope with Communist perversity.

Pericles long ago was confronted with a similar problem. As the leader of the open society of Athens, locked in an irreconcilable conflict with the garrison state of Sparta, he recognized a relatively simple fact which many of the theorists of war in the nuclear age have overlooked, namely, that there are subtle alternatives to the risky and blunt strategy of engaging the enemy in direct and decisive military action. In the protracted conflict known as the Peloponnesian War, Pericles chose to pursue an extended strategy which was designed to avoid a showdown battle while wearing down, by a campaign of economic, political, and psychological attrition, the enemy's will to resist. Liddell Hart pointed out that the Periclean plan was simply a war policy aimed at "draining the enemy's endurance in order to convince him that he could not gain a decision."[1] In today's protracted conflict the United States must maintain and use its power for the same ultimate purpose: to turn the tide of battle against the Communists, to induce them to overextend themselves, to exploit the weakness of their system, to paralyze their will, and to bring about their final collapse. Within the framework of mutual deterrence, both sides can employ the strategy of protracted conflict, and we can do so quite effectively without the dispensation of a jealous and demanding dogma of conflict for conflict's sake.

A psychopolitical offensive, directed against the Communist citadel itself, offers the West its best chance for winning the battle for its own survival and for spoiling the Communist strategy for the subversion of the uncommitted world. Although the currents within the uncommitted world are running against the West, the West need not despair of holding its remaining positions once it has forced the Communists on the psychopolitical defensive by engaging them on the most favorable terrain, namely, the Communists' own "peace zone."

It is rather in the psychological arena than in its technological workshop that the West has displayed its most alarming shortcomings. Objectively, Western strategy has been far more effective than the sensational charges of its critics will have it. It is improbable that either side from now on will be able to achieve decisive technological superiority for more than a temporary, even brief, period. No doubt, our military posture is susceptible to a great deal of improvement. But an exaggerated zeal for improvement, especially when it is triggered by pained surprise at the latest ploy of Communist psychological warfare or considerations of domestic political advantage, might prove to be "counterproductive" in developing our real range of power. Do not let us pour the baby out with the bath water. What we need now more than anything else is an understanding of the comprehensive, complex, subtle, and consistent strategy of our opponent—and the calm resolution to draw the practical consequences.

[1] B. H. Liddell Hart, *Strategy* (New York: Praeger, 1954), p. 31.

3. Can We Survive Technology?

by John von Neumann

The late Dr. Von Neumann, a native of Hungary, was recognized as one of the world's most accomplished mathematicians. His book Theory of Games and Economic Behavior, *which he wrote with the economist Oskar Morgenstern, is regarded as a classic study of strategy in war, business, and poker. In 1933 he joined the Institute for Advanced Study at Princeton, New Jersey, and took leave after President Eisenhower appointed him to the Atomic Energy Commission in 1954. From 1940 on he served as consultant to the armed forces and for his work received two major decorations. Dr. Von Neumann died in 1957 at the age of fifty-three. Although written in 1955, this article's analysis and prognosis is still extremely pertinent to strategic considerations of the 1960s.*

"The great globe itself" is in a rapidly maturing crisis—a crisis attributable to the fact that the environment in which technological progress must occur has become both undersized and underorganized. To define the crisis with any accuracy, and to explore possibilities of dealing with it, we must not only look at relevant facts but also engage in some speculation. The process will illuminate some potential technological developments of the next quarter century.

In the first half of this century the accelerating Industrial Revolution encountered an absolute limitation—not on tech-

In its original form, this selection was published in the June 1955 issue of Fortune. *Copyright 1955, Time, Inc. All rights reserved.*

nological progress as such, but on an essential safety factor. This safety factor, which had permitted the Industrial Revolution to roll on from the mid-eighteenth to the early twentieth century, was essentially a matter of geographical and political lebensraum: an ever broader geographical scope for technological activities, combined with an ever broader political integration of the world. Within this expanding framework it was possible to accommodate the major tensions created by technological progress.

Now this safety mechanism is being sharply inhibited; literally and figuratively, we are running out of room. At long last, we begin to feel the effects of the finite, actual size of the earth in a critical way.

Thus the crisis does not arise from accidental events or human errors. It is inherent in technology's relation to geography on the one hand and to political organization on the other. The crisis was developing visibly in the 1940s, and some phases can be traced back to 1914. In the years between now and 1980 the crisis will probably develop far beyond all earlier patterns. When or how it will end—or to what state of affairs it will yield—nobody can say.

Dangers, Present and Coming

In all its stages the Industrial Revolution consisted of making available more and cheaper energy, more and easier controls of human actions and reactions, and more and faster communications. Each development increased the effectiveness of the other two. All three factors increased the speed of performing large-scale operations—industrial, mercantile, political, and migratory. But throughout the development, increased speed did not so much shorten time requirements of processes as extend the areas of the earth affected by them. The reason is clear. Since most *time* scales are fixed by human reaction times, habits, and other physiological and psychological factors, the effect of the increased speed of technological processes was to enlarge the *size* of units—political, organizational, economic, and cultural—affected by technological operations. That is, instead of performing the same operations as before in less time, now larger-scale operations were performed in the same time. This important evolution has a natural limit, that of the earth's actual size. The limit is now being reached, or at least closely approached.

Indications of this appeared early and with dramatic force in the military sphere. By 1940 even the larger countries of continental western Europe were inadequate as military units. Only Russia could sustain a major military reverse without collapsing. Since 1945, improved aeronautics and communications alone might have sufficed to make any geographical unit, including Russia, inadequate in a future war. The advent of nuclear weapons merely climaxes the development. Now the effectiveness of offensive weapons is such as to stultify all plausible defensive time scales. Soon existing nations will be as unstable in war as a nation the size of Manhattan Island would have been in a contest fought with the weapons of 1900.

Such military instability has already found its political expression. Two superpowers, the United States and the U.S.S.R., represent such enormous destructive potentials as to afford little chance of a purely passive equilibrium. Other countries, including possible "neutrals," are militarily defenseless in the ordinary sense. At best they will acquire destructive capabilities of their own, as Britain is now doing. Consequently, the "concert of powers"—or its equivalent international organization—rests on a basis much more fragile than ever before. The situation is further embroiled by the newly achieved political effectiveness of non-European nationalisms.

These factors would "normally"—that is, in any recent century—have led to war. Will they lead to war before 1980? Or soon thereafter? It would be presumptuous to try to answer such a question firmly. In any case, the present and the near future are both dangerous. While the immediate problem is to cope with the actual danger, it is also essential to envisage how the problem is going to evolve in the next two decades, even assuming that all will go reasonably well for the moment. This does not mean belittling immediate problems of weaponry, of U.S.-U.S.S.R. tensions, of the evolution and revolutions of Asia. These first things must come first. But we must be ready for the follow-up, lest possible immediate successes prove futile. We must think beyond the present forms of problems to those of later decades.

When Reactors Grow Up

Technological evolution is still accelerating. Technologies are always constructive and beneficial, directly or indirectly. Yet their consequences tend to increase instability—a point that will get closer attention after we have had a look at certain aspects of continuing technological evolution.

First of all, there is a rapidly expanding supply of energy. It is generally agreed that even conventional, chemical fuel—coal or oil—will be available in increased quantity in the next two decades. Increasing demand tends to keep fuel prices high, yet improvements in methods of generation seem to bring the price of power down. There is little doubt that the most significant event affecting energy is the advent of nuclear power. Its only available controlled source today is the nuclear-fission reactor. Reactor techniques appear to be approaching a condition in which they will be competitive with conventional (chemical) power sources within the United States; however, because of generally higher fuel prices abroad, they could already be more than competitive in many important foreign areas. Yet reactor technology is but a decade and a half old, and during most of this period effort has been directed primarily not toward power but toward plutonium production. Given a decade of really large-scale industrial effort, the economic characteristics of reactors will undoubtedly surpass those of the present by far.

"Alchemy" and Automation

It is worth emphasizing that the main trend will be systematic exploration of nuclear reactions—that is, the transmutation of elements, or alchemy rather than chemistry. The main point in developing the industrial use of nuclear processes is to make them suitable for large-scale exploitation on the relatively small site that is the earth or, rather, any plausible terrestrial industrial establishment. Nature has, of course, been operating nuclear processes all along, well and massively, but her "natural" sites for this industry are entire stars. There is reason to believe that the minimum space requirements for her way of operating are the minimum sizes of stars. Forced by the limitations of our real estate, we must in this respect do much better than nature. That this may not be impossible has been demonstrated in the somewhat extreme and unnatural instance of fission, that remarkable breakthrough of the past decade.

What massive transmutation of elements will do to technology in general is hard to imagine, but the effects will be radical indeed. This can already be sensed in related fields. The general revolution clearly under way in the military sphere, and its already realized special aspect, the terrible possibilities of mass destruction, should not be viewed as typical of what the nuclear revolution stands for. Yet they may well be typical of how deeply that revolution will transform whatever it touches. And the revolution will probably touch most things technological.

Also likely to evolve fast—and quite apart from nuclear evolution—is automation. Interesting analyses of recent developments in this field, and of near-future potentialities, have appeared in the last few years. Automatic control, of course, is as old as the Industrial Revolution, for the decisive new feature of Watt's steam engine was its automatic valve control, including speed control by a "governor." In our century, however, small electric amplifying and switching devices put automation on an entirely new footing. This development began with the electromechanical (telephone) relay, continued and unfolded with the vacuum tube, and appears to accelerate with various solid-state devices (semiconductor crystals, ferromagnetic cores, etc.). The last decade or two has also witnessed an increasing ability to control and "discipline" large numbers of such devices within one machine. Even in an airplane the number of vacuum tubes now approaches or exceeds a thousand. Other machines, containing up to 10,000 vacuum tubes, up to five times more crystals, and possibly more than 100,000 cores, now operate faultlessly over long periods, performing many millions of regulated, preplanned actions per second, with an expectation of only a few errors per day or week.

Many such machines have been built to perform complicated scientific and engineering calculations and large-scale accounting and logistical surveys. There is no doubt that they will be used for elaborate industrial process control, logistical, economic, and other planning, and many other purposes heretofore lying entirely outside the compass of quantitative and automatic control and preplanning. Thanks to simplified forms of automatic or semiautomatic control, the efficiency of some important branches of industry has increased considerably during recent decades. It is therefore to be expected that the considerably elaborated newer forms, now becoming increasingly available, will effect much more along these lines.

Fundamentally, improvements in control are really improvements in communicating information within an organization or mechanism. The sum total of progress in this sphere is explosive. Improvements in communication in its direct, physical sense—transportation—while less dramatic, have been considerable and steady. If nuclear developments make energy unrestrictedly available, transportation developments are likely to accelerate even more. But even "normal" progress in sea, land, and air media is extremely important. Just such "normal" progress molded the world's economic development, producing the present global ideas in politics and economics.

Controlled Climate

Let us now consider a thoroughly "abnormal" industry and its potentialities—that is, an industry as yet without a place in any list of major activities: the control of weather or, to use a more ambitious but justified term, climate.

Weather control and climate control are much broader than rain making. All major weather phenomena, as well as climate as such, are ultimately controlled by the solar energy that falls on the earth. To modify the amount of solar energy, is, of course, beyond human power. But what really matters is not the amount that hits the earth, but the fraction retained by the earth, since that reflected back into space is no more useful than if it had never arrived. Now, the amount absorbed by the solid earth, the sea, or the atmosphere seems to be subject to delicate influences. True, none of these has so far been substantially controlled by human will, but there are strong indications of control possibilities.

The carbon dioxide released into the atmosphere by industry's burning of coal and oil—more than half of it during the last generation—may have changed the atmosphere's composition sufficiently to account for a general warming of the world by about one degree Fahrenheit. The volcano Krakatoa erupted in 1883 and released an amount of energy by no means exorbitant. Had the dust of the eruption stayed in the stratosphere for fifteen years, reflecting sunlight away from the earth, it might have sufficed to lower the world's temperature by six degrees. This would have been a substantial cooling; the last Ice Age, when half of North America and all of northern and western Europe were under an icecap like that of Greenland or Antarctica, was only fifteen degrees colder than the present age. On the other hand, another fifteen degrees of warming would probably melt the ice of Greenland and Antarctica and produce world-wide tropical to semitropical climate.

The Indifferent Controls

Such developments as free energy, greater automation, improved communications, partial or total climate control, have common traits deserving special mention. First, though all are intrinsically useful, they can lend themselves to destruction. Even the most formidable tools of nuclear destruction are only extreme members of a genus that includes useful methods of energy release or element transmutation. The most constructive schemes for climate control would have to be based on insights and techniques that would also lend themselves to forms of climatic warfare as yet unimagined. Technology—like science—is neutral all through, providing only means of control applicable to any purpose, indifferent to all.

Second, there is in most of these developments a trend toward affecting the earth as a whole, or, to be more exact, toward producing effects that can be projected from any one to any other point on the earth. There is an intrinsic conflict with geography—and institutions based thereon—as understood today. Of course, any technology interacts with geography, and each imposes its own geographical rules and modalities. The technology that is now developing and that will dominate the next decades seems to be in total conflict with traditional and, in the main, momentarily still valid geographical and political units and concepts. This is the maturing crisis of technology.

What kind of action does this situation call for? *Whatever* one feels inclined to do, one decisive trait must be considered: the very techniques that create the dangers and the instabilities are in themselves useful, or closely related to the useful. In fact, the more useful they could be, the more unstabilizing their effects can also be. It is not a particular perverse destructiveness of one particular invention that creates danger. Technological power, technological efficiency as such, is an ambivalent achievement. Its danger is intrinsic.

Science, the Indivisible

In looking for a solution, it is well to exclude one pseudo solution at the start. The crisis will not be resolved by inhibiting this or that apparently particularly obnoxious form of technology. For one thing, the parts of technology, as well as of the underlying sciences, are so intertwined that in the long run nothing less than a total elimination of all technological progress would suffice for inhibition. Also, on a more pedestrian and immediate basis, useful and harmful techniques lie everywhere so close together that it is never possible to separate the lions from the lambs. This is known to all who have so laboriously tried to separate secret, "classified" science or technology (military) from the "open" kind; success is never more—nor intended to be more—than transient, lasting perhaps half a decade. Similarly, a separation into useful and harmful subjects in any technological sphere would probably diffuse into nothing in a decade.

Moreover, in this case successful separation would have to be enduring (unlike the case of military "classification," in

which even a few years' gain may be important). Also, the
proximity of useful techniques to harmful ones, and the possibility of putting the harmful ones to military use, puts a competitive premium on infringement. Hence the banning of
particular technologies would have to be enforced on a world-
wide basis. But the only authority that could do this effectively
would have to be of such scope and perfection as to signal
the *resolution* of international problems rather than the discovery of a *means* to resolve them.

Finally, and most importantly, prohibition of technology is
contrary to the whole ethos of the industrial age. It is irreconcilable with a major mode of intellectuality as our age understands it. It is hard to imagine such a restraint successfully
imposed in our civilization. Only if those disasters that we fear
had already occurred, only if humanity were already completely disillusioned about technological civilization, could
such a step be taken. But not even the disasters of recent wars
have produced that degree of disillusionment, as is proved by
the phenomenal resiliency with which the industrial way of
life recovered even—or particularly—in the worst-hit areas. The
technological system retains enormous vitality, probably more
than ever before, and the counsel of restraint is unlikely to be
heeded.

Awful and More Awful

The problems created by the combination of the presently
possible forms of nuclear warfare and the rather unusually unstable international situation are formidable and not to be
solved easily. Those of the next decades are likely to be similarly vexing, "only more so." The U.S.-U.S.S.R. tension is bad,
but when other nations begin to make felt their full potential
offensive weight, things will not become simpler.

Present awful possibilities of nuclear warfare may give way
to others even more awful. After global climate control becomes possible, perhaps all our present involvements will seem
simple. We should not deceive ourselves: once such possibilities become actual, they will be exploited. It will, therefore, be
necessary to develop suitable new political forms and proce-

dures. All experience shows that even smaller technological changes than those now in the cards profoundly transform political and social relationships. Experience also shows that these transformations are not a priori predictable and that most contemporary "first guesses" concerning them are wrong. For all these reasons, one should take neither present difficulties nor presently proposed reforms too seriously.

The one solid fact is that the difficulties are due to an evolution that, while useful and constructive, is also dangerous. Can we produce the required adjustments with the necessary speed? The most hopeful answer is that the human species has been subjected to similar tests before and seems to have a congenital ability to come through, after varying amounts of trouble. To ask in advance for a complete recipe would be unreasonable. We can specify only the human qualities required: patience, flexibility, intelligence.

4.   The Diminishing Freedom of Choice

by Robert Strausz-Hupé

The United States is heading for the most dangerous stage of its history: it is losing control over its foreign and security policies.

For more than a hundred years, the United States has been able to choose, within an ample margin of discretion, between peace and war. Up until a few years ago, the United States could decide whether it should join international conflict or keep out of it. No other state could make this decision for the United States; no other state could force the United States to go to war against its better judgment or emotional involvement.

In both world wars of this century, the United States was free to decide if and when to join the belligerents and, although popular legends tell of but one alternative, which side to succor. The United States might have kept out of the First World War. Many millions of Americans would have been content to choose this alternative. In the Second World War, the United States could have remained neutral; it could have gone to war and still have withheld support from the Soviet Union. Many millions of Americans would not have caviled at either of these solutions.

One can argue—and it is easy to do so after the event—that national interest and ethical commitment predetermined American participation and alignment in both world wars. The fact is that Americans could take their time determining how compelling was the logic of their interests and hearts. This is, at least, how other peoples saw it. Their leaders were far from sure which way the United States was going to jump, and

Originally published as "U.S. Near Most Dangerous State of Its History," in the August 17, 1956, issue of U.S. News & World Report, an independent weekly news magazine published at Washington. Copyright 1956, United States News Publishing Company.

spared no effort to influence the American decision by every means of persuasion. They may have been prescient enough to see that ultimately the American people would have no choice; they certainly did not act on this supposition. In the eyes of the world, the United States had the freedom of decision.

Since the United States could decide freely to stay at peace or go to war "at times and places of its own choosing," it could —if it so desired—forestall aggression by the timely employment of force. No one can deny that a state has the right, if not the bounden duty, to meet threats of aggression by appropriate military measures. Since international law fully recognizes the right to self-defense in the face of clear and present threats to the peace, the question here is simply one of capability and not one of morality.

Means, Timing, and Self-Defense

A state that decides to use force must not only be reasonably sure that its opponent will indeed become a source of aggression unless blocked by anticipatory action, but it must also exercise a wide latitude of choice as regards means and timing. A state that proposes to forestall a potential aggressor must be strong. No government will venture upon anticipatory military action that does not estimate the chances of victory to be very high. For the penalties of failure, too, are very high: neither domestic nor world opinion looks kindly upon a government's unsuccessful attempt at playing Providence; the potential aggressor might, had he been left unmolested, have changed his mind; no nation has the right to mete out punishment against another nation before the latter is proven guilty of a breach of international law, and presumed intention is insufficient proof; and the worst peace, we are told, is better than the best of wars.

It is because of these homely and practical as well as abstract and elevated considerations that the American people have professed their abiding distaste for using force to resolve international disputes. This popular attitude notwithstanding, the United States has been singularly fitted by natural and contrived circumstances for arbitrating conflict. It is certain that both world wars would have been shorter and mankind would have suffered less had the United States exploited promptly its capabilities for waging preventive war against Germany and Japan. It is hardly debatable that the United States, even though it eschewed the direct road to war, pursued—wittingly or unwittingly—certain policies that contained elements of war strategy: the Germans, in both world wars, and the Japanese, in 1941, were maneuvered into tipping their hands. Granted even that their ultimate designs were aggressive and that they really meant to fight the United States rather than content themselves with regional domination, then U.S. action forced them to change the timetable of their aggressive operation. This was fortunate, although no American statesman has cared to claim the credit for having made the potential aggressor fight just then, when it was time for the United States to go to war.

Among historians, there is still wide disagreement on exactly how the United States came to participate in the last two world wars; among moral philosophers, there has always been, and always will be, wide disagreement as to whether a nation should refrain from using force except as a last resort against all-out armed attack.

The Emerging One-Way Street of Diplomacy

Hardly any American will disagree that his country's capability of fighting a war "at times and places of its own choosing"—no matter whether that capability is used or not—constitutes a healthy restraint on foreign aggression. As matters now stand, it is uncertain, to say the least, that the United States possesses a weapons system that favors decisively offensive operations. More important still, the decision as to whether and when to go to war, preventive or reactive, lies no longer with the United States alone or with its friends or with the United States and its friends together.

The capability of using force is the prerequisite of a foreign policy that is independent rather than reactive. Once the potential aggressor knows that he need not reckon with the anticipatory action of his opponent and that only direct military attack will provoke the intended victim into retaliatory action, he can apply safely any and all stratagems of conquest short of direct military attack. More important still, he can prepare safely that direct military attack itself and even venture upon all kinds of probing actions designed to test the defensive reflexes of the intended victim.

Loss of the capacity to enforce the peace, rather than letting the aggressor determine when and how to break it, marks the end of effective diplomatic negotiation; for the potential aggressor knows that his intended victim will apply the sanction of violence only when it is confronted by outright aggression, that is, when the aggressor sees fit to rupture all diplomatic negotiations and to engage in that most violent of unilateral actions, war.

This does not mean that the potential aggressor will eschew diplomatic negotiations: on the contrary, he will launch himself eagerly upon formal diplomatic negotiations, the more elaborate the better. He need not shirk this contest, for he stands to gain not only concrete concessions but also valuable propaganda advantages; nor need he fear any serious discomfiture, since his opposites will not back up their diplomacy by force except in self-defense against overt military attack.

Diplomacy is thus turned into a one-way street along which the potential aggressor pushes his intended victim—now quieting its fears by hearty smiles and well-advertised, though trivial, concessions; now goading it into angry verbal protests by the summary refusal to make any concessions whatsoever —toward public humiliation, diplomatic isolation, and domestic demoralization. In history, such a strategy has been crowned with not a few "bloodless victories."

Postwar Capabilities

The overarching fact about the postwar relationship between the United States and the Soviet Union is this: The United States possessed, from 1945 to 1951, the capability of waging war, and the Soviet Union did not.

The Communists, steadfast in their purpose and perhaps

crediting the United States with an estimate of Soviet intentions far more realistic than they needed to fear, placed the contingency of an American-initiated war at the top of their calculations. Atomic monopoly and superior air power endowed the United States with the capability required for fighting against Communist forces—provided the United States had been determined to mobilize the total of its "conventional" as well as "unconventional" military resources.

There can be no doubt that the principal objectives of Soviet policy throughout the first decade after World War II was to close the technological gap between the United States and Russia and to dissuade, by diplomatic and psychopolitical means, the United States from launching military action under optimum conditions. In this purpose, Soviet policy succeeded brilliantly.

Up until the end of the Korean War, the logic of the relationship between the American and Soviet weapons system argued conclusively for an American strategy of unrelenting pressure upon the Soviet Union.

For the Soviets, this period was, within their empire, one of consolidation, and, at the periphery, one of defensive sorties and cautious probing actions. In Europe, the Soviets concentrated upon the strengthening of the positions which they had acquired at the end of World War II. In Asia, the Soviets were concerned chiefly with the completion of the Communist conquest of China—in which transaction, incidentally, they refrained discreetly from overt intervention—and the establishment of a working partnership with the new rulers of mainland China.

The Soviet blockade of Berlin, intrusion in Iran, and support of Red China during the Korean War must be viewed in retrospect as probing and diversionary actions which the Soviets broke off as soon as they met determined Western resistance and discerned the danger of an all-out Western riposte—that is, of general war launched by the United States.

No doubt the Soviets would have pressed home these thrusts had they encountered less vigorous opposition, for many of their earlier successes had been won through the skillful exploitation of tactical opportunities. The creation of NATO closed western Europe not only to whatever military adventures along the Elbe or in the Mediterranean the Soviets might have contemplated but also to Communist political warfare on the Czechoslovak model.

In Asia, the deployment of American forces in Korea and the Formosa Strait counseled the Communists to pursue their ends by diplomatic negotiations rather than by military operations. But the true purpose of Soviet maneuvers from Greece to Berlin and from Iran to Korea can now be clearly seen: to screen the build-up of the modernized Red Army and Navy and to divert the West from what, by Soviet logic, should have been its true purpose, namely, to crush Soviet power before it had attained technological parity.

The leaders of the Western democracies vied with one another in renouncing indignantly the very thought of such a "spoiling operation." What mattered to the Soviets was to make doubly sure that the democracies would not deviate from the highroad of self-restraint. Their peace campaigns were designed to confirm the Western peoples in their conviction that to insure peace by preparing for war is wasteful, if not wicked, and that to strike the potential aggressor before he can strike is wastefulness and wickedness compounded.

The Shift in the Power Balance

The Soviets, during the long years of their military "incubation," were keenly aware of the West's capabilities. The West possessed the capability, although not the will, of retaliating against Soviet moves "at times and places of its own choosing." The Soviets' release from the haunting fear of the West's doing just that coincided with the change of rulers in Russia. This accident is at the root of much confusion. No one can tell what Stalin would have done had he been at the helm in 1955, the year of Geneva. More important than conjectures on differences between successive Soviet bosses is the fact that any Soviet ruler or ruling-clique incumbent would have confronted in 1955 the same profound change in the balance of power in favor of the Soviet Union. Nikita Khrushchev was only acknowledging a long-standing fact when he boasted, in his speech to the Supreme Soviet of January 14, 1960, that "a fundamental shift has taken place in the balance of power between the socialist and capitalist states."

That change in the power balance was not due to the altered tactics of Stalin's successor; the "new look" of Soviet diplomacy was the result of the "new look" of the Soviet armed forces. When President Eisenhower declared, at Geneva, that there was "no alternative to peace," he acknowledged implicitly the successful completion of the most daring and dangerous transformation which Soviet power underwent in its daring and dangerous history: the change-over—under the West's atomic guns, so to speak—from the Red Army of 1945, consisting almost entirely of ground forces, to today's Soviet war machine, equipped with nuclear weapons, jet bombers, intercontinental missiles, and long-range submarines.

If their intelligence services should have failed to confirm completely the Soviet leaders' estimates of the situation, then the President's words must have supplied the missing bits and pieces; the West accepted the nuclear stalemate and discarded war as a means of pursuing diplomatic objectives.

Preventive War and Total Conflict

To abjure the use of force under all circumstances except self-defense in a contest with a revolutionary power is a fateful decision. The principal deterrent to the revolutionary aggressor is the *status quo* power's capability of forestalling him with superior force. Bismarck once said that he who counseled a preventive war reminded him of the man who committed suicide because he was afraid to die. This is an apt characterization of preventive war in a world where the furies of revolution have been chained. In the nineteenth century, even the most "dynamic" powers aimed at no more than limited-power political objectives within the existing order, not at the overthrow of that order itself.

By contrast, Hitler proposed to carry the Nazi revolution from one end of Europe to the other and, if luck held, to farther shores. Is it a debatable question that an Anglo-French war against Nazi Germany, as soon as it took the revision of the peace settlement of 1919 into its own hands, would not

have been just and would not have saved mankind from the
worst calamity of its history? Is it possible to argue that the
United States would now be less secure, and the prospect of
human freedom less bright, had the United States wielded its
power diplomatically and, in the last resort, militarily in order
to force the Soviet Union to surrender its unlawful gains and
renounce its sponsorship of international subversion?

Although the full implications of the "atomic stalemate"
and, more important still, of its acceptance by American diplomacy as a fact of life have not yet received that sober and
searching attention which so portentous a development war-
rants, there have been some attempts to show how the United
States can regain, at relatively small cost, its freedom of maneuver and recapture the initiative. It is hoped, for example,
that a bold new program of economic assistance to the "uncommitted" peoples of Asia and a bolder bid for "the minds
of men" will blunt Soviet offensives in these sectors of the cold-
war front and thus give the West a decisive advantage in the
coexistential competition.

Although effective economic policies and imaginative propaganda are integral to the defense of the Free World, they cannot, however, be expected to right the balance of power in
favor of the United States. Is it plausible to assume that even
the most massive economic aid to, let us say, India will dent
the neutralist disposition of its rulers, or that the most skillful
presentation of the West's cultural and moral ascendancy in,
let us say, Afghanistan or Indonesia will transform either of
these countries into bastions of the Free World's defense? The
best one can hope is that neither of these countries will move
closer to the Communist camp than it has to date.

In the Near and Middle East, the alarming inroads of the
Soviets cannot be ascribed to American failures in the fields
of propaganda or economic policy. The Soviets succeeded in
gaining footholds in the Arab world because the United
States and Britain could not, or thought they could not, employ military sanctions, such as a naval blockade and search
of the Arab bloc.

Can We Recapture the Initiative?

The conclusions deduced from the above analysis are as follows: The containment of a revolutionary power aiming at the overthrow of the existing world order rests upon the defender's capability of taking anticipatory action—of forestalling war with force. In the absence of this capability—of which the resolution to use it is an intrinsic element—a military and diplomatic stalemate ensues. This stalemate favors, and can be broken most advantageously by, the revolutionary power; for the contest is thrown from the court of military and diplomatic arbitrament into the arena of psychopolitical warfare, which is the revolutionary's natural habitat. The old doctrines of limited war do not offer practicable alternatives.

The conditions which, in the eighteenth century and, although somewhat attenuated, in the nineteenth century, imposed upon all belligerents a measure of self-restraint no longer obtain. Nor is it likely that the United States can, at this stage of technological development and mass psychological revulsion against war, reproduce at some future occasion the conditions which enabled it to fight a "controlled" war in Korea.

The recapture by the United States of the diplomatic and psychopolitical initiative in the contest with the Communist bloc depends, therefore, either on a massive technological breakthrough which will restore American military superiority, or on the development of new strategic and tactical concepts which will cancel out, in favor of the United States, the parity of American and Soviet matériel, or, finally, on the devotion of a larger portion of America's national product to this effort. None of these alternatives are now in public sight. The two remaining alternatives are the transformation of the Soviet Union into a *status quo* power or the adoption by the United States of the revolutionary techniques of international conflict. The former contingency lies beyond the control of the United States; the latter implies radical alteration of American society as now constituted and a complete change of context in the world-wide ideological struggle. These alternatives, too, fail to furnish, here and now, an escape from the American dilemma in world politics.

In sum, the position of the United States in relation to the Soviet Union has worsened. Unless the American people realize that time is no longer on their side and take the actions necessary to right the scales which are tipping now against them, their position will continue to worsen and worsen critically. Then American foreign policy will vainly seek to recapture its historic freedom of choice, and the fortunes of the American people will be controlled increasingly by the incalculable decisions of a hostile power.

The adverse implications of this conclusion call for corrective effort, not resigned acceptance. For history is made by men: nothing is inevitable except when men make it so by their acts of commission or omission. The American people can regain their freedom of choice in world politics. They will do so whenever their leaders demand those sacrifices which Americans have never failed to bring in times of national peril.

PART TWO

COMMUNISM: ITS NATURE, STRENGTHS, AND WEAKNESSES

INTRODUCTION

The faces of communism are many.

Communism is an ideology propounded by Marx and Engels, expanded by Lenin, and tailored by his successors to the concrete requirements of the Soviet state and the global revolution. Although tarnished by time and Communist practice, the utopian appeal of this ideology continues to beckon powerfully to the uprooted, the disinherited, and the impressionable.

Communism is a social system, ruthlessly disciplined, rigidly organized, and cut to an over-all blueprint of society. It is a system in the throes of change, but the trajectory of this transition is yet indistinct.

Communism is a global revolutionary movement, centered in an empire stretching from the Elbe River to the far reaches of the Pacific Ocean and guided by a central intelligence. Shaken by recent explosions, this empire is groping slowly for a new organizational basis. The strength of this movement is undeniable. Yet the all-powerful "monolith" which allegedly is communism is more a myth contrived by the Kremlin's propagandists than a fact of international life. Communism's inherent contradictions are ready to be exploited—if only the Free World can muster the requisite means and determination.

5.   The Ideological Core of Communism

by Gerhart Niemeyer

A native of Germany, Dr. Niemeyer is widely recognized as an authority on the history and nature of communism. He studied at the universities of Cambridge and Munich and received his doctorate from Kiel University. He has taught at the universities of Frankfurt and Madrid, and at Princeton, Oglethorpe, Yale, and Columbia universities. From 1950 to 1953 he was planning adviser in the U. S. Department of State. Since 1955 he has been professor of political science at the University of Notre Dame. In 1959 he was on leave as a member of the Department of Political Affairs of the National War College.

"Communism" to some people connotes the present regime in the Soviet Union, to others the Communist Party and its activities, to still others a set of ideas about history and society. Actually, communism is essentially the ensemble of these three aspects. The regime in the Soviet Union would not be a threat if it were not meant to be forcefully imposed on other countries as well and if it did not command a world-wide network of Communist organizations which serve this very purpose of the Soviet regime. The Communist Party system, in turn, would not be dangerous if it were not governed by a doctrinaire ideology which links it to the power aspirations of the Soviet Union. And the set of ideas that identify communism would hardly be a threat if they did not constitute the creedal

This is an expanded version of the address given by Dr. Niemeyer at the National Strategy Seminar for Reserve Officers.

core of a strictly disciplined combat organization operating under the direction of the Soviet Union. Bearing in mind that, in the phenomenon of communism, ideology is intertwined with party organization and the power of a large bloc of nations, we now turn to the ideological roots from which this complex phenomenon has grown.

The Ideological Origins of Communism

There is a widespread misconception that Communist ideology emanated from a burning sense of injustice, or compassion for human suffering, which supposedly inspired the "founding fathers" of the Communist Party.

Nothing could be further from the truth. Lenin, the creator of present-day communism, drew his ideas from the philosophy of Friedrich Engels and Karl Marx, and Marx, in turn, developed his ideas chiefly from philosophical impulses he received from the philosophers Hegel and Feuerbach. From Hegel he received the idea that history is a process by which an underlying logic of change works itself out in the events of society. Hegel himself ascribed this underlying logic to something he called the *Absolute Spirit,* a kind of impersonal Mind that he conceived as realizing itself through progressive historical developments. Feuerbach criticized this as a kind of religious concept. He maintained that all religion is nothing but a fiction of human imagination and that, in reality, there is nothing but nature and man. Feuerbach was, in other words, a materialist, that is, a thinker who asserted that matter is all the reality there is, and consequently he denied the reality of the spirit. Marx accepted materialism from Feuerbach and combined it with Hegel's view of history. The result was *historical materialism,* the idea that history occurs because of changes in material, economic conditions, which make for changes in human existence and which proceed according to an inherent logic.

Before any Communist program of action was ever planned, Karl Marx thus developed a world view, a comprehensive explanation of human existence, social development, and the meaning of historical change. The basic tenets of this world view can be summarized as follows: (1) Life is fundamentally not a relation between man and God, but a relation between man and matter. (2) There are laws of history; they can be scientifically determined; and the Marxist interpretation of change in terms of developing modes of economic production is the only "scientific" key to the knowledge of history. (3) Because history is essentially a process in which the inherent logic of human affairs works itself out, one can find general truth about human affairs only by participating in historical change, not by abstractly speculating about it—so that the point of philosophy is not to interpret but rather actively to change the world.

From this last idea flows the revolutionary activity which Marx and Lenin considered not as a mere implementation of a program but rather as a way of life; from the second tenet is derived the Communist's confidence in the almighty power of History, whom he has decided to serve; from the first principle flows the Communist's certainty that his beliefs are corroborated by scientific proof. Communism thus began as a world view, and its main appeal today is still that of a world view. Its concern with economics is only an elaboration of certain detailed "proofs." Its revolutionary, destructive will is inspired by its vision of an eventual "true" society, which is expected to arrive, according to history's "laws," after the present "false" society has been utterly conquered. This, however, leads to the question of what, according to Marx, the "laws of history" decree.

The centerpiece of the Communist teaching about society and its historical changes is the doctrine that all societies above the primitive level are split into classes, and that these classes are engaged in an unceasing and irreconcilable struggle. Power is interpreted basically as the rule of one class over others. According to communism, it is private ownership of the means of production which enables a class to rule. Those who own the means of economic production can use their property to exploit others who do not own means of production. Political struggles are explained in terms of the determination of the ruling class to hold on to power at a time when new means of production have already enabled a new class to form and to make a bid for the ruling position. Thus communism does not merely observe different classes according to ownership, but also attributes to these classes the will and the capability to act in history. It assumes that human consciousness is essentially class consciousness, that is, that men act according to interests derived from their class environment. It also takes it for granted that people belonging to a given class think sufficiently alike to be able to act in history without being organized for common action. Above all, Communists, for these reasons, think of society not in terms of peace, unity, and order, but rather in terms of continuous struggle. For Communists, struggle is not an abnormal condition, but rather the characteristic trait of all historically recorded societies. If the Christian looks upon life as a "vale of tears," the Communist regards it as the scene of unceasing battle.

The Bourgeois-Proletarian Polarity

The perennial class struggle, according to communism, has taken on a peculiarly sharp and significant form in the present-day, or bourgeois, society. Each type of society is characterized by the rule of a particular class. The ruling class of the present-day society is the bourgeoisie, the class of factory owners, who produce commodities through hired wage labor. Under the rule of this class, the class struggle has narrowed down to a conflict between the propertied bourgeoisie on the one hand and the propertyless wage workers on the other— between the *bourgeoisie* and the *proletariat*. Within the womb of bourgeois society, the proletariat is supposed to be the revolutionary force which one day will overthrow the rule of capitalists.

The coming revolution of the proletariat, however, is a revolution which differs markedly from the other upheavals of history. In the past, all classes which overthrew a previously ruling class owned some new type of means of production, which they sought to protect as soon as they had gained ascendancy. The proletariat is supposed to differ from all these revolutionary classes because it possesses no means of production. Since only property can allegedly engender class rule, the proletariat, being without property, cannot set up another class rule by its victory. The revolution of the proletariat is therefore expected to end all class rule and to inaugurate a new type of society, in which there will be no classes, no exploitation, and no need for political power—socialist society.

Phases of Historical Development

Even more important than this view of the present-day society, however, is the Communist doctrine that all human societies pass necessarily through successive phases of development which must eventually lead them to the present bourgeois-proletarian polarity. Communists distinguish between types of society in terms of techniques of production and the corresponding rule of certain classes over others. Working back in history, they trace bourgeois society to the preceding feudal society (in the European West), the feudal society to the slaveholding society of antiquity, and that, in turn, to the primitive society on the tribal level, in which classes were not yet discernible. They insist that these constitute general patterns of social organization which are necessarily bound to succeed each other as "phases" of historical development. Thus, not only in the West but everywhere, from primitive beginnings a slaveholding society would develop, from that a feudal society, from that a bourgeois society, and from that, by means of a proletarian revolution, a socialist society. According to this scheme, a Communist future is thus assured by the "laws of history." Official Communist ideology denies that there are any other than these five "phases" of societal development, even though Marx himself, and, at times, Lenin, recognized at least one other type: Asiatic society. This is a society in which power is wielded not by owners of private property but by the state bureaucracy, and the people are held not in private slavery, serfdom, or labor contract, but rather in what Marx called "general slavery." It turned out that the fact of Asiatic society did not fit the Communist scheme, for not only had this society been stable for thousands of years and never been essentially changed by revolutions but it also had not issued into feudal society. Once the dangerous implications of this concept were realized by the

leading Communists, references to Asiatic society were first
ignored and then suppressed in Communist ideology.

It is clear that the entire body of ideas about history, class
struggle, proletarian revolution, and phases of society constitutes not so much scientific knowledge as a kind of mythology
in scientific garb. Together, these ideas give to Communists
their sense of direction, the justification for their actions, and
their confidence in ultimate success. The class struggle is seen
as a kind of curse which is fastened on mankind as the result
of the introduction of private property. Because of private
property and the class struggle, men have been alienated from
one another, classes have used oppressive power, a machinery
for oppression—the state—has been invented, and wealth has
been generated only at the price of poverty. All this will not
be ended until the curse is removed and a human society free
from class rule emerges. Hence Communists not only are confident that, in the course of the immutable "laws of history,"
socialism will eventually come to pass but they also look upon
their image of the future as the "true" reality of human life
and consequently reject all of the present world as "false,"
unreal, and doomed. It is to these judgments about the present-
day world that we must now turn.

The Basic Legacy of Marx

The Communists' views on present-day society flow from
ideas developed by Karl Marx in his main work, *Capital*, in
which he elaborated his analysis of bourgeois society already
contained in the earlier *Communist Manifesto*. One can summarize the significance of this work by saying that Marx left
to his followers these ideas about the society in which they
live: (1) In bourgeois society, all men are ruled by the capitalists, who exploit the people for the sake of profit. (2) The evil
of this system is not the personal intention of the exploiters but
inheres in the system as such and cannot be removed except
by the destruction of the entire system. (3) The inherent contradictions of the capitalist system will necessarily bring about
its collapse, its overthrow by the proletariat, and socialism as
the successor society. In other words, Marx furnished his fol-

lowers with a target for hostility (the bourgeoisie), a motive for irreconcilable hatred of the present-day society (the inherent evil of exploitation), and the prediction of a catastrophic but hopeful end (collapse and revolution).

Marx supposedly proved the exploitation of the workers by the capitalists through his doctrine of surplus value, which in turn is based on the so-called labor theory of value. The capitalists buy from the worker his labor power. The value of labor power, according to Marx, is what it takes to keep the laborer in physical existence. This is what the capitalist pays him. The worker himself, toiling for the capitalist, earns his own keep. For that, however, no more than a part of the full workday is required. The capitalist, who hires the worker for a full day, thus obtains from the worker a surplus over and above what it costs to buy the worker's labor power. This is called surplus value, which allegedly is the source of profit and capital formation. The capitalist, who, according to Marx, holds all the trump cards, squeezes the wealth of society out of the worker but uses it himself. The entire system is based on the wage contract, which enables the capitalist to pocket the surplus value, which he, allegedly, had no share in producing.

This system, however, is, according to Marx, beset by inner contradictions which will lead to its downfall. It is based on competition. As a result, workers' wages will be pressed lower and lower. Capital will be gathered in fewer and fewer hands. Increasing wealth will accumulate on one side, increasing misery on the other. Wider and wider masses will be drawn into the proletariat. Periodically, capitalism will fall into crises in which overproduction will glut the market and result in stagnation. These crises will increase in severity and eventually lead to complete paralysis. At this point, the indignation of the masses, the reaction to their suffering, will have reached the breaking point. A revolution of the proletariat will break the fetters that have held them down. The "expropriators will be expropriated."

Lenin's Addenda

These ideas, developed at full length in Marx's *Capital*, were essentially transformed by Lenin. The analysis of capitalism which Lenin made in his book *Imperialism* provides now the formulas in which Communists think about the present-day society. While Lenin's description of capitalism seems to differ in important points from that of Marx, he also points out to his followers a target for hostility (the imperialist countries), a motive for undying hatred (the imperialist tendency toward war), and the prediction of a catastrophic but hopeful end (the defeat of imperialism by the colonial and socialist forces).

Lenin explained that capitalism has now moved into a monopolistic stage, which, so he asserted, is capitalism's "final" stage. Monopoly having replaced competition, capitalism now requires the political control of markets and resource areas. The ruling power is in the hand of financiers, and their main need is the export of capital. Industrial countries are thus driven to conquer and dominate colonial areas. Having divided up the world among them, they proceed to redivide it again and again, thus becoming embroiled in conflicts from which wars are inevitably born. Capitalism in its "imperialist" stage is, in other words, at the end of its tether, and thus the capitalist nations turn on each other in mutually destructive wars. The "inherent contradictions" are here seen as essentially political contradictions.

Just as Marx saw hope in the rise of a revolutionary force in the womb of capitalist society, so Lenin looked for redemption through the victory of the enemies which imperialism begets through its exploitation of the colonial peoples. These peoples, together with the revolutionary workers of the industrial countries, will rise against the oppressive capitalist rule. The entire world scene has thus become the theater of a great conflict between two camps: the industrial countries on the one hand and the camp of socialism and anti-imperialism on the other. The eventual victory of the latter over the former will supposedly not only destroy capitalism, imperialism, and exploitation but also the tendency to war. The socialist and anti-imperialist "camp" comprises, according to Lenin, the "overwhelming majority" of the world's population, just as, in the analysis of Marx, the proletariat, at the time of the revolution, would constitute the "overwhelming majority" of the people. Thus, the revolutionary cause is presented as the cause of the "overwhelming majority" and thereby given a kind of democratic justification.

Without giving up the idea of an irreconcilable class struggle and without abandoning Marx's total rejection of present-day society, Lenin thus managed to explain why capitalism, sixty years after Marx, had not yet collapsed, why the workers' lot in industrial countries had improved, and why more workers had not become revolutionists. His answers were that capitalism had not yet collapsed because it had found new fields of exploitation in the colonies, that the lot of workers in industrial countries had improved at the expense of the colonial peoples, and that the "upper" part of the working class had allowed itself to be "bribed" by a share of capitalist wealth. At the same time, Lenin saw the struggle of the revolutionary forces against capitalism as a world-wide struggle between two international "camps" and claimed that it is a struggle not only against capitalist oppression but also against war. Revolutionary cause and world politics here are merged into a single pattern.

The Myth of the Revolution

One can reduce Marxism-Leninism to one central proposition: The present-day society, which is rotten beyond any hope of redemption, will be destroyed in a great epochal conflict, and from that conflict will rise a new society, in which, for the first time, man will enjoy the fullness of real life. Communist ideology, in other words, centers in the tension between two societies: the "false" one of the present and the "real" one of the future. The chief business of Communists, according to the ideology, is to fight the struggle of the future against the present. This struggle is the Socialist Revolution, or simply "the Revolution."

The doctrine of the Revolution (1) predicts the inevitable

and catastrophic end of the present-day society, (2) issues a call to all "toilers" to unify under the leadership of the Communist Party, for the purpose of fighting the revolutionary struggle, and (3) justifies any method required in that struggle in the name of the eventual hoped-for result. The prediction says that the rule of the bourgeoisie will engender its own "gravediggers," who eventually will rise up and overthrow capitalism. The call for action insists that deliberate action and political organization are required to bring about the downfall of the present-day society. The justification presents the future society in terms of such ideal harmony that no sacrifices can be deemed excessive in the struggle for its realization. All this together constitutes what one might call the myth of the Revolution, a myth centering in the notion of the proletariat as a class with the historical mission to redeem mankind from the curse of the class-divided society. On the basis of this myth, Communists have developed their typical attitude, which considers everything "revolutionary" as hallowed.

The myth of the Revolution is, however, not the same as the operational doctrine of the Communist struggle. The latter is the chief guide for Communist practice and theory. There is a widespread misconception that Communist ideology contains the blueprint of an ideal society which Communists, if true to their faith, should consistently seek to implement. Any failure to hew to the line of this implementation is scored as a "weakening of the revolutionary ideology."

Actually, Communist ideology does not draw up a blueprint for an ideal society. The future society is not designed but rather expected, as an automatic result from victory of the revolutionary forces over the forces of the present-day society. Communist ideology, therefore, focuses entirely on the struggle against now existing societies, institutions, ideas, and ways of life. In this struggle, the brilliance of a hoped-for future serves as a promise of eventual good to come from bitter strife, rather than as an immediate object to be realized.

The operational doctrine of communism is thus concerned mainly with the requirements of the struggle in which Communists see themselves engaged for an indefinite time to come. This doctrine was shaped entirely by Lenin, who also insisted on the indefinite duration of the period of struggle. In the vision of Marx and Engels, the Revolution had appeared as a kind of climactic event, a single, mighty upthrust that would, at one fell swoop, usher in the new society. Lenin taught that the struggle would continue with undiminished fury, not only against external but also against internal enemies, long after Communists had seized power. He thus changed the idea of the Revolution, for practical purposes, from that of a single upheaval to that of a "protracted struggle." With respect to that struggle, Communist ideology now teaches important doctrines concerning (1) the Communist Party and its relation to the masses, (2) principles of Communist strategy, (3) the use of the state by Communists, and (4) the role of the Soviet Union.

The Role of the Party

The Party, in Communist ideology, is defined as the "vanguard" of the proletariat. Lenin did not believe that the proletariat, by itself, could have the "socialist consciousness" required to carry out its mission. Without "socialist consciousness," however, there could be no Socialist Revolution. "Socialist consciousness" can be developed only by a small group steeped in the theoretical knowledge of the "laws of history," a group guarded by the strictest discipline against any deviation from the sole correct ideology. The Communist Party, in Lenin's concept, is thus not only a quasi-military combat organization of professional revolutionaries but also a priesthood of the "truth of history" and, as such, ranking high above the masses, including those of the proletariat.

As the keeper of revolutionary theory, which is, by definition, the most "advanced" thinking, the Party is infallible. This does not mean that it cannot be mistaken; it means that nobody else can be as "advanced" in his thinking as the Party is. The Party is, therefore, necessarily the judge of the correctness of anyone's thought. Deviations from its "line" must be tantamount to hostility to the Revolution and sympathy for the bourgeoisie. Because there can only be one truth, the Party must be centralized, disciplined like an army, and united under its leadership. Membership in the Party is not merely a full-time job but a twenty-four-hours-a-day dedication to the profession of revolution.

Since this kind of Party must of necessity remain relatively small, the masses cannot belong to the Party. Rather, the masses are mobilized to support the Party by means of so-called "transmission belts." Transmission belts are non-Party organizations and institutions in which Communists hold controlling positions. The masses are manipulated through the appeals of non-Party institutions rather than through the direct appeal of Communist control, which often remains concealed.

The Doctrine of the Two Revolutions

The fundamental premise of Lenin's doctrine of the Communist Party is that it will remain numerically small and will forever constitute a minority among the population. From this a number of strategic principles were developed, all of which turn on the problem of how a small but compact organization can control large-scale revolutionary movements and changes. Most of them teach Communists how to use revolutions made by others, chiefly by bourgeois revolutionary movements.

The "doctrine of the two revolutions" states that in countries like Russia a revolution by the bourgeoisie must precede the Socialist Revolution. It demands that the "bourgeois" revolution, no less than the Socialist Revolution, be led and controlled by the Communists, but by Communists acting under bourgeois rather than Communist slogans and programs (for example, "land for the peasants"). The Communists, according to this doctrine, can come to power only as the leaders of non-Communist and even nonproletarian masses. The power they would thus set up would be a dictatorship of the proletariat and the peasantry. Only after full consolidation of this (bourgeois) revolution would the Communists proceed to carry out their own (Socialist) revolution, this time against their erstwhile allies.

From this flows another strategic principle, which bids Communists to seek the "alliance" of all kinds of discontented forces whose additional strength is required to help Communists obtain power. Among these forces are nationalistic movements, the bourgeoisie of colonial peoples, peasants, and intellectuals. The Party, however, is exhorted to "watch its ally as if he were an enemy."

A third strategic principle is that of "neutralization." It calls on Communists to divide their enemies into three parts: those who by some means can be induced to support the Party, those who are irreconcilably hostile to the Party, and those who are undecided. The hostile part must be attacked and destroyed. This will be possible only after the undecided part has been "neutralized," that is, made to sit out the struggle on the side lines.

A fourth principle teaches the Party to engage always in both "legal and illegal activities." As a minority group, the Party is supposed to work as a conspiracy and to organize an underground apparatus. At the same time, however, aboveground activities within the legal framework of nonparty and even nonpolitical organizations are considered necessary, because the Party, being a minority, is admittedly too weak to conquer all resistance by direct action.

The Role of the State

In the Communist teaching on the state, dogma is curiously mixed with operational prescriptions. The state, Lenin insisted along with Marx and Engels, will "wither away" when classes have disappeared and there is "nothing any more to suppress." The "withering away" of the state will alone bring about a society of full freedom. The road, however, leads through the "dictatorship of the proletariat." In other words, until that promised day arrives, the state has to be used dictatorially, as a "rule based upon force and unlimited by law." Thus, Communists look upon a state controlled by them as an instrument of class warfare. They use it to destroy everything suspected of hostility to the Party and to control and manipulate all human activities and thoughts. At the same time, somewhat irrationally, they expect this kind of totalitarian dictatorship eventually to issue into a society free from any state power. At any rate, the state is for Communists not an order of the common good but a basis for combat operations of the Party.

The Place of the Soviet Union

The last of the Communist operational doctrines concerns the place of the Soviet Union in the revolutionary struggle. After the seizure of power in Russia, the Party faced the choice between instigating a chain reaction of proletarian revolutions in one after another of the industrial countries on the one hand, and consolidating its power in Russia on the other. It decided on the latter alternative. The implications of this decision were embodied in the strategic principle called "socialism in one country." As "socialism in one country" was elevated to the rank of a revolutionary strategic principle, Soviet Russia became a chief instrument of the world revolution and the Communist International the tool of Soviet Russia—roles which would have been reversed had the Party chosen the first alternative. Henceforth the national power, national security, and national expansion of the Soviet Union came to be intertwined with communism as an ideological cause, so that Soviet national interests and Communist objectives have become well-nigh indistinguishable.

As a result, Soviet foreign policy was incorporated into the arsenal of methods by which the revolutionary struggle is to be carried on. The problem of war assumed new significance. Before the seizure of power, Communists faced only the decision whether or not to support a given war effort as a Party. Now their choice became one between war or peace as a national policy. Too weak to think of a frontal attack on their class enemies, the Soviets devised a "strategy from weakness" similar to that applied to the operations of the Party as such. "Peaceful coexistence" is a term actually introduced by Stalin, but, as a principle, it was formulated by Lenin. Periods of advance would alternate with periods of equilibrium, during which one had to make concessions to the enemy. These "compromises," however, should never be allowed to weaken the basic Communist determination to win the life-and-death struggle. War between the Soviet Union and its enemies is considered "inevitable" only if the enemies choose to resist. In any war in which the Soviet Union is engaged, though, it actually fights for "peace," because it combats imperialism, which is the true cause of war. The Soviet Union, standing for the cause of peace, represents not merely its own national interests but the interests of the whole of mankind, which will be "liberated" by the victorious struggle of the Soviet camp against the camp of imperialist capitalism.

The Power of Ideology

In conclusion, it should be pointed out that the motivating force of the Communist ideology is not weakened either by the inherent contradictions of its teachings or by the repeated changes to which it has been subjected. It belongs to the class of total, apocalyptic, and chiliastic views of the world, society, and history which have turned out to have an irresistible appeal to people despite all difficulties in keeping the various parts together. In addition, the Communist ideology holds an undisputed monopoly in the education, publication, art, and public discussion of one third of the globe. In the countries of the Soviet bloc, the meaning and justification of the entire social system rests squarely on ideological foundations. Were these foundations to be removed, neither Communist rulers nor their subjects would know what actions to take from one day to the next.

For the Communist masters of these countries, the ideology contains the meaning of their lives, the hope that inspires them, and the assurance of what they believe to be their ultimate success. Communism has been called a "philosophy in action." More accurately, it should be described as a closed and doctrinaire ideology equipped with the entire arsenal of modern material means of power.

6. The Appeals of Communism

by J. Edgar Hoover

> *Mr. Hoover entered the Department of Justice in 1917, became special assistant to the Attorney General in 1919, and two years later assistant director of the Federal Bureau of Investigation. In 1924 he was appointed director of the Bureau and has served in that office ever since. In 1938 he published* Persons in Hiding *and has contributed articles to numerous magazines, law reviews, and police journals. His most widely acclaimed book,* Masters of Deceit, *was published in 1959.*

Communism is the great tempter of our time. It promises all things to all men. Its all-embracing philosophy purports to explain man's origin, development, and destiny. Like Mephistopheles in *Faust*, communism promises man the world in exchange for his sovereign soul. It holds forth the utopian vision of a world-wide society in which complete equality and material abundance will prevail and in which the exploitation of man by his fellow man will be ended. It offers a comprehensive program of political action to achieve these goals. The appeal of communism, therefore, is a universal one.

By its very nature, communism impinges upon every facet of man's existence. No phase of human experience, economic, sociological, political, psychological—to mention just the broad categories—is immune. The combination of communism's all-embracing appeal, the complexities of human nature, and the wide variations in the social, political, and economic levels of the nations of the world makes it impossible to isolate any one factor as the predominant appeal of communism. Although one appeal may prove more decisive than another in a specific case, the acceptance of communism, in most instances, has been due to the interaction of two, or more, or even all, of these appeals.

Communism openly proclaims its intention of changing the world. It insists that all non-Communist systems contain inherent contradictions which cannot be alleviated by mere reforms. Communism is offered, therefore, as the only alternative. In its dedication to the complete transformation of all non-Communist societies, communism continuously exploits both the negative and the positive aspect of each appeal. Negatively, communism stimulates the desire for a fundamental change in any society in which such problems as unemployment, discrimination, and political instability persist. Positively, communism invites the non-Communist world to join in creating what it alleges will be the best possible future.

Today, the major Communist appeals are being presented within the framework of a world-wide propaganda campaign. The tactical slogans are "peaceful coexistence" and "peaceful competition." This campaign is clearly designed to exploit the almost instinctive yearning of mankind for international peace as the precondition for all further progress.

Economic Appeals

The economic field is frequently, but incorrectly, regarded as the particular province of communism. With unflagging enthusiasm, communism hammers at its themes of economic and historical determinism in an attempt to convince the world that the triumph of communism is not only desirable but also inevitable. Yet, the Communist appeal in the economic realm is largely a negative one. By distorting economic issues, communism foments hatred of the existing order and demands its complete destruction as the first step in resolving all economic difficulties.

The importance of the economic appeal is illustrated by the Communist-bloc emphasis on trade and aid. These programs embody a number of significant implications—political as well as economic—particularly for the underdeveloped nations, many of which are still uncommitted in the struggle between freedom and communism. This adroit Communist economic offensive lends a certain amount of credence to the sincerity of the peaceful-coexistence campaign. It creates an impression that there is relative prosperity in the Communist nations. It is used in support of the spurious claim that the Soviet Union, which has been transformed from a largely agricultural nation to the second-ranking industrial nation in the world within forty years, should be the model for all underdeveloped countries in their efforts toward rapid economic growth.

Sociological Appeals

Communism's sociological appeal, while often not as obvious as the economic, is probably more chronic. The attraction of the Communist economic appeal tends to diminish during periods of economic prosperity. This is not true of the sociological appeal, based as it is on problems of a more deep-rooted, persistent nature which are rarely susceptible to quick solution. There are probably as many Communist appeals in the sociological field as there are social issues throughout the non-Communist world.

Dissatisfaction and frustration over sociological issues—real or imagined—are exploited by communism to incite rebellion against non-Communist societies. Dissatisfaction may arise from such factors as discrimination in any form, the prevalence of crime, and corruption in public life. Frustration may be caused by such personal experiences as poor housing, the lack of educational opportunities, inadequate medical care, and even domestic difficulties. Claiming the only solution to these and similar issues, communism portrays itself, in non-Communist nations, as the champion of social protest. Today, communism asserts that peaceful coexistence would make it possible, particularly for the major non-Communist nations, to divert current large expenditures from armaments to extensive social-welfare programs for the benefit of their citizens.

Political Appeals

Communism boasts that its political system is responsible for the significant progress of the Soviet Union within the comparatively short period of forty years. If this claim is accepted uncritically, the political appeal of communism becomes obvious. Communist "efficiency" could easily dazzle the underdeveloped nations, all of which are intent on rapid progress. Moreover, leaders of some nations which are troubled by political instability may look to the totalitarian discipline of communism as the solution to that problem.

The political appeal of communism is being enhanced by the peaceful-coexistence campaign. In many areas of the world, the Communist political system is gaining additional prestige because Communist propaganda is, to some extent, erasing the image of the Soviet Union as a totalitarian, imperialistic power attempting to impose its domination upon the entire world.

Psychological Appeals

The heart of the Communist peaceful-coexistence campaign is its psychological appeal. Aimed at the instinctive longing for peace essential to the successful pursuit of man's destiny, this campaign touches on every phase of human endeavor. It is here, too, in the psychological area, that the interrelation of all the broad appeals of communism is most evident. Communist propaganda urging, for example, disarmament and an end to the testing of nuclear weapons carries with it implications which go far beyond immediate military considerations.

Without any factual justification, communism insists that Marxism-Leninism is the product of a "scientific" analysis of nature, man, and history. The claim is made that communism, rather than reacting to historical developments, plans the organization and direction of society according to "scientific" principles. According to Marxism-Leninism, the progress of society toward communism is not only desirable but also historically inevitable. Viewed in this perspective, communism fraudulently appeals as the invincible "wave of the future," against which all opposition seems futile.

A Tarnished Image

However, it is in the psychological field that communism exposes a serious, inherent vulnerability. In this area, as in so many others, Communist practices refute Communist theories. Communism's dependence on the psychological appeal implicitly affirms what communism openly denies—that man has fundamental spiritual needs, values, and ideals which transcend the material necessities of life.

The large number of Americans who, at one time or another, were members of the Communist Party, U.S.A., attests to the deceptive attraction of Communist promises. Yet, in our country today there are many more ex-Communists than members of the Party—clear evidence that Communist appeals are illusory. There is no one word which completely describes the experience of these former Communists. If there were such a word, it would be one with the connotation of disillusionment.

Rarely, if ever, has any other movement promised so much to so many. Rarely, if ever, has any other movement so flagrantly reneged on its promises. History has proved that those who have been deluded by the Communist dream have, to their sorrow, awakened to a grotesque reality.

7. Whither Soviet Evolution?

by Vladimir Petrov

Mr. Petrov fled his native Russia in 1944, after seven years of forced labor in a Siberian gold mine. At Yale since 1947, from 1955 to 1957 he served as editor of the Russian-language broadcasts of the Voice of America transmitter in Munich. At present lecturer in Slavic languages and literature again at Yale University, he is the author of Soviet Gold *(1949) and* My Retreat from Russia *(1950).*

Few observers of the Russian scene would question the fact that Soviet society is given to significant change. True, these mutations take place within the rigid framework of a monolithic state. Nevertheless, ever since the Revolution of 1917, life in Russia has undergone profound change.

This change is not reflected so much in official policy. To gauge Russia's future on the basis of the twists and turns of the Kremlin's pronouncements would be illusory. The very nature of dictatorship, with its power of arbitrary decision making and its disregard for the desires of the masses, renders any sound prognosis unthinkable.

Nonetheless, Communist leaders are not completely free agents. Their freedom of action is limited not only by external forces and developments within the vast Communist world but also by the underlying trends and moods of the Soviet masses. No matter how unlimited may seem the range of options open to the Soviet dictatorship at any given time, the success of its policies depends, at least to some extent, on the

Revision of an article which appeared in the Fall 1959 issue of Orbis. *Reprinted by permission.*

co-operation of the people. To a much greater degree than in Stalin's time, the present Party leadership is forced to court various segments of the population.

Policy in a dictatorship is conditioned primarily by the necessity of self-preservation. The Party, to preserve itself in power, must not only maintain its control over the machinery of the state but must also command the loyalties of certain strata of the population. The postwar expansion of the U.S.S.R. created the need for many thousands of trusted agents charged with carrying out the dictatorship's policies throughout the world: in the satellites, in China, in the uncommitted nations of Asia and Africa, and in the West. Industrialization, which has immensely complicated the internal relationships of Soviet society, requires the voluntary and loyal co-operation of millions of technicians and administrators. Without their loyalty, the Soviet economy—and the foreign policy of the government—would falter and eventually collapse.

This dependence of the government upon the co-operation of its people suggests that some clues to the future course of Soviet communism may be found not in official Soviet policy but in a relatively stable element of the Soviet scene: Soviet society itself. The adverb "relatively" needs to be stressed. In 1913 almost three quarters of the Russian population were peasants; today only 40 per cent of the Soviet people tend the soil. The old bourgeois and landowning classes have disappeared, and the number of noncollectivized peasants and independent artisans is negligible. The number of industrial workers and technicians has increased many times. And a new class—the ruling class of the Soviet nation—has been born.

Russia has become more literate. Although its population has increased by only 25 per cent since 1914, there are today seven times as many colleges and universities and fifteen times as many students. Thirty million children attend the elementary and secondary schools of the Soviet Union—a threefold increase over 1914.

These are symptoms of tremendous changes which have taken place over a span of forty years. In part they were the product of time: the old generation—or that part of it which survived the civil war and the bloody purges of the Stalin era —is rapidly passing from the scene. In another ten or twenty years no one in the Soviet Union will remember pre-Revolutionary Russia: its life, traditions, and values. This eclipse is of particular importance in Russia, since the intrusion of Communist doctrine and ideology into all spheres of culture shattered, in effect, the normal continuity of the cultural history of the nation. The old classics, both Russian and foreign, are still published and widely read, but everything that contradicts Communist doctrine has long ago been removed from the library shelves and from the publishers' lists.

Still, this eclipse in the mentality of a nation, significant though it is, should not be overestimated. It would be absurd to assume that forty years have undone the character of a great nation compounded by a thousand years of history. Russian sons understand their fathers, though with an effort, and the appreciation of old Russian cultural achievements is deep. There are young *kolkhozniks* whose craving for a plot of land of their own is no less intense than that of their grandfathers. Members of the Komsomol, despite forty years of violent anti-religious propaganda, occasionally venture to marry in church and bring their children to be baptized.

Behind all progress, whether social or material, lies discontent with existing conditions. But discontent alone cannot trigger sociopolitical improvement; equally essential is an understanding of the forces which move society. Soviet society lacks a "thinking minority" which can formulate discontent and channel it toward desirable political goals. The "thinking people" in the Soviet Union are, for all practical purposes, either absorbed into or fully controlled by the Party. This does not mean, of course, that there may not be people in Russia who have pondered the implications of Communist rule and are capable of projecting the future course of the nation along lines different from those of the Communists. But we know nothing of them, and we may safely assume that the Soviet public at large knows nothing of them.

The Communist rulers of Russia have been eminently successful in solving the problem of opposition to their regime: the most gifted and energetic elements either have been attracted by the promise of better living conditions and other rewards or, if they refuse to play along, have been eliminated. There is no doubt that many of those who have chosen to be loyal to the regime are dissatisfied with conditions at large or in their individual fields of endeavor. However, this dissatisfaction finds loyal rather than hostile expression. Their criticism, if voiced at all, remains constructive: it must appear to further the improvement of the Soviet way of life. Never do these critics take a negative attitude toward the regime as such; never are their demands radical.

Unconcealed hostility toward the Soviet regime is manifested only in the lower strata of society: among the peasants, the workers, and the Soviet youth. But this opposition is inarticulate, disorganized, unaccustomed to action, and lacks spokesmen among the representatives of the "leading class." It presents no real danger to the regime—at least so long as a massive police apparatus regulates Soviet life.

Organization of Soviet Society

Contemporary Soviet society is a pyramidlike structure, topped by the Central Committee of the Communist Party of the Soviet Union and its Presidium. Below these lofty bodies we find: (1) the leading members of the government and of the army command and (2) the technical and scientific elites, leading writers and artists, and members of the state and Party bureaucracy.

These two groups, which may constitute about 2 per cent of the population (about 5 per cent if we include the members of their families), represent the upper layer of Soviet society, its "new class," deeply committed to the preservation of the regime. Much further below on the social scale are the rank and file of the intelligentsia—professional men, school and college teachers, and minor specialists—the workers, and, finally, the peasants.

For the members of the last three groups, access to the upper layer is barred except through a Party career. But such a career is usually chosen only by those incapable of achieving success in other fields of endeavor, by the unscrupulous, and by men indifferent to the opinions of others. Some of the most loyal Soviet subjects regard Party membership as at best an unavoidable evil.

A Soviet citizen, even one with a college education, has at best a nebulous idea of the forces which shape his life. Soviet mass psychology has succeeded in confusing him. It has inculcated in him a number of taboos—forbidden topics of thought. And he has developed an extraordinary ability to shed from his mind all disturbing questions. He has learned from childhood that it is the Party which thinks and decides for him, and that whatever initiative he himself can muster must be limited to the range of his immediate competence: his kolkhoz, his factory, his office—wherever he may "legitimately" claim to be an expert. He knows that all meetings and demonstrations are organized by the Party alone, that strikes are forbidden, and that outspoken criticism of the Party leadership is a punishable crime. And although in his everyday life a Soviet citizen may violate many regulations and laws which stand in the way of the improvement of his standard of living, he is psychologically incapable of assuming the role of an "enemy of the Party." He has long ago learned that "enemy of the Party" means "enemy of the people" or "political criminal" (an opprobrium far more serious than that of common criminal).

Demonstrations against the regime or its evil manifestations are extremely rare. It is interesting to note that even in the Russian territories occupied by the Germans during the Second World War there were extremely few instances of the Russian people's physically harming Soviet officials who stayed behind. They were not allowed to participate in local affairs; sometimes they were reported to the Gestapo; but rarely were they subjected to violence even when violence could go unpunished.

Is Democracy Possible in Russia?

To evaluate the prospects for democracy in Russia one has to imagine the conditions under which formal democracy might replace the totalitarian regime. It is obvious that political democracy would have to come first, for little experience in genuine self-government, let alone a democratic tradition, can be developed under a totalitarian regime of the oppressive kind which rules Russia.

There are only two conceivable ways in which a formal democracy can be established in Russia. One is by force, through an overthrow of the Soviets. Another is through the evolution of the Soviet regime. The overthrow may take place as a result of war, of a *coup d'état,* or of a revolution. The chances of war or *coup d'état* are beyond predictability. We can assert with reasonable confidence, however, that the possibility of a revolution is almost nil. The emergence, under the watchful eyes of a well-organized totalitarian state, of a mass clandestine organization capable of overthrowing the government, is less than unlikely. Local insurrections should not be ruled out—and there have been several such risings in the past forty years—but the mighty police machine can easily cope with such trifling challenges.

Besides the Communist Party there are two nation-wide organizations in Russia: the Army and the Church. Neither has the means or the desire to engage in purposeful political action; both are effectively controlled by the Party. The army leadership, even if it chafes occasionally under government policy, is fully aware of its dependence on the Party and its inability to rule the enormous nation.

Occasionally we hear of proposals to activate latent anti-Soviet forces in Soviet territories populated by non-Russian ethnic groups. Fervent nationalism, we are told, pits the Ukrainians, the Georgians, and the Armenians unalterably against their Russian overlords. These forces, it is argued, can trigger a general insurrection against Moscow's domination and thus bring about the downfall of the Soviet state.

This theory does not merit serious consideration. First of all, the non-Russian territories of the U.S.S.R. have their own leading class, whose survival depends entirely on the preservation of the *status quo.* For the last thirty years, no more overt discontent has been evident in these areas than in Great Russia proper.

There have been no movements approaching the scale of, let us say, the Greek underground on Cyprus. Then, too, any uprising in the Caucasus or in Central Asia would necessarily be a local one and would be quickly crushed by the central government. There were reports of mass demonstrations in Tbilisi, Georgia, on the third anniversary of Stalin's death; yet, it still is not clear whether these were anti-Soviet riots or protests by Stalin's compatriots against Khrushchev's denigration of the late dictator.

In brief, there are many forces at work in the Soviet Union which can complicate the life of Soviet policy makers and Party leaders. None of these forces, however, seems powerful enough to pose a serious challenge to the Soviet regime. Barring war or other unforeseen developments, the regime's iron grip over Soviet society is not likely to loosen.

Government versus Party Controls

Although the chances of a peaceful transformation of the Soviet system into a Western type of democracy appear to be nil, it may be useful to explore the possibilities of its evolution toward a less rigid and more enlightened form of dictatorship. To what extent can a Communist state "relax" without ceasing to be itself? What elements of democracy could be introduced in the Soviet Union in years to come? In order to form some tentative conclusions, let us first project the most favorable conditions possible.

Since Stalin's death we have witnessed changes in the Soviet Union which could be interpreted as a trend toward liberalization. There has been, for example, a noticeable departure from Communist economic dogma. The new leadership decided to abandon rigidly centralized planning in favor of a partial decentralization of the economy, thus giving local leaders more say in local affairs. The fact that, following the inauguration of this program, there were signs of the reins being tightened again is not necessarily discouraging; rather, it appears that the original plan was not thought out properly and the Soviet leaders decided to slow the pace of decentralization pending a more comprehensive blueprint.

Even more significant has been the apparently sincere desire of the post-Stalin leadership to improve the standard of living of the population as a whole. A standard of minimum wages (low as they are) has been made into law. Pensions for the aged and for invalids have been increased. The peasants have been given certain incentives to produce more; the machine-tractor stations, those embodiments of "socialism," have been dissolved, and the machinery has been turned over to the collective farms. The current Seven-Year Plan provides, at least on paper, for a considerable rise in the production of consumer goods. An attempt has been made to make Soviet statistics somewhat more honest, and some unflattering figures have been published in Moscow. One may argue that these measures were dictated by necessity, expedience, and plain common sense. Whatever the motivations, however, doctrine and its rigid practice never before have been sacrificed with such nonchalant abandon.

Since Stalin's death, the government apparatus, which formed the backbone of the Soviet system during the twilight of Stalin's rule, has yielded in importance to the Party. This has meant a relative diminution of the role of the so-called managerial class and a growth in the power of Party professionals. As during the first decade after the Revolution, the Party represents the only stepladder to social improvement. This function by the Party gives its leadership full control over individuals in commanding positions, whom it can reward or punish through Party channels without having to bother with the cumbersome formalities of a government bureaucracy.

To secure the loyalty of Party members the new leadership has offered them certain personal guarantees. Ever since the Twentieth Party Congress in 1956, the power—and the autonomy—of the police have been curtailed. Nowadays, the arrest of a Party member involves a rather complex procedure; the Party professionals are further beyond the law than ever before. At the same time, the revised Penal Code, while making legal procedures more orderly and less arbitrary, provides for considerably stricter punishment for "crimes against the state"—that is, for attempts to weaken or overthrow the rule of the Party. As before, the Party remains above the law, which it writes and rewrites at will.

There has been little change in the cultural field. The period of the "thaw," which flourished in 1955–56, has been brought to an end: apparently the Party considered it fraught with too many dangers. Nevertheless, the new conformity does not resemble the rigid synchronization of Soviet society under Stalin. Although the right to oppose the official line is still denied, the right to dissent under certain circumstances exists in fact, if not as a recognized principle.

These changes are significant. Yet precisely how significant? Do they signify a meaningful evolution of the Soviet state into a more mellow and liberal society? Are they likely to lead to democratic reforms?

A careful study of Russian history indicates that suppression in Russia—including the police terror—has always been a measure of the internal and external insecurity of the regime. This cause-and-effect relationship remains true today: the present regime cannot permit "relaxation" to the point where it would infringe upon the sense of security of Party professionals.

It can be argued that the Soviet leadership should, by all rights, feel more secure today than ever before. The Soviet Union, after all, has emerged as a military power of the first rank and may claim to be strong enough to destroy its enemies in the event of war. Yet the ruling elite knows that the next war may totally destroy the power base which it has wrought with such enormous effort. True, the "socialist" camp, including China and eastern Europe, possesses a tremendous potential in terms of human and industrial resources—a potential unprecedented in its history. At the same time, events in Poland and Hungary have demonstrated that Communist assets can quickly turn into dangerous liabilities. The Soviet leaders clearly realize that no accounting sheet can be drawn today which could show a comfortable balance in their favor. This basic insecurity to a great extent lies behind the baffling contradiction of themes in Soviet propaganda: the mixture of overtures for "peace" with blustering threats of war.

At home, the Soviet leadership has attempted to buy security by bidding for the loyalty of larger segments of the people. Under Stalin, hostility to the regime was deep and pervasive, fed as it was by an oppressive machine of terror; today, dreary resignation has given way to hopefulness and expectation. New and glowing promises have been made to the population at large, and recent improvements in its standard of living spur the hope that these promises will be fulfilled.

Yet disillusionment is certain to set in. Khrushchev's "horn of plenty" is limited by the productive capacity of the Soviet economy and by the staggering commitments of the Soviet state. Despite all efforts, per capita agricultural production in Russia is still below that of 1913. The cost of armaments is colossal. The efficiency of the Russian industrial establishment is well below the standards of the average capitalist enterprise. If one adds to these burdens the Soviet foreign-aid commitments, the astronomical cost of the propaganda machine, and the subsidies for "progressive" movements abroad, it becomes clear that little is left over for appreciably raising the standard of living of the rank-and-file citizen. Then, too, the Soviet leadership has to support an army of Party professionals, perhaps three million strong—a completely nonproductive and parasitic body—and to support it on a lavish scale.

Although this privileged group tends to grow—in fact, there has been a noticeable effort to enroll new members into the Party in the last few years—it is likely to remain an exclusive club. The Soviet Communist of today is a realist. He has not read much of Marx or Lenin, and he cares little for doctrine. He would favor decentralization of industry if this measure could be justified economically to his satisfaction. He would agree to the loosening of controls over collectivized agriculture (a move which would cause Stalin to turn in his grave), if he felt confident that this would benefit him directly.

But there is one thing which the Party professional would resist to the bitter end: the loosening of the Party's grip on the people. He himself may be disdainful of Communist doctrine, but he will allow no one else to question it, since all his claims to a privileged position in Soviet society, as well as his Party's sole claim to power, are based on doctrine. Whatever the citizens may think in the solitude of their minds, they must conform outwardly. The Party will maintain its monopoly on the means of communication for no other reason than to check the spread of "heresy." Criticism of Marxism, the Party, or the policies of the leadership will remain a punishable crime. Soviet citizens will continue to be denied any but official sources of information and forced to accept the official interpretation of events.

In short, no matter what the intentions of the ruling group

in the Soviet Union may be, its actions are guided, first and foremost, by the need of self-preservation. The Party will continue to be above the law, for the law is its major weapon against real or imagined opposition within the country; and it will employ the full power of the State to enforce its decisions. This means that any grants of liberties or social improvements to the population would carry no guarantee other than the convenience of the Party leadership.

The precise point at which "relaxation" would endanger the regime is indeterminable. Probably nothing short of world domination—if that—will make Soviet leadership completely confident of its ability to survive. History does not know of an autocratic regime which reformed itself voluntarily, and there is little reason to believe that the Soviet Union will be an exception to this rule.

The Illusion of Freedom in Russia

If revolution in Russia is thus out of the question and if liberalization of the regime cannot proceed beyond certain rigid limits, what hope—if any—does the future hold for Soviet man? Perhaps more significantly, what hope is there for the Free World?

In seeking an answer to these questions, we must, first of all, shed the illusion that the drive for freedom is inexorable and universal. The majority of Russians do not resent the absence of political freedom—they do not for the simple reason that they cannot miss something which they never possessed. Lacking any other choice, they can reconcile themselves to a one-party system. They can learn to tolerate the dullness of their press and the monotony of their literature, movies, and drama. They can continue to do the Party's bidding and remain loyal to the regime, for experience has shown them that, in order to survive, they must adjust to the harsh realities of Soviet life.

There is, however, one variable in the Soviet equation: namely, the material and social aspirations of the Russian people. Sooner or later, Soviet citizens will expect some rewards for submission and loyalty. Sooner or later—if not already today—they will expect a reasonably high standard of living, which has been promised to them so often by so many of their leaders. They will expect that a man of "low" social background be given at least a modest opportunity to ascend the social ladder. They will expect that, as long as they are loyal to the regime, they should be trusted more, and not treated like retarded children incapable of deciding even the most trivial matter for themselves. And they will expect from their government a little more fairness and honesty.

Few of these expectations are likely to be met in the foreseeable future. Russia is a class society in which the privileged class, hypersensitive to real and imagined threats to its existence, jealously guards its privileges. There may be some concessions in the economic realm. Barring war or other calamity, the material lot of the Soviet man should continue to improve. He may never reach the level of well-being of the average man in the West, but eventually his basic needs in food, clothing, and housing will be satisfied. As the output of the economy increases, however, the appetite of the public will grow commensurately—a dangerous trend in a society which functions on the principle that the state determines all individual needs.

With the general improvement in the Soviet economy, its material benefits will be more evenly distributed among the Soviet aristocracy. At the same time, membership in the elite, while it may widen somewhat, will tend increasingly to become hereditary. The appetites of the "haves" are likely to grow faster than the economy of the nation, and they will have to be given first priority. Although the country's gross national product will become considerably greater, the workers' and peasants' share in it will tend to be proportionately smaller. There will be an increasing disparity within Soviet society.

Thus, the cycle which began with the death of Stalin will have run its full course. Even though, in the end, Soviet man may be better off materially, popular moods are rarely determined by absolute want. The present leadership fully realizes this and is attempting to close the gap somewhat between the "haves" and the "have nots." These attempts cannot be successful, for the simple reason that the Soviet economy, even if it becomes more efficient and productive, will never be able to give to everyone "according to his needs." The members of the elite will secure as high a standard for themselves as possible at the expense of the masses; and the leadership, dependent as it is upon the elite, will have to assist them in this quest.

As this process continues, the present hope of the pariahs of Soviet society will fade. Their disillusionment inevitably will lead them to question the justice of the social order which, while ostensibly dedicated to the goal of a "classless society," withholds from them their rightful share in the fruits of their labors. There is no way of telling what form this discontent will take. It is clear, however, that the Party, in order to keep it in check, will be forced to restore full power to the police, to reduce or eliminate the few liberties of the post-Stalin era, and to suppress the opposition by the traditional methods of dictatorship.

The terror is not likely to affect the elite. The members of the Soviet aristocracy, as they develop a more prodigious taste for the comforts of life, will tend to become more avaricious and close their ranks still tighter. The regime will be protected from external attack by the powerful deterrent of a few thousand perfected ICBMs, with push buttons on the desk of the First Secretary of the Party. It will be protected at home by a mighty police machine surpassing even Stalin's fondest dreams.

Under these conditions—prosperity and relative freedom for some, and austerity and repression for the rest—the Communist state may be able to exist indefinitely. The Roman Empire was in decline for four centuries, and would have lasted still longer had it not suffered invasion by more dynamic conquerors.

Yet all empires have their life span. In time, the Soviets, unwilling to risk an uneasy stability at home in doubtful adventures abroad, may gradually shed the dynamics of their revolutionary faith. Thus, while the future holds little promise for the average Soviet citizen, there is hope, albeit a distant one, for the Free World. The West, if it weathers the challenges of the present aggressive "flow period" of Soviet power, may yet witness a reversal of the Communist tide. The prospects are not uniformly bright. There is always the danger that the Soviet leadership, sensing that the "dialectic of history" is turning against it, will in desperation detonate the nuclear Armageddon. But short of a pre-emptive war, a war which contravenes the very ethos of Western society, the West has no alternative except steadfastness, courage, and patience —and the hope that time will reap what man cannot.

8. Communist Vulnerabilities

by Bertram D. Wolfe

> *Mr. Wolfe, who writes in the fields of both
> history and political science, ranks among
> the outstanding Soviet experts of the United
> States. Born in Brooklyn, New York, he re-
> ceived his B.A. from the College of the City
> of New York and his M.A. from Columbia
> University. He has held senior fellowships in
> Slavic studies at Stanford and Columbia and
> set up and headed the Ideological Advisory
> Staff of the State Department for the Voice
> of America. Among his books are* Three Who
> Made a Revolution *(1948) and* Khrushchev
> and Stalin's Ghost *(1957). He is at present
> at work upon the second volume of his his-
> tory of the Russian Revolution.*

Vulnerability implies an alert and determined opponent, ready
to take advantage of every weakness and every opening. Only
then do weaknesses and inconsistencies become vulnerabilities.
But this determination and this readiness are today lacking in
the Free World.

The Communists know that they are engaged in what Professor Robert Strausz-Hupé and his associates at the Foreign
Policy Research Institute of the University of Pennsylvania
have called "a protracted war." They know that they are engaged in a war to the finish, a war for the world. Every separate issue, every negotiation, every conference, every utter-

Originally published in the September 7, 1959, issue of the New
Leader, *this is based on an address Mr. Wolfe gave to the National
Strategy Seminar for Reserve Officers. Reprinted by permission of
the author and the* New Leader.

ance, they regard as a move in that war, whereas for us in the
West each is treated as a separate concrete issue to be settled
once and for all in order that we may relax.

We aim to persuade our opponents that our intentions are
friendly. We aim to "reassure" the Soviets as to their "security." We aim to trade concessions, which in practice means
only to give away positions we possess, so that the other side,
which offers nothing in exchange, can renew the battle from
a more advantageous position.

Edward Gibbon once wrote, "Persuasion is the resource of
the feeble; and the feeble can seldom persuade." We are not
feeble. Actually, America and the Free World are at this moment stronger economically and militarily than the opponent
who is determined to destroy us. But we are acting as though
from feebleness, thus endangering peace by making the Communists underestimate our strength and luring them, without
intending to do so, into the folly of an attack. Thus, the very
moves we make to preserve peace are moves which profoundly
endanger the peace.

Insofar as we act as if we were weak, as if our task were
to persuade the unpersuadable and to settle what cannot be
settled; insofar as we have permitted the Communists to divide
the world into their "peace zone," where we may not and do
not intervene, and our "war zone," where the entire world and
the United Nations and they also may intervene—to that extent it is not they but we who are vulnerable. We are proving
vulnerable because of our incapacity and unwillingness to use
the openings which their system has provided, does provide,
and will continue to provide.

What we need, first of all, is an understanding of this universal, unitary, unending war to the finish. Second, we need
a revolutionary strategy, to put the revolutionary forces of our
time at our disposal and deny the Communists their use and
exploitation. Only then will their system prove more vulnerable than ours, as potentially it is. With this caveat in mind,
let us examine first their theoretical foundations and, second,
their strategical and tactical vulnerabilities.

The Theoretical Foundation: Marxism

The Communist theoretical foundation lies in something called Marxism. We must first examine the self-refuting inconsistencies in Marxism and its prophecies that have been refuted by history.

One hundred and ten years ago, Karl Marx and Friedrich Engels issued their call to arms in the *Communist Manifesto*, with its dogmatic pronouncements and apocalyptic expectations. A decade later, Marx undertook to lay bare "the law of motion" of industrial society in a work called *Contribution to the Critique of Political Economy*. Those 110 years have not dealt kindly with Marx's predictions and have mocked and refuted the very "law of motion" which he claimed to have discovered.

The heart of those works was an expectation of an early apocalypse. The world was headed toward immediate and total catastrophe. In 1848, this catastrophe was only days, or at most weeks, away. It would come with the next street skirmish. Before the year was up, it was to come with the next war, within the year. When it came neither with the street skirmishes nor with the wars which Marx advocated, he decided it would come with the next downswing in the business cycle. But the apocalypse failed to appear.

The second startling thing about the *Communist Manifesto*, which aimed to be the program for the Revolution of 1848, is that it prophesied the end of nationalism. Yet 1848 witnessed the greatest explosion of nationalism in the history of Europe. And now, in the twentieth century, two world wars and their revolutionary aftermaths have proved that nationalism is the one great cause for which millions are ready to fight and die. It has spread from Europe, which was its home, to Asia and Africa, which in Marx's time knew not the nation. National feeling provides great vulnerabilities in the Soviet empire, if we have the wit to exploit them. At the same time, it provides great vulnerabilities for the Free World in Asia and Africa, because the men in the Kremlin do have the wit to exploit the nationalism which the *Communist Manifesto* said was on the way out or was already out.

Marx's third prophecy dealt with the increasing polarization of society. It treated industrial society, in mythical Hegelian terms, as a system all the parts of which were so connected that no change could be made in it; the system could not be improved or reformed; it could not evolve; it could only be scrapped. The defects were treated as integral to the system and incapable of being removed defect by defect and replaced by other structures or circumstances; they could only be shattered and replaced by another system. The special mission to do the shattering was assigned by Marx to the working class. When this did not come immediately, as the *Communist Manifesto* anticipated, Marx began his long work to give a "scientific" foundation to this expectation of the apocalypse.

Marx's *Capital* has this as its function. The book is strangely constructed, so that most of it consists of empirical evidence, striking descriptions of the workings of industrial society, drawn from the England of Marx's day, or rather the England of the day before Marx's day. He took most of the evidence from the Parliamentary Blue Books, reports of a Parliament that had already investigated the evils of early industrialism and was busy regulating, moderating, reforming, and removing the evil excrescences of industrialization. His book thus gives overwhelming evidence of this evolution and reform, as he himself is compelled finally to point out. When he is discussing the achievement of the ten-hour-work law, regulation of child labor, and other such achievements of the England of his day, he writes: "Capital is under compulsion from society. The factory magnates have resigned themselves to the inevitable. The power of resistance of capital has gradually weakened. The power of attack of the working class has grown with the number of its allies. Hence, the comparatively rapid advance since 1860."

If one reads Marx's *Capital* as an empirical student should read it, the overwhelming evidence of the Blue Books drives one, as it drove him, to this conclusion. Yet when one comes to the last chapter, "the last for which the first was made," a chapter called "The Historical Tendency of Capitalist Accumulation," one finds that capital came into the world conceived in original sin, "a congenital bloodstain on its cheek, dripping with blood and dirt from head to foot, from every pore." And it is destined to leave it now in a fearful cataclysm, a day of wrath and doom, by the workings of "the immanent laws of capitalist production itself."

"One capitalist kills many"; all other classes are destined to be proletarianized; and, as if by mitosis, society is to be polarized. "Along with the constantly diminishing number of magnates of capital . . . grows the mass of misery, oppression, slavery, degradation, exploitation; but with this grows, too, the revolt of the working class. . . . The monopoly of capital becomes a fetter upon the mode of production. Centralization of the means of production, and socialization of labor, at last reach a point where they become incompatible with their capitalist integument. This integument is burst asunder. The knell of capitalist private property sounds. The expropriators are expropriated." Thus, the conclusion of 1848 is tacked on again after the mass of empirical material to the contrary which makes up the bulk of the volume. But for this it was not necessary to study the Parliamentary Blue Books.

Such has been the perversity of history that it has not vouchsafed the revolution Marx expected in the countries of advanced industry, but has vouchsafed revolutions which invoke Marx's name only in underdeveloped countries on the eve or in the incipient stages of industrialization, in countries shaken by the impact of the West's economy and equality upon autocratic institutions which Marx regarded not as pre-socialist but as pre-bourgeois or non-bourgeois.

Another thing which would startle Marx were he to be resurrected today is the succession of industrial revolutions which followed his "industrial revolution." He knew the development from cottage artisanship to machinofacture, from the use of wind and water and animal and manpower to the use of steam power. This was the industrial revolution that Marx studied. But the industrial revolution is unending. He thought that industrial society had reached "the end of its development" in 1848, when he pronounced its doom so stirringly. Actually it was but at the beginning of the development of its productive forces. Since then have come the age of electricity, conveyor belt, combustion engine, synthetic chemistry, electronics, automation, fission, fusion; and the end is nowhere in sight, unless atomic war should bring a cataclysm indeed, but not Marx's cataclysm.

The society which he thought was to polarize until it had reached the breaking point of total polarization has actually been depolarizing. Intermediate classes have not disappeared; they have multiplied. The industrial proletariat has not become the whole of society; it has lost in numerical weight in society while it has gained in status and in economic and political power. Classes have become more fluid and more equalized—not merely in comparatively classless America but in once caste-ridden England and France and Germany as well.

In America—absurdly, Marx would think—one man, woman, and child in every eight is today a stockholder in the great corporations which he thought were going to provide the little "handful" of capitalists to be destroyed. Main Street frequently exercises more power than Wall Street, and labor and farmers have more influence on legislation than corporation executives or bankers. The latter could only fume impotently and curse "that man in the White House" while we went through the tremendous revolution in our society known as the New Deal. And even the "owning class" was divided in its attitude.

The state thus has proved refractory to Marxist prophecies. In place of becoming an executive committee of a shrinking bourgeoisie, as he described it, it has been increasingly democratized, subjected to pressure of the labor vote, the farm vote, and the intermediate-class votes, even to the pressure of strategically located minorities such as the Negroes in the big cities of the North. Out of labor's influence on government, and out of the classless pressure of the whole of society, has come a state regulation of economic life, a legal limitation of the hours of work, a minimum wage, collective bargaining, the legislated right to organize, and a whole sweep of social-security legislation. "The state," as the French socialist Marcel Déat wrote, "has undergone a process of socialization, while socialism has undergone a process of nationalization."

The Supremacy of Politics over Economics

In Marx's day there was a general superstition, of which Marx was the most prominent advocate but which was general for most of the leading thinkers of his age: the superstition that "economics determines politics." The twentieth century has made it a commonplace that politics tends to determine economics. In fact, totalitarianism is, from this angle, an attempt totally to determine the economic and social structure of society by putting one's hand on the powerful political lever, the lever of unified centralized and exclusive power.

Thus, what has happened to the economy is that it has been increasingly politicalized. Moreover, the whole notion of an autonomous economy, with its own autonomic laws, on which Marx based himself and on which Marx's opponents in the mid-nineteenth century based themselves no less—all this has become obsolete and has revealed itself as no longer a workable hypothesis. In its place has come the increasing social and political regulation of the economy. Politics determines economics through tariffs, protectionism, quotas of export and import, currency regulation and manipulation, regulation of the interest rate, deficit spending, price floors, price ceilings, parities, subsidies, state fostering of cartelization as in Germany, state persecution or prosecution of cartelization as in our anti-trust acts in the United States, and supranational economies like Benelux, the "inner-six common market," the "outer-seven free-trade area," and all the other supranational economies that are beginning to grow up. And in vast areas of the world there is total politicalization and autarchy. Not a word of what Marx has written is helpful in approaching the problems of our era. Whether these features are to be welcomed or to be feared, they have surely produced a world which makes the projections of Marx and the projections of his nineteenth-century opponents alike irrelevant.

Unkindest cut of all, the worker himself has not consented to be increasingly proletarianized, increasingly impoverished, and to have thrust upon him the mission with which Marx endowed him. If the worker has engaged in a "class struggle,"

it has been one to put off from himself this increasing pro-
letarianization and impoverishment and this mission which
Marx and the Marxists would confer upon him. In this struggle, the workers have displayed stubbornness, tirelessness,
courage, selfishness, solidarity, skill, incapacity to recognize
when they are defeated, and the power to enlist the sympathy
of the rest of society in fighting off this prophetic destiny and
this prophetic assignment.

Unlike the intellectuals who offered them socialist leadership, they have no stomach for being reduced to nought, the
better to prepare themselves for becoming all. To win the suf-
frage on the continent of Europe, to influence and exert control over government, to legalize and contractualize improvements in the hours of their lives that are spent in labor, to
win some security and dignity within the system in which they
live, to become "something" in the world in which they have
their being, rather than to be "everything" in the world which
exists only in the fantasy of the utopians, of whom Marx was
perhaps the greatest—it is to these aims that they have rallied.
For this they have fought their struggle, and to these aims
they have succeeded in rallying most of modern society.

Those who "being nought were to become all" having become something, the whole scheme loses its tidy outlines. Thus,
the flaw in the foundation itself, the theory on which communism claims to build, lies in the fact that a hundred years
of subsequent history have reduced every theoretical tenet of
Marxism to a shambles.

Marxism as an "Ism"

Insofar as it has claimed to be a science, Marxism is dead.
Marx and Engels in their last years were uncomfortably aware
of this and were beginning an uneasy and reluctant patching
or revising of their dogmas. But after their death the revision-
ists who followed were outlawed and condemned, and ceased
to be Marxists, and those who claimed to be Marxists survived
only with the aid of the frozen orthodoxy of a dogmatic creed
no longer subject to scientific examination or revision. Indeed,
in this lies the strength and the staying powers of Marxism

after Marxism as a "science" has proved itself bankrupt. As a science, it has produced only invalid results, but it is also an "ism"—Marxism. There is no "Lockeism," no "Smithism," "Millism," "Durkheimism," "Micheletism," "Rankeism" or "Gibbonism," but there is a Marxism. And this is a fundamental difference which we must strive to understand.

Besides having claimed to be a science, it has been a creed which can be clung to by faith when the intellect questions and rebels. While as a theory Marxism can be refuted by intellect talking to intellect, the strength of the Marxist movement as such lies not in the realm of ideas but in the realm of emotions. It is an ersatz religion, and this is harder to reach with rational argument and harder to cope with.

Though the Marxist revolution never occurred, and is not likely to occur, we do indeed live in an age of revolution, a revolution which began before Marx's time and which will outlast our own lifetime. It is not the revolution which Marx predicted; nor did it grow from the seeds he sowed. His theory was but one of the misunderstandings of this revolution. The West's rapid expansion to all the continents of the world upset all the world's surviving civilizations. Western society planted everywhere the seeds of its own creativeness, its own problems, and its own dissensions.

This is a world revolution in the true sense. The Communists did not create it, but they study ceaselessly to utilize it for the spread of their power and for the destruction of ours. We did create it. But we do not try to understand or to utilize it, or to aid it in finding new forms of abundance and of freedom. The Communists seek to give neither abundance nor freedom. What they propose to do is to extend their power and their zone; to set up regimes of specialized productivity for power and for war, not regimes of plenty and freedom; to link the revolutionary forces afoot in the world to their war for the winning of the world. Whoever harnesses the forces of that revolution which the West has set in motion yet has not striven to understand, whichever side manages to put to its own use these forces in politics and economics, in science and technology, in all fields of life, and to deny them to its opponent, that side will win the struggle for the world.

Insofar as the Communists are doing just that and we are

not, they are slowly winning the war and will continue to win the war which will occupy the rest of our century. And therefore, in spite of the inconsistencies, cruelties, and absurdities of their system, the balance of vulnerability has been swinging from their side to ours.

The Strategy and Tactics of Leninism

Leninism is the strategy and tactics for waging this war, for utilizing the revolutionary forces afloat in the world for the purpose of building totalitarian single-party power throughout the world. Leninism claims to be Marxism: the Marxism "of the period of imperialism, world war, and world revolution." Leninism claims to be Marxism, yet in all essential respects it has stood Marxism on its head as Marx claims to have stood Hegelianism on its head.

Marx: Economics determines politics. *Lenin:* Politics determines economics.

Marx: Revolution comes after capitalism has reached its pinnacle and comes first in the most advanced countries. *Lenin:* Revolution comes first where capitalism is weakest—"the break in the system at the point of its weakest link."

Marx: The revolution will come first in England, or perhaps Germany or France. *Lenin:* The revolution comes first in Russia, where capitalism is weakest, and then we carry the revolution to advanced Europe, or, failing in that, to Asia and Africa from backward Russia in order to deny to the advanced countries their outlets and markets, cut them off from the backward part of the world, and cut the undeveloped countries off from them.

Marx: The working class is destined to develop its own consciousness, its own theory, its own organization, its own party, and its own revolution. *Lenin:* The working class left to itself is capable only of bourgeois thought. Not the "bourgeois-minded and vacillating" working class, but a revolutionary elite, a classless vanguard party, is the guardian of the working class. It dictates to the working class. It rules over the working class—and all other classes. It uses the working class as a battering-ram because the urban working class is the most unified and concentrated, but it uses the peasantry as a battering-ram, too, and it tries to use discontent in all classes. And piling up the discontents, it aims to put in power not the working class but its own elite vanguard nonclass party.

If this is so, a revolution can be made in a backward country where the working class is not ripe, and the vanguard party can profess to be establishing a dictatorship in the name of the proletariat where it is only beginning to come into existence. Or, as in China, the peasantry can be used as the battering-ram. And when the scepter of power has been seized, the vanguard party can claim that it has established the dictatorship of a proletariat which does not yet exist. Or where is the proletariat of North Vietnam? Ho Chi Minh, dictator in the name of a dictatorship of a nonexistent proletariat through a nonexistent party of the proletariat, dictates over a society which is not only not socialist but is still pre-capitalist.

Leninism can be understood as a strategy and tactics for the conquest of power, for the maintenance and expansion of power, for making that power absolute and total; as a prescription for the building of a party designed to seize and hold power; as a strategy and tactics for the utilization of the discontents, the unrests, the disturbances, and the revolutionary forces which the West has set afloat in the world—to the end of subverting and destroying all that the West stands for and all that the West dreams of. It is a revolutionary strategy for the winning of the world and for the remaking of man according to Lenin's blueprint. As such, it is, of course, highly vulnerable if it is confronted by an alert, determined, and watchful opponent, ready to utilize the revolutionary situations and strategies and to contest for the leadership of the forces set free by Western civilization itself.

The Russian Revolution—Promise and Performance

The Russian Revolution is now over forty years old. In the four decades that this new power has existed and become total, all of its original promises have turned into their opposites. Here is where an alert opponent would find more vulnerabilities than he would know what to do with if he were really on the job.

1. It promised "land to the peasants." But in the end it took away even the land which the peasants had under the Czars, and it herded them into a new state-owned serfdom.

2. It promised "perpetual peace." Instead it has produced a totalitarian state which forever wages a twofold war—a war on its own people to remake them according to its blueprint and a war upon the world. And the word "war" is meant not figuratively but literally. When it wages war on its own people, it is a real war, a war of nerves, a war of quarantine (the Iron Curtain), a war of propaganda, of agitation, of conditioning, of psychological warfare, of physical warfare, of prisons, of concentration camps, of bombardment by loud-speakers and press and movies and all the means of cultural conditioning, and, when necessary, a bullet in the base of the brain. At the same time it has used this war upon its own people to keep them mobilized for unending war to win the world.

3. It promised "production for use," that is, for the sake of the consumer and consumers' goods. Instead it has set up production for production's sake, for the sake of expanding the oppressive power of the producer-owner state.

4. It promised "plenty," and it has produced perpetual scarcity of all the goods that make life gracious, pleasant, easy, cultured, rewarding, full of promise and possibility.

5. The state that was "to wither away" has expanded to totality. Lenin promised that "every cook is to become master of the affairs of the state." Now the state is the master of the affairs of every cook.

6. It promised "freedom," and it has abolished all freedoms.

7. It promised "the workers' paradise," and it has immured its people behind an impenetrable wall and turned their country into a prison for their thoughts and for their very lives, which cannot be penetrated by learning what happens on the outside or by the freedom to discuss what is happening to themselves on the inside.

8. It has raised the banner of "national self-determination" and "anti-imperialism," but it has become the most aggressive, the most oppressive, the most rapidly expanding imperialist power in the history of man.

Thus—and the above are only a few of communism's potential vulnerabilities—all the revolutionary slogans which Lenin sought to use, and which the Kremlin uses today against all peoples, governments, and institutions, could easily be turned by a determined opponent, in tune with our age and ready to use revolutionary strategy, into weapons in our hands. The Communists' hands would prove nerveless and lifeless if we would but grasp the weapons which they are using against us, which are not theirs by right and which by right can be made to belong to us, for they are indeed our weapons.

We, not they, are today the advocates of genuine agrarian reform and the right of each man to till his own land. There is no country in the world more badly in need of agrarian reform than the U.S.S.R. itself.

We, not they, are the advocates of a just and enduring peace, based on the respect for the rights and the existence of all nations in being or a-borning or yet to be.

We, not they, are the champions of the rights and freedoms of workingmen, the freedom of movement, the freedom to change jobs, the freedom to build organizations of their own choosing under their own control, the right to elect their own officials, to formulate and negotiate their own demands, the right to strike, the right to vote for a party and a program and candidates of their own choice.

We, not they, are able to call the armies to "fraternize across the trenches," for it is they who must cut off their armies from the news of what is happening in the West, and we who must make our armies and theirs understand what is happening in their land.

We, not they, are the champions of the freedom of the human spirit, of the freedom of the arts and sciences, freedom of conscience, freedom of belief and worship, freedom from scarcity and want and from the tyranny of irresponsible and omnipotent officials. Though, in all these things, the Free World has its own imperfections and lapses, these are the things that the Free World stands for and in good measure realizes, and these are the things which totalitarianism completely destroys and makes high treason even to think upon.

In the battle for the future shape of the world, all the creative and explosive weapons are in our hands if we have the wit and the understanding to take them up. If we do not, then there are no psychological or ideological vulnerabilities of communism. If we do, the Communists are vulnerable on every front and at every moment and in every layer of their society. Whether the answer to this question is "Yes" or "No" will determine the outcome of the protracted war that is likely to occupy the rest of our lives and the rest of our century.

PART THREE

COMMUNIST STRATEGY AND TACTICS

INTRODUCTION

In little more than four decades, communism has grown from a rented room in Zurich, Switzerland, into an empire covering nearly one third of the earth's surface. The mainspring of this thrust to power has been a revolutionary strategy—to wit, the strategy of protracted conflict. The salient characteristics of this strategy are: the careful blending and co-ordination of all available techniques of conflict, from the "nonviolent" methods of subversion and infiltration to the ultimate annihilative blow; a broader view of the terrain of struggle; a greater understanding of—and, therefore, a greater capacity to exploit—the forces which shape, or misshape, international society; and, finally, a deeper insight into the psychological matrix of human beings —their motivations, actions, and interactions.

9. The Orchestration of Crisis

by Colonel William R. Kintner, U.S.A.

*Presently assigned to the Office of the Chief
of Research and Development, Department
of the Army, Colonel Kintner was deputy
commandant of the first National Strategy
Seminar for Reserve Officers. He graduated
from the United States Military Academy
in 1940 and received his Ph.D. from Georgetown University in 1949. He served in Europe during World War II and commanded
an infantry battalion during the Korean
War. He is recognized as one of the Army's
outstanding students of international affairs,
and he is currently working on a special project with the Foreign Policy Research Institute of the University of Pennsylvania. He is
the author and coauthor of several books, including* Protracted Conflict, *and contributes
frequently to national magazines.*

The master plans for world conquest have often depended to a
great extent on the inertia and ignorance of the proposed victims. Ironically enough, many of these plans, even those as
recent as Hitler's *Mein Kampf* and the Japanese *Tanaka Me-
morial,* were available to the ignorant well in advance of the
onslaught. And though advanced students at Moscow's Lenin
School of Strategic Studies are not allowed to take notes from
their classes, the master plan of Communist strategy is clear,
too, for anyone willing to study and analyze not only the bla-
tant Communist record of aggrandizement but also the pub-

Reprinted from Esquire, *May 1959. Copyright 1959 by Esquire, Inc.*

lished writings of Lenin, Stalin, and Mao Tse-tung. To one who understands the Communist formula, the seemingly disparate crises of the past decades become interlocking parts of an over-all pattern of conflict with but a single purpose: to destroy the Western world and make Communist totalitarianism supreme everywhere.

The Strategy of Protracted Conflict

The Communist plan is the strategy of protracted conflict. A hard look at protracted conflict—at its meaning, at its historical development, at the many ways it is currently used against us to forward the aims of a relentless enemy—might provide us with a key for survival.

The term "protracted conflict" was first used by Mao Tse-tung. Mao's term aptly describes the multifront, multiweapons nature of Communist operations. Most generally, it is, by its very name, a method of conflict whereby weaker powers, in time, gain the strength necessary to overcome stronger ones. This strength is gained not only through warfare—which is often, in fact, a last resort—but through other, subtler means of conflict as well: political, economic, and even psychological. It is a method requiring infinite patience; the purpose of each action, military or otherwise, is not to gain an immediate smashing victory but rather to enhance the relative power position of the weaker at the expense of the stronger. The parallel to a game of chess is unmistakable. White's disadvantage is black's advantage. Poker players, as we are in the West, always hoping for the lucky draw, are helpless before it.

Of course, there are those who would say that Soviet technology has so developed in recent years that *we* have become the weaker in this life-and-death game. This is too extreme a view; on balance, the West still appears to be the stronger. Even if we have lost ground, we have definitely not lost the power of enormous, possibly fatal, retaliation. And one cardinal principle of Communist operational doctrine is well understood: the Soviet Union, the base of the world revolution, must not be risked in the pursuit of any one objective. Thus the problem of Communist strategists is now (as it was in the departed days of decisive U.S. nuclear superiority): How can the greatest freedom of maneuver be maintained so that power and space may be gradually amassed without the risk of being plunged into a full-scale atomic war?

Protracted conflict is the obvious answer. A strategy of limited actions, of indirect threats, it is also one in which no single move constitutes adequate provocation for the unleashing of the West's engines of nuclear destruction. And for its success it relies most heavily on our fears that any introduction of such weapons would surely produce a global chain reaction. Because Western strategy has been mainly predicated on the concept that war, if it comes, will be total in character, involving maximum violence, we are still ill equipped to meet the diffuse and dangerous challenges offered by that form of conflict at which the men in Moscow and Peiping are most proficient.

Examples of Piecemeal Strategy

A brief backward look at the Korean War is instructive in a discussion of the Communist piecemeal strategy. In June 1950, the Soviets, testing the firmness of U.S. intentions in the Far East, acted indirectly by manipulating the puppet regime of North Korea to launch an attack on its neighbor to the south. They then parried the affirmative American response which followed by inducing the Communist Chinese to enter the war, doubtless by persuading them that here was their golden opportunity to establish themselves as a major power. Even after 1950 the United States was inclined to think that the war *in* Korea was still *over* Korea, with the additional feature of Chinese intervention superimposed. A mental block obscured the fact that this was now a conflict between Communist China and the West, which refused to extend operations even after the meaning of the war itself had been extended. The chief fear was that an expansion of the theater of action (by air raids on Chinese bases north of the Yalu) and of the weapons system (by the use of tactical nuclear arms) might have sparked the Soviets into action and brought on a general war. There is good reason now to conclude that the West's fear was more emotional than logical. However they bluster, the Soviets seem manifestly reluctant to leap into an all-out fight. At any rate, the West failed in Korea to revise its strategy to meet the new situation.

There are other examples. Also in Asia, the conquest of Indochina constitutes a striking example of Communist ingenuity and energy. There, following hard on Korea, a modern mechanized French military machine, numbering more than half a million troops and backed by practically unlimited conventional war supplies from the United States, was less defeated than neutralized in a rapid culmination of events that startled the world, reoriented the thinking of numerous opportunistic Easterners, and brought a perjured peace in which a nation was bisected in a ceremony humiliating to the West at Geneva in 1954.

The conflict in Indochina was a convincing demonstration of the versatility of Red strategists simultaneously employing the various weapons of protracted warfare on two continents. In Europe, especially in France, the tools were political pressure, intrigue, propaganda, and economic strife. And in the actual target area, the instances were rare that the Communists made attempts to match military muscle with the French. Yet when the situation was ripe and the battle was all but won by an eight-year campaign of subversion, terror, and guerrilla warfare, a conventional but resounding military triumph was engineered at Dien Bien Phu to complete the discomfiture of the West and to pave the way for new conflicts of the protracted war.

Contrasting Concepts of War and Peace

Study of the historical development of U.S. and Western attitudes toward war is enlightening because it reveals the wellsprings of the general concept which today permits the depredations of protracted conflict. In general, the Western tradition, until the latter part of the nineteenth century, vindicated the use of force to defend the moral order. And at the same time it emphasized that there must be limitations of warfare for ethical reasons. For example, the nonmilitary or purely civilian components of the warring societies were to be protected against direct assaults.

But on the level of intellectual theory, the concept of war in the mind of the West has suffered a schizophrenic split. In one ideological extreme there has been a gradual tendency to exalt power and war until they become exciting ends in themselves. By World War II a succession of theorists stretching as far back as Machiavelli in the sixteenth century had helped prepare the way for an almost unquestioning faith in a series of decisive, crushing sledge-hammer blows as the surest way to a strategic victory. But on the other ideological extreme there has been a tendency to become so skeptical about war that peace and the total abolition of force from the international scene become ends in themselves.

The competition of the total-war advocates and the total-peace advocates for the allegiance of the Western mind has helped prepare that mind to take it for granted that the issue today is total nuclear war or some state of nonviolent suspension which masquerades as peace. Especially since August 1945, when the atomic age was ushered in over Hiroshima, it has been difficult for Western man to imagine how another war involving major powers could possibly be anything but a push-button affair in which the atmosphere over the combating nations would be instantly and indiscriminately speckled with mushroom clouds. The idea of conflict involving limited stakes and less apocalyptic means became as meaningless to the twentieth-century American as the idea of total war, involving whole populations, would have been to a twelfth-century knight.

The Undesirable Status Quo

"We both fear war," Stalin is reported to have said to a high-ranking Western diplomat. "But you fear it more than we do." Precisely this fear of total war, or, rather, the belief that it is but one of two alternatives, is the motivation of much of Western policy. It is the reason we most often tend to sidle forward to meet each new Communist thrust, the reason why, in the ever briefer periods of relative quiet, we strive only to maintain an often undesirable *status quo*. It thwarts all initiative and makes it almost unthinkable, even in the minds of U.S. statesmen and prominent military planners, that we can undertake limited offensives without the certain risk of absolute war. The Communists are not similarly inhibited.

The roots of present-day Soviet concepts of conflict do not go much further back in time than the nineteenth century. On the other hand, Chinese ideas, which today are virtually the same as their partner's, are founded in the ancient writings of the military writer Sun-tzu, who lived during the sixth century B.C. Sun-tzu is of particular importance because he foreshadowed the modern Chinese concept of protracted conflict when he made the simple suggestion that it is most advantageous to defeat the enemy without doing battle. Central to his teaching was the principle that the most effective strategy should either avoid the use of force altogether or employ force only to consummate a victory already won in political, moral, espionage, logistic, and territorial terms. Under no circumstances should an enemy be faced with annihilation: such an enemy would fight to the utmost and inflict more damage on the victor than the annihilation of his forces would be worth. At any given point the enemy should be allowed to retreat to a position of further disadvantage. Successive retreats to worse and worse positions would end in the final loss of the enemy's military effectiveness.

Mao Tse-tung is a student of Sun-tzu, fond of uttering such aphorisms from the master as: "Know your enemy and know yourself," "Avoid the enemy when he is full of dash, and strike him when he withdraws exhausted," and "Make a noise in the East, but strike in the West."

In the mid-twenties Mao dedicated himself and his then few followers to an unending war for power whose final outcome even he did not pretend to know. He preached war for its own sake as a means of furthering the revolution. "To learn warfare through warfare," he declares, "this is our chief method." And Mao has never been afraid that prolonged warfare might sap the moral courage of his people. On the contrary, he says: "In the course of such a long and ruthless war, the Chinese people will receive excellent steeling."

Mao is the world's leading opponent of the concept of calculated warfare. "A military expert," he has written, "cannot expect victory in war by going beyond the limits imposed by material conditions, but within these limits he can and must fight to win." He firmly believes that when a weaker power is engaged in a struggle with a stronger, protracted warfare is the only way in which the weaker can move toward ultimate victory. It is the central principle of his strategy. By limiting the scope of the action and keeping its tempos perfectly under control, the victory may finally be won. And the greater the disparity and the strengths of the antagonists, the longer must be the range of view which the weaker side adopts in its planning.

Mao constantly warns against military adventurism and makes it clear that the objective of war is not only to annihilate the enemy but to preserve oneself. In the Korean War he always kept open the avenues of retreat in the event the United States showed any inclination to strike at the source of Chinese Communist power. War is seen not as a destroyer, as the Western nations view it, but as a creator of strength. Using this notion of protracted conflict, Chinese Communist military and political forces have often won against overwhelming odds (particularly over the Japanese and the forces of Chiang Kaishek) by maintaining a consistent and cumulative process of attack, pretense of attack, retreat, and renewed attack.

The War of Attrition

The elements of the indirect Chinese approach fit very well into Soviet thinking. The doctrine of the war of attrition has been adopted by many Communist leaders, beginning with Marx and Engels, and subsequently Lenin, Trotsky, and Stalin. Soviet Communists see the world revolution essentially as a gigantic war of attrition which will last a hundred years or so, a war undertaken for the purpose not only of destroying individual forces of the capitalist nations but also of changing the whole structure of capitalist society. Consequently, Communist forces should avoid all-out engagements except when they have an impressive tactical superiority. One Bolshevik doctrine postulates that even the weakest and smallest forces can make a definite contribution and that in conflict all available forces should be used in some way, without, however, exposing the main strength to extreme risks. Thus, the numerically small Communist Party in Iraq, playing on the shadow of Soviet power to the north, contributed substantially to the 1958 *coup d'état* in Baghdad.

Lenin contributed much to the growing strategic consciousness of communism and stressed particularly the need for fitting its entire organization and all methods to the single objective of conquest. As Mao is of Sun-tzu, Lenin was a great admirer of Clausewitz, the celebrated German military theoretician who once said: "War is a continuation of politics by other means."

From his studies of Clausewitz, Lenin finally developed a definition of strategy which epitomizes the central concept of protracted war: "The soundest strategy in war is to postpone operations until the moral disintegration of the enemy renders the delivery of the mortal blow both possible and easy."

The memory of Lenin's fearsome successor, Joseph Stalin, is far from sacred in Russia today. Yet his operational theories have not been rendered obsolete by the ruthless downgrading process which has gone on since 1953. The basic conflict doctrine is not substantially affected by personality changes within the Soviet structure. The unlamented Stalin's works serve to illustrate only more concretely the methodically planned opportunism of the Communists. Witness his pact with Hitler in 1939. And it was Stalin who adopted the older Russian methods of extended strategy, in which indirect means, such as bribery, espionage, and subterfuge, are preferred to direct military ventures outside the homeland. Stalin prophesied in 1925 that, through a situation of gradual "socialist encirclement," the capitalist states "will consider it expedient 'voluntarily' to make substantial concessions to the proletariat." The Communist tune of world domination through protracted conflict does not change, no matter which leader plays it.

With the advent of nuclear weapons, the United States has emerged as the chief opponent of communism. The world cannot be won for bolshevism until the United States has been disarmed and destroyed as a political entity. To this end the Soviets and their partners have bent every effort in the past decade and a half, at the same time putting forth a truly gigantic effort to overcome our atomic lead. Not only have they caught up with us in weapons technology, they have materially advanced Stalin's "socialist encirclement" all over the globe. And, simultaneously, they have avoided the ultimate showdown. All of their provocations in Europe, such as the Berlin blockade, were conceived within the framework of a piecemeal strategy. In Korea and Indochina, the U.S.S.R. has been able to exploit the blindly legalistic attitudes of the Western nations toward conflict to evade responsibility for actions which have been controlled from Moscow, and thereby to escape the danger of a major war. Even in the Middle East, where up to present years Russia had obtained no real influence, the Communists have accumulated masked but important power by the simple expedient of promoting unrest in an area where we are futilely resisting the irresistible forces of exploding nationalism. The protracted-conflict battle lines are everywhere.

The Communist doctrine of conflict, then, synthesizes all the techniques which history has proved to be workable, everything from persuasion through coercion to the most modern forms of military warfare. While some of the doctrine's central concepts have been kept secret, a study of the record over the past half century clarifies the aims as well as the methods of the Communists. These seem to be: (1) undermining anti-Communist morale; (2) disrupting the social and economic structure of non-Communist nations; (3) weakening their military capabilities; (4) infiltrating and disrupting their institutions and organizations; (5) causing them to make false political and strategic decisions; (6) cultivating an unreal sense of security abroad; (7) creating local disaffections and internal crises which might induce a nation to acquiesce in a Communist "solution." Concurrently with all these, the Communists strive to build up both their technological and military positions. They do not place their reliance most heavily in any single aspect of this doctrine. Their real skill lies in their ability to vary the combinations in any given situation.

In time, the Communists are confident they can find ways to exploit any set of conditions to their own advantage. And their task is made simpler by virtue of the fact that the independent policies of their enemies are rarely co-ordinated. This condition enabled the Communists to divide the West in the postwar decade by starting peripheral wars in three different areas, none of which was a focal point of the interests of all three major Western allies. The French were kept busy in Indochina, the British by the risings in Malaya, and the United States by aggression in Korea. The Communists are masters at the organized promotion of orchestrated crisis.

And the struggle need not always be based on violence, which is rarely sufficient unto itself and indeed is sometimes unnecessary. Violence must always be preceded, accompanied by, and followed with nonviolent-conflict techniques, such as agitation, propaganda, infiltration, and political sabotage. This not only renders the violence less risky, it makes it more effective.

Ethics-in-Reverse Concept of Conflict

Essentially, the entire Communist concept of conflict boils down to a crystalline-hard summation: Gain strength by weakening your opponent; do unto your opponent exactly the opposite of what you want him to do unto you. This code calls for no moral indignation, as we of the West seem to need before we can take positive action. It simply involves a kind of ethics-in-reverse that has maddened us, addled us, and left us apparently powerless to do anything appropriate about it. In short, protracted conflict is working precisely according to plan.

What can we expect in the future? Barring a technological breakthrough as momentous as the atomic bomb, it is virtually certain that the Communists will continue to prefer the indirect approach rather than risk a sudden life-and-death engagement. The Soviets will likely persist in acting by proxy instead of directly confronting the United States. If more trouble comes in the Middle East, it may be stirred up by Afghanistan or Iraq. If it continues in North Africa, it will be quarterbacked by Egypt, a nation which, incidentally, might well beware of indirect Communist assaults which could damage its ambitions. Meanwhile, the U.S.S.R. will remain free of military entanglements to become more active in the political, economic, and psychological penetration of south and southeast Asia, the Middle East, Africa, and Latin America.

The gradual Communist build-up not only minimizes the chances of decisive counteraction, it is also conducive to temporizing on the part of the West. If the United States does come into conflict, the Communist theory goes, it will come in tentatively, furnishing aid "too little and too late."

The Communists will probably be reluctant to undertake forceful expansion in a direction which would prove offensive to neutralist nations like India as long as these neutralists serve useful purposes and other targets are available. This means that areas of potential military conflict in the foreseeable future may be limited. There is a high probability that, if any treaty partner of the United States is chosen as a target, the Communists will carefully avoid anything that looks like conventional war. Instead, they will instigate rebellion and civil insurrection against those governments so that U.S. support could be labeled "intervention," such as happened in Lebanon in 1958. Tacit Soviet backing of Arab nationalism, for example, represents an almost ideal embodiment of Communist conflict doctrine in the nuclear age.

The Instruments of Terror

The forecast is unmistakably grim. And it is rendered still more grim by the knowledge that the weapons for utterly concluding the conflict, should the moment ripen sufficiently or desperation demand it, are firmly in Soviet hands. Clearly, they seem less interested in even pretending to want an agreement. At the very best, nuclear weapons and operational intercontinental ballistic missiles are persuasive instruments of terror in the protracted conflict.

The great dilemma, unquestionably the most critical of this or any other age, remains: What can we do about it? How, within the framework of our Western traditions and ethics, can we save ourselves? We must continue certainly to *react* to present danger. Much more than that, however, we must learn to *act*, to seize an initiative that is now never ours. To cope with future dangers, the United States needs to develop its own concept for dealing with continuous conflict, not, to be sure, one so cynically aggrandizing as the Communists', but one in which our vital interests would be forwarded as well as protected. And to do this we must be very sure we know exactly what our interests are. We must develop a clear sense of national purpose, and act on it, not defensively, but positively in the sure knowledge of our convictions.

10. The Larger Strategic Vision

by Alvin J. Cottrell and James E. Dougherty

A Research Fellow, Foreign Policy Research Institute, University of Pennsylvania, Dr. Cottrell is an instructor in the Political Science Department and assistant to the chairman of the International Relations Group Committee, University of Pennsylvania. He is co-author of several books, including Protracted Conflict, *and frequently contributes articles to national publications, such as* U.S. News & World Report, Orbis, *and the* U. S. Naval Institute Proceedings.

Dr. Dougherty is assistant professor of political theory and international relations at St. Joseph's College, Philadelphia, and a Research Fellow, Foreign Policy Research Institute, University of Pennsylvania. Together with his colleague, Alvin J. Cottrell, he addressed the first National Strategy Seminar for Reserve Officers. He has contributed articles to such publications as Orbis, *the* Political Science Quarterly, *and the* U. S. Naval Institute Proceedings.

Within four decades, Communist power grew from a gleam in Lenin's eye to the absolute domination of nearly a billion people. One of the principal reasons for the Communists' enormous gains has been their ability to conceive of the struggle

Adapted from Chapter 3 of Protracted Conflict *(Harper & Brothers, 1959), by Robert Strausz-Hupé, William R. Kintner, Alvin J. Cottrell, and James E. Dougherty.*

for power—its terms, its theater, its methods, and its goals—
in larger dimensions than their opponents.

The dialectic theory of history, first formulated by Marx and
Engels, is a theory of universal and protracted conflict: the
whole world is transformed into a battlefield upon which socio-
economic forces are locked in a titanic contest of indefinite
duration. Marx and Engels bequeathed to the revolutionary
Communists a conceptual framework which enabled them to
relate the meaning of events to a wider historical process governed by immutable laws and moving toward a predictable
end. Lenin acknowledged the debt of Bolshevik political and
military strategy to Marxist historical analysis:

"Marxism asks that the various types of struggle be analyzed
within their historical framework. To discuss conflict outside
of its historical and concrete setting is to misunderstand elementary dialectic materialism. At various junctures of the economic evolution, and depending upon changing political, national, cultural, social, and other conditions, differing types of
struggle may become important and even predominant. As a
result of those sociological transformations, secondary and subordinate forms of action may change their significance. To try
and answer positively or negatively the question of whether a
certain tactic is usable, without at the same time studying the
concrete conditions confronting [the movement at] a given
moment [and] at a precise point of its development, would
mean a complete negation of Marxism."[1]

The Globe as a Battlefield

This strategy, as developed and refined by revolutionary
communism, transforms the entire globe into a theater of war.
Nations are mere salients to be reduced and continents mere
flanks to be turned.[2] While the military commander confines
his analysis of the logistical situation to the immediate theater
of war, the Communist conflict manager extends his evaluation
to the performance of entire rival economic and technological
systems. The morale of one's own forces is a question of education, training, indoctrination, and other modes of social control; the morale of the enemy is marked as the target of

psychopolitical attacks, especially through the enemy's own media of mass communications. In this broader dimension, it is not sufficient to study a single leader, his character, his training, and his strategic preconceptions. The strategist of global, protracted conflict must seek to gain insights into the society which he is bent on conquering: its cultural matrix, its institutional structure, its popular emotions and neuroses, and its decision-making machinery. Moreover, he must vary the modes of his approach—military, paramilitary, political, psychological, technological, and economic—and suit them to the place and the time. He must phase his tactical operations over large geographical areas and long periods of time, and he must subordinate all operations to the larger strategic goal; a local military victory, for example, may have to be forfeited for the sake of more enduring political gains.

As the geographic setting of conflict analysis widens, the time needed to consummate the strategic operation must be lengthened and broadened commensurately. In turn, the extension of scale calls for suitable organizational techniques and instruments. In protracted-conflict strategy, five-year logistical plans are meshed with decades of the tactical movement of forces and the careful phasing of political, economic, psychological, and military or paramilitary operations. Hence, the side which knows how to conceive of the conflict in the appropriate dimensions of time enjoys the advantage—and can even afford the luxury of policy mistakes, for the opponent is ill equipped to recognize and comprehend their significance in time to exploit them.

The Interchangeability of Military and Political Instruments

From the outset, Communist conflict doctrine revealed a remarkable affinity to military thought. The idea that military and political instruments are interchangeable in the execution of one vast strategic plan, central to Clausewitz's thought, is the pith of Communist doctrine. In his personal copy of the great German theoretician's famous book, *On War*, Lenin underscored the following passage:

If War belongs to policy, it will naturally take its character from thence. If policy is great and powerful, so also will be the War, and this may be carried to the point at which War attains to its absolute form.

It is only through this kind of view that War recovers unity; only by it can we see all Wars as things of one kind and only thus can we attain the true and perfect basis and point of view from which great plans may be traced out and determined upon.

There is upon the whole nothing more important in life than to find out the right point of view from which things should be looked at and judged of and then to keep to that point, for we can only apprehend the mass of events in the unity from one standpoint, and it is only the keeping to one point of view that guards us from inconsistency.[3]

In sum, war, be it fought with military hardware or with nonviolent political and psychological instruments, is a unity. "Hot" and "cold" are phases of intensity in one and the same war.

If Clausewitz was the unwitting prophet of the Communist doctrine of protracted conflict, its most incisive modern spokesman is Mao Tse-tung. The wide strategic vision of the Chinese Communist leader derives at least in part from the oriental tradition of warfare.

As conceived by Mao, the strategy of protracted conflict is the lever for effecting a gradual change in the relative strength of the two sides—the revolutionary and the *status quo*. As the war is prolonged, various forces—political, economic, psychological, and military—which are unfavorable to the enemy and favorable to the revolutionaries can be set in motion, shaped, and nourished. The Communists will grow in military experience, technology, and organizational ability and gain increasingly the international mass support. Conversely, the Communists' foes will suffer changes for the worse: exhaustion of resources, disintegration of morale, the alienation of world opinion, and confusion over the proper policy to be pursued.[4] At every turn in the protracted war, the Communists can, by adopting all kinds of deceptive measures, effectively drive the enemy into the pitfall of making erroneous judgments.[5] Mao, in one famous passage, distilled the essence of his extended strategy to sixteen words: "Enemy advances, we retreat; enemy halts, we harass; enemy tires, we attack; enemy retreats, we pursue."[6] The import of Mao's writings is that both time and wisdom are on the side of the Communists and that, inescapably, the forces of the *status quo*, lacking a conceptual framework of the conflict, will succumb in the enveloping tide of revolutionary Communism.

In keeping with the broad strategic vision advocated by Clausewitz and Mao, the Communists have acquired a spectrum of weapons much more variegated than that which composes the arsenal of the West. They discern weapons where the West sees only the implements of peaceful international relations. According to the Communists' doctrine of protracted conflict, war, politics, diplomacy, law, psychology, science, and economics—all form a continuum and all are closely integrated in the conduct of foreign policy. Moreover, the Communists have developed political, psychological, and organizational strategies far more sophisticated than the mere physical seizure of territory. They have mastered the technique of staging aggression against social institutions and human minds, without physically violating political borders and thus posing a *casus belli*.

The Ebb and Flow of the Revolutionary Tide

What particular method or mixture of conflict methods is to be used depends upon given capabilities and opportunities. Psychologically prepared for an indefinitely prolonged struggle, the Communists are steeled against temporary setbacks. They remain undaunted in the face of adversity, for they are convinced that their reverses are only partial, or local, or short-lived. If the Communists suffer an acute loss in one area, they can take comfort from the victories wrought in another. All reversals are thus seen as relative; new strength can be drawn from the lessons which they contain. Every retreat becomes a "strategic retreat," calculated to produce greater gains subsequently. If plans are blocked and rendered invalid by unanticipated events on the terrain of conflict, these events can

sooner or later be reconciled to the global blueprint, or else
the blueprint can be modified to accommodate them. This concept, that is, the "ebb and flow" of the world revolutionary
tide, is fundamental in Communist strategic thought.[7]

The Treaty of Brest-Litovsk constitutes one of the earliest
and most interesting applications of the "ebb and flow" concept. Lenin, upon coming to power in 1917, confronted one
overarching problem, namely, how to end Russia's participation in the world war as quickly as possible, so that the Bolsheviks could concentrate their resources on consolidating their
first territorial foothold, the launching platform of future conflict operations. Lenin realized that unless peace were made
soon, the fledgling Soviet state might be crushed in the vise of
foreign war and internal armed resistance. So far as Lenin was
concerned, the internal enemy—that is, the White Russian
forces—was more to be feared than the external foe. In order
to guarantee the continuation of his Communist regime, he
came to terms with Germany at a heavy cost to Russia. Under
the Treaty of Brest-Litovsk, Lenin ceded 32 per cent of Russia's arable land, 34 per cent of her population, 89 per cent
of her coal resources, and 54 per cent of her total industrial
capacity.[8]

Lenin, however, perceived his strategic problem in larger dimensions than did the "triumphant" leaders of Imperial Germany. The severe conditions of the Treaty of Brest-Litovsk
did not disconcert Lenin in the least. In fact, the Soviet leader,
by yielding to the demands of the victorious, albeit exhausted
Germans, showed a consummate mastery of a strategic technique which was by no means new in Russian history—trading
space for time. This technique, as applied by Lenin, reflects
what may be aptly termed a "four-dimensional" approach to
conflict. No retreat or loss need be considered fatal for communism if communism thereby strengthens itself or enhances
its capabilities of carrying on future conflict. In due time, everything that has been conceded will be taken back.

Exploiting the Colonial Struggle

An excellent illustration of the Communists' larger strategic vision—their ability to widen the global dimensions of the battlefield on which the protracted conflict is being waged—can be found in their policy toward the colonial areas. At the end of the First World War, the Communist leadership realized that the Asian and African continents were entering a period of revolutionary transformation. They proposed to harness the power of the social forces which were about to inundate the colonial regions. The Communists perceived that developments impending in these regions would have a direct and important bearing upon the success of their strategy against the West. As early as 1921, Stalin called attention to this relationship:

> If Europe and America may be called the front, the scene of the main engagements between socialism and imperialism, the nonsovereign nations and the colonies, with their raw materials, fuel, food, and vast store of human material should be regarded as the rear, the reserve of imperialism. In order to win a war, one must not only triumph at the front but also revolutionize the enemy's rear, his reserves.[9]

Perhaps Lenin never actually uttered the famous aphorism which is so often attributed to him: "The road to Paris lies through Peking." Whether he did or not, it is clear that Lenin and his successors saw the important part which the anticolonial struggle would play in softening up the West for the final, decisive phase of the protracted conflict. Today, few would deny the significant role played by the colonial areas in the struggle between communism and the West. Yet Lenin foresaw this role as early as 1916, when he quoted the following passage by Rudolf Hilferding:

> The thousand-year-old agrarian isolation of countries situated outside the main current of history is broken, and they are dragged into the capitalist whirlpool. Capitalism itself gradually procures for the vanquished the means

*and resources for emancipating themselves. And they set
out to obtain the objective which once seemed to the European nations to be the highest objective: national unity
as a means to obtain economic and cultural freedom. This
movement for national independence threatens European
capital in its valuable field of exploitation, where the ra-
diant prospects are opening up before it, and in those
places European capital can only maintain its domination
by continually increasing its military forces.*[10]

Military Conflict for Political Objectives

The conduct of the Soviets immediately prior to and during
World War II furnished instructive examples of the manner
in which the Communists apply their conflict strategy to concrete historical situations.

The Communists, when waging actual military operations,
are not guided by the same set of canons that inform Western
wartime policy. Americans in particular, once they have
thrown themselves into the effort to defeat the enemy with
sheer physical power, are inclined to postpone consideration
of political objectives until after the cessation of hostilities.
Thus, American leaders in World War II planned and conducted an exclusively military strategy which was designed to
produce a crushing victory as rapidly as possible. It is indeed
a paradox of our time that democracies, once fully mobilized
for military conflict, are apt to outdo the dictatorships in waging total military war—the war for unconditional surrender.
This paradox derives from the democracies' instability of mood
—the oscillation between the aversion against all things military and a war psychosis that can be appeased only by total
victory and the severe punishment of the enemy.

When the war against Germany entered its final phase and
the Soviets took the offensive, Stalin became increasingly concerned with Russia's postwar position in central and eastern
Europe. Earlier, at Teheran, he had exerted his influence to
bring about a Western "second front" in France rather than
in the Balkans, where an attack would have thwarted Russia's postwar objectives. His primary objective of winning the

war already assured, Stalin now concentrated his efforts upon the problem of how to exploit the war in its closing stages in order to maximize Russian political gains. Instead of maintaining unrelenting pressure upon the retreating German forces, the Soviets paced their military operations to the attainment of political objectives beyond military victory: they sought to insure Moscow's postwar domination of the eastern European governments. An eyewitness of the Soviet conquest of Hungary wrote:

> These operations were directed solely by political expediency and as a result of that, they were momentarily illogical from a military point of view. . . . The aim of all these operations was to eliminate the existence of strong pro-Ally and anti-German resistance forces in Poland, Bulgaria, and Hungary, which, after the liberation of their countries, could have been significant obstacles on the avenue to Bolshevization, due to their non-Communist character. The military procedure applied was that of indirect extermination, indirect co-operation with the German Army.[11]

The U.S.S.R. disdained the opportunity to negotiate armistices with the indigenous governments of the former Nazi satellites, which were anxious to end their participation in the war as speedily as possible. Instead, the Soviets sought, even at the risk of delaying their westward military advance, to create a political vacuum in each of the eastern European countries which could later be filled by a Communist provisional government. The best-documented incident of this truly Machiavellian strategy occurred in Poland. As the Red Army approached Warsaw in July 1944, the Soviet radio repeatedly urged the underground army of Polish patriots in the capital, led by General Bor, to rise up and fight the Nazis. But when the Poles launched their insurrection, the Soviet forces immediately brought their offensive to a standstill outside Warsaw and waited patiently while the Nazis liquidated General Bor's forty thousand men. The Russians refused to make the slightest effort to extend aid and declared that they would not allow British and American aircraft to use Soviet airfields if they attempted to fly supplies to Warsaw. As a result of Stalin's pol-

icy, the Polish uprising proved a complete failure. After the
Home Guards had been totally destroyed, the Red Army resumed its advance, "liberated" Warsaw, and established the
hand-picked Lublin Communist government in power.

Soviet Controlled Warfare

The manner in which the Soviet Union dealt with Japanese
peace overtures in early 1945 furnishes another instructive example of controlled warfare.

Although the first Japanese attempt to obtain Soviet media-
tion was made in Tokyo during February 1945, the Soviet
Government concealed this information from the United States
until the Potsdam Conference, five months later. Obviously,
Stalin did not wish to see the Pacific war end "prematurely."
He intended to exploit it in two ways: first, by extracting maximum concessions from the United States for his promise to
enter the war against Japan, and second, by using his actual
participation in the war to establish his claim to a major voice
in the Far Eastern postwar settlement. There is now little question that the Soviet Union held it within its power to take a
step which could have led to the termination of hostilities even
before the dropping of the atomic bombs. Japan had sought
Soviet help in obtaining from the West a less severe armistice
formula than "unconditional surrender." But the Soviet Union
could not accede to such a request without forfeiting the
chance to profit politically from having taken a belligerent's
part in the defeat of Japan. Nor could the U.S.S.R. flatly reject
Japan's overtures without prompting Tokyo to make a more
direct appeal to the West.

Thus, Stalin shrewdly led the Japanese to believe that there
was some chance of softening the harsh terms of unconditional
surrender. At the same time, Stalin assured the Western leaders of his loyal adherence to the policy of "unconditional surrender." That he fully intended to enter the Pacific war at the
most advantageous juncture is borne out by the hasty Soviet
military assault on Japan just forty-eight hours after the first
American atomic bomb dropped on Hiroshima.[12]

The Larger Dimensions of Conflict

Thus, unlike most Western strategists, who have tradition-ally equated war with the clash of arms, Communist leaders are trained to think of conflict in much larger dimensions. Mili-tary action for them is but one of many forms of warfare. Other forms of conflict—political, sociological, ideological, psy-chological, technological, and economic—are just as important or, under certain circumstances, even more important. Quick, decisive military victory, which for centuries has been the prime objective of Western strategic planning, does not hold an equally exalted place in Communist conflict science.

The Western strategist is inclined to consider his job done once crushing victory has been won on the battlefield; the re-sponsibility for advancing the nation's political objectives is then shunted conveniently from the military commanders to the diplomatists. This delineation of functions reflects Western democracy's traditional image of war: an aberration from in-ternational normalcy, resulting from a breakdown in ortho-dox diplomacy. For the Communists, by contrast, policy and war are but two sides of one coin. The coin is strategy.

Notes

1. V. I. Lenin, "Partisan Warfare," *Orbis*, II, 196. The above is a translation of the article "Partisanskaya Voina," which has been reprinted in all four Russian editions of Lenin's *Sochineniya* (*Collected Works*).

2. The Party must make all appraisals "on a sufficiently broad scale, that is, precisely on a world scale." Nathan Leites, *The Operational Code of the Politburo* (New York: McGraw-Hill, 1951), p. 15.

3. Cf. Byron Dexter, "Clausewitz and Soviet Strategy," *Foreign Affairs*, XXIX (October 1950), 49–50.

4. *Selected Works of Mao Tse-tung* (5 vols.; London: Lawrence & Wishart, Ltd., 1954), II, 189.

5. Ibid., p. 216.

6. Ibid., p. 164.

7. "The Communist movement never should swim against the trend of the historic cycle. During revolutionary ebbs and non-Communist tides, it should avoid risk and protect its position while simultaneously accumulating strength." Stefan T. Possony, *A Century of Conflict: Communist Techniques of World Revolution* (Chicago: Regnery, 1953), p. 394.

8. John W. Wheeler-Bennett, "The Meaning of Brest-Litovsk To-day," *Foreign Affairs*, XVII (October 1938), 139.

9. Joseph Stalin, *Marxism and the National and Colonial Question* (New York: International Publishers, n.d.), p. 115.

10. Cited in V. I. Lenin, *Imperialism: The State and Revolution* (New York: Vanguard Press, 1929), p. 101.

11. John A. Lukacs, "Political Expediency and Soviet Russian Military Operations," *Journal of Central European Affairs*, VIII (January 1949), 402.

12. Paul Kecskemeti, *Strategic Surrender* (a RAND Corporation Research Study) (Stanford: Stanford University Press, 1958), pp. 155–211.

11. Communist Psychological Warfare

by Stefan T. Possony

*Born in Vienna, Dr. Possony received his
Ph.D. from the University of Vienna and
subsequently studied in Rome and Paris.
Since 1947 he has been professor of international politics in the Graduate School,
Georgetown University. He is an associate of
the Foreign Policy Research Institute, University of Pennsylvania. He lectured at the
first National Strategy Seminar for Reserve
Officers.*

Perhaps the most striking characteristic of Communist propaganda is how dull and unconvincing it is. Its arguments are
not logically persuasive, and their presentation, more often
than not, is repellent and unattractive. The fact that, nevertheless, communism has been able to achieve considerable successes, even in the intellectual domain, has been puzzling to
many analysts. One explanation of this apparent mystery may
be found in the circumstance that the Communists do not at
all aim to "persuade" the mind. Instead, they seem to be ori-
enting the souls of their audience.

If we accept this as our first hypothesis, we should assume
next that the techniques of "soul surgery" should become clear-
est in situations where they are easiest to apply. Hence, instead of looking for such techniques in the field of international
diplomacy, we should expect the Communist "psywar" techniques to be revealed most dramatically in the indoctrination

Published originally in the January 1959 issue of The Officer Magazine, *by the Reserve Officers Association. Reprinted by permission.*

of Party members and in the activities commonly called "brain-washing" or "brain changing." The treatment of war and political prisoners, including Party members, of young Party recruits, and of captive populations may give more valuable hints about the Communists' secret doctrine of psychological warfare than their purely verbal efforts in so-called propaganda campaigns.

The Conditioned Reflex

The Communists have acknowledged that they owe a considerable debt to Ivan P. Pavlov and his discovery of the conditioned reflex. This theory, especially if reinterpreted, can be evolved as a supplement to the basic theorem of Marxism, that a change in social conditions will transform men. In addition to rejecting the "subjective," or "will," factor, the Pavlovian or post-Pavlovian theory asserts that man's reflexes and behavior are controlled by signals—social conditions, words, and mass communications—which in turn are controllable by scientific procedures. Thus, man's behavior is decided by "objective" factors and, to the extent that those factors can be manipulated, is determinable. The person is "other-directed" by state or Party or, in their absence, by economic "forces"; psychological processes can be managed, fixed, or altered; and man can be "transformed."

Fundamentally, the Communists hold that behavior, especially the behavior of groups, classes, and nations, can be manipulated through the conditioning of reflexes, a circumstance which is particularly important for those situations where the human animal is denied food and treated to overdoses of ringing bells. To a large extent, this theory underlies Soviet propaganda, especially its insistence on monotonous repetition and its capture of all the symbolic words which, so to speak, "ring a bell."

Undoubtedly, the Communists learned from Pavlov how to influence behavior through proper regulation of work, food, and leisure, that is, to get at the mind through the body. More important is the probability that the Communists are making conscious use of Pavlov's findings concerning methods whereby psychological disturbances can be induced in living organisms. Pavlov has shown that by manipulation of stimuli the desire for independent action, or what he called the "freedom urge," can be weakened or extinguished and neurotic behavior induced.

The artificial creation of insanity—a device which the Communists have applied to their prisoners by subjecting them to various forms of "invisible torture," such as uncertainty, fear, sleeplessness, strong light effects, and kneeling or standing—may not lend itself to the treatment of large numbers of people. However, unpredictable behavior, the acceleration and calming of disturbances and crises, alterations between smiles and growls, and the maintenance of tension at perpetuity may induce quasi-neurotic behavior, increase the values of the "signal" (as, for example, those of the bell as against the food), and facilitate the acceptance of new word signals. Whatever one may think of the determinism inherent in Pavlovian thinking, a deliberate application of such techniques makes it possible to implant in human minds numerous notions, such as "A follows B," which are not only false to fact but also inhibit the learning of the proper sequences. The ensuing disorientation cannot but fail to produce lasting mental crises or, at least, serious maladjustments.

The Use of Freud's Theories

Perhaps more surprising than the Communist loans from Pavlov are their unacknowledged adoptions of the findings of Sigmund Freud. By interfering with family life and placing major emphasis on public education of infants, the father image is vested in an external and nonhuman entity, the state or the Party. This method of rearing children probably induces them to become more submissive to higher authority.

The value systems which are being inculcated by the Soviets exploit pre-existing Russian patterns. The Soviets make sure that the human herd obeys the "signals" of authority, while the individual and initiative remain underdeveloped. The relegation of sex and other types of affection to minor and regressive roles induces, or rather is expected to induce, "sublimation" through productive work and Party chores. This particular technique is employed to transform human beings into mere cogs within a gigantic machine.

The Psychoanalytic Interview

The Communists have adopted the basic techniques of psychoanalysis, in particular the psychoanalytic interview. Normally, such an interview is designed to determine the causes of psychological disturbances. It aims at the removal of these causes. The psychoanalytic interview between physician and patient obviously would be impractical if patients were to be treated in large numbers. Hence the Communists have developed more streamlined methods, which allow the mass production not of cures but of "complexes" and "traumas." These techniques include the compulsory writing of diaries, autobiographies, and histories of one's thought development; of oral interviews with Party members; of hearings before ideological commissions and the political police; and of public "confessions."

The purpose of these interviews, which may be repeated many times, is to inculcate in the "patient" feelings of error, guilt, shame, and fear, as well as desires for repentance and revenge—and to make available to the Party powerful levers of blackmail. The expectation is that, through this process, the patient's conscience will be weakened, his will to obey and believe increased, and all his survival instincts made pliable for Party purposes.

Normally, these procedures will be successful: since practically everyone is actually or potentially "guilty" within the framework of the Communist code—because no one ever failed to doubt the dogma or to wish escape from Party discipline, and because every sane person has family and property instincts—the average "patient" can be relied upon to produce the trauma by himself. Whenever a person shows himself capable of resisting, treatment may vary between outright pressure and terror, and "persuasion" of the kind described in Arthur Koestler's *Darkness at Noon*.

These processes aim, as does psychoanalysis, at the cleansing of old thoughts and emotions. While the therapist wants to eliminate the sources of trouble, the Communist psychological manipulator works toward the destruction of the self-reliant personality. To employ modern terms, he tries his hand at "brainwashing." Once this operation has been completed, a supplementary activity, "brain changing," must be undertaken. The brain is emptied of mundane thoughts, while simultaneously the body is weakened and the sensuous drives are subdued by fatigue, hunger, deprivation, and anguish. The mind enters a state of receptivity and exaltation. At this point, thoughts, ideas, symbols, and emotions—in short, "visions"—are put into the cleansed mind. The "patient"—who may be a member of a Western Communist Party or a student at a Party "university"—is invited to learn by rote some of the basic texts of the Communist literature. He is asked to write down the various thoughts which he considers the right ones and to apply the doctrine to current and concrete issues. He may even be asked to participate in conspiratorial activities and to commit himself through acts of immorality, which may range all of the way from informing and spying to the betrayal of one's parents, from leading a lynching party to straight murder.

Hypnosis and Suggestion

Hypnotic and suggestive techniques seem to be used extensively. The "patient" must indulge in autosuggestion and tell himself, often by mechanical repetition, that he is becoming a better Communist, that he is cutting himself loose from all the black shadows of the past, and that he desires to sacrifice himself to the cause. In addition, his manipulators follow the standard practices of hypnosis or, in any event, of suggestion, to make sure that the suitable thoughts really stick. An interesting aspect of this process is that the "patients" themselves, while learning and acquiring the proper reflexes, must emit the signals to which they themselves and the others must react. The insistence on parrotlike repetition is designed to harden the conditioned reflexes, to maintain a system of mutual suggestion or hypnosis, and to "fix" the desired complexes.

Two key terms of modern psychotherapy have special importance: frustration and guilt. By identifying existing frustrations and stimulating them, the Communists gain recruits and undermine foreign societies. The Communists try to exploit professional, social (and racial) status, and intellectual-cultural frustrations among the persons who place themselves outside the pale of their own society. The intent is not to allow these frustrations to incapacitate the man but, on the contrary, to transform them into aggressive impulses. The international manipulation of guilt complexes comes out in the Communist emphasis on the distinction between "just" and "unjust" wars. Command efficiency and troop morale are lowered through guilt feelings. A nation is more likely to win in conflict if it considers its cause to be just. Hence the Communists try to arrange matters in such a way that any war *they* are fighting will be a *just* war, while any war fought by a democratic nation will be *unjust*. The purpose is to inculcate into the Free World guilt feelings about resistance to communism and at the same time immunize the "Soviet peoples" with a sort of ideological vaccination against any notion that Communist wars or even "aggressions" may be something less than emanations of an exalted sense of justice. The Free World has been infected to some degree by bad conscience and guilt feelings. Hence, partly at least, the often surprising paralysis of democratic will.

Communism and Religion

In their attempts to undermine hostile societies, the Communists make every effort to destroy religious, ethical, and other higher motivations, in the expectation that the preoccupation with immediate, mundane, material, and private interests and the destruction of spiritual reserves will create frustrations and "atomize" society. As religious beliefs wane, the number of possible recruits for communism tends to increase. This is so, not only because there is a mechanical relationship between communism and atheism but, more significantly, because the human hunger for redemption and assurance must be stilled and because the desire for a God craves satisfaction.

Communism redeems on earth and proclaims *man* to be "God." The revolution is seen as the crucial "religious" event which transforms man from the "object" into the "subject" of history, that is, into the "creator" of the perfect society of history. Paradise is moved from the origin to the destination of man's wandering.

The Communists' most powerful weapon in their onslaught on religion is "social criticism" addressed to economic hardship, oppression, racial tension, delinquency, family trouble, and the shortcomings of religious organizations. The purpose of "social criticism" is to produce frustration consciousness and persuade people that they cannot take such frustrations in their stride, let alone sublimate them by religious abnegation and hope for the hereafter. Instead, they must overcome them by revolutionary and violent action, and by active sacrifice. Frustration, let us note, is a forerunner of aggressiveness, especially if aggressive impulses can be stimulated artificially.

To the extent, therefore, that religion is eliminated as the Basic Premise, the individual is thrown back onto his own mental resources. He looks for another Basic Premise and abandons himself to pleasure seeking and other selfish drives. Most importantly, having been deprived of the basis of certainty, he loses judgment and, above all, the Job-like steadfastness in trouble.

By contrast, the Communists must find for the societies under their rule a substitute for religion as a foundation of mental health. They cannot adopt religion, certainly not openly, because this would sensitize human conscience and thus undermine the foundations of their state and their world movement. Neither can they condone hedonistic tendencies or any openminded and multivalued thinking, which would jeopardize their dogmatic ideology and, most significantly in our context, preclude the effective application of psywar, Communist style. Their obvious solution is, first, to peddle the pseudo religion of materialistic communism; second, to retain aspects of religions: faith, brotherhood, initiation, salvation, redemption, grace, paradise, consecration, guilt, sin, sacrifice, atonement, asceticism—all of which have their counterparts in the Communist ideology; and third, to be excessively dogmatic about it all.

Communist Sociological Assumptions

Many schools of psychology are agreed on the importance of fear and anxiety. Fear and anxiety are considered to be among the main factors which hinder the proper working of the mind. There is little doubt that fear is the disintegrating factor par excellence. This, of course, is not a new discovery from the political practitioner. It is not surprising that the Communists have always laid great stress on terror, violence, and purges and nowadays have enlisted the specter of nuclear war in their strategy of terror. In the dimension of psychological warfare, they do not expect that much will come from further readings of the *Communist Manifesto*, but they usually obtain good results from giving the impression that they are willing to go *beyond* the "brink of war."

However, the Communists have added an "improvement" to the age-old art of inducing fright. Men no longer fear a phenomenon once its nature has been understood and its behavior has become predictable. A danger perceived may become a stimulant for action—a most unwelcome possibility. Consequently, the Communists have adopted the techniques of erecting impenetrable "curtains" and of acting unpredictably and capriciously; for example, by alternating smiles with growls, arresting the innocent and freeing the guilty, keeping prisoners in captivity beyond their terms but releasing them at any odd moment, and in general showing themselves impervious to reasonable argument and immovable by counsels of moderation. Deliberately, the impression is being created that one can never know what is going to happen next; even if everything is calm now, the "next" disturbance may be of unparalleled violence.

Let us look at one example of Soviet "irrational" behavior. The Soviet habit of giving consistently an inflated impression of Communist strength is unsound according to all rules of the military art. Schlieffen's motto, generally accepted by thinking soldiers, was, "Be more than you seem." Specifically, this method was considered sound by a foremost Soviet expert,

Marshal Boris Shaposhnikov. But the opposite axiom: "Appear stronger than you really are," is the most rewarding one for the purposes of psychological operations, especially if the victim's reactions to the Soviet strategy of terror can be inhibited by a show of phony friendliness. The technique of blowing hot and cold and of alternating confusing signals was used by Pavlov to instigate "neurotic" behavior in his dogs. It is entirely acceptable to international politics.

Another important cause of mental disturbances has been identified by Emile Durkheim in his concept of *anomie*. Other sociologists have amplified this concept by pointing out that, to be psychologically healthy, the individual needs a close community life. Precisely because society has changed into a functional and utilitarian association, the individual needs emotional security and close human relations. The structure of the over-all society must be intelligible, so that the individual can orient himself within it. His dependence on the large group must offer gratifications sufficient to evoke in him feelings of loyalty, pride of membership, dedication, conviction, etc.

The Communists aim to produce *anomie* through propaganda, class warfare, infiltration, disintegration, policy sabotage, and other revolutionary and subversive operations. The psychological effects are not long in coming. Given an anomic situation, it is relatively easy to induce in large numbers of people some kind of neurotic behavior characterized by hopelessness, obsessions, compulsions, and fears of failure. Protracted disturbances undermine motivation, dedication, loyalty, the community spirit, and all those attitudes which keep society going. As this assault bears fruit and creates defeatism and listlessness, *anomie* grows with cumulative force.

Communist Crowd Psychology

It will come as no surprise that the Communists are close students of crowd psychology. They have learned Gustave Le Bon's fundamental postulate that crowd behavior is characterized by the temporary weakening or loss of restraint and reason. Crowds are suggestible, aggressive, and destructive.

"Crowd mentality," that is, the loss of impulse and action controls, is contagious. Going beyond Le Bon, the Communists have discovered that "crowds" are not formed just by direct physical contacts among a mass of people, such as in meetings or demonstrations, but that, in modern times, crowd attitudes can be created among people who are physically isolated. It is merely necessary to arouse excessive fears, exploit a calamity, stimulate a panicky attitude, give signals for action against scapegoats or for actions with a symbolic character, and keep the majority of the population paralyzed. It is easy to see how the application of conditioned reflexes and fears to otherwise straightforward propaganda operations can contribute greatly to the *Vermassung* of modern man. One of the great objectives is to induce in all hostile groups the attitude of "no will."

However, the Communists know that crowds do not originate or move by themselves but must be created and led. Activating concepts are as necessary as paralyzing ideas. Therefore, the principal aim of Communist activities is to render the revolutionary leadership group capable of performing the "rape of the masses." This leadership group must be endowed with one predominant characteristic: "iron will," impervious to the attrition of time. The Communists have borrowed Nietzsche's concept of the "length of will." Will is iron only if the commitment is total in all dimensions, time included. The Communist leader is a person who cannot turn his back on communism, and the comrades see to it that defections of leaders do not really occur, even in the case of expulsions and purges.

12. Soviet Strategy of Disarmament

by Thomas W. Wolfe

Dr. Wolfe is a long-time student of Soviet affairs. A native of California, he received his M.A. degree from Columbia University and his Ph.D. degree from Georgetown University. He is also a graduate of the Russian Institute of Columbia University.

Soviet disarmament proposals are an integral part of a strategy aimed at degrading Western strengths and reducing the risks of nuclear war while the Soviets are in the process of building up their own over-all power position.

The implications of Soviet disarmament initiatives for the West are sometimes lost in the search for an unequivocal answer to the question: Do the Soviets expect to win the struggle for world supremacy via processes of "historical development" short of major military conflict, as Premier Nikita S. Khrushchev publicly proclaimed, or do they privately believe that military power will be required ultimately to bring the West to its knees?

No categorical answer can be given to this question, which for all practical purposes can be answered only by events. In fact, the question itself is misleading, for it fails to distinguish between Soviet preferences and the strategic necessities which confront them in their quest to dominate the world. By implication, the question also neglects the back-up role of military power for diplomatic blackmail and other forms of nonviolent Soviet aggression.

Preferred Strategy and Dictates of Reality

The Soviet Union's *preferred* strategy undoubtedly would be to force the West—and above all, the United States—to capitulate without war. However, the Soviet leaders are realists, brought up in a hard school which teaches that power in its various strategically significant forms is what counts when great historical issues are to be decided.

As realists they know that strategies grow out of the interaction between competitors in the power struggle, and not out of unilateral preferences. Whatever their preferences might be, therefore, the men in the Kremlin can scarcely shirk their historic duty of preparing the Soviet camp to subdue the West by force if it refuses to be disarmed. Moreover, they have inherited a weighty legacy of doctrine and experience which, while cautioning against military "adventurism," nevertheless clearly prescribes that force and violence are essential levers in the overthrow of one historic order of society by another.

Marx, for example, who preached that "war is the midwife of revolution," wrote that "the last word of social science on the eve of each general reconstruction of society will always remain: 'struggle or death, bloody war or nothingness.'"[1] Lenin said, "Great historical questions can be solved only by violence,"[2] while a contemporary Communist theoretician, Mao Tse-tung, has written:

> *Every communist must grasp the truth that political power grows out of the barrel of a gun, . . . in fact, we can say that the whole world can be remolded only with the gun.*[3]

Khrushchev himself has not hewn strictly to the traditional Communist line on the role of war in the struggle between the Communist and non-Communist camps, although neither has he strayed as far from it as some observers are wont to believe. Khrushchev's amendment at the Twentieth Party Congress in 1956 of the Leninist dogma of inevitable war so long as capitalism exists is largely responsible for the reputation he has acquired as a doctrinal innovator. Holding that the Communist camp has become "a mighty force" with "not only the moral but also the material means to prevent aggression,"[4] Khrushchev advanced the notion, novel to Communist ears, that a world war might not be necessary before the final global victory of communism. However, his much publicized assertion that "war is not a fatal inevitability" was, and subsequently has been, carefully qualified. According to Khrushchev:

> As long as imperialism exists, the economic base giving rise to wars will also remain. . . . As long as capitalism survives in the world, reactionary forces, representing the interests of the capitalist monopolies, will continue their drive toward military gambles and aggression and may try to unleash war. But war is not a fatalistic inevitability. Today there are mighty social and political forces possessing formidable means to prevent the imperialists from unleashing war, and, if they try to start it, to give a smashing rebuff to the aggressors and frustrate their adventurist plans.[5]

He stated on another occasion:

> Leninism teaches that the ruling classes do not surrender their power voluntarily. However, the greater or lesser intensity which the struggle may assume, the use or nonuse of violence in the transition to socialism, depend on the resistance of the exploiters . . . rather than on the proletariat.[6]

Just and Unjust Wars

Khrushchev's doctrinal position on war can perhaps be best understood in light of the distinction between just and unjust wars which Communists have always drawn. By Communist definition, just wars are "wars of liberation" from "capitalist slavery," from the "yoke of imperialism" and in defense against foreign attack, whereas wars by capitalist states against each other or against Communist states are unjust, or predatory, wars, "wars of conquest waged to conquer and enslave foreign countries."[7] By definition, Communists cannot fight an unjust war, even if they initiate it, because wars fought by communism are always progressive and revolutionary, that is, just wars.

Khrushchev has carefully maintained the distinction between just and unjust wars, even when denying most vociferously that Communists have any intention of trying to achieve their aims by force of arms. Thus, for example, in a speech in Budapest on December 1, 1959, he said:

> The Socialist countries have no reason whatsoever to start war, to propagate their ideas by force of arms. . . . No Communist party anywhere, if it really is Communist, has ever said that it hopes to achieve its aims through war.
>
> Consistent struggle against unjust wars of conquest has been an integral part of the international working class movement since its very inception.[8]

In his remarks in Peiping on September 30, 1959, at the tenth anniversary of the founding of Communist China, he said:

> Marxists have always recognized only . . . just wars and they have always condemned imperialistic aggressive wars. This is one of the characteristics of Marxist-Leninist theory.[9]

Again, addressing the Supreme Soviet in October 1959, Khrushchev took a strong stand against predatory and imperialistic wars.

The point of these and similar statements by Khrushchev, which reiterate classical Communist doctrine on just and unjust wars, is that war remains a permissible instrument of revolutionary change so long as it serves the interests of communism and so long as conditions are suitable for waging it.

His estimate of the probability of an open battle between the "Soviet camp" and the "camp of imperialism" rests on "a calculation of the chances of effective resistance" by the latter.[10]

From the point of view of experience, no less than from a doctrinal standpoint, there is ample evidence for supposing that Communist leaders like Khrushchev are fully aware of the relationship between military power and Communist expansion. History shows that not a single country in the world has been brought under Communist domination except where nonviolent revolutionary techniques have been backed up by armed conquest or the close presence of Communist military power. In Western countries with traditionally strong Communist movements, like Italy, France, and Greece, the Communist revolution has made no headway in the absence of direct Soviet military support, as Stalin privately pointed out in his correspondence with Tito in 1948.[11]

To suppose that hard-boiled realists like the Soviet leaders are unreservedly optimistic about the likelihood of bringing off a Communist revolution in the United States without an assist from Soviet arms is to imply that they have drawn no lessons from some forty years of Communist experience.

Explicit recognition of the historical dependence of communism on war can be found in a new Soviet textbook, *Foundations of Marxism-Leninism*. Discussing the question "Is revolution obligatorily linked with war?" the text states:

> *Up to now historical development adds up to the fact that revolutionary overthrow of capitalism has been linked each time with world wars. Both the first and second world wars served as powerful accelerators of revolutionary explosions.*[12]

After noting Communist gains from these two wars, the text goes on:

> *From these historical facts the conclusion can be fully drawn that in the epoch of imperialism, world wars— which sharpen the social-political contradictions of capitalist society to the extreme—inevitably lead to revolutionary upheavals.*[13]

The textbook also reiterates the traditional Communist doctrine that war is not "an obligatory prerequisite," applying this notion, however, only to national-liberation revolutions. Recent examples cited to support the point were the revolutions in Iraq (1958) and Cuba (1959).[14]

Both the English and the American revolutions also were what the Communists term "bourgeois democratic" revolutions. Like the "national liberation" types, they were not "proletarian revolutions." Therefore, the implication is clear to any trained Communist. Other forms of revolution may occur peacefully, but "proletarian revolutions" require the exercise of some degree of violence.

Avoidance of Frontal Military Encounter

The strategy of the post-Stalin leadership has been marked by the tendency carefully to steer away from any major frontal military encounter with the West. This exercise of elementary caution, which is fully consistent with the Bolshevik schooling that the realities of power must be weighed carefully at all times, probably has served more than anything else to sustain the image of Khrushchev as an advocate of peaceful conquest.

It is doubtless evident to the Soviet leaders that, so long as the West maintains its global nuclear power unimpaired, Communist ambitions would be placed in jeopardy under any of the calculable situations in which major military power of the Soviet and Western camps might become engaged. These situations would be: (1) the case of Western reaction to a war started by the Soviet bloc; (2) the case of a war started by the West, such as the "desperate lashing out" of moribund capitalism, in line with Marxist doctrine; and (3) the case of a major war which might grow out of limited war, or otherwise occur by accident or miscalculation.

Seen in this light, the central aim of the Soviet disarmament campaign is to clear the strategic landscape of a serious roadblock to world revolution by engineering the nuclear disarmament of the West. If this can be accomplished, not only would the Soviets gain elbow room to pursue a more aggressive political strategy but, fully as important, the stage would be set for seeking a decisive reversal of the military balance.

From the Soviet viewpoint, reversal of the military balance by the brute process of trying to outbuild the United States on a massive scale in modern weapons probably has not looked as a particularly promising task. Even forging ahead of the United States in a new weapons system like the ICBM might well seem to offer only a transient advantage in a situation of unrestricted arms competition. As a powerful industrial nation put on notice that its survival depended on success in an all-out arms race, the United States would plainly be capable of upping the ante and canceling out the Soviet advantage. Indeed, this sort of aboveboard arms competition is undoubtedly what Khrushchev had in mind when he deemed it "high time to put an end to the arms race." The logic of the Soviet disarmament campaign is to avoid just such an open competition, the more so at a time when the Soviets may calculate that they have managed to pull ahead.

Dual Approach to the Power Struggle

Much more in keeping with the classical Soviet approach would be the dual process of immobilizing the nuclear weapons systems on which American military power is mainly based, while at the same time accumulating advantages on the Soviet side through such means as technological and psychological surprise, hidden military preparations, clandestine storage of decisive weapons, and the like.

In fact, it can be said without exaggeration that the Soviet disarmament campaign has become the *central strategic battle* of the times. Rather than constituting a Soviet acknowledgment that the path to world revolution is henceforth closed to all but peaceful means of competition, the disarmament campaign represents a major attempt to keep this path open to all means of struggle, including whatever use of military force may be necessary to reach the Communist goal of world domination.

There is also another element of deep strategic significance behind the Soviet disarmament campaign. Since the level of armaments and over-all security posture of the Free World represent fundamentally a defensive stance against Communist aggression, acceptance of any precipitate program of disarmament by the West would mean, in a basic strategic sense, that the West no longer felt capable of insuring its own survival. This acknowledgment alone would constitute for the West a strategic defeat of enormous magnitude, leaving an irresolute Western world only the recourse of seeking accommodation with an aggressive movement which is dedicated to achieving mastery of the globe.

Soviet Proposals of Full and Partial Disarmament

Soviet disarmament proposals fall into two categories: first, the "full and complete" disarmament scheme advanced by Khrushchev before the U. N. General Assembly on September 18, 1959; and second, a group of partial-disarmament measures, including earlier Soviet proposals of 1955, upon which the Soviet Union has declared itself ready to negotiate if the Western countries "do not for some reason or other express their willingness to agree to general and complete disarmament."

Tactically, the sweeping Khrushchev proposal was meant to put the West on the defensive and to create a climate in which the West could be maneuvered into accepting less radical but nevertheless crippling disarmament measures. If by outside chance the West should lose its balance completely and go along with the scheme of total disarmament in four years, this would be regarded by the Soviets as a pure windfall. The control and inspection provisions of the Soviet proposal are so vague, and its period of execution so brief, that it could not possibly provide the conditions necessary for a stable and orderly transition to a peaceful world. The basic object of the plan is to confuse Western opinion, paralyze Western decision-making processes, slow down Western defense efforts, and forestall the marshaling of effective opposition during a vital phase in the historical process of reversing the power balance between the Communist and non-Communist camps.

From the Communist viewpoint, the world is now passing through a significant and possibly decisive phase of transition between two historical periods. "Capitalist encirclement" has been broken. "Communist encirclement" does not yet exist, but the rapidly growing strength of the Communist camp "is opening up new prospects for it."[15] Allowing for the fact that Communist advances are deliberately exaggerated for psychological effect, there is nevertheless ample evidence that the Communist leadership now sees a real prospect ahead for "turning the corner," as it were, and reversing once and for all the power balance between the Communist camp and the Free World. In a basic sense, the Kremlin's great strategic task is to turn this historical corner without a collision which might throw the whole Communist movement for a fatal loss. Its peaceful-coexistence strategy—of which disarmament is the most dramatic concomitant—is calculated to help carry off this task successfully.

Aside from the tactical and strategic purposes noted above, advocacy of total disarmament serves Soviet pursuit of the East-West struggle in other ways. It strengthens a diplomatic-propaganda offensive against the West during a period of important international negotiations and gives dramatic support to the Soviet effort to pose as the champion of world peace and security for all peoples. It also enables the Soviet leadership to shift the blame on the West for any difficulties its domestic programs may encounter. For example, Khrushchev hinted to the Soviet people that if benefits like a six-hour working day are not widely realized during the present Seven-Year Plan, it will be because the West refuses to accept his total-disarmament proposal.[16]

The partial-disarmament proposals which have been advanced by the Soviets offer little novelty. One proposal calls for a European inspection zone and reduction of foreign troops in the NATO area, designed to bring about a weakening of the NATO "shield." A second calls for a "denuclearized zone" in central Europe along lines of the Rapacki Plan of 1957, the object of which is to divest NATO forces of their tactical nuclear weapons and to prevent the nuclear arming of West Germany. Another proposal is for total withdrawal of foreign forces from Europe, but this is conditioned by the stipulation that foreign military bases everywhere be liquidated—a provision aimed at the world-wide deployment of American strategic forces. In return for what they ask, these and other partial disarmament proposals give up very little and are clearly calculated to advance basic Soviet military and political objectives.

To the extent that both the total-disarmament scheme and the various partial-disarmament steps would call for a lengthy period of negotiations, the Kremlin may well calculate that

Western parliamentary governments, operating under the pressure of public opinion, can be encouraged to slacken their defense efforts while the closed Soviet system presses on with its own military preparations.

A drawn-out period of negotiations on the crucial issue of disarmament might also hold another interesting prospect for the Communists. The Soviets consistently regard the negotiation of agreements as a means of registering and confirming the power balance. They may look on an arms-negotiating period as one during which further build-up of Soviet-bloc economic and military power can be expected to tip the scales decisively in Soviet favor, particularly if the negotiations serve at the same time to put a brake on Western defense preparations.

For example, the "missile lag," which is calculated to grow to Soviet advantage in the early sixties, would coincide with a series of disarmament discussions. If the talks themselves yielded nothing but interminable sparring over control and inspection problems, like the Geneva nuclear-test-ban negotiations, they might nevertheless take the steam out of Western attempts to overcome the Soviet missile lead while, behind the curtain of Soviet secrecy, Soviet missile plants and research establishments would go on preparing further "surprises" for the West at the negotiating table.

Soviet expectation of the gains to be derived from disarmament negotiations with the West will be conditioned to a considerable extent, of course, by their estimate of the firmness and unity of the Western camp. If the West shows no disposition to accept agreements on terms other than those which serve its own vital security interests, the Soviets conceivably could be forced to reconsider their whole approach to the disarmament issue. There is, despite the mutual incompatibility of basic Soviet and Western goals, some possibility that the Soviets might be brought around to acceptance of genuine arms-control measures on conditions compatible with Western security.

Will Soviet Disarmament Strategy Change?

Several factors which might motivate a Soviet interest in some types of "genuine" arms-control agreements can be adduced, although it remains to be demonstrated whether any of them are compelling enough to dictate a real change in Soviet attitudes and behavior.

One of these is concern over the danger of war by accident or miscalculation. Soviet leaders have alluded to this danger frequently, although usually attributing it in a propaganda context to Western military activities and deployments. At bottom, there may be real uneasiness among the Soviet leadership that accidental war represents an incalculable element over which they have no control. However, there is little good evidence to date that the Soviets are yet sufficiently concerned over the "accident factor" to accept the kind of control and inspection measures which would be necessary to alleviate the danger.

Economic pressure is another factor which might influence the Soviet attitude toward disarmament. The rising costs and rapid turnover rates of modern weapons systems may give pause to the Kremlin's planners, even though their growing economy allows more leeway than in the past for military allocation of resources. Manpower might also pose a particular problem at this time, due to the coincidence of World War II aftereffects and the expanding labor-force requirements of the Seven-Year Plan. However, as suggested by Khrushchev's January 14, 1960, speech on armed-force reductions,[17] this need is being met in part at least by rational readjustment of the Soviet military establishment to cut down its oversized troop strength and substitute the firepower of modern arms. On balance, the Soviets appear to be under no great compulsion to offer significant disarmament concessions out of economic necessity.

The possibility also exists that the Communists may be willing to pay a price at the disarmament negotiating table for insuring further consolidation of the Soviet bloc and reducing potential sources of internal stability. Some types of agreements might appeal to the Kremlin—for example, if they would put a seal on Soviet-dominated regimes in eastern Europe and smother any lingering hopes of deliverance. The Soviets might also find some interest in arrangements which would discourage the growth of too much military capability in Communist China, particularly attainment of independent nuclear status.

While such factors as these may have some influence on the attitude which the Soviet leaders take toward disarmament negotiations with the West, there is still no reason to assume that their real view of disarmament is less hardheaded and calculating than that of their forerunner, Lenin, who said: "Only *after* the proletariat has disarmed the bourgeoisie will it be able, without betraying its world-historical mission, to throw all armaments on the scrap heap! . . ."[18]

Notes

1. Karl Marx, *The Poverty of Philosophy* (London: Martin Lawrence, Ltd., 1936), p. 147.

2. V. I. Lenin, *Selected Works* (New York: International Publishers, 1943), III, 313.

3. Mao Tse-tung, *Selected Works* (New York: International Publishers, 1954), II, 272–73.

4. Leo Gruliow (ed.), *Current Soviet Policies II: The Documentary Record of the 20th Party Congress and Its Aftermath* (New York: Praeger, 1956), p. 37.

5. Ibid.

6. Ibid., p. 38.

7. *Short History of the CPSU (b)* (Moscow: Foreign Languages Publishing House, 1945), pp. 168–69.

8. The New York *Times,* December 2, 1959.

9. Ibid., October 1, 1959.

10. *Facts on Communism,* Vol. I: *The Communist Ideology,* Committee on Un-American Activities, House of Representatives, December 1959, p. 115. Dr. Gerhart Niemeyer of Notre Dame University is credited with this analysis.

11. *The Soviet-Yugoslav Dispute,* Text of the Published Correspondence (London: Royal Institute of International Affairs, 1948), p. 51.

12. O. V. Kousinen (ed.), *Osnovi Marksisma-Leninisma* (*Foundations of Marxism-Leninism*) (Moscow: State Publishing House of Political Literature, 1959), p. 519.

13. Ibid.

14. Ibid., p. 520.

15. See *Khrushchev on the Shifting Balance of World Forces*, U. S. Senate Document No. 57 (Washington: Legislative Reference Service of the Library of Congress, September 1959), p. 2.

16. *Pravda*, November 18, 1959.

17. Ibid., January 15, 1960.

18. V. I. Lenin, "Military Program of Proletarian Revolution," *Collected Works* (New York: International Publishers, 1942), XIX, 366.

13.   Changes in Soviet Conflict Doctrine

by Anne M. Jonas

*Mrs. Jonas has been engaged in full-time re-
search on the U.S.S.R. in Washington, D.C.,
since 1951. A graduate of the University of
Virginia, she has also studied at American
University and Georgetown University. Her
extensive knowledge of Russian has enabled
her to monitor in depth the shifts in Soviet
strategic thinking.*

Slowly but surely, the U.S.S.R. is adapting its strategy and
tactics to the realities of the technological world revolution.
This adaptation is being accomplished within the framework
of Communist orthodoxy. Briefly summarized, the orthodox
teaching has been, and still is: direct all efforts toward the
main goal of achieving global victory for communism, but
change tactics and techniques to conform to concrete conditions.

These broad tactical shifts can be attributed to two factors.
First, the U.S.S.R. has acquired new weapons—nuclear explosives and advanced means of delivery. Second, it possesses
greater fundamental strength than ever before—economic,
technological, and psychopolitical.

Khrushchev's Strategic Innovations

Khrushchev's innovations have been twofold. First, he has
placed increasing emphasis on attempts to strengthen Communist capabilities for relatively "bloodless" world revolution.
Second, he has adapted military-force structure to nuclear

realities—an attempt to prepare Communist forces for world revolution through conquest, if necessary.

Khrushchev's combination of a "peaceful coexistence" campaign and a sweeping modernization of the military establishment is true to the best Communist style and conforms fully to the doctrine of "dialectics." But in strategic sophistication and tactical variety, intensity, and scope, his innovations exceed those of earlier days. True, Khrushchev commands new and far more powerful tools in the historical struggle for world domination. Yet the problems posed by nuclear firepower have become more difficult to solve. Khrushchev's moves are an attempt to find an original solution to the risks and complexities of nuclear war.

Far from abandoning hope for completing the world Communist revolution, he has voiced new confidence in the likelihood of its success. Nuclear long-range weapons have furnished, for the first time in history, a capability to attack the principal capitalist power—the United States, which, heretofore, was beyond the access of the Soviet military machine. Khrushchev has stated that, if all-out nuclear war occurred, *capitalism* would vanish. Presumably, in his belief, the U.S.S.R. would survive a new world war, to lead the international Communist movement to definitive victory on a global scale.

How well will Khrushchev succeed in his attempts to extend Communist power without unleashing nuclear war? Failing decisive success in this endeavor, under what conditions is he most likely to initiate war? An analysis of the challenges with which Khrushchev has confronted us may provide a partial answer.

Although dozens of factors are involved, an examination of four key elements within Communist conflict doctrine may furnish clarification. These crucial factors are: the role of nuclear weapons, the role of peaceful revolution, the role of war, and the conditions for initiating war.

The Role of Nuclear Weapons

When President Truman first told Stalin about joint U.S.-British work on the atomic bomb, Stalin appeared indifferent.

After the first bomb fell on Hiroshima, propagandists, and Stalin himself, took pains to disparage atomic weapons and to deny their military effectiveness. The subsequent record proved, as should have been expected, that this was but another example of deception. While the Soviet leaders publicly were berating the effectiveness of atomic weapons, simultaneous development of across-the-board atomic capabilities was enjoying highest priority. Apparently as early as 1943, Stalin had ordered Russian physicists to resume their prewar research, and espionage networks had been requested to collect as much Western nuclear information as possible.[1]

Despite these intensive efforts, though apparently unplanned, the strategy of the counteroffensive proved, once more, in World War II, to be Stalin's winning strategy.[2] The concept of luring the enemy deep into the great spaces of Russia and defeating him at the far end of his logistics lines had succeeded several times in the past. Yet if this strategy was to predominate, it would permit no more than the exercise of tactical and technological surprise. It ruled out strategic surprise, which already was evolving as the key to success in nuclear conflict.

After Stalin's death, Soviet military publications publicly debated the changed strategic significance of surprise and pre-emption in the nuclear age.[3] It was now "admitted" openly that surprise could be of decisive importance; hence there arose the need to "pre-empt" a hostile strike before it is launched.

Khrushchev has been somewhat circuitous in admitting the strategic importance of a surprise nuclear blow in current Soviet doctrine. In a speech to the Supreme Soviet, he refrained from going beyond the hint that, to minimize retaliation, the attacker should try to wipe out all enemy ICBM sites and nuclear stockpiles with the first blow.[4] In addition, he admitted the obvious—future wars would begin not on the frontiers, as formerly, but with massed missile attacks during the first minutes of the war on strategic targets in the heart of the warring countries.[5] Khrushchev pointed out that the U.S.S.R. was developing a potent deterrent against defeat by surprise attack—namely, a second-strike capability. "We deploy our missile complexes in such a way that duplication and triplication is guaranteed. The territory of our country is huge; we are able to disperse our missile complexes and to camouflage them well."[6] The West, Khrushchev asserted, was more vulnerable than the Soviet Union:

> *In the event of a new world war . . . we, too, would suffer great calamities; we would have many losses, yet we would survive. Our territory is immense; our population is less concentrated in major industrial centers. . . . The West would suffer incomparably more. . . . A new war not only would be their last war, it would also be the end of capitalism.*[7]

In announcing a one-third reduction of the officers and men constituting the military establishment, Khrushchev left no doubt about his views on the decisive importance of nuclear and hydrogen weapons in contemporary warfare. "The defense potential of a country depends, to a decisive extent, on the total firepower and the means of delivery."[8]

Marshal Rodion Malinovsky, U.S.S.R. Minister of Defense, bluntly stated: "Our premise is that a future war will be waged with mass use of nuclear weapons." Also, he went beyond Khrushchev and stressed the advantages of ICBMs in terms of global targeting flexibility and ground and in-flight invulnerability. He told the Supreme Soviet:

> *Present-day ballistic missiles guarantee a high probability of inflicting powerful strikes simultaneously on a great variety of targets. The tremendous range and speed of missiles make it possible to redirect firepower quickly, shifting the decisive thrust from one target or one theater of operations to the other, and by means of massed nuclear strikes to influence and change the situation to one's own advantage. . . . The launching sites of missiles are easy to camouflage and even to conceal completely (ukryt'), and thus possess the highest probability of survival and invulnerability. . . . Destroying a ship at sea or bringing down an airplane or destroying an aircraft projectile in the air causes no great difficulty when present-day means . . . are employed. But neutralizing a ballistic missile to destroy it in flight so far is impossible—it hits the target relentlessly.*[9]

In accepting the importance of nuclear firepower and various missile-delivery systems, Khrushchev has modernized, but not abandoned, Communist doctrine on the need for a mixed-force structure, the combination of all arms, and the continuous variation and modernization of the weapons of conflict. He is adapting his force structure to permit all-out surprise attack. In addition, he is retaining a spectrum of capabilities to wage all types of warfare. At the two extremes of his force structure are nuclear-delivery systems and proxy guerrillas. His views that no single weapons system is decisive under all conditions conforms to traditional guidelines of Communist strategy. New in the Communist operational lexicon is the realization that nuclear weapons must figure, in one way or another, in any attempt to defeat the United States and its major allies.

In addition to recognizing the military advantages of nuclear-thermonuclear-missile weapons systems, the Soviet leaders have demonstrated, both by word and deed, keen appreciation of their inherent psychopolitical potentialities. Outside the bloc, the fears about nuclear weapons and their various means of delivery have become the keystone in one of the most intensive efforts at neutralization through military blackmail in the history of communism.

The Role of Peaceful Revolution

Three basic motivations underlie current Communist efforts to accomplish world domination by peaceful means: the dilemma presented by the risk of all-out nuclear war; the emergence of new states in a period of technological revolution; and, corollary to these phenomena, changed estimates on the rapidity of the world revolution.

The "contradictions" inherent in these motivations are, briefly, these:

1. For the first time, the Soviet Union has the capability of attacking the chief capitalist enemy, the United States, and of accomplishing the world revolution by military means.

2. Contrary noises from the Kremlin notwithstanding, many obstacles prohibit decisive—and even "adequate"—victory over the United States at the moment, and presumably for the near

future. Two principal obstacles obtrude. The first of these is the *political* intent of Communist conquest—wars are not won until occupation is accomplished and a Communist regime installed. Even though a Soviet surprise attack may prove to be devastating, it will not necessarily vault the Communists into power in the United States. Second, a fundamental Communist doctrinal tenet holds that the "base of the world revolution"—the U.S.S.R.—must be kept inviolate. Even if Khrushchev is prepared to have the Soviet countries absorb the destruction of nuclear war, as he insists, unrest in the satellites, in China, and perhaps in Russia itself cannot be ruled out; nor can a vicious intra-Party struggle. Hence nuclear war poses extreme danger to the continued solidarity and stability of the Communist bloc. It is most unlikely that the Kremlin is oblivious to this hazard.

On the other hand, aggressive nuclear war waged under favorable conditions against the United States would considerably spur the world revolution.

The Communist view of the rapidity of the world revolution has changed several times. Events disproved earlier predictions of a cataclysmic and global crisis of capitalism which, if exploited by the proletariat, would flame into immediate world revolution. After some hesitancy, the Communists adopted the concept of protracted conflict—the notion that the world revolution cannot be triggered by a single global crisis, but will be accomplished, instead, in installments and over the span of an entire "era." In the interim the Soviet Union was to be forged into the main power base of the world revolution—primarily through a build-up of war potential and of the armed forces as the chief instrument of the revolution. The role of foreign Communist parties also changed: they should act, in most cases, as auxiliaries of Soviet power.

In an attempt to reconcile the risks and promises implicit in the new weapons, Khrushchev has opted for an assortment of tactics. As Stalin phrased it, "in order to win a war, one must not only triumph at the front but also revolutionize the enemy's rear."[10] This effort is conducted according to the unwritten "inverted golden rule" of Communist doctrine: "Do unto your opponent exactly the opposite of what you want him to do unto you."[11]

Against the major powers, the principal Communist tactics under Khrushchev have been: deterrence to gain time; paralyzation and demoralization of will through nuclear blackmail; and attempts at force degradation through "disarmament" and "coexistence" moves.[12] The strategy is obviously a phased one. The objectives are, first, to inhibit progressively the Free World's responses to Soviet gambits and, second, to achieve the active—though perhaps unwitting—co-operation of forces within the West.

Paralyzing the Will of the West

According to standard Communist procedure, the predominant enemy group should not be attacked in any decisive manner *before* its leaders and cadres have become unsure of their capabilities, intentions, and rights and, above all, of their chances of success. Through the neutralization of allies and the paralyzation of principal sources of domestic support, the leadership elite in the chief enemy country can be made to vacillate. As it falls victim to paralyzing ideas and political and ideological splits, and suffers from progressive loss of sociopolitical group cohesion, the military and security forces at its command are infected, become unreliable and ineffective. This degradation of military strength, in turn, emasculates the political leadership. "Disarmament" tactics are among the preferred means of accomplishing these objectives. Another method is the wooing of political parties, which, for one reason or the other, can be induced to seek "accommodation" with the Soviet Union. Simultaneously with attempts to neutralize the principal opponent and his allies, indirect gains must be achieved in the "intermediate strata"—the rest of the world. The principal tactics now being applied are attempts at "socialist encirclement" of the United States through: (1) disparagement of "imperialism" and encouragement of national liberation and bourgeois democratic revolutions; (2) exploitation of fears of nuclear war to create hostility toward the United States and its allies; and (3) exercise of "political sabotage" through parliamentary infiltration and penetration, particularly in unstable countries.

For the latter purpose, the Socialist parties have assumed new importance: the period when they were described as "social Fascists" has passed. Now they are considered, in a number of nations, to be "stirrup holders" to Communists eager to get into the saddle.

To the extent that the will of the chief opponent can be paralyzed, the neutralization of his allies and of non-allied powers will progress more rapidly. Khrushchev, in his speech to the Supreme Soviet in January 1960, reiterated the concept of "socialist encirclement" of the United States. The greater the degree of isolation of this country and other key members of the Free World alliance, the more easily some minor countries may loosen their ties with the West and even shift their loyalty to the "revolution."

As these strata break away, the disintegrating processes within the anti-Communist nucleus is accentuated in turn. The ultimate purpose of this dialectic process is to break the entire nonrevolutionary camp into small and disjointed fragments and to prevent its standing cohesively and firmly against external and internal revolutionary attack.

The Communists appear confident that their tactics are proving effective. They claim that the "forces of peace" are gaining ground throughout the world, while more and more people in the principal nations of the Free World—including the United States—are becoming fatalistic, are losing their faith in the future, and are adopting a passive attitude toward all aspects of life. This is the principal justification for Khrushchev's changed "estimate" that war is not likely *at present* and that the world balance of forces now favors the Communist camp.

Total paralysis of Western will and debilitation of Western military, economic, and political power—this is the ultimate aim of Khrushchev's "peaceful coexistence" campaign. Once general moral dislocation has been brought about, but not before, the optimum time has come for the decisive contest—provided the military capability of the Soviet Union to launch an effective surprise attack and subsequent blows of exploitation has been brought to the qualitative and quantitative level required, and provided the risks of the contest are considered acceptable.

The Role of War

There are no valid indications that Khrushchev has abandoned Lenin's expressed acceptance of Clausewitz's formulation of the role of war to further political objectives. "War is part of a whole, the whole is politics," stated Lenin. Yet the Communists long have believed that, when a critical historical change is in process, extreme caution must be exercised. This caution is particularly necessary during the "period of transition from socialism to communism." The advent of nuclear weapons, in their estimation, has accentuated the requirement of resisting "adventurism." Nor is there any coercion to hurry at the wrong time. The United States is deemed to be deterred; neutralization is progressing effectively. Meanwhile, the U.S.S.R. is acquiring the necessary economic and technological strengths prerequisite to total war. If and when the appropriate moment arrives, the U.S.S.R. is prepared to attack, if this should be necessary.

Much of the confusion which leads some observers to conclude that the U.S.S.R. does not plan to employ war as an instrument of policy stems from a misunderstanding of the orthodox Communist distinction between "just" and "predatory" wars. Khrushchev, good strategist that he is, recognizes the importance of deceiving the potential enemy. He also recognizes the need *not* to abrogate Communist doctrine. His solution to the problem of how to preach war and peace simultaneously is to denounce "predatory" war and keep silent about the types of war which the Party considers both permissible and inevitable. However, on at least one occasion since his return from his visit to the United States in 1959, Khrushchev specifically told a Communist audience that the traditional Communist doctrine of "just" warfare still applied. "The Marxists have always recognized only liberative, just wars; . . . have always condemned aggressive imperialist wars."[13]

"Just" wars may take any form or combination of forms, from world nuclear conflict to guerrilla skirmishes, provided the Communists fight them. The Soviet leaders do not think that the less intense or less bloody war also is the less unjust.

Hence, it is important to understand Soviet doctrine on limited war. Khrushchev's views are closely related to his assessment that capitalist encirclement of the U.S.S.R. is being replaced gradually by socialist encirclement of the United States. They are also related to his belief that the United States is, at the moment, effectively deterred.

Khrushchev's note of November 5, 1956, to England and France during the Suez crisis—which contained vague threats of Soviet missile retaliation if these states failed to withdraw their forces from Egypt—is credited, *post factum*, with having prevented the crisis from developing into total war.[14] It is argued, also, that the "peace forces" prevented the United States from using atomic bombs in Korea.[15]

The Soviet leaders aver that limited war would expand into all-out war under two conditions: (1) if nuclear weapons were used and (2) if both the United States and the U.S.S.R. became directly involved.

Since 1957, or earlier, Soviet writers have been attempting to convince the United States that tactical nuclear weapons cannot be used without expansion of the conflict.[16] Khrushchev himself has said, "The theory of so-called local or minor wars with the use of mass-destruction weapons has sprung up now in the West. . . . Should such wars break out, they could soon grow into a world war."[17]

On the question of total war resulting from both U.S. and Soviet involvement, Khrushchev has been less specific. However, at a White House dinner during his visit to the United States, after downgrading the destructiveness small nations could inflict on one another, he went on to point out: "If strong nations like the United States and the Soviet Union quarrel, then not only will our two countries suffer tremendous damage but other countries will inevitably be involved in a world catastrophe."[18]

The doctrine, if read in conjunction with the historical record, seems to state that, if possible, the U.S.S.R. should refrain from direct participation in limited wars when a major Western power is involved. Nuclear blackmail and other forms of psychopolitical conflict—insurrection, proxy support, secret arms shipments, and "volunteers"—are equally effective tactics. The latter involve fewer risks and lower costs. However, various situations could arise which would motivate a reassessment of this strategy—for example, timing and provocation considerations, changed views of the degree of effective deterrence of the United States, prestige and political pressures, and the like.

By contrast, the orthodox doctrine that limited wars between lesser powers will continue to occur still applies; if and when a "revolutionary situation" results, Communist forces should exploit the opportunity to seize power, or may have no option but to intervene.[19]

Under the newly announced plan to restructure the military establishment, a large force of trained reserves will be available for immediate call-up.[20] The U.S.S.R. has retained its capability to wage limited or "conventional" war if and when the situation requires it.

The argument sometimes has been advanced that the U.S.S.R., since Khrushchev's revision of the orthodox Communist position, no longer considers war to be "inevitable" during the lifetime of capitalism. At the Twentieth Congress of the CPSU in 1956, Khrushchev held that, given the changed balance of world forces, war was no longer a "fatalistic inevitability."[21] He iterated this thesis at the Twenty-first Congress in January 1959. More recent data clarify the fact that, according to current Communist thinking, the inevitability—or avoidability—of war depends on the degree of success achieved through nonviolent means. Late in 1959, a new, authoritative textbook on Communist doctrine and tactics was published. Written at the direction of the Central Committee, apparently it is meant to replace Stalin's *Problems of Leninism*. Without doubt, it updates Communist doctrine and adjusts it to current international conditions.

Taking their cue from such factors as the growth of Communist strength and the alleged spread of socialist ideas in non-Communist nations—an assessment of dubious validity—the authors maintain that peaceful revolution now is a possibility under certain conditions. However, they go on to emphasize the following:

> In taking into account the possibility of peaceful revolution, the Marxist-Leninists have in no way accepted the

*reformist position. . . . They know that any revolution—
peaceful or nonpeaceful—is the result of class struggle.
Peaceful or nonpeaceful, a socialist revolution remains
just as much of a revolution if it decides the question of
transferring authority from the hands of the reactionary
class to the hands of the people.*

*The reformists believe that the peaceful road is the only
road to socialism. Marxist-Leninists, while noting the
emergence of the possibility of peaceful revolution, understand the interrelationships between one and the other:
the inevitability, in a number of instances, of a sharp ag-
gravation of the class struggle. Thus, in cases where the
military-police forces of the reactionary bourgeoisie are
strong, the working class will encounter fierce resistance.*
There can be no doubt that in a number of capitalist
countries the overthrow of the bourgeois dictatorship by
means of armed class struggle will be inevitable.[22]

After Khrushchev's return from the United States, this passage was quoted in the leading theoretical journal of the international Communist movement as one of the most important
points made in the new textbook.[23] It should be noted that
the phrase "armed class struggle" can have all and any meaning within the spectrum of violent conflict. Under certain conditions it can be a synonym for "war."

Initiation of War

Clearly, the question of whether or not the U.S.S.R. will
initiate war—and, if so, what type of war and when—cannot
be answered by considering any single factor or set of factors.
Existing weapons systems permit Khrushchev broad freedom
of choice, and he himself has said that an assortment of more
advanced weapons are in various stages of development. He
told the Supreme Soviet:

*The armament which we now have is formidable arma-
ment. The armament under development is even more
perfect and more formidable. The armament which is be-*

*ing created and which is to be found in the folders of the
scientists and designers is truly unbelievable armament.*[24]

In addition, numerous considerations other than military
ones would be involved in a decision to initiate war. Nevertheless, the principal points relating to the problem of whether,
in the future, Khrushchev will be content to apply his military
capabilities psychopolitically or will decide to wage war are:
(1) the degree of success of his neutralization strategy and
(2) the margin of over-all force superiority—military, psychopolitical, economic, and technological—at the time when an
attack is contemplated or required. Moreover, Khrushchev has
disclosed his preoccupation with the problem of timing. As
the tempo of the technological race quickens, force superiori-
ties may become transitory.[25] If the Soviets fail to attack at
a time when their forces are clearly qualitatively and quantitatively superior, they would be guilty of the Bolshevik sin
of flaunting historical opportunity.

There have been indications recently that, in the future,
"outside influences" may have a new and important bearing on
the Communist decision to initiate war.

Under Stalin, the tendency was to overemphasize "organization" to the detriment of "spontaneity"—a tendency motivated, in large part, by fears of being drawn into battle prematurely and at the wrong place. Yet, increased strength leads
to an increased willingness to take chances. "Spontaneity," together with the concept that in nuclear war "capitalism" can
be dealt quick deathblows, may lead the latter-day Communists to exhume old notions on the "rapidity of world revolution." Under such circumstances, if a situation arose in which
communism gathered effective and world-wide spontaneous
support, the temptation to accelerate the world revolution
through all-out nuclear war might become overpowering
enough to offset fears for the security of the revolutionary
"home base."

The Search for a Strategic Synthesis

Briefly, then, the principal elements in Khrushchev's conflict strategy as it had evolved by 1960 can be summarized as follows: (1) employment of combined military and non-military weapons to degrade and neutralize the opponent while building up Soviet strength; (2) preparations directed toward attaining a capability to initiate a surprise attack—should the proper combination of propitious circumstances arise—or to pre-empt an enemy attack by military or nonmilitary means, or a combination thereof; (3) retention of sufficient "conventional" forces to wage whatever type of war the occasion demands; and (4) emergence of appreciation of "spontaneity."

What is Khrushchev's strategic pattern? According to one possible interpretation, based upon one set of his statements, Khrushchev is veering in the direction of strategic nuclear war and its peacetime version, deterrence. In other words, he is adopting his own variant of American strategy as reflected by SAC and the Polaris concept. According to another interpretation based on a second set of Khrushchev dicta, he is upgrading political and insurrectional techniques. In other words, he is reverting to a modern counterpart of the "classical" revolution envisaged by Marx and Engels.

Both interpretations seem to be right, but neither is valid by itself. Khrushchev appears intent not on reconciling but on *combining* these two strands of strategic thinking. Nuclear ICBMs and IRBMs are the canopy under which "classical" revolution, guerrilla operations, and up-to-date political conquests can be executed, or a "revolution from without" imposed by communist forces. Political warfare culminating in paralysis of government or seizures of power can serve as the prelude to nuclear surprise attack and as insurance for the effectiveness of the surprise blow; or it can heighten the psychological impact of nuclear blackmail and lead the victim toward ultimate surrender. Should nuclear conflict eventuate, guerrilla and insurrectional techniques (perhaps strengthened by "small" nuclear weapons) could effect a favorable outcome of the "broken back" phase of the Armageddon.

Clearly, Khrushchev is reaching out, in the best dialectic tradition, for a *synthesis*. We would do well not to underrate his capability to develop a genuinely original doctrine truly applicable to modern conditions. Already he has eliminated from Soviet doctrine many parts which had become dogmatized and, in many ways, inapplicable. Some—like the notion of constant pressure—had become self-defeating. Second, he has modernized Soviet strategy and attuned it to technological reality. Third, he has upgraded the use of broadly conceived techniques of degradation aimed at neutralization through disarmament, demoralization, and nuclear blackmail. Fourth, he has displayed great tactical skill and flexibility in his execution of the more or less perennial strategy of communism. Finally, he is exuding renewed confidence in the chances of completing the world Communist revolution.

It cannot be said that, *as yet*, Khrushchev has proved himself an innovator in strategy. But he has demonstrated that he is indeed a formidable opponent—infinitely more resourceful and dangerous than his predecessors. He has been "one up" on Machiavelli: capable of roaring like a true lion, he also has shown himself to be one of the most cunning of all the political foxes of the twentieth century.

Notes

1. Arnold Kramish, *Atomic Energy in the Soviet Union* (Stanford: Stanford University Press, 1959), p. 36; *The Report of the Royal Commission . . . to Investigate . . . the Circumstances Surrounding the Communication . . . of Secret . . . Information to . . . a Foreign Power* (Ottawa: H. M. Stationery Office, 1946), pp. 694–95.
2. See Stalin's letter to Colonel Razin citing the historic successes of "Scythian strategy" against Charles XII, Napoleon, and Hitler. *Military Affairs*, XIII, No. 2 (Summer 1949), 77.
3. The pioneering study is H. S. Dinerstein's *War and the Soviet Union: Nuclear Weapons and the Revolution in Soviet Military and Political Thinking* (New York: Praeger, 1959). Changed Soviet views on the role of strategic surprise and pre-emption

as they evolved during 1955–58 are analyzed in detail (pp. 167–212). The author is indebted to Arnold Horelick, of the RAND Corporation, for pertinent comments concerning more recent developments, and to Wlodzimierz Baczkowski, of the Library of Congress, for drawing my attention to the interrelationships, in Czarist Russian military doctrine, of the concepts of offense, initiative, and surprise and to Soviet adaptations of them.

4. *Pravda*, January 15, 1960.

5. Ibid.

6. Ibid.

7. Ibid.

8. Ibid.

9. Ibid. (emphasis added).

10. *Marxism and the National and Colonial Question* (New York: International Publishers, n.d.), p. 115.

11. Cf. Stefan T. Possony, *A Century of Conflict: Communist Techniques of World Revolution* (Chicago: Regnery, 1953), pp. 377–83, especially p. 379.

12. Elsewhere in this book, Dr. Thomas W. Wolfe discusses Soviet disarmament tactics in detail. One of the most useful works on coexistence is Wladyslaw W. Kulski's *Peaceful Co-existence: An Analysis of Soviet Foreign Policy* (Chicago: Regnery, 1959).

13. Speech on the tenth anniversary of the Chinese People's Republic, *Pravda*, October 1, 1959.

14. O. V. Kousinen (ed.), *Osnovi Marksisma-Leninisma (The Foundations of Marxism-Leninism)* (Moscow: State Publishing House of Political Literature, 1959), p. 501.

15. Ibid., p. 500.

16. See Kulski, op. cit., pp. 129–30.

17. Reply to questions from a Brazilian journalist, November 21, 1957, *Za Prochnyi Mir i Mirnoe Sosushchestvovanie (For a Lasting Peace . . .)* (Moscow, 1958), p. 282.

18. *Zhit' v Mire i Druzhbe! Prebyvanie . . . N. S. Khrushcheva v SShA, 15–27 sentiabria 1959 g. (Live in Peace and Friendship! N.S. Khrushchev's Visit to the U.S.A., (September 15–27, 1959)* (Moscow, 1959), p. 55.

19. Kousinen, op. cit., pp. 507, 520–23, 528–29.

20. *Pravda*, January 15, 1960.

21. *Pravda*, February 15, 1956, quoted in Kulski, op. cit., p. 92. Note that the Communists have been talking about this "changed balance" of power since 1950.

22. Kousinen, op. cit., p. 529 (emphasis added).

23. "Scientific Foundations of a Revolutionary Policy," *World Marxist Review*, II, No. 12 (December 1959), 43.

24. *Pravda*, January 15, 1960.

25. "In the . . . competition with capitalism . . . the question of the time it takes to solve economic tasks is of exceptional and vital importance. . . . The question of the time factor, of gaining time in economic development . . . is the main question." (Speech to the All-Union Conference of Power Industry Construction, November 28, 1959; broadcast by Radio Moscow, December 13, 1959.)

PART FOUR

PROBLEMS OF MILITARY STRATEGY

INTRODUCTION

Ever since 1914, the countenance of peace has been as blurred as that of war. As conflict has become total, so have the strategies designed to wage it. The spectrum of conflict today embraces, in effect, the entire range of human actions.

This spectrum is expanding rapidly. Technology is the major, but not the only, spur to this expansion. The number of nations which, for one reason or another, want to engage in conflict continues to increase. Methods of psychopolitical warfare continue to become more refined and more sophisticated. In the coming years, potential theaters of conflict will encompass ever greater dimensions. They will include the spheres of outer space and the depths of the oceans; they will witness "invisible weapons" and implements which, like computers, "conquer time."

The new element in the strategic equation is the nuclear weapon. This new weapon will not abolish the traditional spectrum of conflict as it has been waged throughout history. Conflict will not lose its multidimensional character. But the nuclear weapon *will* become the prime mover of conflict techniques. Already, all types of conflict systems and techniques, with nuclear weapons as their core, are being merged into the most powerful instruments of conquest history has ever known. The essential consequence of the across-the-spectrum integration is a continual extension and sophistica-

This introduction is based on a lecture given by Dr. Stefan T. Possony at the National Strategy Seminar for Reserve Officers.

tion of strategy and tactics. More important, with increasing rapidity the problems of security and survival are becoming synonymous.

What are the basic characteristics of the conflict spectrum as it exists at mid-century and as it is likely to evolve in the future? To a considerable extent, the answer depends on the areas of conflict, the frequency of conflict, the interrelationships between varying types of military and technological conflict on the one hand, and psychopolitical, economic, and other nonviolent techniques on the other.

"War" against an unstable, weak, and unsophisticated government can be waged at minimum cost, merely by employing psychopolitical weapons of pressure and coercion and, in later stages, by resorting to revolution or other forms of "local violence." Yet, victorious conflict against a stable, powerful, sophisticated state requires more than the employment of revolutionary techniques. At some time within the span of a given conflict, it requires the defeat and destruction of the hostile state as a prerequisite to military occupation or political-revolutionary seizure of power, or surrender.

We must sharpen our understanding of how the spectrum of conflict is operating in today's world. We must recognize that the cold war is a means of waging a momentous conflict through the use of economic and technological progress as a substitute for more recognizable and orthodox means of warfare. At the same time, we must accept the fact that if we do not surrender at the terminus of the cold war, we will be required to defend our way of life with force and sacrifice.

The Communist system is based on the assumption that conflict is all and all is conflict. War and peace are mutually supplementary forms. Military principles, in their traditional version and as reformulated by Communist innovators, apply both to open warfare and to what Westerners think of as "peaceful endeavor" or "competitive coexistence"—in brief, to all aspects of life and historical developments. To our opponents, struggle is the essence of life. They believe that force and violence are integral parts of the relentless and "dialectic" process of history.

The first task of free government, if it is to survive, is to master the intellectual challenge—to rethink the pattern of conflict. Our partial approach to portions of the spectrum and our infatuation with the purely "legal" and artificial distinction of "war" and "peace" must give way to organic comprehension of the *whole* problem. It is only through such comprehension of the conflict spectrum in its entire breadth that we shall be able to manage our strategy effectively, in a mélange of techniques suitable to our own purposes. It is only on such a basis that we shall be able to obtain maximum advantage from our vast resources, potential and actual.

14. Values, Power, and Strategy

As manager of the Air Defense Evaluation Program, Stanford Research Institute, Mr. Foster directs an interdisciplinary research team in evaluating programs for the active and passive defense of the United States and western Europe against air and missile attacks. The value of his work has been recognized by the Department of the Army, which gave him the Patriotic Civilian Service Award. A graduate of the University of California in philosophy, his publications include articles on techniques of production management and functional scheduling as well as the paper "The Lead Time Race" for the President's Advisory Committee on Government Organization.

In the twilight of the 1950s, a prediction by De Tocqueville published in 1835 has come true. America and the Soviet Union each sway the destiny of half the globe. Vast differences of values and in ways of life separate the Free World—led by America—and the Communist bloc—led by the Soviet Union. But no matter how profound the differences in starting point and in the courses that have led the two countries to this polarity of world power, they have some fundamental problems in common. Perhaps the most critical problem is that which results from the twentieth-century explosion of science and technology. Each nation is forced to tame the exploding

From the Stanford Research Institute Journal, Fourth Quarter 1959. Reprinted by permission.

technologies that have resulted in weapons of such power that they may effectively destroy the values and the culture of either side, and of western Europe as well.

The Power of Nuclear Weapons and Fundamental Values

Both sides are faced with the ancient moral problem of the relation of power and value. Each side must find new answers to govern the use and containment of what appears to be almost unlimited power. The thermonuclear weapon is not just another explosive; the ICBM is not just another delivery weapon. Together they represent a quantum jump in the power to destroy the most basic of all values—people, wealth, culture, and history. The possible annihilation of culture by the use of such potent military armament brings both sides face to face with the physical consequences of annihilation and its moral corollary, nihilism.

Wars between great powers are fought to achieve objectives that lie beyond war. Present and future United States and Soviet leaders will seek to preserve their values and will strive to limit wars to those in which their nations can survive and prevail in the long term. Aside from the danger of unilateral annihilation, there is a real possibility of a war of mutual annihilation initiated by accident or by a nihilist who rejects all values. In the coming age of the ballistic missile, the danger of such a war by accident increases unless both sides make a supreme effort at control.

The Free World and the Communist bloc share a common humanity. In the face of the destructive force of nuclear weapons in abundance, the two sides of the bipolar world must agree on fundamental values that will constrain the use of their latent powers of annihilation. At least two areas of agreement have already automatically been reached by sane men:

1. Wars that threaten to destroy all or a major fraction of the human race are universally rejected by men of reason.

2. All such men agree that life is better lived with others, and that the social fabric in which they live is worth preserving.

A third area of agreement is emerging as a consequence of

the increasing danger of an accidental nuclear war. If all sane men agree on these two fundamental values, then an agreement on lessening the danger of such an accidental war is in the self-interest of both sides of the bipolar world. The impetus behind such a weapons-control agreement is a mutual fear of a purposeless war that may in fact turn out to be so destructive that neither side would survive as a nation if it occurred before either side was prepared. On the other hand, Khrushchev's proposal to the United Nations for total disarmament in four years would have to be based on mutual trust—a trust which does not now exist.

Polarity of Power and Formulation of Strategy

Let us focus our attention on some of the consequences of the polarity of power between America and the Soviet Union as a first step in evolving a national strategy for the next decade. We must recognize, first, that the polarity of power is also in part a polarity of values, although the values of the United States and the U.S.S.R. overlap to a degree not yet explored. Second, use of power by either side is constrained and directed by strategies, and these strategies are, in turn, contained in a framework of national values and objectives. Third, these national values and objectives of both sides are in a context of values of the rest of the world. Each side is making a claim to the common humanity of all nations. Each side is courting the public opinion of the world.

How well are we doing in this competition? Presently, our power is greater than the Soviet Union's, and our values make a greater claim on the faith of a larger share of humanity; the Soviets have an advantage in that their strategy is more coherent and covers a larger area of their economy and of the daily life of their people than does ours. They may also have a future advantage in that the rate of growth of their military power relative to ours is greater.

Finally, each side is seeking both to preserve its values against the use of force by the other side and to extend its power in all ways—economic, political, military. Traditionally, the objectives of the use of military power by civilized peoples have been to seek out and destroy the enemy's military forces in the field, not to exterminate people and cultural values. But too often the problem of values is either ignored or unconsciously assumed when a military strategy is being formulated.

The relationships between steps of decision in formulating strategy are more complex. Aside from the sequence of decisions that lead to the adoption of a strategy are reservoirs of undirected power, such as science and technology, or physical and economic resources. At the base of the decision sequence lies the most profound statement of human, moral and religious values that man can make. This is the basis of the public opinion of the world. Within this framework are our national values, which, in turn, prescribe our national goals and objectives. On the basis of these objectives we lay out policies that to a large extent determine the way in which we will allocate our resources. Next up the scale is the selection of a national strategy, including foreign policy, trade, and aid, and the like. Within the framework of the national strategy, military strategies are conceived. Military strategy is both art and science. It is still more art than science, although a very considerable effort in the past few years has gone into the problem of reducing military strategy to more measurable terms, particularly in the relation of strategy to technology. It is in this area that a radical improvement in the quality of our military planning can be made. Strategy, then, helps select the military forces and weapons to secure the objectives of the nation and is determined by those objectives. The weapon choice is based on a selection of technologies out of the scientific and technological base, and is constrained by policy decisions that allocate economic resources.

This complex and dynamic interaction of national values, policy, allocation of resources, military strategy, and technology that results in a selection of a strategy by one side influences and is influenced by a similar selection made on the other side. There is continuous action and counteraction in this two-way selection process. However, too often choices of technology and economic-allocation decisions dictate strategy with little concern for either values or the reactions of the enemy.

As we attempt to see why the United States finds itself in the position of having to face the possibility of annihilation, a melancholy fact emerges. A critical turning point was the adoption of the massive-retaliation strategy announced in 1954 by the United States. Two things emerge: First, we took no long-term view of the ethical basis for the strategy. Hence we are now faced with a profound moral crisis. Second, as a consequence of this decision, certain technologies were most fully exploited to support it. Our selection was primarily of those technologies that give rise to the weapons with the largest "kills per dollar"—that is, thermonuclear weapons and the long-range delivery systems that can apply these weapons against a whole nation.

We overlook the fact that strategy is two-sided. We find that we exploited a short-term power advantage. The Soviets have essentially caught up with us in nuclear technology and are probably ahead in the ballistic-missile field. The United States no longer has the comfort of a monopoly of massive retaliation.

Thus, the United States made a narrow selection out of a wide range of technologies available for consideration, in the belief that we could get more security at less cost. Instead, we bought rigidity of posture, and to a certain extent, forced rigidity on the Soviet Union. There were different technologies, different kinds of weapons, different kinds of forces available for choice, some of which could have led to more flexible strategies. Our ability to wage limited wars for limited objectives in defense of not only our values but those of our allies and other free nations is withering away. We can no longer solve the basic issues between ourselves and the Soviet Union by a thermonuclear exchange; nor can we initiate a thermonuclear war against the Soviet Union and hope to escape unscathed.

Choice of a thermonuclear war has never been in consonance with our national values. Yet we can predict that force of some kind will be used to resolve some of these issues. We find ourselves in a more and more rigid posture, with strategic flexibility rapidly diminishing. Our strategic thinking and planning have been too narrow in scope, of too low a quality, and too short-term. Can we do better in the next decade?

Planning and Uncertainty

As we enter the 1960s we are faced with a complex and difficult problem: we must evolve long-range plans for greater strategic flexibility in the face of great uncertainties. Hopefully, there are feasible solutions to this difficulty. The first requirement for a solution is to identify and characterize the uncertainties; the second is to put them into perspective. Only by taking a very long-term view of both our national values and where we want to go as a nation do we make these uncertainties recede into their proper perspective. Some of the more important areas of uncertainty as they affect military strategic planning are:

1. *Technological change.* On the one hand, the lead time to recognize applications of new technologies and then to incorporate them into an operational weapon is very long—five to ten years at least. On the other hand, the technological base is exploding at a fantastic rate. Future technologies will make obsolete some weapons now in development before they are fully deployed.

2. *Intelligence.* Much of our planning must be based on estimates of Soviet capabilities—present and future. This is extremely difficult, particularly because our intelligence on present Soviet capabilities is imperfect at best, and we can only project into the future from an estimate of the present.

3. *Planning.* After we have decided on a strategy with its weapons, there remain many uncertainties of planning. Will our selected weapons meet their predicted schedules and performance goals within the estimated cost?

4. *Political stability.* Although we may seek to stabilize a mutual deterrent to general nuclear war, we cannot stabilize the political situation of a world in ferment—as in Africa, Asia, the Near East, and South America.

5. *Accidental war.* We have discussed how both the United States and the Soviet Union mutually desire the reduction of this danger.

6. *Strategic balance of power.* The balance of power may shift radically at any time. For example, if one side exploits

new breakthroughs in defense technology, the other side's ballistic-missile force may become obsolete; or if a disarmament agreement is reached and one side disarms more rapidly than the other side, the balance could change very swiftly.

7. *Values.* Here an immeasurable difficulty exists. Can we predict with any certainty the level of damage the Soviets are willing to sustain under all possible future political conditions? For example, a high-tension international situation may cause Soviet leaders to estimate that nuclear war was the least undesirable course of action open to them. Furthermore, World War II proved they can absorb a tremendous loss of life and still prevail and survive over the long term.

8. *Feasibility of nuclear war.* This is by all odds the most important uncertainty of all. We will examine some of the implications of this problem as they affect the formulation of a United States military strategy for the next decade; for example, can stability be achieved in a mutual-deterrence posture with an "all-offense" system?

Yet, in the face of these uncertainties, long-range strategic planning is still necessary and desirable, and, moreover, our achieving it may be more likely than we think. Nuclear weapons are here, and their existence faces us too plainly with the necessity for making a proper choice of strategies for the future so that we do not lose the race.

Relative Advantages in the Balance of Power

Before we can formulate long-range plans and strategic concepts for the future, it is well to list the advantages that each side will have throughout the next decade. Some of the principal advantages which favor the Soviet Union might be listed as follows:

1. *Geopolitical.* Location in the heartland of the Eurasian continent enables the U.S.S.R. to threaten to use their land forces for the forcible occupation of western Europe—the first prize of the power struggle. If during the 1960s we achieve a relatively stable balance of power for general nuclear war, so that both sides are mutually deterred, then the Soviets

might estimate that they can fight—and win—a conventional ground war in order to capture Europe.

2. *Relative population density.* The United States has a much higher proportion of its population in metropolitan areas than do the Soviets. Hence the Soviet Union can cause greater destruction of life with the same number of nuclear weapons.

3. *The organization of government.* A highly centralized form of government gives the Soviet leaders virtually complete control over allocation of their economy. In a real sense, the U.S.S.R. is a military state that can set long-range goals and maintain the discipline necessary to meet them. Their rapid decision-making capability enables them to shorten lead times and to exploit the military advantages of new technologies much more rapidly than in the United States. In addition, the Russian people are subject to Party and other controls, enabling Soviet leaders to install a civil-defense program with far greater ease and celerity than in a democracy.

4. *Will.* Related to the organization of government is the problem of will—or willingness to go to war. The ICBM with a thermonuclear warhead gives a tremendous advantage to the side that can decide to strike first, particularly with surprise, and the Soviet leaders apparently do not rule out this advantage.

5. *Intelligence access.* The Soviet Union has an advantage in this area. For example, the Iron Curtain makes it relatively hard for the West to obtain information on new Soviet weapon developments, on possible ICBM launching sites, and on their military intentions. On the other hand, the open societies of the West make all of these intelligence tasks fairly easy for the Soviets.

The above is a formidable listing of power advantages on the side of the Soviet Union. These advantages will not go away if we ignore them; our future strategies must take them into account. However, many of the advantages accorded the Soviet Union by some United States planners and policy makers are not borne out by the facts. For example, let us look at the so-called Soviet military manpower advantage; a comparison of census figures for the United States and its NATO allies with those of the Soviets indicates a preponderant military manpower advantage on the side of the West. In the face of the real advantages of the Soviet Union, the United States has at least two extremely important—and, we hope, decisive—advantages on its side for the next decade. How we make use of them is a test of our national resolution and of the depth of the faith of our convictions. These are:

1. *Economic supremacy.* It is unlikely that the Soviet economy can achieve parity with that of the United States by 1970. Their economy is strained; ours has a large additional capacity and expansibility whose limits have not yet been tested. Theirs is rigid; ours has a flexibility yet unmatched in the world's history. Their labor supply is short; ours has untapped sources, as World War II demonstrated. The Soviet agricultural economy strains to produce a minimum supply of food with 40 per cent of their labor; ours produces unmanageable surpluses with less than 10 per cent of our labor. The list could be extended. But this advantage can be thrown away in the next decade unless we recognize the challenge of the rate of growth of the Soviet economy, and if we fail to allocate our economic resources wisely.

2. *Our national values.* Too often we forget that the source of our strength is derived from the wellspring of our values—the freedom and dignity of the individual; the right to liberty combined with the voluntary sense of responsibility to our community; the exaltation that lies in the vision of the grandeur of a free man's destiny in a world where a high sense of purpose awaits and invites each individual's participation. The character of our institutions—the Constitution; the law and the independent courts; the free-enterprise system with its judicious balance of opportunities and of rewards for individual effort, and its claims on almost all of us to contribute to our mutual well-being—reflects these basic values.

De Tocqueville's eloquent statement that "the principal instrument of [America] is freedom; of [Russia] servitude," contrasts the two systems of values. Our NATO and other Free World allies are joined with us because we hold that these basic values are the property of all mankind, and because we have shown our resolution to defend them with our wealth and the lives of our youth in two great wars and in Korea in this century.

We can take pride in the maturity with which we have

abjured colonialism and the temptations of empire. We have given not only freedom to former colonial possessions but also our wealth to support them as nascent democracies, as in the Philippines. We can contrast our behavior with that of the Soviets after World War II. We utilized our resources and our power not only to rebuild the economies of our western European allies but also to rebuild our erstwhile enemies—Japan, Germany, Italy. The Soviets captured whole nations, enslaved their peoples, and stripped their resources and their economies to enhance Soviet power. Within the framework of this contrasting behavior, let us look more closely at the nature of the Soviet challenge.

Power, Value, and National Resolve

Khrushchev, in his recent unprecedented visit to the United States in 1959 and in his article "On Peaceful Coexistence" in the October 1959 issue of *Foreign Affairs*, stated with great conviction that he believes in his values and in the Communist way of life. He expressed a confidence in the Soviet military might and warned America: "Should a world war break out, no country will be able to shut itself off from a crushing blow." He challenged the West to a transformation from conflict to competition and expressed his determination and resolve to use the resources—human and material—of the Soviets to win over the West in the long term. Although we and the Communists share a common humanity, it would be worse than folly to ignore the fundamental differences between their objectives and methods and those of the West. No doubt the Soviet leadership will use all of the power advantages on their side—including military action. They will exploit uncertainty, indecision, irresolution, and confused thinking wherever and whenever these factors in the United States leadership and in the Western alliance appear. We cannot afford gaps anywhere in the spectrum of conflict with the Communist bloc—nor is there any need for this to happen. With a resolution at least equal to Khrushchev's, the two advantages on our side—economic supremacy and our national values—represent the basis for meeting the Communist challenge without resorting to strategies of extermination.

No low-cost strategies are available to us. We cannot "buy" our way through the next decade with little or no sacrifice. We cannot afford either complacency or naïveté in the face of the implacable enmity the Communist leaders have shown toward Western social and cultural values.

Western ideas of conduct and of fair play are not accorded the same role in the Communist bloc—in which the ends of the state justify any means—as they are in the Western democracies. The Communist society is, by Western standards, led by moral strangers; the Marxist-Leninist philosophy produces the technocratic man, a moral neuter, who is an instrument of the apparatus of the Party.

Yet these newcomers in world affairs understand and respect power and resolution. An effective national resolve of the United States must be strong enough to present the Communist leaders with but two alternatives: the mutual rewards that derive from respect for the rules of civilized conduct in the community of nations, or an unacceptable price they would have to pay for conduct that ignores and destroys these rules.

Value Considerations Related to Strategic Problems

We can isolate three issues that are particularly relevant to a discussion of the relation of values and power in the formulation of strategy:

1. Is there an ethical basis for deterrence by the threat of retaliation? The answer to this hinges largely on what actions we are trying to deter. Self-preservation is a first law of nature: so long as the Soviets have the power to destroy or greatly damage us as a nation, we are obligated to make that use of Soviet power an unacceptable course of action to Soviet leaders. But a simple statement of national survival is not sufficient. Why is it important not only to us but also to the rest of the Free World that we survive as a major power? We have not begun either to ask ourselves or to answer this question in a serious way.

2. In the "balance of terror" can stability of mutual deter-

rence be achieved easily and cheaply? A stable and reliable deterrence to general nuclear war is difficult to achieve. We may go through a period of extreme instability in which the Soviet military planners may calculate that they can strike the first blow at our nuclear retaliatory forces and thus reduce the level of damage they might sustain from the crippled residual United States SAC force to one which would be acceptable, taking into account their defensive measures—both active and passive.

Although all strategists do not wholly accept this thesis, all responsible military strategists agree that the military objective of first priority is to achieve a stable deterrent to a direct Soviet nuclear attack on the United States based primarily on a capability to retaliate on the Soviet Union. All agree that this is an absolute requirement for all other strategic objectives.

There is a great controversy, however, about the cost of such a deterrent system, and about the conditions of stability. Once again, as in the beginning of the past decade, one strategic concept is emerging that has a principal appeal—low cost. The basic weapon system proposed is essentially an all-offense system, with no real effort made to defend the United States. Some of the weaknesses of this minimum-deterrence strategy have been discussed by competent analysts. However, two fallacies in the reasoning related to the problems of power and value should also be pointed out.

The first fallacy lies in a part of the moral argument. Efforts of the United States to defend its cities and preserve its values constitute no direct threat to the Soviet's values. An all-offense system, directed solely at destroying Soviet values, may be looked upon by the rest of the world and by the Soviets as a strategy of annihilation—a suicide pact—reflecting the Communist prediction of the "bankruptcy of Western capitalist-imperialist values." From the value side, the United States build-up of an all-offense system for general nuclear war directed solely toward the threatened destruction of Soviet values may look to Soviet planners as an extremely unstable situation and thus invite a pre-emptive attack on United States general-nuclear-war forces before the relatively invulnerable all-offensive deterrent forces can be deployed in quantity.

The second fallacy lies in the assumption about United

States knowledge of Communist values—that is, some of the strategists think they can estimate the level of damage that any future Soviet leader will be willing to sustain under all conceivable political situations. Usually a single strategic value criterion is selected, such as the destruction of major industrial concentrations. This is then said to constitute unacceptable damage to the Soviet Union. Thus the Soviet leaders will be deterred. This estimate of Soviet values, as we have noted, is a major uncertainty that must be taken into account in planning strategies for the next decade. For example, the Soviets may adopt a plan to evacuate their cities, putting their population in fallout shelters and giving up a part of their industrial base. This base could then be rebuilt if their armies could capture western Europe intact, and use the western European economy to rebuild that portion of their industrial base destroyed by a United States retaliatory raid—unless we would also be willing to destroy western Europe to deny these resources to the Soviets.

There are other dangers and fallacies in this proposal. Essentially, it is a proposal that erects a national strategy on the characteristics of a few offensive weapons. The proponents have not taken a long-term view of either the effect of the offense-defense balance on the balance of power or the ethical basis for the strategy. War in the next decade is much too complex to allow for such simple strategies.

3. What is the role of the scientist in formulating strategy? Following the brilliant discoveries of the scientists in World War II and the increasing impact of technology on strategy, there has grown a tendency to give the scientist responsibility for formulating strategy and, in some cases, policy. To the extent that this has been done, our military and civilian leaders have been abdicating some responsibilities in the face of the enormous complexities of science and technology. But science and technology are merely a part of the reservoirs of undirected power from which we make choices. The strategist and policy maker must understand science and, in addition, know the nature of warfare, doctrine, and tactics; economics; politics; foreign policy; and philosophy—disciplines in which the scientist is generally not trained. The policy maker can do no

less, for the grave burden of choice rests on him alone and not on his advisers.

Your and My Responsibility

A participation in the choice of a national strategy by a more widely informed public is vital to the continued existence of a democracy.

We cannot turn back the pages of history and pretend that thermonuclear weapons with their long-range delivery systems —bombers, ballistic missiles—do not exist. They do—and on both sides. The price that will be exacted of us for our own survival and for the purposes beyond survival is more than material; it requires, in addition, an examination of the ethical basis of our strategies within the perspective of long-term moral consequences.

The premium we might pay for morally acceptable and flexible military strategies that would extend our capabilities beyond the rigidity of primary reliance on nuclear-weapon technology is unpredictable today. But we can predict that the price of freedom will be high. The advantages on our side —those of economic supremacy and flexibility, political freedom, and Western cultural values—need only our resolve and hard work to crystallize them into strategies that cover the entire spectrum of conflict. We can meet the Soviets in all forms of conflict and competition without ourselves calling into account the issue of national survival for each side at every turn in the political and diplomatic road.

Such a choice requires the participation of all of us. At the minimum we will have to mobilize our resources. But it will take a considerable economic sacrifice to achieve the long-term goals and national values. Such goals and values require that we explore and exploit areas of agreement, starting with the Soviet Union. Victory in the conflict and competition requires that we work hard at reaching areas of agreement with our allies and between the political parties, management and labor, and the military services. A supreme effort is required to close the gap between scientists and policy makers if we are to bring the power released by scientific discovery under the control of our enduring values.

The American genius that De Tocqueville noted as a pragmatic and analytical approach to life must be supplemented with another fact of the American genius—that of unifying disparate and often conflicting elements of our society for achieving a common purpose. We have achieved this feeling of unity and sense of high purpose during wartime and during emergencies. The next decade will demonstrate whether or not we can achieve it in a period of uneasy peace.

15.   Strategy on Trial

by John F. Loosbrock

Mr. Loosbrock has been the editor of Air Force Magazine *since 1957. A graduate of the College of Journalism at Marquette University, Mr. Loosbrock rose from private to captain during World War II and served with the 1st Infantry Division in North Africa and Sicily. He was formerly an associate editor of the* Infantry Journal *and Washington editor of* Popular Science Monthly. *He was the editor of the book* Space Weapons, *co-ordinated the editing of* A History of the U.S.A.F.—1903–1957, *and has lectured at the Air University on Air Force doctrine.*

It is a strange paradox that, in a time when science is making profound impacts on the tools and concepts of war, military planners are denied, and happily so, the advantage of the ultimate in scientific procedure—the controlled experiment to determine the validity of their theories. Revolutionary new weapons, strategy, and tactics must now be considered and accepted without prior trial in war. Nor can bets be hedged by retaining the tried and true while adding the new. There are no Indian campaigns, no border skirmishes to test our forces and try our new weapons. We must choose, now, and accept the risks. We must be prepared at any moment to go with what we have.

This is a hard burden, for coupled with this essentially military problem is a dynamic power struggle between two large blocs of nations, each led by countries almost equally rich in essential elements of military power but with antithetic political ideologies. Thus, in a world which is politically and militarily unstable, military plans must be under constant review. They are conditioned by such factors as national policy, relations with allies, enemy capabilities, technological developments, and, not least, the economic price the nation is willing to pay. Some of these factors can be predicted quite accurately; others cannot. But plans must be laid on the basis of what is known or can be perceived. And we can arrive only at guidelines, not dogmas.

On this basis, three general military requirements appear to be valid for this nation into the 1970s. They are proposed in the interest of avoiding a general war through a combination of measures and of deterring, or localizing, lesser conflicts so that the basic position of the Free World is not substantially threatened. Should the deterrent posture fail to deter, then the resulting conflict must be won. And, indeed, the weight of evidence indicates that a posture that can win a general war is by its very nature the kind of posture that can deter both it and lesser conflicts.

Within this framework, the first requirement is for strategic delivery forces, able to absorb a surprise attack and still deal a crushing blow. These forces are the heart and core of deterrence, both of general and of limited war, the *sine qua non* which establishes the context in which all other forces and actions must be studied.

The second requirement is for defense measures, both active and passive, should the enemy, either through an irrational act or a wrong evaluation of our offensive power, attempt to overpower us with a massive, surprise onslaught. Active defenses against a determined air attack do not have an encouraging history. The Battle of Britain was won with a defense that was less than 10 per cent effective, not close to good enough against thermonuclear weapons. Intercontinental missiles have made the problem all the more difficult to solve, but there will always be a place for active defense as part of an ante-raising proposition to discourage attack. Passive measures, to protect our retaliatory forces and our civil population, are still another card in the ante raising and one which, by and large, has been neglected.

The combination of offensive and defensive strength which serves to deter the enemy from launching a general war is likely also to discourage lesser forms of military aggression. The small war may get out of control and bring down the full strength of our offensive power upon the enemy homeland. Nevertheless, he may be willing to take that chance, and we must be prepared for such an eventuality.

The third military requirement, therefore, is to be prepared to meet limited aggression, wherever it may occur, quickly and in a manner best suited to achieve our national objectives. The forces to accomplish this must be based on careful consideration of the probable extent and nature of limited war, the weapons which may be used, and the size and nature of the threat to our national objectives.

The Margin of Deterrence

Since defeat in a general war would mean the end of our free existence as a nation, it is clearly the more serious threat. Likewise, the threat of limited aggression is related directly to the relative general-war postures of the United States and the Soviet Union. So long as we maintain a superior general-war capability, so long as we maintain a clearly definable deterrent margin, all forms of Soviet military and political aggression will be inhibited. If the deterrent margin shrinks, or disappears, the Soviet Union will have almost complete freedom of action, militarily and politically.

The ability to retaliate swiftly and decisively, then, stands as the keystone of our deterrent philosophy.

In happier, less complicated days, even as recently as a decade ago, the doctrine of deterrence was comparatively simple to enunciate and to carry out. It was not much more involved than Teddy Roosevelt's dictum to "walk softly and carry a big stick." Perhaps even less complicated, since during the pre-Korean period the United States not only possessed the only big stick in the world but held a monopoly on the means to deliver it as well.

These days are gone forever. The technological revolution has also exploded behind the Iron Curtain, where it is being exploited shrewdly and with great determination. Deterrence is becoming a two-way street and, with this evolution, has taken on subtle and sophisticated overtones. The big stick grows ever bigger, yet it must now be handled with the delicacy and finesse of a rapier.

One arrives at a complicated equation, not susceptible of the kind of simplification usually resorted to in public debate over "missile gaps." The effectiveness of our retaliatory force, and hence of our deterrent posture, is not just a matter of quantity, or of quality, although neither factor can be ignored and their relative importance will vary according to the weight of other factors. If the problem can be simplified, perhaps it is fair to say it boils down to survival and penetration. The force must be able to leave here and get there.

Survival and Penetration

For purposes of discussion, the problems of survivability and penetration capability will be considered separately, although even this dichotomy will necessarily be artificial.

One way to insure the survival of enough of the force to retaliate decisively is through sheer weight of numbers. The more bombers and missiles we have, the more the enemy must destroy in order to cut his homeland damage down to an acceptable level. Numbers will never cease to be important.

Another element of survivability is the state of the active air-defense system. Every enemy bomber or missile stopped short of target adds to the number of weapons delivered on his homeland targets.

A third element is reaction time, which is steadily shrinking under the impact of increasing speeds of delivery systems. If you have moved from the target by the time the enemy's blow arrives, he cannot hit you—but you still have the power to hit him.

Dispersal is still another factor in survivability. It multiplies the number of targets which the enemy must destroy before he feels that retaliatory destruction is reduced to a level he can accept. In the case of manned bombers, the ultimate in dispersal is the so-called air-borne alert—vertical, rather than horizontal, dispersal.

Still another method of reducing the vulnerability of the

retaliatory force is through hardening—placing weapons and their command and control systems far enough underground that almost a direct hit is needed to put them out of commission.

Mobility—land-borne, sea-borne, air-borne—also is a key method of reducing vulnerability and one that is taking on increasing importance.

But in an age of intercontinental missiles, with thirty minutes' travel time from launch to a target six thousand miles away, perhaps the most single significant element in reducing vulnerability lies in the field of warning against surprise attack—both tactical warning that an attack is actually on the way and strategic warning of signs that an attack is imminent. The latter truly encompasses the broad field of intelligence.

Thus it is seen that technology has introduced no radically new elements into the survival equation. One increases the size of his forces, one either digs in or moves about, one learns all he can of both the enemy's capabilities and his intentions so as to survive and counterattack. What technology has done is, in effect, to turn the entire world into a battlefield, with room for error eliminated for all practical purposes. There are no opportunities for muddling through. Either you are right or you are dead.

Through a combination of all or part of the above measures, a substantial part of the retaliatory force will be spared in even a surprise attack and will be dispatched against enemy targets. The effectiveness of this measure will be measured in terms of its penetration capability—how many warheads get through to how many targets and with what degree of accuracy. Looking to the future once more, the advent of the intercontinental ballistic missile has simplified the penetration problem, inasmuch as, at the moment, there is small prospect of an active defense system that can detect, identify, intercept, and destroy a warhead before it reaches its target. Likewise, the manned bomber, using the so-called stand-off missile or air-launched ballistic missile, is less likely to have to fight its way through active defenses to the target. The thermonuclear warhead has an area of destruction which puts a much lower premium on accuracy than in the past, although both U.S. and Soviet achievements in missile accuracy have been little short of phenomenal. This latter factor, incidentally, is important because (1) it reduces the number of missiles required to inflict an unacceptable level of damage and (2) it makes of the intercontinental missile a truly counterforce weapon rather than a city-destroying instrument of vengeance.

Technological developments of the past two decades, then, have vastly increased and complicated the problems of survivability of the retaliatory force while vastly easing the problems of penetration to target. The pendulum of advantage has swung far in favor of attack versus defense and, concomitantly, in the political context of the times, has given the potential aggressor, with the twin advantages of surprise and initiative, a well-nigh incalculable degree of superiority, all else being equal.

On the brighter side, however, the same technological successes which have brought us to this impasse may well carry within themselves the seeds for solutions to the very problems which they have created. More on this later.

The Idea of Mutual Invulnerability

In terms of hardware, our strategic forces are in a period of transition from a manned-bomber force to one composed of both missiles and bombers. The mixed force, our military planners feel strongly, will give a flexibility of employment above that of either an all-bomber or an all-missile force. Through this decade the mix will be progressively weighted in favor of missiles until by 1970 substantially more than half of the long-range delivery forces will be equipped with Atlas, Titan, Minuteman, and later-generation intercontinental ballistic missiles, reinforced by intermediate-range ballistic missiles in the hands of our western European allies. If the logic of survivability is followed, these weapons will be securely housed in hardened sites and dispersed both within the continental limits of the United States and in overseas bases. In addition, the mobility element will be introduced, with Polaris intermediate-range ballistic missiles in submarines at sea, and with Minuteman and its follow-on missiles, which are designed for land-borne mobility.

An unforeseeable fraction of the force will be invested in space-borne systems within the decade, if not in delivery systems as such, then at least in early-warning, surveillance, and command and control systems. No one can predict with accuracy all of the military applications that will result from exploitation of space technology. However, it appears that the advent of space vehicles, manned and unmanned, will provide the ultimate in target accessibility, intelligence, and early warning.

In the period under discussion there will continue to be tasks which manned bombers can perform better than missiles. Among these are the destruction of mobile or ill-defined targets which require extreme accuracy, combat patrol missions, exploitation of an enemy defense system which has been degraded through missile attacks, and missions which require on-the-spot human judgment. The latter, of course, has to do with the great advantage of having part of your retaliatory force subject to recall in case of false alarm or concessions on the part of the enemy. It is highly dubious that we will ever wish to stake all on a missile system that must continue on to target once launched. The stakes are too high and the danger of war through accident or miscalculation too great.

The strategic progression of the United States and Russia over the next decade, short of general war, appears to be toward the development of two mutually invulnerable strategic delivery systems, forces which can wreak unacceptable damage upon the other nation regardless of who starts what, or when, or how. In such a case, a true nuclear stalemate will have been reached, and there are many who feel that such a stalemate is the only chance for world stability.

But stalemates do not last forever, and the rewards for breaking one of this magnitude will be high, high enough to tempt an aggressor into actions designed to do so. As a result, it will be to our advantage to explore methods of reducing the mutuality of deterrence, placing us once more in a position where our deterrent factor is positive and measurable, as it was when we possessed a monopoly of nuclear weapons and their delivery systems.

There are several ways through which this goal may be pursued, and while their pursuit should not divert us from our quest for an invulnerable retaliatory force, neither should their importance be sloughed off as incidental to the main problem. They must be sought in addition to, and coincidentally with, the achievement of invulnerability. Indeed, they may be said to contribute directly and indirectly to our overall deterrent posture.

One of these is the development of an improved limited-war capability above that provided by the protective umbrella of the retaliatory force. This is essentially a tactical job, with forces designed for quick reaction, global mobility, and selective application of power to include non-nuclear weapons if the situation should so dictate. It includes a modernized airlift capability for small numbers of ground troops to act as the "starch in the collar" for indigenous forces, hopefully to be supplied by the enlightened self-interest of our allies.

A second field for exploitation is that of protection of our military and civil population against fallout and other radiation hazards, provision of continuity of government on local, state, and national levels, and insurance of national economic recovery following a general war. Herein would appear to lie a fruitful and purposeful mission for the bulk of our Reserve forces.

The third field for exploitation in the stalemate lies in space. Actually, the need for military space vehicles is part and parcel of our guarantee of invulnerability of the force, but it has been selected for separate discussion because (1) the ramifications and implications project far beyond the time period under discussion and (2) because the potential for peace-seeking objectives in essentially military space systems has largely been overlooked.

Controlled Peace

Warning against surprise attack is the key to invulnerability. That is why we disperse our aircraft and place them on airborne alert; why we harden our missile sites and extend our radar; why we seek mobility through the Minuteman and Polaris missile systems. But mainly it is a problem of getting high enough and seeing far enough. Up to now, our line of sight has been limited technically by restrictions imposed by air-borne vehicles and politically by the existence, recognized in international law, of national frontiers in the atmosphere —frontiers which cannot be violated with impunity. Now our progress in ballistic-missile technology can be coupled with what some term "the electronic revolution" to allow us to keep sensitive warning, surveillance, and command and control devices in orbit to provide constant warning and control of aggression wherever in the world it might occur. Positive warning coupled with positive retaliation may indeed offer the world its first hope for intelligent, purposeful control of arms on a practical, rather than an idealistic, basis. Disarmament has long been a goal of well-meaning people, in the mistaken belief that disarmament was synonymous with peace. Now it is possible realistically to think of peace under positive control by weapons of war, leading, in the end, to practical reductions in the world's crushing arms burden without opening the door of weakness to an aggressor.

It becomes obvious that we cannot do all that is to be done in the forthcoming decade within the economic restrictions currently imposed on military budgets. We are lagging behind in almost every field under discussion. Granted, there is waste and duplication of effort imposed by the current defense organization, with its artificial lines of demarcation between service interests and responsibilities. We can immeasurably ease the economic burden by an organization which can concentrate resources where they are needed most.

But above and beyond this must come a realization that peace is not a penny-ante affair, that the competition will get rougher all the way along the line, and that we must make an investment large enough to insure our security beyond a peradventure of a doubt or the billions we have invested to date will be a total loss.

Our strategy of deterrence cannot be a matter of trial and error. It is constantly on trial and there can be no room for error.

16. The Delicate Balance of Terror

by Albert Wohlstetter

Mr. Wohlstetter is a Fellow of the Council on Foreign Relations on leave from the RAND Corporation, where he is Associate Director of Projects. At RAND, beginning in 1951, he conducted a series of studies concerned principally with problems of deterring general war and the vulnerability of retaliatory forces. He engaged also in studies of the active and passive defense of the United States and of methods and problems of arms control. A native of New York City, Mr. Wohlstetter was trained in mathematical logic and in economics at Columbia University.

The first shock administered by the Soviet launching of Sputnik has almost dissipated. The flurry of statements and investigations and improvised responses has died down, leaving a small residue: a slight increase in the schedule of bomber and ballistic-missile production, with a resulting small increment in our defense expenditures for the current fiscal year; a considerable enthusiasm for space travel; and some stirrings of interest in the teaching of mathematics and physics in the secondary schools. Western defense policy has almost returned to the level of activity and the emphasis suited to the basic assumptions which were controlling before Sputnik.

One of the most important of these assumptions—that a general thermonuclear war is extremely unlikely—is held in com-

Abridged version of an article by the same title which appeared in the January 1959 issue of Foreign Affairs *and reprinted by special permission. Copyright 1959 by Council on Foreign Relations, Inc., New York.*

mon by most of the critics of our defense policy as well as by
its proponents. Because of its crucial role in the Western strategy of defense, I should like to examine the stability of the
thermonuclear balance, which, it is generally supposed, would
make aggression irrational or even insane. The balance, I believe, is in fact precarious, and this fact has critical implications for policy. Deterrence in the 1960s is neither assured nor
impossible but will be the product of sustained intelligent effort and hard choices responsibly made. As a major illustration important both for defense and foreign policy, I shall treat
the particularly stringent conditions for deterrence which affect forces based close to the enemy, whether they are U.S.
forces or those of our allies, under single or joint control. I
shall comment also on the inadequacy as well as the necessity
of deterrence, on the problem of accidental outbreak of war,
and on disarmament.

The Presumed Automatic Balance

I emphasize that requirements for deterrence are stringent.
We have heard so much about the atomic stalemate and the
receding probability of war which it has produced that this
may strike the reader as something of an exaggeration. Is deterrence a necessary consequence of both sides having a nuclear delivery capability, and is all-out war nearly obsolete?
Is mutual extinction the only outcome of a general war? This
belief, frequently expressed by references to Dr. Oppenhei-
mer's simile of the two scorpions in a bottle, is perhaps the
prevalent one.

Deterrence, however, is not automatic. While feasible, it
will be much harder to achieve in the 1960s than is generally
believed. One of the most disturbing features of current opinion is the underestimation of this difficulty. This is due partly
to a misconstruction of the technological race as a problem
in matching striking forces, partly to a wishful analysis of the
Soviet ability to strike first.

Since Sputnik, the United States has made several moves
to assure the world (that is, the enemy, but more especially
our allies and ourselves) that we will match or overmatch

Soviet technology and, specifically, Soviet offense technology. We have, for example, accelerated the bomber and ballistic-missile programs, in particular the intermediate-range ballistic missiles. The problem has been conceived as more or better bombers—or rockets; or sputniks; or engineers. This has meant confusing deterrence with matching or exceeding the enemy's ability to strike first. Matching weapons, however, misconstrues the nature of the technological race. Not, as is frequently said, because only a few bombs owned by the defender can make aggression fruitless, but because even many might not. One outmoded A-bomb dropped from an obsolete bomber might destroy a great many supersonic jets and ballistic missiles. To deter an attack means being able to strike back in spite of it. It means, in other words, a capability to strike second. In the last year or two there has been a growing awareness of the importance of the distinction between a "strike first" and a "strike second" capability, but little, if any, recognition of the implications of this distinction for the balance-of-terror theory.

Where the published writings have not simply underestimated Soviet capabilities and the advantages of a first strike, they have in general placed artificial constraints on the Soviet use of the capabilities attributed to them. They assume, for example, that the enemy will attack in mass over the Arctic through our Distant Early Warning Line, with bombers refueled over Canada—all resulting in plenty of warning. Most hopefully, it is sometimes assumed that such attacks will be preceded by days of visible preparations for moving ground troops. Such assumptions suggest that the Soviet leaders will be rather bumbling or, better, co-operative. However attractive it may be for us to narrow Soviet alternatives to these, they would be low in the order of preference of any reasonable Russians planning war.

The Quantitative Nature of the Problem and the Uncertainties

In treating Soviet strategies it is important to consider Soviet rather than Western advantage and to consider the strategy of both sides quantitatively. The effectiveness of our own choices will depend on a most complex numerical interaction of Soviet and Western plans. Unfortunately, both the privileged and unprivileged information on these matters is precarious. As a result, competent people have been led into critical error in evaluating the prospects for deterrence. Western journalists have greatly overestimated the difficulties of a Soviet surprise attack with thermonuclear weapons and vastly underestimated the complexity of the Western problem of retaliation.

Perhaps the first step in dispelling the nearly universal optimism about the stability of deterrence would be to recognize the difficulties in analyzing the uncertainties and interactions between our own wide range of choices and the moves open to the Soviets. On our side we must consider an enormous variety of strategic weapons which might compose our force, and for each of these, several alternative methods of basing and operation. These are the choices that determine whether a weapons system will have any genuine capability in the realistic circumstances of a war. Besides the B-47E and the B-52 bombers which are in the United States strategic force now, alternatives will include the B-52G (a longer-range version of the B-52); the Mach-2 B-58A bomber and a "growth" version of it; the Mach-3 B-70 bomber; a nuclear-powered bomber possibly carrying long-range air-to-surface missiles; the Dynasoar, a manned glide rocket; the Thor and the Jupiter, liquid-fueled intermediate-range ballistic missiles; the Snark intercontinental cruise missile; the Atlas and the Titan intercontinental ballistic missiles; the submarine-launched Polaris and Atlantis rockets; Minuteman, one potential solid-fueled successor to the Thor and Titan; possibly unmanned bombardment satellites; and many others which are not yet gleams in anyone's eye and some that are just that.

The difficulty of describing in one chapter the best mixture of weapons for the long-term future beginning in 1960, their base requirements, their potentiality for stabilizing or upsetting the balance among the great powers, and their implications for the alliance, is not just a matter of space or the constraint of security. The difficulty in fact stems from some rather basic insecurities. These matters are widely uncertain; we are talking about weapons and vehicles that are some time off and, even if the precise performances currently hoped for and claimed by contractors were in the public domain, it would be a good idea to doubt them.

Recently some of my colleagues picked their way through the graveyard of early claims about various missiles and aircraft: their dates of availability, costs, and performance. These claims are seldom revisited or talked about: *de mortuis nil nisi bonum*. The errors were large and almost always in one direction. And the less we knew, the more hopeful we were. Accordingly, the missiles benefited in particular. For example, the estimated cost of one missile increased by a factor of over 50—from about $35,000 in 1949 to some $2,000,000 in 1957. This uncertainty is critical. Some but not all of the systems listed can be chosen, and the problem of choice is essentially quantitative. The complexities of the problem, if they were more widely understood, would discourage the oracular confidence of writers on the subject of deterrence.

Some of the complexities can be suggested by referring to the successive obstacles to be hurdled by any system providing a capability to strike second, that is, to strike back. Such deterrent systems must have (1) a stable, "steady-state" peacetime operation within feasible budgets (besides the logistic and operational costs there are, for example, problems of false alarms and accidents). They must have also the ability (2) to survive enemy attacks, (3) to make and communicate the decision to retaliate, (4) to reach enemy territory with fuel enough to complete their mission, (5) to penetrate enemy active defenses, that is, fighters and surface-to-air missiles, and (6) to destroy the target in spite of any "passive" civil defense in the form of dispersal or protective construction or evacuation of the target itself.

Within limits, the enemy is free to use his offensive and defensive forces so as to exploit the weaknesses of each of our systems. He will also be free, within limits, in the 1960s to choose that composition of forces which will make life as difficult as possible for the various systems we might select. It would be quite wrong to assume that we have the same degree of flexibility or that the uncertainties I have described affect a totalitarian aggressor and the party attacked equally.

A totalitarian country can preserve secrecy about the capabilities and disposition of his forces very much better than a Western democracy. And the aggressor has, among other enormous advantages of the first strike, the ability to weigh continually our performance at each of the six barriers and to choose that precise time and circumstance for attack which will reduce uncertainty. It is important not to confuse our uncertainty with his. Strangely enough, some military commentators have not made this distinction and have founded their certainty of deterrence on the fact simply that there are uncertainties.

The Delicacy of the Balance of Terror

The most important conclusion is that we must expect a vast increase in the weight of attack which the Soviets can deliver with little warning and the growth of a significant Russian capability for an essentially warningless attack. As a result, strategic deterrence, while feasible, will be extremely difficult to achieve, and at critical junctures in the 1960s we may not have the power to deter attack. Whether we have it or not will depend on some difficult strategic choices as to the future composition of the deterrent forces as well as hard choices on its basing, operations, and defense.

Manned bombers will continue to make up the predominant part of our striking force in the early 1960s. None of the popular remedies for their defense will suffice—not, for example, mere increase of alertness (which will be offset by the Soviets' increasing capability for attack without significant warning), nor simple dispersal or sheltering alone or mobility taken by itself, nor a mere piling up of interceptors and defense missiles around SAC bases. Especially extravagant expectations have been placed on the air-borne alert—an extreme form of defense by mobility. The impression is rather widespread that one third of the SAC bombers are in the air and ready for combat at all times. This belief is belied by the public record. According to the Symington Committee hearings in 1956, our bombers averaged 31 hours of flying per month, which is about 4 per cent of the average 732-hour month. An Air Force representative expressed the hope that within a couple of years, with an increase in the ratio of crews to aircraft, the bombers would reach 45 hours of flight per month—which is 6 per cent. This 4 to 6 per cent of the force includes bombers partially fueled and without bombs. It is, moreover, only an average, admitting variance down as well as up. Some increase in the number of armed bombers aloft is to be expected. However, for the current generation of bombers, which have been designed for speed and range rather than endurance, a continuous air patrol of one third of the force would be extremely expensive.

On the other hand, it would be unwise to look for miracles in the new weapons systems, which by the mid-1960s may constitute a considerable portion of the United States force. After the Thor, Atlas, and Titan there are a number of promising developments. The solid-fueled rockets, Minuteman and Polaris, promise in particular to be extremely significant components of the deterrent force. Today they are being touted as making the problem of deterrence easy to solve and, in fact, guaranteeing its solution. But none of the new developments in vehicles is likely to do that. For the complex job of deterrence, they all have limitations. The unvarying immoderate claims for each new weapons system should make us wary of the latest "technological breakthroughs." Only a very short time ago the ballistic missile itself was supposed to be invulnerable on the ground. It is now more generally understood that its survival is likely to depend on a variety of choices in its defense.

It is hard to talk with confidence about the mid- and late 1960s. A systematic study of an optimal or a good deterrent force which considered all the major factors affecting choice and dealt adequately with the uncertainties would be a formidable task. In lieu of this, I shall mention briefly why none of the many systems available or projected dominates the others in any obvious way. My comments will take the form of a swift run-through of the characteristic advantages and disadvantages of various strategic systems at each of the six successive hurdles mentioned earlier.

The first hurdle to be surmounted is the attainment of a stable, steady-state peacetime operation. Systems which depend for their survival on extreme decentralization of controls, as may be the case with large-scale dispersal and some of the mobile weapons, raise problems of accidents, and over a long period of peacetime operation this leads, in turn, to serious political problems. Systems relying on extensive movement by land, perhaps by truck caravan, are an obvious example; the introduction of these on European roads, as is sometimes suggested, would raise grave questions for the governments of some of our allies. Any extensive increase in the armed air alert will increase the hazard of accident and intensify the concern already expressed among our allies. Some of the proposals for bombardment satellites may involve such hazards of unintended bomb release as to make them out of the question.

The cost to buy and operate various weapons systems must be seriously considered. Some systems buy their ability to negotiate a given hurdle—say, surviving the enemy attack—only at prohibitive cost. Then the number that can be bought out of a given budget will be small and this will affect the relative performance of competing systems at various other hurdles, for example, penetrating enemy defenses. Some of the relevant cost comparisons, then, are between competing systems; others concern the extra costs to the enemy of canceling an additional expenditure of our own. For example, some dispersal is essential, though usually it is expensive; if the dispersed bases are within a warning net, dispersal can help to provide warning against some sorts of attack, since it forces the attacker to increase the size of his raid and so makes it more liable to detection as well as somewhat harder to co-ordinate. But as the sole or principal defense of our offensive force, dispersal has only a brief useful life and can be justified financially only up to a point. For against our costs of construction, maintenance, and operation of an additional base must be set the enemy's much lower costs of delivering one extra weapon. And, in general, any feasible degree of dispersal leaves a considerable concentration of value at a single target point. For example, a squadron of heavy bombers costing, with their associated tankers and penetration aids, perhaps $500,000,000 over five years, might be eliminated, if it were otherwise unprotected, by an enemy intercontinental ballistic missile costing perhaps $16,000,000. After making allowance for the unreliability and inaccuracy of the missile, this means a ratio of some ten for one or better. To achieve safety by *brute* numbers in so unfavorable a competition is not likely to be viable economically or politically. However, a viable peacetime operation is only the first hurdle to be surmounted.

At the second hurdle—surviving the enemy offense—ground alert systems placed deep within a warning net look good against a manned-bomber attack, much less good against intercontinental ballistic missiles, and not good at all against ballistic missiles launched from the sea. In the last case, systems such as the Minuteman, which may be sheltered and dispersed as well as being alert, would do well. Systems involving launching platforms which are mobile and concealed, such as Polaris submarines, have particular advantage for surviving an enemy offense.

However, there is a third hurdle to be surmounted—namely, that of making the decision to retaliate and communicating it. Here, Polaris, the combat air patrol of B-52s, and in fact all of the mobile platforms—under water, on the surface, in the air, and above the air—have severe problems. Long-distance communication may be jammed and, most important, communication centers may be destroyed.

At the fourth hurdle—ability to reach enemy territory with fuel enough to complete the mission—several of our short-legged systems have operational problems such as co-ordination with tankers and using bases close to the enemy. For a good many years to come, up to the mid-1960s in fact, this will be a formidable hurdle for the greater part of our deterrent force. The next section of this article deals with this problem at some length.

The fifth hurdle is the aggressor's long-range interceptors and close-in missile defenses. To get past these might require large numbers of planes and missiles. (If the high cost of overcoming an earlier obstacle—using extreme dispersal or airborne alert or the like—limits the number of planes or missiles bought, our capability is likely to be penalized disproportionately here.) Or getting through may involve carrying heavy loads of radar decoys, electronic jammers, and other aids to defense penetration. For example, vehicles like Minuteman and Polaris, which were made small to facilitate dispersal or mobility, may suffer here because they can carry fewer penetration aids.

At the final hurdle—destroying the target in spite of the passive defenses that may protect it—low-payload and low-accuracy systems, such as Minuteman and Polaris, may be frustrated by blast-resistant shelter. For example, five half-megaton weapons with an average inaccuracy of two miles might be expected to destroy half the population of a city of 900,000 spread over forty square miles, provided the inhabitants are without shelters. But if they are provided with shelters capable of resisting overpressures of 100 pounds per square inch, approximately sixty such weapons would be required; and deep rock shelters might force the total up to over a thousand.

Prizes for a retaliatory capability are not distributed for getting over one of these jumps. A system must get over all six. I hope these illustrations will suggest that assuring ourselves the power to strike back after a massive thermonuclear surprise attack is by no means as automatic as is widely believed.

In counteracting the general optimism as to the ease and, in fact, the inevitability of deterrence, I should like to avoid creating the extreme opposite impression. Deterrence demands hard, continuing, intelligent work, but it can be achieved. The job of deterring rational attack by guaranteeing great damage to an aggressor is, for example, very much less difficult than erecting a nearly airtight defense of cities in the face of full-scale thermonuclear surprise attack. Protecting manned bombers and missiles is much easier because they may be dispersed, sheltered, or kept mobile, and they can respond to warning with greater speed. Mixtures of these and other defenses with complementary strengths can preserve a powerful remainder after attack. Obviously not all our bombers and missiles need to survive in order to fulfill their mission. To preserve the majority of our cities intact in the face of surprise attack is immensely more difficult, if not impossible. (This does not mean that the aggressor has the same problem in preserving his cities from retaliation by a poorly protected, badly damaged force. And it does not mean that *we* should not do more to limit the extent of the catastrophe to our cities in case deterrence fails. I believe we should.) Deterrence, however, provided we work at it, is feasible, and, what is more, it is a crucial objective of national policy.

What can be said, then, as to whether general war is unlikely? Would not a general thermonuclear war mean "extinction" for the aggressor as well as the defender? "Extinction" is a state that badly needs analysis. Russian casualties in World War II were more than 20,000,000. Yet Russia recovered extremely well from this catastrophe. There are several quite plausible circumstances in the future when the Russians might be quite confident of being able to limit damage to considerably less than this number—they make sensible strategic choices and we do not. On the other hand, the risks of not striking might at some juncture appear very great to the Soviets, involving, for example, disastrous defeat in peripheral war, loss of key satellites with danger of revolt spreading—possibly to Russia itself—or fear of an attack by ourselves. Then, striking first, by surprise, would be the sensible choice for them, and from their point of view the smaller risk.

It should be clear that it is not fruitful to talk about the likelihood of general war without specifying the range of alternatives that are pressing on the aggressor and the strategic postures of both the Soviet bloc and the West. Deterrence is a matter of comparative risks. The balance is not automatic. First, since thermonuclear weapons give an enormous advantage to the aggressor, it takes great ingenuity and realism at any given level of nuclear technology to devise a stable equilibrium. And second, this technology itself is changing with fantastic speed. Deterrence will require an urgent and continuing effort.

The Uses and Risks of Bases Close to the Soviets

It may now be useful to focus attention on the special problems of deterrent forces close to the Soviet Union. First, overseas areas have played an important role in the past and have a continuing though less certain role today. Second, the recent acceleration of production of intermediate-range ballistic missiles and the negotiation of agreements with various NATO powers for their basing and operation have given our overseas bases a renewed importance in deterring attack on the United States—or so it would appear at first blush. Third, an analysis can throw some light on the problems faced by our allies in developing an independent ability to deter all-out attack on themselves, and in this way it can clarify the much agitated question of nuclear sharing. Finally, overseas bases affect in many critical ways, political and economic as well as military, the status of the alliance.

At the end of the last decade, overseas bases appeared to be an advantageous means of achieving the radius extension needed by our short-legged bombers, of permitting them to use several axes of attack, and of increasing the number of sorties possible in the course of an extended campaign. With the growth of our own thermonuclear stockpile, it became apparent that a long campaign involving many re-uses of a large proportion of our bombers was not likely to be necessary. With the growth of a Russian nuclear-delivery capability, it became clear that this was most unlikely to be feasible.

Our overseas bases now have the disadvantage of high vulnerability. Because they are closer than the United States to the Soviet Union, they are subject to a vastly greater attack by a larger variety as well as number of vehicles. With given resources, the Soviets might deliver on nearby bases a freight of bombs with something like fifty to one hundred times the yield that they could muster at intercontinental range. Missile accuracy would more than double. Because there is not much space for obtaining warning—in any case, there are no deep-warning radar nets—and since most of our overseas bases are close to deep water from which submarines might launch missiles, the warning problem is very much more severe than for bases in the interior of the United States.

As a result, early in the 1950s the U. S. Air Force decided to recall many of our bombers to the continental United States and to use the overseas bases chiefly for refueling, particularly poststrike ground refueling. This reduced drastically the vulnerability of U.S. bombers and at the same time retained many of the advantages of overseas operation. For some years now SAC has been reducing the number of aircraft usually deployed overseas. The purpose is to reduce vulnerability and has little to do with any increasing radius of SAC aircraft. The early B-52 radius is roughly that of the B-36; the B-47, roughly that of the B-50 or B-29. In fact, the radius limitation, and therefore the basing requirements we have discussed, will not change substantially for some time to come. We can talk with comparative confidence here, because the U.S. strategic force is itself largely determined for this period. Such a force changes more slowly than is generally realized. The vast majority of the force will consist of manned bombers, and most of these will be of medium range. *Some* U.S. bombers will be able to reach *some* targets from *some* U.S. bases within the continental United States without landing on the way back. On the other hand, some bomber-target combinations are not feasible without pre-target landing (and are therefore doubtful). The Atlas, Titan, and Polaris rockets, when available, can of course do without overseas bases (though the proportion of Polaris submarines kept at sea can be made larger by the use of submarine tenders based overseas). But even with the projected force of aerial tankers, the greater part of our force, which will be manned bombers, cannot be used at all in attacks on the Soviet Union without at least some use of overseas areas.

What of the bases for Thor and Jupiter, our first intermediate-range ballistic missiles? These have to be close to the enemy, and they must of course be operating bases, not merely refueling stations. The Thors and Jupiters will be continuously in range of an enormous Soviet potential for surprise attack. These installations therefore reopen, in a most acute form, some of the serious questions of ground vulnerability that were raised about six years ago in connection with our overseas bomber bases. The decision to station the Thor and Jupiter missiles overseas has been our principal public response to the Russian advances in rocketry, and perhaps our most plausible response. Because it involves our ballistic missiles, it appears directly to answer the Russian rockets. Because it involves using European bases, it appears to make up for the range superiority of the Russian intercontinental missile. And most important, it directly involves the NATO powers and gives them an element of control.

There is no question that it was genuinely urgent not only to meet the Russian threat but to do so visibly, in order to save the loosening NATO alliance. Our allies were fearful that the Soviet ballistic missiles might mean that we were no longer able or willing to retaliate against the Soviet Union in case of an attack on them. We hastened to make public a reaction which would restore their confidence. This move surely appears to increase our own power to strike back, and also to give our allies a deterrent of their own, independent of our decision. It has also been argued that in this respect it merely advances the inevitable date at which our allies will acquire "modern" weapons of their own, and that it widens the range of Soviet challenges which Europe can meet. But we must face seriously the question whether this move will in fact assure either the ability to retaliate or the decision to attempt it, on the part of our allies or ourselves. And we should ask at the very least whether further expansion of this policy will buy as much retaliatory power as other ways of spending the considerable sums involved. Finally, it is important to be clear whether the Thor and Jupiter actually increase the flexibility or range of response available to our allies.

One justification for this move is that it disperses retaliatory weapons and that this is the most effective sanction against the thermonuclear aggressor. The limitations of dispersal have already been discussed, but it remains to examine the argument that overseas bases provide *widespread* dispersal, which imposes on the aggressor insoluble problems of co-ordination.

There is, of course, something in the notion that forcing the enemy to attack many political entities increases the seriousness of his decision, but there is very little in the notion that dispersal in several countries makes the problem of destruction more difficult in the military sense. Dispersal does not require separation by the distance of oceans—just by the lethal diameters of enemy bombs. And the task of co-ordinating bomber attacks on Europe and the eastern coast of the United States, say, is not appreciably more difficult than co-ordinating attacks on our east and west coasts. In the case of ballistic missiles, the elapsed time from firing to impact on the target can be calculated with high accuracy. Although there will be some failures and delays, times of firing can be arranged so that impact on many dispersed points is almost simultaneous —on Okinawa and the United Kingdom, for instance, as well as on California and Ohio. Moreover, it is important to keep in mind that these far-flung bases, while distant from each other and from the United States, are on the whole close to the enemy. To eliminate them, therefore, requires a smaller expenditure of resources on his part than targets at intercontinental range. For close-in targets he can use a wider variety of weapons carrying larger payloads and with higher accuracy.

The seeming appositeness of an overseas-based Thor and Jupiter as an answer to a Russian intercontinental ballistic missile stems not so much from any careful analysis of their retaliatory power under attack as from the directness of the comparison they suggest: a rocket equals a rocket, an intercontinental missile equals an intermediate-range missile based at closer range to the target. But this again mistakes the nature of the technological race. It conceives the problem of deterrence as that of simply matching or exceeding the aggressor's capability to strike first.

The basis for the hopeful impression that they will not is rather vague, including a mixture of hypothetical properties of ballistic missiles in which perhaps the dominant element is their supposedly much more rapid, "push button" response. What needs to be considered here are the response time of such missiles (including decision, preparation, and launch times) and how they are to be defended.

The decision to fire a missile with a thermonuclear warhead is much harder to make than a decision simply to start a manned aircraft on its way, with orders to return to base unless instructed to continue to its assigned target. This is the "fail-safe" procedure practiced by the U. S. Air Force. In contrast, once a missile is launched, there is no method of recall or deflection which is not subject to risks of electronic or mechanical failure. Therefore, such a decision must wait for much more unambiguous evidence of enemy intentions. It must and will take a longer time to make and is less likely to be made at all. Where more than one country is involved, the joint decision is harder still, since there is opportunity to disagree about the ambiguity of the evidence, as well as to reach quite different interpretations of national interest. On much less momentous matters the process of making decisions in NATO is complicated, and it should be recognized that such complexity has much to do with the genuine concern of the various NATO powers about the danger of accidentally starting World War III. Such fears will not be diminished with the advent of IRBMs. In fact, widespread dispersion of nuclear-armed missiles raises measurably the possibility of accidental war.

Second, it is quite erroneous to suppose that by contrast with manned bombers the first IRBMs can be launched almost as simply as pressing a button. Countdown procedures for early missiles are liable to interruption, and the characteristics of the liquid-oxygen fuel limits the readiness of their response. Unlike JP-4, the fuel used in jet bombers, liquid oxygen cannot be held for long periods of time in these vehicles. In this respect, such missiles will be *less* ready than alert bombers. Third, the smaller warning time available overseas makes more difficult any response. This includes, in particular, any active defense, not only against ballistic-missile attacks but, for example, against low-altitude or various circuitous attacks by manned aircraft.

Finally, passive defense by means of shelter is more difficult, given the larger bomb yields, better accuracies, and larger forces available to the Russians at such close range. And if the press reports are correct, the plans for IRBM installations do not call for bomb-resistant shelters. If this is so, i should be taken into account in measuring the actual contribution of these installations to the West's retaliatory power. Viewed as a contribution to deterring all-out attack on the United States, the Thor and Jupiter bases seem unlikely to compare favorably with other alternatives. If newspaper references to hard bargaining by some of our future hosts are to be believed, it would seem that such negotiations have been conducted under misapprehensions on both sides as to the benefits to the United States.

But many proponents of the distribution of Thor and Jupiter —and possibly some of our allies—have in mind not an increase in U.S. deterrence but the development of an independent capability in several of the NATO countries to deter all-out attack against themselves. This would be a useful thing if it can be managed at supportable cost and if it does not entail the sacrifice of even more critical measures of protection. But aside from the special problems of joint control, which would affect the certainty of response adversely, precisely who their legal owner is will not affect the retaliatory power of the Thors and Jupiters one way or the other. They would not be able to deter an attack which they could not survive. It is curious that many who question the utility of American overseas bases (for example, our bomber bases in the United Kingdom) simply assume that, for our allies, possession of strategic nuclear weapons is one with deterrence.

There remains the view that the provision of these weapons will broaden the range of response open to our allies. Insofar as this view rests on the belief that the intermediate-range ballistic missile is adapted to limited war, it is wide of the mark. The inaccuracy of an IRBM requires high-yield warheads, and such a combination of inaccuracy and high yield, while quite appropriate and adequate against unprotected targets in a general war, would scarcely come within even the most lax, in fact reckless, definition of limited war. Such a weapon is inappropriate for even the nuclear variety of limited war, and it is totally useless for meeting the wide variety of provocation that is well below the threshold of nuclear response. Insofar as these missiles will be costly for our allies to install, operate, and support, they are likely to displace a conventional capability that might be genuinely useful in limited engagements. More important, they are likely to be used as an excuse for budget cutting. In this way they will accelerate the general trend toward dependence on all-out response and so will have the opposite effect to the one claimed.

Nevertheless, if the Thor and Jupiter have these defects, might not some future weapon be free of them? Some of these defects, of course, will be overcome in time. Solid fuels or storable liquids will eventually replace liquid oxygen, reliabilities will increase, various forms of mobility or portability will become feasible, accuracies may even be so improved that such weapons can be used in limited wars. But these developments are all years away. In consequence, the discussion will be advanced if a little more precision is given such terms as "missiles" or "modern" or "advanced weapons." We are not distributing a generic "modern" weapon with all the virtues of flexibility in varying circumstances and of invulnerability in all-out war. But even with advances in the state of the art on our side, it will remain difficult to maintain a deterrent, especially close in under the enemy's guns.

It follows that, though a wider distribution of nuclear weapons may be inevitable, or at any rate likely, and though some countries in addition to the Soviet Union and the United States may even develop an independent deterrent, it is by no means inevitable or even very likely that the power to deter all-out thermonuclear attack will be widespread. This is true even though a minor power would not need to guarantee as large a retaliation as we in order to deter attack on itself. Unfortunately, the minor powers have smaller resources as well as poorer strategic locations.[1] Mere membership in the nuclear club might carry with it prestige, as the applicants and nominees expect, but it will be rather expensive, and in time it will be clear that it does not necessarily confer any of the expected privileges enjoyed by the two charter members. The burden of deterring a general war as distinct from limited wars is still likely to be on the United States and therefore, so far as our allies are concerned, on the military alliance.

There is one final consideration. Missiles placed near the enemy, even if they could not retaliate, would have a potent capability for striking first by surprise. And it might not be easy for the enemy to discern their purpose. The existence of such a force might be a considerable provocation and, in fact a dangerous one, in the sense that it would place a great burden on our deterrent force, which more than ever would have to guarantee extreme risks to the attacker—worse than the risks of waiting in the face of this danger. When not coupled with the ability to strike in retaliation, such a capability might suggest—erroneously, to be sure, in the case of the democracies —an intention to strike first. If so, it would tend to provoke rather than to deter, general war.

I have dealt here with only one of the functions of overseas bases: their use as a support for the strategic deterrent force They have a variety of important military, political, and economic roles which are beyond the scope of this chapter. Expenditures in connection with the construction or operation of our bases, for example, are a form of economic aid and, moreover, a form that is rather palatable to the Congress. Ther are other functions in a central war where their importance may be very considerable and their usefulness in a limited war might be substantial.

Indeed, nothing said here should suggest that deterrence is in itself an adequate strategy. The complementary requirements of a sufficient military policy certainly include a more serious development of power to meet limited aggression, especially with more advanced conventional weapons than those now available. They also include more energetic provision for active and passive defenses to limit the dimensions of the catastrophe in case deterrence should fail. For example, an economically feasible shelter program in the United States might make the difference between 50,000,000 survivors and 120,000,000 survivors.

But it would be a fatal mistake to suppose that because strategic deterrence is inadequate by itself it can be dispensed with. Deterrence is not dispensable. If the picture of the world I have drawn is rather bleak, it could nonetheless be cataclysmically worse. Suppose both the United States and the Soviet Union, given the opportunity to administer the opening blow, had the power to destroy each other's retaliatory forces and society. The situation would then be something like the old-fashioned Western gun duel. It would be extraordinarily risky for one side *not* to attempt to destroy the other, or to delay doing so, not only because it can emerge unscathed by striking first but because this is the sole way it can reasonably hope to emerge at all. Evidently such a situation is extremely unstable. On the other hand, if it is clear that the aggressor, too, will suffer catastrophic damage in the event of his aggression, he then has strong reason not to attack, even though he can administer great damage. A protected retaliatory capability has a stabilizing influence not only in deterring rational attack but also in offering every inducement to both powers to reduce the chance of accidental war.

The critics who feel that deterrence is "bankrupt" sometimes say that we stress deterrence too much. I believe this is quite wrong if it means that we are devoting too much effort to protect our power to retaliate; but I think it is quite right if it means that we have talked too much of a strategic threat as a substitute for many things it cannot replace. If there were no real danger of a rational attack, then accidents and the "nth" country problem would be the only problems. As I have indicated, they are serious problems, and some sorts of limitation and inspection agreement might diminish them. But if there is to be any prospect of realistic and useful agreement, we must reject the theory of automatic deterrence. And we must bear in mind that the more extensive a disarmament agreement is, the smaller the force that a violator would have to hide in order to achieve complete domination. Most obviously, *"the abolition* of the weapons necessary in a general or 'unlimited' war"* would offer the most insuperable obstacles to an inspection plan, since the violator could gain an overwhelming advantage from the concealment of even a few weapons. The need for a deterrent, in this connection too, is ineradicable.

Summary

Almost everyone seems concerned with the need to relax tension. However, relaxation of tension, which everyone thinks is good, is not easily distinguished from relaxing one's guard, which almost everyone thinks is bad. Relaxation, like Miltown, is not an end in itself. Not all danger comes from tension. To be tense where there is danger is only rational.

What can we say then, in sum, on the balance-of-terror theory of automatic deterrence? It is a contribution to the rhetoric rather than the logic of war in the thermonuclear age. The notion that a carefully planned surprise attack can be checkmated almost effortlessly, that, in short, we may resume our deep pre-Sputnik sleep, is wrong and its nearly universal acceptance is terribly dangerous. Though deterrence is not enough in itself, it is vital. There are two principal points.

First, deterring general war in both the early and late 1960s will be hard at best, and hardest both for ourselves and our allies wherever we use forces based near the enemy.

Second, even if we can deter general war by a strenuous and continuing effort, this will by no means be the whole of a military, much less a foreign, policy. Such a policy would not of itself remove the danger of accidental outbreak or limit the damage in case deterrence failed; nor would it be at all adequate for crises on the periphery.

A generally useful way of concluding a grim argument of this kind would be to affirm that we have the resources, intelligence, and courage to make the correct decisions. That is, of course, the case. And there is a good chance that we will do so. But perhaps, as a small aid toward making such decisions more likely, we should contemplate the possibility that they may *not* be made. They *are* hard, *do* involve sacrifice, *are* affected by great uncertainties, and concern matters in which much is altogether unknown and much else must be hedged by secrecy; and, above all, they entail a new image of ourselves in a world of persistent danger. It is by no means *certain* that we shall meet the test.

Note

1. General Gallois argues that, while alliances will offer no guarantee, "a small number of bombs and a small number of carriers suffice for a threatened power to protect itself against atomic destruction" (*Réalités*, November 1958, p. 71). His numerical illustrations give the defender some 400 underground launching sites (ibid., p. 22, and the *Reporter*, September 18, 1958, p. 25) and suggest that their elimination would require 5000 to 25,000 missiles —which is "more or less impossible"—and that in any case the aggressor would not survive the fallout from his own weapons. Whether these are large numbers of targets from the standpoint of the aggressor will depend on the accuracy, yield, and reliability of offense weapons as well as the resistance of the defender's shelters and a number of other matters not specified in the argument. General Gallois is aware that the expectation of survival depends on distance even in the ballistic-missile age and that our allies are not so fortunate in this respect. Close-in missiles have better bomb yields and accuracies. Moreover, manned aircraft—with still better yields and accuracies—can be used by an aggressor here since warning of their approach is very short. Suffice it to say that the numerical advantage General Gallois cites is greatly exaggerated. Furthermore, he exaggerates the destructiveness of the retaliatory blow against the aggressor's cities by the remnants of the defender's missile force—even assuming the aggressor would take no special measures to protect his cities. But particularly for the aggressor—who does not lack warning—a civil-defense program can moderate the damage

done by a poorly organized attack. Finally, the suggestion that the aggressor would not survive the fallout from his own weapons is simply in error. The rapid-decay fission products which are the major lethal problem in the locality of a surface burst are not a serious difficulty for the aggressor. The amount of the slow-decay products, strontium 90 and cesium 137, in the atmosphere would rise considerably. If nothing were done to counter it, this might, for example, increase by many times the incidence of such relatively rare diseases as bone cancer and leukemia. However, such a calamity, implying an increase of, say, 20,000 deaths per year for a nation of 200,000,-000, is of an entirely different order from the catastrophe involving tens of millions of deaths, which General Gallois contemplates elsewhere. And there are measures that might reduce even this effect drastically. (See the RAND Corporation Report R-322-RC, *Report on a Study of Non-Military Defense,* July 1, 1958.)

17. The Nature and Feasibility of War and Deterrence

by Herman Kahn

Mr. Kahn is recognized today as one of the nation's best-informed authorities on civil-defense problems. A physicist, he received his academic training at the University of California and the California Institute of Technology. A visiting research associate to the Center of International Studies, Princeton University, in 1959, he has been a consultant to the Gaither Committee, the Office of Civil and Defense Mobilization, and the Atomic Energy Commission. He spent eleven years at the RAND Corporation studying problems of weapons design, weapons systems, and strategy.

On July 16, 1960, the world entered the sixteenth year of the nuclear era. Yet we are increasingly aware that after living with nuclear bombs for fifteen years we still have a great deal to learn about the possible effects of a nuclear war. We have even more to learn about conducting international relations in a world in which force tends to be both increasingly more available, increasingly more dangerous to use, and therefore in practice increasingly less usable. As a result, basic foreign and defense policies formulated early in the nuclear era badly need review and examination.

This paper summarizes, sometimes rather cursorily, some of the points discussed by the author in his book Thermonuclear War: Three Lectures and Several Suggestions, *published by the Princeton University Press in 1960. It appeared originally as a portion of a longer article in the Stanford Research Institute Journal, Fourth Quarter 1959. Reprinted by permission.*

Possibly of first importance is the casting of doubt on the widely accepted theory that the very existence of nuclear weapons creates a reliable balance of terror. This theory commonly holds that a thermonuclear war would mean certain and automatic annihilation of both antagonists, perhaps even the end of civilization. This concept of certain "mutual homicide" has been comforting to some. It makes plausible the widely held conviction that as soon as governments are informed of the terrible consequences of a nuclear war, their leaders will realize that there can be no victors and, therefore, no sense to such a war. No sane leader would ever start one! According to this view, the very violence of nuclear war will act to deter it.

The mutual-annihilation view is not unique to the West. Malenkov introduced it to the Soviet Union several years ago, apparently arguing in the now classical fashion that with nuclear war entailing the end of civilization, the capitalists would not attack; the Soviet Union, he said, could afford to reduce investment in heavy industry and military products and concentrate on consumer goods. A different view seems to have been held by Khrushchev and the Soviet military. They agreed that war would be horrible, but at the same time they argued that this was no reason for the Soviet Union to drop its guard: given sufficient preparations, only the capitalists would be destroyed. With some modifications their views seem to have prevailed.

Much depends on the validity of this notion of the balance of terror. Is it really true? Would only an insane man initiate a thermonuclear war? Is war, at least of the thermonuclear variety, completely obsolete? Or are there circumstances in which a nation's leaders might rationally decide that a thermonuclear war would be the least undesirable of the possible alternatives?

It should be clear that if either the Soviets or the Americans ever become careless in the operation of their alert forces, it is conceivable that a war might start as a result of an accident, some miscalculation, or even irresponsible behavior. But the situation seems worse than this, for one can conclude that with current technology there are plausible circumstances in which leaders might decide that war was their best alternative. To recognize such possibilities is certainly not to endorse them.

Some experts have come to a quite different set of conclusions. They believe that the balance of terror is indeed stable and that a war could start only as a result of an accident or miscalculation. They argue that a thermonuclear war would inevitably signal the end of our civilization; that even if there were survivors "these survivors would envy the dead." It is true that the world will not recover completely from a thermonuclear war. The environment will be permanently (that is, for perhaps 10,000 years) more hostile to human life as a result of such a war. Therefore, if the question "Can we restore the prewar conditions of life?" is asked, the answer must be "No!" But there are other relevant questions. How much more hostile will the environment be? Will it be so hostile that we or our descendants would prefer death to life? Perhaps even more pertinent is this one: How happy or normal a life can the survivors and their descendants hope to have? Objective studies indicate that although human tragedy would be increased immeasurably in the postwar world, it would not be increased to the extent that normal and happy lives became impossible.

One such study of the possibilities for alleviating the consequences of a thermonuclear war was conducted by the RAND Corporation several years ago. That study[1] was as searching and objective as we could make it with the resources, information, and intellectual tools available to us. *We concluded that for at least the next decade or so, any assumption of total world annihilation appears to be wrong, irrespective of the military course of events.* Equally important, the assumption of total disaster is not likely to apply even to the two antagonists. Barring an extraordinary course for the war, or technical developments not yet foreseen, one and perhaps both of the antagonists should be able to restore a reasonable semblance of prewar conditions quite rapidly. Typical estimates run between one and ten years for a well-prepared and reasonably successful attacker and somewhat more for the defender, depending mainly on the tactics of the attacker and the preparations of the defender. In the RAND study we shied away from optimistic assumptions. Thus, we believe that while the uncertainties are large enough so that the actual situation could be worse than we estimated, it is more likely than not to be more favorable than the findings of the study indicated.

To support this assertion about the "feasibility" of thermonuclear war, it is necessary to describe and evaluate the total impact of a thermonuclear war and to describe the kinds of risks that might cause decision makers to weigh the alternatives of going to war and not going to war. For the purpose of this analysis, it is convenient to describe a thermonuclear war as being composed of eight stages:

1. Various time-phased programs for deterrence and defense and their possible impact on us, our allies, and others.
2. Wartime performance under different pre-attack and attack conditions.
3. Acute fallout problems.
4. Survival and patch-up.
5. Maintenance of economic momentum.
6. Long-term recuperation.
7. Postwar medical problems.
8. Genetic problems.

To survive a war it is necessary to negotiate *all eight* stages. If there is a catastrophic failure on any one of them, there will be little value in being able to handle the other seven. Differences among exponents of different strategic views can often be traced to the different estimates they make on the difficulty of handling one or more of these eight stages. While all of them present difficulties, most civilian military experts seem to consider the *last six* the critical ones. Nevertheless, most discussions among "classical" military experts concentrate on the *first two*. To get a sober and balanced view of the problem, one must examine *all eight*. It is of great urgency that this examination be done well enough so that a "national debate" can be conducted on which of the alternative strategies should be chosen. While this debate will probably have to be carried on continuously, it is important that there be a clear-cut tentative choice so that military planning on the lower levels for specific items and weapons systems can be conducted in a context and so that the security and foreign policy consequences of the decision can be examined inside and outside of government. However, in this paper we will concentrate on the first of the eight stages. A systematic discussion of the other seven stages can be found in the RAND report already referred to or in my book *Thermonuclear War*.

Damage versus Commitments

Even if one accepts the balance-of-terror theory and we don't have to worry about a deliberate Soviet attack on the United States, we are still faced with important strategic problems. In 1914 and 1939 it was the British who declared war, not the Germans. Such a circumstance might arise again; but if the balance of terror were reliable, then we would be as likely to be deterred from striking the Soviets as they would be from striking us, and it would be doubtful that the United States would resort to an all-out attack on the Soviets, even to correct or avenge, for example, a major Soviet aggression limited to Europe.

That this now is plausible can be seen by Christian Herter's response on the occasion of the hearings on his nomination: "I cannot conceive of any President involving us in an all-out nuclear war unless the facts showed clearly we are in danger of all-out devastation ourselves, *or that actual moves have been made toward devastating ourselves.*"

A thermonuclear balance of terror is equivalent to signing a nonaggression treaty that neither the Soviets nor the Americans will initiate an all-out attack—no matter how provoking the other side may become. Sometimes people do not understand the full implications of this figurative nonaggression treaty. Let me illustrate what it can mean if we accept absolutely the notion that there is no provocation that would cause us to strike the Soviets other than an immediately impending or an actual Soviet attack on the United States. Imagine that the Soviets have dropped bombs on London, Berlin, Rome, Paris, and Bonn but have made no detectable preparations for attacking the United States, and that our retaliatory force looks good enough to deter them from such an attack. Suppose also that there is a device that restrains the President of the United States from acting for about twenty-four hours.

The President would presumably call together his advisers during this time. Most of these advisers would probably urge strongly that the United States fulfill its obligation and strike the Soviets. Now let us further suppose that the President is also told by his advisers that even though we will kill almost every Russian if we strike the Soviets, we will not be able to destroy all of the Soviet strategic forces, and that these surviving Soviet forces will (by radiation, or strontium 90, or something) kill every American in their retaliatory blow.

While such an attack might prompt us to declare war on the Soviet Union and engage in various military actions, it is difficult to believe that under these circumstances any President of the United States would initiate a *thermonuclear war* by retaliating against the Soviets with the Strategic Air Command. There is no objective of public policy that would justify ending life for everyone. It should be clear that we would not restore Europe by our retaliation; we could only succeed in further destroying it, either as a by-product of our actions or because the Soviets would destroy Europe as well as the United States.

There were two important caveats in the situation described: the President would have twenty-four hours to think about his response, and 180 million Americans would be killed. Let us consider the latter first. If 180 million dead is too high a price to pay for punishing the Soviets for their original aggression, how many American dead would we accept as the cost of our retaliation? I have discussed this question with many Americans, and after about fifteen minutes of discussion their estimates of an acceptable price generally fall between 10 and 60 million dead. No American that I have spoken to who was at all serious about the matter believed that U.S. retaliation would be justified—no matter what our commitments were—if more than half of our population would be killed.

The twenty-four-hour delay is a more subtle device. It is the equivalent of asking: Can the Soviets force the President to act in cold blood, rather than in the immediate anger of the moment? The answer depends not only on the time he has to ponder the effects that would accrue from his actions but also on how deeply and seriously the President and his advisers had thought about the problem in advance. This latter, in turn, could depend on whether there had been any tense situations or crises that forced the President and the people to face the concept that war is something that can happen, rather than something that is reliably deterred by some declaratory policy that is never acted on.

I have discussed with many Europeans the question of how many casualties Americans would be willing to envisage and still live up to their obligations. Their estimates, perhaps not surprisingly, range much lower than the estimates of Americans—that is, roughly 2 to 20 million.

Published unclassified estimates of the casualties that the United States would suffer in a nuclear war generally run from 50 to 90 million. If these estimates are relevant (which is doubtful, since they generally assume a Soviet surprise attack on an unalert United States), we are already deterred from living up to our alliance obligations. If they are not relevant, we ought to make relevant estimates for now and the future.

The critical point is whether the Soviets and the Europeans believe that we can keep our casualties and the other effects of a war to a level we would find acceptable, whatever that level may be. In such an eventuality the Soviets would be deterred from very provocative acts, such as a ground attack on Europe, Hitler-type blackmail threats, or even evacuating their cities and presenting us with an ultimatum. But if they do not believe that we can keep casualties to a level we would find acceptable, the Soviets may feel safe in undertaking these extremely provocative adventures. Or at least the Europeans may believe that the Soviets will feel safe, and this in itself creates an extremely dangerous situation for pressure and blackmail.

Type 1 Deterrence (Deterrence against a Direct Attack)

It is important to distinguish three types of deterrence. The first of these is: Type 1 Deterrence, or deterrence against a direct attack.

Most experts today argue that we must make this type of deterrence work, that we simply cannot face the possibility of a

failure. Never have the stakes on success or failure of prevention been so high. Although the extreme view, that deterrence is everything and that alleviation is hopeless, is questionable, clearly Type 1 Deterrence must have first priority.

Typically, discussions of the capability of the United States
to deter a direct attack compare the pre-attack inventory of
our forces with the pre-attack inventory of the Russian forces
—that is, the number of planes, missiles, army divisions, and
submarines of the two countries are directly compared. This
is a World War I and World War II approach.

The really essential numbers, however, are estimates of the
damage that the retaliatory forces can inflict after being hit.
Evaluation must take into account that the Russians could
strike *at a time and with tactics of their choosing*. We strike
back with a *damaged* and perhaps *un-co-ordinated* force
which must conduct its operations in the *post-attack environment*. The Soviets may use *blackmail* threats to intimidate
our response. The Russian defense is completely *alerted*. If
the strike has been preceded by a tense period, their active
defense forces have been *augmented* and their cities have been
at least partially *evacuated*. Any of the emphasized words can
be very important, but almost all of them are ignored in most
discussions of Type 1 Deterrence.

The first step in this calculation—analysis of the effects of
the Russian strike on U.S. retaliatory ability—depends critically on the enemy's tactics and capabilities. The question of
warning is generally uppermost. Analyses of the effect of the
enemy's first strike often neglect the most important part of
the problem by assuming that warning will be effective and
that our forces get off the ground and are sent on their way
to their targets. Actually, without effective warning, attrition
on the ground can be much more important than attrition in
the air. The enemy may not only use tactics that limit our
warning but he may do other things to counter our defensive
measures, such as interfering with command and control arrangements. Thus it is important in evaluating enemy capabilities to look not only at the tactics that past history and
standard assumptions lead us to expect but also at any other
tactics that a clever enemy might use. We should not always
assume what Albert Wohlstetter has called "U.S.-preferred at-

tacks" in estimating the performance of our system. We should also look at "U.S.S.R.-preferred attacks"—a sensible Soviet planner may prefer them!

The enemy, by choosing the timing of an attack, has several factors in his favor. He can select a *time* calculated to force our manned-bomber force to retaliate in the daytime, when his day fighters and his air-defense systems will be much more effective. In addition, he can choose the *season* so that his post-war agricultural problems and fallout-protection problems will be less difficult.

The second part of the calculation—consequences of the lack of co-ordination of the surviving U.S. forces—depends greatly on our tactics and the flexibility of our plans. If, for example, our offensive force is assigned a large target system, so that it is spread thinly, and if because of a large or successful Russian attack the Russians have succeeded in destroying much of our force, many important Russian targets would go unattacked. If, on the other hand, to avoid this we double or triple the assignment to important targets, we might overdestroy many targets, especially if the Soviets had not struck us successfully. For this and other reasons, it would be wise to evaluate the damage and then retarget the surviving forces. Whether this can be done depends critically on the timing of the attack, the nature of the targeting process, and our post-attack capability for evaluation, command, and control.

Our attack may also be degraded because of problems of grouping, timing, and refueling; in some instances our manned bombers might be forced to infiltrate in small groups into Soviet air territory and lose the advantage of saturation of the Soviet defenses. Whether or not this would be disastrous depends a great deal on the quality of the Russian air-defense system, especially on whether it has any holes we can exploit, and the kind and number of penetration aids we use. This aspect is complicated and classified.

Another point that may be of great importance is that modern nuclear weapons are so powerful that even if they don't destroy their target, they may change the environment so as to cause the retaliating weapons system to be inoperable. The various effects of nuclear weapons include blast, thermal and electromagnetic radiation, ground shock, debris, dust, and ionizing radiation—any of which may affect people, equipment, propagation of electromagnetic signals, and so on. One might say that the problem of operating in a post-attack environment after training in the peacetime environment is similar to training at the Equator and then moving a major but incomplete part (that is, a damaged system) to the Arctic and expecting this incomplete system to work efficiently the first time it is tried. This is particularly implausible if, as is often true, the intact system is barely operable at the Equator (that is, in peacetime).

In addition to attacking the system, the enemy may attempt to attack our resolve. Imagine, for example, that we had a pure Polaris system invulnerable to an all-out simultaneous enemy attack (invulnerable by assumption and not by analysis) and the enemy started to destroy our submarines one at a time at sea. Suppose an American President were told that if we started an all-out war in retaliation, the Soviets could and would destroy every American because of limitations in our offense and our active and passive defenses. Now if the President has a chance to think about the problem, he simply cannot initiate this kind of war even with such provocation.

One of the most important and yet the most neglected elements of the retaliatory calculation is the effect of the Russian civil-defense measures. The Russians are seldom credited with even modest preparedness in civil defense. A much more reasonable alternative that would apply in many situations—that the Russians might at some point evacuate their city population to places affording existing or improvisable fallout protection—is almost never realistically examined. If the Russians should take steps to evacuate their cities, the vulnerability of their population would be dramatically reduced.

The Soviets also know that they can take an enormous amount of economic damage and be set back only a few years in their development. Not only did they do something like this after World War II, but, what is even more impressive, they fought a war *after* the Germans had destroyed most of their existing military power and occupied an area that contained about 40 per cent of the prewar Soviet population—the most industrialized 40 per cent.

The difficulties of Type 1 Deterrence arise mainly from the

fact that the deterring nation must strike second. These difficulties are compounded by the rapidity with which the technology of war changes and the special difficulty the defender has in reacting quickly and adequately to changes in the offense. The so-called missile gap illustrates the problem. The Russians announced in August 1957 that they had tested an ICBM. Evidence of their technical ability to do this was furnished by Sputnik I, sent aloft in October of that year. Early in 1959 Khrushchev boasted that the Soviet Union had intercontinental rockets in serial production. We have little reason to believe that they won't have appreciable numbers of operational ICBMs about three years after their successful test —which would be in August 1960.

Suppose that in 1957 and 1958 we had refused to react to this "hypothetical" threat, so that when the autumn of 1960 appeared we had not completed the needed modifications to our defenses to accommodate this development. What kind of risk would we have run?

I will assume (on the basis of newspaper reports and congressional testimony) that we had approximately 25 *unalert* SAC *home* bases in 1957. In accordance with the proposed hypothesis of doing nothing, I will (incorrectly) assume that we still have 25 bases in 1960. The number of missiles that the Russians would need in order, hypothetically, to destroy these 25 SAC bases depends on their technology. Assume that their missile has a probability of one in two of successfully completing its countdown and destroying the SAC base at which it is launched. What would we have risked? Simple calculation indicates that our risk would have been substantial. For example, if the Russians had 125 missiles, then even if their firing time were spread out over an hour or so, it would still be possible for Mr. Khrushchev's aides to push 125 buttons and expect that there would be a better than even chance that they would destroy all of the aircraft on the ground at SAC home bases, about one chance in three that only one such base would survive, and a very small probability that two or more bases would survive. The Soviets could well believe that their air defense would easily handle any attacks launched by aircraft from one or two bases. If they are prepared to accept the risk involved in facing an attack from, say, four or five bases, then they need only about 75 missiles, each with a single-shot probability of one half; if they had 150 missiles, the single-shot probability could be as low as one third and still be satisfactory to a Soviet planner willing to accept retaliation from four or five surviving bases.

This kind of missile attack is much more calculable than almost any other kind of attack. It is so calculable that many people believe that the results of such an attack can be predicted just by applying well-known principles of engineering and physics. It looks so calculable that even a cautious Soviet planner might believe that he could rely on the correctness of his estimates; *he might find it the path of caution to attack while the opportunity was still available.*

Actually, even with tested missiles, results of attacks are not really mathematically predictable. The probability of extreme variations in performance, the upper and lower limits, cannot be calculated accurately. But laymen or narrow professionals persist in regarding the matter as a simple problem in engineering and physics. Therefore, unless sophisticated objections on the possibilities of intelligence leaks, firing discipline, reliability of the basic data, field degradation, and others, are raised, even an inarticulate Russian general could probably force the following conclusions on a group of hostile, skeptical, and busy civilians, whether they wanted to believe them or not: that in this hypothetical case (where the Russians had 125 missiles, each with a single-shot probability of one half) if they were to push these 125 buttons and also launch a supplementary co-ordinated attack with ICBMs and tactical bombers on U.S. and allied overseas bases, there would be a reasonable chance that the Soviet Union would get away scot free; that there would be a good chance that they would suffer very little damage; and that there would be no chance at all that they would suffer as much damage as they suffered in World War II.

Let us consider some of the caveats that this Russian general would have to concede if somebody raised them, and try to judge how serious Khrushchev or the Presidium would find them.

The first is that there be no intelligence leak. Given the small number of missiles involved and the tight security in the Russian empire, this might look like a reasonably safe assumption. But whether the Russians would be willing to rely on our lack of intelligence is very hard to say.

The second caveat concerns firing discipline, that is, that nobody fires either prematurely or too late. If we work on our original assumption that the U.S. posture remains unchanged since 1957, when alerts were measured in hours or so, this is not a rigid requirement. However, if we give ourselves credit for a fifteen-minute alert, this would mean that the Russian missile is so reliable that when they press the buttons the majority of the missiles are actually ready to be fired. Given that the Soviet missiles have a "hold" capability, this may not be a much smaller number than if we define reliability as the probability that the missile takes off within a few hours of the assigned firing time. A small reduction in missile "reliability"—that is, the probability that it takes off within a few minutes of the assigned firing time—would simply mean that the Russians would need a few more ICBMs. A large reduction would most likely put the Soviets out of business.

There is an interesting interaction between firing discipline and measures designed to reduce the possibility of intelligence leaks. If the Soviets trained with very realistic exercises, so that even the people involved in the exercises could not distinguish until the last minute the exercise from the real thing, then such exercises could be used to disguise preparations for attack. But there would be a tendency for somebody to fire prematurely, perhaps causing an accidental war. If, on the contrary, the Soviets try to prevent this breach of firing discipline by the use of severe threats and indoctrination so that nobody will fire prematurely, then they run the opposite risk, that people will refuse to believe the order when it comes, unless alerted ahead of time.

The third caveat is that they must have accurate intelligence about the U.S. military posture. Given U.S. security practices currently in vogue about the position and use of our SAC bases and the ease with which information could be obtained about last-minute changes, this also could look feasible. Probably the only requirement is to try to get the information. Much more important, they need accurate data about themselves—the yield, accuracy, and reliability of their ICBMs, for example. While it is surprisingly hard to get reliable estimates of these quantities, only very sophisticated people will know this. If the Soviets have some extra margin of performance for insurance—that is, if they have a much better technological capability than they need—then they do not require extremely accurate estimates of this capability. On the other hand, if their equipment is just marginally satisfactory, then even though they have an adequate capability they are unlikely to know this.

Last and most important is the question of field degradation. Let us go back to our Russian general's persuasion problem. It is perfectly possible, for example, for this general to take the members of the Presidium out to the range and show them, say, five or ten ICBMs lined up and ask them to select one and make a cross on the map. The range personnel could proceed to fire that ICBM and hit near enough to the cross to make the general's point. Or even more convincingly, they might fire all five or ten ICBMs at once.

This would be an impressive demonstration, but a question arises. What happens when the missiles are operated in the field by regular military personnel? How far off from range performance will they be?

It should also be noted that, so long as our strategic bases are soft, missile attacks present the Russians with possibilities for the use of a post-attack blackmail strategy almost as extreme as the one mentioned previously. If the Russians concentrate their attack solely against strategic bases and air-burst their weapons (which is the most efficient way to use a weapon against a soft target), there will be no local fallout effects. Then, unless one of the weapons goes astray and hits a major city, deaths would be limited to a few million Americans as the result of blast and thermal effects. The Soviets could then point out (unless we had appreciable levels of air offense, air defense, and civil defense surviving) that they could totally *destroy* our country (while we could only *hurt* them), and ask us whether we really wanted to pick this moment to initiate the use of nuclear weapons against open cities.

While it would take a moderately reckless Soviet decision maker to press the 125 ICBM buttons even if the assumptions were as favorable as originally hypothesized, it would be even more reckless for the United States to rely on extreme Soviet caution and responsibility as a defense. The need for quick reaction to even "hypothetical" changes in the enemy's posture is likely to be true for the indefinite future, in spite of the popularity of the theory that once we get over our current difficulties we will have a so-called minimum nuclear deterrent force that will solve the Type 1 Deterrence problem. Some even maintain that it will solve all strategic problems.

Type 2 Deterrence (Deterrence of Extreme Provocation)

A quite different calculation is relevant to U.S. Type 2 Deterrence, although it is still a Soviet calculation (but this time a Soviet calculation of an American calculation). Type 2 Deterrence is defined as using strategic threats to deter an enemy from engaging in very provocative acts other than a direct attack on the United States itself. The Soviet planner asks himself: If I make this very provocative move, will the Americans strike us? Whether the Soviets then proceed with the contemplated provocation will be influenced by their estimate of the American calculation as to what happens if the tables are reversed. That is, what happens if the Americans strike and damage the Russian strategic air force and the Russians strike back un-co-ordinated in the teeth of an alerted U.S. air defense and possibly against an evacuated U.S. population? If this possibility is to be credible to the Soviets, it must be because they recognize that their own Type 1 Deterrence can fail. If Khrushchev is a convinced adherent of the balance-of-terror theory and does not believe that his Type 1 Deterrence can fail, then he may just go ahead with the provocative action.

It is important to realize that the operation of Type 2 Deterrence will involve the possibility that the United States will obtain the first strategic strike or some temporizing move, such as evacuation. Many people talk about the importance of having adequate civil and air defense to back our foreign policy. However, calculations made in evaluating the performance of a proposed civil- and air-defense program invariably assume a Russian surprise attack and—to make the problem even harder—a surprise attack directed mostly against civilians. This is unnecessarily pessimistic. The calculation in which one looks at a U.S. first strike in retaliation for a Russian provocation is probably more relevant in trying to evaluate the role that the offense and defense play in affecting some important aspects of foreign policy.

Under this assumption, if we have even a moderate non-military defense program, its performance is likely to look impressive to the Russians and probably to most Europeans. For example, the crucial problem of obtaining adequate warning will have been greatly lessened, at least in the eyes of the Soviets. They are also likely to think that we have more freedom than we will have. The Soviets may believe that we are not worried by the possibility that they will get strategic or premature tactical warning. This could be true in spite of the fact that in actual practice such an attack would probably involve a considerable risk that the Soviets would get some warning. Any planning would have to be tempered by the sobering realization that a disclosure or mistake could bring a pre-emptive Russian attack.

The possibility of augmenting our active and passive defense is very important. That is, rather than striking the Russians if they do something very provocative, we might prefer to evacuate our city population to fallout protection, "beef up" our air defense and air offense, and then tell the Russians that we had put ourselves into a much stronger position to initiate hostilities. After we had put ourselves in a position in which the Russian retaliatory strike would inflict much less than a total catastrophe, the Russians would have just three broad classes of alternatives:

1. To initiate some kind of strike.

2. To prolong the crisis, even though it would then be very credible that we would strike if they continued to provoke us.

3. To back down or compromise the crisis satisfactorily.

Hopefully the Soviets would end up preferring the third alternative, because our Type 1 Deterrence would make the first choice sufficiently unattractive and our Type 2 Deterrence would do the same for the second.

Type 3 Deterrence (Deterrence of Moderate Provocation)

Type 3 Deterrence might be called *"tit-for-tat* deterrence." It refers to those acts that are deterred because the potential aggressor is afraid that the defender or others will then take limited actions, military or nonmilitary, that will make the aggression unprofitable.

The most obvious threat that we could muster under Type 3 Deterrence would be the capability to fight a limited war of some sort. Because this subject is complicated and space is limited, I will not discuss this particular Type 3 Deterrence capability—although it is important and necessary. Instead, I shall consider some of the nonmilitary gambits open to us.

Insofar as day-to-day activities are concerned, the things that seemingly regulate the other man's behavior are nonmilitary. For example, among other things, a potential provocation may be deterred by any of the following effects or reactions:

1. Internal reactions or costs.
2. Loss of friends or antagonizing of neutrals.
3. Creation or strengthening of hostile coalitions.
4. Lowering of the reaction threshold of potential opponents.
5. Diplomatic or economic retaliation.
6. Moral or ethical inhibitions.
7. An increase in the military capability of the potential opponent.

Space permits discussion of only the last subject, which is both very important and badly neglected. It has become fashionable among the more sober military experts to regard mobilization capabilities as examples of wishful thinking. And indeed, in the few *hours* or few *days* of a modern war, large-scale production of military goods will not be possible.

What deters the Russians from a series of Koreas and Indochinas? It is probably less the fear of a direct U.S. attack with its current forces than the probability that the United States and her allies would greatly increase both their military strength and their resolve in response to such crises. The deterrent effect of this possibility can be increased by making explicit preparations so that we can increase our strength very rapidly whenever the other side provokes us. For example, in June 1950 the United States was engaged in a great debate on whether the defense budget should be 14, 15, or 16 billion dollars. Along came Korea. Congress quickly authorized 60 billion dollars, an increase by a factor of four!

No matter what successes the Communist cause had in Korea, that authorization represents an enormous military defeat for the Soviets. However, it was almost three years before that authorization was fully translated into increased expenditures and corresponding military power. It is very valuable to be able to increase our defense expenditures, but this ability becomes many times more valuable if authorizations can be translated into military strength in a year or so. If the Russians know that deterioration in international relations will push us into a crash program, they may be much less willing to let international relations deteriorate. The problem is: Would we have time to put in a useful program? After all, the basic military posture (including installations) must be of the proper sort if it is to be possible to expand it within a year or so to the point where it is prepared to fight a war in addition to being able to deter one. Our current posture (1960) is probably far from optimal for doing this.

If preparations like these were at least moderately expensive and very explicit, the Russians might find it credible that the United States would initiate and carry through such a program if they were provocative even, say, on the scale of Korea or less. The Russians would then be presented with the following three alternatives:

1. They could strike the United States before the build-up got very far. This might look very unattractive, especially since the build-up would almost certainly be accompanied by an increased alert and other measures to reduce the vulnerability of SAC.

2. They could try to match the U.S. program. This would be very expensive.

3. They could accept a position of inferiority. Such an acceptance would be serious, since the United States would now

have a "fight the war" capability as well as a "deter the war" capability.

In each case the costs and risks of their provocation would have been increased, and it is likely that the Soviets would take these extra costs and risks into account before attempting any provocation. If they were not deterred, we could launch the crash program. Then we would be in a position to correct the results of their past provocation or at least to deter them in the future from exploiting these results.

It might be particularly valuable to have credible and explicit plans to institute crash programs for civil defense[2] and limited-war capabilities. It seems to be particularly feasible to maintain inexpensive and effective mobilization bases in these two fields, and the institution of a crash program would make it very credible to the Russians, our allies, and neutrals that we would go to war at an appropriate level if we were provoked again.

This is one of the major threats we can bring to bear on the Russians. If we are not aware that we have this threat, if we believe that doubling the budget would really mean immediate bankruptcy or other financial catastrophe, then the Russians can present us with alternatives that may in the end result in their winning the diplomatic, political, and foreign-policy victory. It is important that we understand our own strengths as well as our possible weaknesses.

Notes

1. RAND Corporation Report R-322-RC, *Report on a Study of Non-Military Defense,* July 1, 1958.
2. For a discussion of the possibilities, see Herman Kahn, *Some Specific Suggestions for Achieving Early Non-Military Defense Capabilities and Initiating Long-Range Programs,* The RAND Corporation, Research Memorandum RM-2206-RC, January 2, 1958, revised July 1, 1958.

18. The Lead-Time Problem and Technological Waste

by Ellis Johnson

Dr. Johnson has since 1948 been director of the Johns Hopkins University's Operations Research Office, which operates under contract to the U. S. Army. During World War II he was the principal physicist at the U. S. Navy's Ordnance Laboratory. For the past several years he has devoted his attention chiefly to the nation's technological progress.

In the continuing race for global power, one fact has thrown an elongated shadow over efforts by the United States to maintain technological supremacy over the Soviet Union: the fact that Russia can develop a new weapons system in approximately five years, while the same task takes the United States roughly twice that time.

What is the nature of this problem of "lead time," the gap between conception and use of new technological devices?

The Cost Factor

The problem is, first of all, a function of cost. The effect of increasing physical knowledge on the cost of weapons in a weapons system has been very great in terms of money and complexity. For example, the cost of aircraft increased tenfold from 1945 to 1955. As would be expected, the over-all increase was a function of the cost of important elements of the weapon.

The cost of electronics in fighter aircraft has increased from $3000 in 1939 to $300,000 in 1954. Factors other than cost are increased by technical advance. In bombers, the weight of the bombsight has increased from 125 pounds in 1940 to 2000 pounds in 1955. Each pound added to equipment increases the gross weight of the bomber as much as ten pounds over-all. Affected also are complexity and reliability. In aircraft gas turbines, the number of parts has increased from 9000 in 1946 to 20,000 in 1957. Of precious engineering hours, 17,000 were required to design a fighter aircraft in 1940 and 1,400,000 in 1955.

All of these technically caused increases, rising at a tremendous rate as a function of time, stem from the basic fact that knowledge in the physical sciences is itself increasing exponentially. This is well illustrated by the number of choices available to the designer in 1935 in the design of a major bomber weapons system. Then there were on the order of two major choices available to the designer; in 1955 there were more than 360 choices available.

The explanation for the observed increase in cost and complexity in attack and defensive systems is that they result from the very existence of such a large number of choices and from the regenerative interaction between attack and defense. When an enemy attack system appears, the defense reacts by using more modern technology to reduce the effectiveness of the attack system. Some years after the original attack system is first established, the attack system itself reacts to the improved defense by choosing, from among the many new alternative possible improvements that have appeared in the interim, one or more alternatives that will produce a new attack system of increased effectiveness, inevitably of increased complexity and cost.

In a second cycle, the defensive system in its turn reacts again from an even greater increase in the number of choices available. The cycle repeats itself continuously, and the attack and defense systems become ever more complex and costly. The executive is often almost a helpless observer in this process, which results from technological competition and the executive's expressed desire for the "best" or "most effective" weapons system. Once loose, such forces of technology are not easily turned off or reharnessed.

These questions arise: Do we necessarily have to let ourselves be driven to more and more expensive choices? Can we not find more timeless solutions in cost in which the military budget does not have to double every few years? Let us next examine these questions.

The Effect of Lead Times and Obsolescence Policy

Because a war can now be decided in days instead of years, it is argued that relative military power now depends more importantly upon making choices in a minimum time and in achieving the minimum possible lead time between decisions and the availability of a weapons system for use. As I said at the outset, it presently appears that Soviet lead time between concept and use may be about five years, on the average, while the U.S. lead time may be about ten years.

In examining the effect of the disparity in lead times in the competition between a Soviet air-attack system and a U.S. air-defense system, let us assume that the Soviet Union decided upon a particular weapons system in 1955. Let us say that at that time there were about 200 choices available. It is reasonable to assume that the Soviet Union is able to keep its technical choices secret from us from one to two years. Under these circumstances, it would have been 1957 before we became aware of the probable characteristics of the forthcoming Soviet weapons system, which is scheduled by them to become fully operational in 1960. Then suppose that we reacted by making a decision in 1957 to counter this new Soviet attack system by an adequate defense system within our economic capability. At that time we had 500 choices available, which gave us an improved situation with respect to the Soviet system generated two years before, despite the fact that the Soviets will be able to incorporate at least some of the improvements generated in the interim. There are, however, serious limitations as to how many improvements can be actually incorporated by the U.S.S.R. if the original Soviet schedule is held to. However, with a ten-year lead time, the U.S. defense system will not come into being as an operationally effective system until 1967—seven years after the Soviet capability first became operational.

We now have to consider obsolescence policy on the part

of the Soviet Union. The meager data bearing on this problem indicate that the policies of the Soviet Union and the United States in air-attack systems are such that weapons systems have an operational life of between five to seven years. In our case, therefore, the Soviet weapons system, which became operational in 1960, will have been phased out sometime between 1965 and 1967 and will have been replaced by a new weapons system based upon the technology of about 1960 and 1962, and the U.S. defensive technology will thus come into being *after* the Soviet attack system which it was designed to counter is superseded by a superior Soviet attack system. Furthermore, the new Soviet attack system which will come into being between 1965 and 1967 will be based upon the technology of 1960 to 1962, at which time there will have been available roughly 5000 choices, as compared with the 200 choices available to them at the time of their design of the original system. Under these circumstances, the U.S. defense system will come into operational being against a technologically superior attack system, against which it may have a negligible or very reduced effectiveness and indeed may be completely ineffective.

It is perhaps obvious that a particular weapon cannot usually be improved indefinitely. Instead, it approaches a technological limit in effectiveness after a period of reasonably intensive development and needs marginal improvement thereafter primarily to maintain production feasibility (in the use of new or currently available raw materials) and efficiency. Sometimes the increase in scientific knowledge permits a bigger spurt in the improvement of the weapon, but this is rare. The rifle is an example of an essential, good, but stable weapon. Weapons systems, often built around a major weapon or tactical concept—the manned bomber is an example—also evolve in this sigmoid cycle. This does not for long limit the practical application of increased scientific knowledge which turns to alternative weapons systems, that is, to the ICBM as a replacement for the bomber.

The arguments given above make it crystal clear that if physical knowledge is advancing as fast as appears to be the case, then, assuming equivalent technological capability within each culture as is indicated by current evidence, the struggle between offense and defense can be maintained at parity only if there are no more than a few months' lag between Soviet decisions on their attack system and U.S. decisions on its defense system, and if U.S. lead time is equal to or shorter than the Soviet lead time.

The Dilemma of the Optimum

If there are thousands of choices from which particular weapons systems can be chosen, the executive is faced with the cruel dilemma of having to choose from among the tempting array which he must pay for with limited resources in raw materials, manpower, time, and energy. Presumably he should choose the "best" buy. But this can hardly be done by the nontechnical executive *only* with the aid of intuition, as in earlier times. What he is usually forced to do is to have "staff" studies, or "systems analysis," or "operations research," etc., made which will narrow down the choices to a manageable few. The trouble with such studies is that, if they are to have a high reliability, they often take from one to four years to make and thus add to the already long lead time. They may often, because of long study time, be concerned with choices already conceptually obsolete at the time they are completed.

The need to choose the "optimum" out of complexity is thus antagonistic to the need for speed in going from choice to operation. A "quick" weapon, technically inferior because the optimum was not chosen, may be just as fatal to the user when battle is joined as a weapon that is technically inferior due to obsolescence because too much time was taken to bring it into being.

Effect on Military-Economic Competition

The effect of new technological choices and improvements forces the side with the longer lead time into the development of military defense systems that are never able to match the opposing attack systems. The side defending against an attack system will be able to meet the gambits of the attacking side in time, although perhaps not economically, *only* if its lead time is short in comparison with the other side and if lag in intelligence on enemy decisions is short. In fact, the sum of intelligence lags plus technological lag time must be shorter for the defense system than for the attack system. Other things being equal, the side with a grave disadvantage in lead time, as is now the case with the United States, runs an unreasonable risk of being outgamed politically, strategically, and economically in both offense and defense strategies and of losing the military-economic race.

But what about the size of the military budget? It appears from our analysis that the increase in the rate of generation of knowledge has greatly increased rather than decreased costs. If we are to protect the nation, we are forced to match our military budget to that of our opponent, or if the military-economic exchange rate is adverse, as is the likely case in defense versus attack, we may need to spend *more* for defense than the enemy spends on attack systems. In the long run, therefore, the effect of improved technology is to exacerbate the requirement for the *maximum* possible military budget acceptable to the nation.

The Cumbersome Industrial-Military System

Let us turn to a consideration of the factors that make the present U.S. lead time so long.

Military research and development in the United States is now achieved in a system whose components are primarily industry and the Department of Defense. Although there are a few great "in-house" military laboratories that do creative work in their own right, most of the creative weapons development and design is done by defense industry.

In theory, the guidance and management of this effort comes from the military officers of the Department of Defense. It is of the greatest importance to note that civilians with military research and development experience have, except for a small and relatively unimportant residue, been organized out of all of the positions of management responsibility and authority for military research and development programs in the Department of Defense. This was a deliberate action taken by the three services, acting in concert, beginning shortly after the end of World War II. The concentrated effort followed the dissolution of the Office of Scientific Research and Development and culminated in the dissolution of the Research and Development Board.

The direct influence of science and engineering within the Department of Defense and at higher echelons of the government now is channeled through the shadowy façade of scientific advisory committees. These committees actually have no responsibility or authority for the development programs, have negligible influence upon these programs, and are relatively unacquainted with the substantive content of the military-technical problems involved. Almost the entire creative burden of weapons development, therefore, falls upon industry, yet there is no formal and systematic method to keep industry informed of the tactical and strategic military requirements. It is obvious that this random procedure not only extends the time from concept to initiation of development but it operates under the most severe handicap possible with respect to any high assurance that the development is best suited to meet the strategic requirements of the United States.

Assuming, however, that the development is a desirable one, a number of requirements must be met by industry. First, in order to survive at all, industry must make a profit, a profit adequate to assure the survival of the company—survival that hinges primarily upon production contracts that follow successful development. The second requirement is that steady employment for scientists and engineers be assured within the industrial development laboratories. It takes approximately two years for a new employee in a company to become fully productive. This makes it impracticable to hire and fire research and development people on a short-term basis and still retain the competence necessary for successful development. A steady work load can be assured only by having a large backlog of development projects. In this case, the development time for each project is stretched out, increasing the lead time, while each project awaits its turn on the priority list. On the other hand, if there is no backlog of development contracts, the work program on the current contract is rigidly scheduled on a stretch-out basis while the sales engineers of the company work desperately to get the new contracts that will insure survival of the development laboratory. In this case, development time is also prolonged, again increasing the lead time.

There are two other unfortunate effects in this industry-defense system as it is now designed. The company must make the profit required for survival on the production of the new weapon. This means that the company will tend to choose and process developments that have a very high probability of being successful. This leads to development that is heavily weighted in the direction of product improvement, since high-profit, high-risk development programs are too uncertain to provide assurance that the production facilities of the company will be employed. Thus, our present industrial-military partnership tends to result in slow, steady, but mediocre progress.

Another unfortunate factor is use of cost-plus-fixed-fee contracts by the Department of Defense. These contracts have two effects. They tend to result in an exorbitant use of technical personnel in each development, since the fee is always tied to the total cost; the greater the cost (that is, the greater the number of scientists and engineers working on a weapons development), the higher the profit to the industry. There is thus no incentive toward economical use of scientific and engineering personnel. A second unfortunate effect of the cost-plus-fixed-fee contract is that there is no incentive to take a high risk which might result in a high profit, because there is no particular immediate reward for success or punishment for failure. In times past, success in weapons development was accompanied by high profits. This provided a desirable and effective incentive to industry.

There are a number of additional factors that greatly increase weapons-development lead time. The overriding desire of the Department of Defense is for an immediate payoff in useful end-item weapons systems. This strong desire for immediate results has led to a tremendous neglect of applied research and component-subsystems development for weapons. In practice, the prior and independent development of good components (a rocket of high thrust, for example, is a *component* of a missile or satellite launcher) has been relatively neglected. Such development is time-consuming and, because there is little prestige to the officer-manager within his tour of duty, there is little interest among the operating group. Far too small a portion of defense funds have been allocated to component and subsystem development. Thus, when a weapons-system development is determined upon, the applied research and the component and subsystems development must be initiated if it is critical to the system development, or else the development must be frozen at the existing state of the art.

How Security Regulations Can Increase Lead Time

Before leaving the subject of the difficulties of industrial weapons development, another most serious problem must be mentioned: the effect of security regulations upon industry. These regulations are rigidly enforced, so that not only is industry unable to make proposals based upon the most forward-looking tactical and strategic requirements but also industry does not, in general, have adequate access to the tremendous amount of prior or parallel work of other industry or military laboratories. As a result, the classified libraries of industry are inadequate relative to their need for classified information.

Another effect of the "need to know" restriction is that this so limits communications within the Department of Defense that there is unnecessary duplication of work. This does not mean competition in development, but the actual re-solving of old problems. The effect is again to increase development time, because, if problems have already been solved, the solutions should be adopted instead of wasting technical manpower to solve the problems again.

The "need to know" crisis is the result of lack of experience on the part of the higher-ranking military personnel, especially with respect to the requirement of "tautological" information on the part of research and development personnel. We actually are keeping our secrets so closely that this has aided the Soviet Union to draw ahead of us.

Forgotten Lessons of World War II

During World War II, the United States and other countries were tremendously productive in developing many new weapons. A variety of management methods were used in different laboratories. Yet several factors stood out.

First, most of the great weapons systems were developed in systems laboratories independent of production control. This was true in Germany and in Great Britain as well. Second, and most important, every laboratory was treated as though it were a facility. There was never a question as to whether there would be enough work to do; there was never the need to stretch out the development time, because every laboratory had more work than it could do during the entire war. The laboratories worked at maximum speed and concentrated on each weapons system, usually one by one. There was no difficult tie-in between development and production from the viewpoint of profit. There was an acceptance of high-risk, high-profit development tasks, and failures were generally forgiven if the effort to make the development successful had been a great and honest one. There was, in general, a high and sophisticated support of component and subsystem development, as well as of all the necessary applied research. All of these led to the short lead times of one to five years that were achieved in American weapons-development systems during World War II.

There were, of course, some other factors. The best scientists in the country joined in weapons development during the war. Most of them returned to universities or other research centers at the end of the war. And finally, the motivations were high. Not only was our goal lofty, but we were sure that we could achieve it.

Research, in general, was managed by civilians, since most of the military personnel were then engaged in military operations or in training the military cadres. Another striking factor during World War II was the very free exchange of classified information within and between industry and Department of War management. We had then not achieved our preeminence in weapons systems. The present excessively severe security rules had not been formulated or designed. Communications thus were free. This undoubtedly speeded up development time.

Examination of the current methods used by the Soviet Union in weapons development indicates that they treat their laboratories as facilities. There is never an idleness problem; there is steady employment for all research and development personnel. Then, too, everything indicates that the Soviets provide heavy support to applied research, to component development, and to subsystem development prior to or parallel with and independent of the specific end-item weapons systems. This is exactly the method we used during the war, especially in the Office of Scientific Research and Development. Did the Soviet Union learn these lessons from our techniques, the ones we have forgotten?

To summarize the principal factors which contributed to success on the part of the Free World during World War II in weapons development, and which appear to lead to important successes now on the part of the Soviet Union: First, development laboratories were treated as facilities, were organized as weapons-systems laboratories, and their development programs were not tied on a one-to-one basis to production. Second, the communication of classified information was provided on an adequately free basis, permitting maximum utilization of progress made, regardless of where results were obtained in the over-all system. Third, management was primarily in the hands of competent civilians trained in research and development. Fourth, the motivations were to obtain maximum technical progress, rather than an absolute assurance of reaching the production stage.

If we are to compete with the Soviet Union in weapons design, if we are to cut our lead times to effective proportions, we must remember these lessons of World War II.

19.   Limited War

by Hanson W. Baldwin

*A native of Maryland, Mr. Baldwin gradu-
ated from the United States Naval Academy
in 1924. He resigned his commission three
years later to begin a writing career which
has brought him wide recognition as an an-
alyst of military affairs. He is the author of
twelve books and is a frequent contributor
of articles to many magazines, including
the* Saturday Evening Post, *the* Atlantic
Monthly, Reader's Digest, *and the* Marine
Corps Gazette. *For many years he has lectured at the several colleges of the armed
services. Mr. Baldwin became military editor of the New York* Times *in 1942 and the
following year was awarded the Pulitzer
Prize for reporting from the Pacific battle
areas.*

In early 1959, a three-star admiral publicly admitted the most
significant politico-military heresy yet confessed by a man in
uniform. Vice-Admiral "Cat" Brown answered a question at
the National Press Club in Washington with a simple negation which struck at the heart of many of the nation's military policies. "I have no faith," he said, "in the so-called controlled use of atomic weapons. . . . I would not recommend
the use of any atomic weapon, no matter how small, when
both sides have the power to destroy the world." Admiral
Brown added that he did not believe there was any dependa-

This selection originally appeared in the May 1959 issue of the
Atlantic Monthly. *Reprinted by permission of Willis Kingsley Wing.
Copyright 1959, by Hanson W. Baldwin.*

ble distinction between tactical, or localized and restricted, targets or situations and strategic, or unlimited, situations.

Admiral Brown, being human, may well be wrong. But he has been a serious student of modern war, both at the Air War College and the Naval War College, and he exercised for two years one of the most important sea commands the Navy can offer—the Sixth Fleet in the Mediterranean—during the period of the Anglo-French-Israeli attack on Egypt, a succession of Syrian crises, the Iraqi coup, and in the summer of 1958 intervention by the United States in Lebanon. Faced repeatedly in the troubled Middle East with the possibility of limited wars which might become unlimited, Brown renounced the use of battlefield nuclear weapons as too risky.

Brown's statement in Washington is representative of the opinions of other students of war who feel that Henry A. Kissinger, in his book *Nuclear Weapons and Foreign Policy*, was guilty of oversimplification. Kissinger's major thesis—with which nearly all students of war and politics in the atomic age will agree—was that the nation must be prepared to fight and win limited wars. But he advocated the waging of limited wars with small tactical nuclear weapons, and he implied that the development and proper employment of such weapons would compensate for our inferiority in land strength compared with that of the Communist powers. Our advanced nuclear technology was the answer to the hordes from the East.

But, as Roger Hilsman remarked in a paper, "On NATO Strategy" (written for the Washington Center of Foreign Policy Research), "there is nothing to indicate . . . that a good big atomic army would not be able to defeat a good little atomic army." And it is clear that Russia will have, in time, small tactical nuclear weapons in plenty; we may have a tactical nuclear advantage today, but we shall not have that advantage tomorrow.

There are many who challenge the comfortable thesis that limited wars can be fought and won despite inferiority in numbers and conventional arms by utilizing small, or battlefield, nuclear weapons. They challenge this thesis on two grounds: that of Admiral Brown, that the utilization of any kind of nuclear weapon is likely to spread the conflagration and to risk unlimited war; that of Mr. Hilsman, that, other things being equal, a small atomic army is at a disadvantage compared with a big atomic army.

This debate, which deals in its broadest terms with life or death for our nation—indeed, for civilization—requires a cold-blooded, dispassionate, objective analysis and discussion. This chapter has been tailored to try to fit these guidelines, not because the author is unaware of the justifiable fears and emotional pressures of the nuclear age, but because only rational judgments can help us to avoid the catastrophe of nuclear war.

The debate calls for definitions, then for some answers to these questions: Is limited war possible? If so, how can it be fought successfully without undue risk of spreading the conflict into an unlimited one? Can nuclear weapons be used, without such undue risks, in limited wars? If they can, would their military advantages compensate for their admitted political and psychological liabilities?

What Is "Limited" War?

In the Pentagon today, general war—that is, unlimited war —is usually defined as any war in which U.S. and U.S.S.R. armed forces meet face to face. There are a few, particularly in the Army, who believe that a war between the United States (and its allies) and Soviet Russia (and its satellites) might possibly be fought without the use, or with restricted use, of nuclear weapons. But such a war—a war roughly similar to World War II—scarcely fits the definition of "limited"; it would certainly be unlimited as to area, and the chances of keeping it non-nuclear would be slight. If there is a world war, unlimited as to area, between the United States and Russia, no holds will be barred.

A limited war might be any war in which U.S. and Soviet forces are not fighting each other. Such a war, in a sense, was Korea, where Russia fought against the United States chiefly by proxy, utilizing North Koreans and Chinese equipped with Soviet arms. The Indochinese war, with communism directly involved ideologically but with Russian participation limited to economic aid, weaponry, and perhaps some technological advice and assistance, was another limited war.

Yet, on a small scale, Russian and U.S. armed forces have frequently opposed each other since World War II in shooting and nonshooting incidents without general war resulting.

Again and again and again, U.S. and Soviet planes have clashed in actual shooting frays, from the Sea of Japan and the vicinity of Kamchatka to the Baltic and Armenia. Numerous U.S. planes, and probably some Russian planes, have been lost in these clashes, yet there has been no war. In Korea, Russian-speaking Soviet pilots flying Soviet planes rose to do battle with U.S. pilots and planes. Again there was no general war.

Any definition of limited war, therefore, as one in which U.S. and Soviet forces do not oppose each other is too narrow. Under certain restraining circumstances (for example, in Korea the Soviet pilots utilized the fighting chiefly for training, as both the Nazis and the Communists did in the Spanish Civil War) U.S. and Soviet forces might actually fight each other without general war resulting.

Limited war is limited not so much by the nationalities of the combatants as by the objectives of both sides, the weapons and methods employed (in other words, the degree of force), and the geography and extent of the fighting. The nationalities involved are, of course, important from a prestige viewpoint, but communism can always, if it desires and if its objectives are limited, conceal participation of Russian forces under the guise of "people's volunteers" or in other ways.

World history demonstrates that limited wars are the only kind that have occurred since World War II. About twenty-three limited wars or war situations have been recorded since 1945. General Maxwell D. Taylor, former Army chief of staff, studied seventeen of these wars and pointed out that they have not necessarily been small or short wars. "By striking a statistical time-manpower balance of all seventeen limited wars," he said, "one finds that they have averaged about two and a half years in duration and nearly six hundred thousand men engaged."

In none of these wars have atomic weapons been used, though they have been available in several instances and at least once their use was threatened (the Soviet missile threat at the time of the Anglo-French-Israeli attack upon Egypt).

These limited conflicts or situations have ranged in scope from Korea (where a total of half a million Americans were engaged over a three-year period at a cost of more than thirty thousand U.S. lives—our fourth-largest conflict) to the Lebanese expedition of 1958, in which a total of some fifteen to sixteen thousand U. S. Marines and soldiers landed in the Levant, backed up by the U. S. Sixth Fleet. A few of these situations, like Lebanon, did not involve actual shooting for U.S. forces; the vast majority of them, including the revolt in Hungary, involved the employment by one side or the other or both of all types of ground arms available—and often many types of air and naval armaments—short of nuclear weapons.

Thus, the lessons of history are plain: limited wars continue even in the shadow of the atomic age. General Taylor's "inference that they will continue and that the rate of occurrence may increase" seems logical, based on past experience.

The answer to the first question—Is limited war possible?—is therefore clearly an affirmative one. But history gives us no clue as to whether or not nuclear weapons could be used in such conflicts without spreading them. For in none of the twenty-three wars since World War II have nuclear weapons of any sort actually been utilized.

Can Wars Be Kept from Spreading?

Whether or not nuclear weapons can, under certain circumstances, be employed or whether, if we want to keep war limited, they must be relegated to a background role depends fundamentally upon the answer to the second question: How can a limited war be fought without undue risk of spreading into an unlimited one?

A limited war, if it is to be kept limited, must be fought for limited and well-defined political objectives, with limited military force, and, generally, in a limited geographic area.

A limited war must be limited first and fundamentally by the objectives, intentions, and will of the participants. As Kissinger correctly stresses, the primary requirement for keeping a war limited is the limitation of the political and military objectives for which the war is fought. The destruction of Carthage, the unconditional surrender of Germany, were unlimited aims which helped to induce unlimited wars. No war which has as its objective the absolute destruction of Russian power or the complete elimination of communism can be limited; in fact, one can say, with the sure support of history, that ideological wars have always led to unlimited conflicts. An idea has peculiar vitality; it cannot be destroyed by the sword; from death and destruction it springs phoenixlike to new dimensions. A war of fuzzy, ill-defined, or unlimited aims encourages unlimited means. The fundamental requirement to keep war limited is to know what you are fighting for, to define the price you are willing to pay for the objectives you are determined to gain, to make certain that those objectives are realizable without forcing the main enemy, Russia, into the position of a cornered wolf—desperate, irrational, fighting back with all-out effort.

The Korean War, under the ground rules imposed (by ourselves, our allies, and our enemies), was a war of limited objectives. One could quarrel with those objectives, with the strategic and tactical means we used to try to achieve those objectives, and with our fluctuating policies; nevertheless, in Korea, probably for the first time in our history, we fought for something besides victory unlimited.

And despite General Douglas MacArthur's dictum that the object of war is victory, future wars, if they are to remain limited and if victory is to have any tangible meaning, must similarly stress limited objectives. For unless military victory is defined in tangible political terms, in limited terms, war is not only slaughter but senseless, irrational carnage.

Hitler started World War II with definite and attainable limited objectives: the elimination of the Polish Corridor and the conquest of Poland. But his ambitions, plus the fact that he forced his adversaries into a corner, led him to substitute an unattainable and unlimited objective: the conquest of Europe and Russia—in fact, mastery of the world. The Allies, in opposing Hitler's ends, postulated a fuzzy and unlimited aim—unconditional surrender—for what should have been well-defined political objectives.

The Need for Clear Objectives Clearly Defined

The first requirement for a limited war, then, is a limited, well-defined political objective attainable by limited military strength. It should be stated and restated that war is not an end in itself; war is justifiable only if it is a servant of policy, if it is invoked to achieve a definite political aim, if it is fought for the vital interests of the nation, and if it results in increased security for the nation and in a more stable world.

These limited objectives require statement and restatement, emphasis and re-emphasis, throughout the conflict. This is important for two reasons: the effect upon our own people and our friends and the effect upon the enemy. When war starts, fear, hysteria, and emotion are powerful allies of unreason; they tend toward the war's extension, the substitution of unlimited means for unlimited ends. This trend, so pronounced in Korea, can be checked and controlled only by clear-cut definitions of our aims, understandable not only and not primarily to a schoolboy but also to the parents of the boys who must die for limited ends. Reason, indeed, may not be able to cope with emotion, but unless there is a rational checkrein the end is chaos.

Similarly, such a statement is essential if a national frustration, such as that which developed during the latter stages of the Korean War, is to be avoided. The enemy, too, must be assured and reassured that our objective is limited, that we do not intend his complete destruction, that there is a way out, lest through fear he extend the conflict to an unlimited one. The corollary to this, of course, is the tacit threat—a threat credible to him—that unless he, too, keeps his aims and methods limited we shall clobber him.

The devastating power of nuclear weapons and the speed and elusiveness of their carriers—jet planes, rockets, atomic submarines—mean that the first requirement for keeping a limited war limited is, ironically, the capability of extending it. The rifleman of today and tomorrow fights under the awful shadow of the wings of global death. The capability of invoking all-out nuclear retribution is the most certain military sanction—the surest, though an imperfect, guarantee—that a limited war will remain limited, that an enemy will not extend it lest he suffer terribly and unacceptably in retribution. Thus national psychology, as well as national aims, plays a part in limited war.

But if war is to be limited, we clearly cannot use unlimited means to attain limited ends. Limited war implies not only a tangible definition of restricted and attainable objectives but also a restraint on the use of force, a limitation of the means and weapons.

Nuclear Bombs Mean Total War

All-out military power today—power unlimited, power unrestrained—implies clearly the death of civilization as we know it. Enough atomic weapons now exist to destroy, if delivered, the principal cities of Russia and the West, to leave large areas of irradiated earth uninhabitable, to kill probably hundreds of millions of people. Clearly the use of large numbers of nuclear weapons implies an ever expanding and unlimited war. Equally clearly, discrimination as to the power and size of the weapons employed is essential if a war is to be limited, for a limited war means limited devastation.

A metropolis-busting "thermonuke" with explosive power of at least a megaton (one million tons of TNT equivalent) is an area weapon. Its blast and heat effects, though finite, are tremendous. A megaton weapon, for instance, would devastate sixty to seventy square miles and cause grave damage well beyond this area.

The bomb's invisible killer, radioactivity, would pose a far less finite and far less calculable effect. The burst of neutrons and gamma rays released at the instant of the blast would be dangerous about as far as the blast and heat. But some of the atomic fission products of the explosion, strontium 90 and other long-lived particles, would be sucked up into the stratosphere and deposited around the earth gradually through months and even years, with physiological and genetic results still imprecisely known. Even more dangerous would be the local fallout, in a wide elliptical swath downwind from the explosion, of

dust and dirt particles impregnated with radioactivity by the blast. Local fallout may vary from negligible—if the fireball is well above the earth and rain or snow does not quickly precipitate the fission products and residual particles—to very heavy —if the earth is scourged and beaten and particles are sucked up into the vortex of the atomic cloud. As the Japanese fishermen on the ill-named *Lucky Dragon* discovered, dangerous radioactivity from local fallout can lay a blanket of death across hundreds of miles.

The Effects of Nuclear Weapons, a Department of Defense and Atomic Energy Commission handbook, states that "if only five per cent of a one megaton bomb's energy" is spent in scourging the earth with its fireball, "something like 20,000 tons of vaporized soil material will be added to the normal constituents of the fireball. In addition, the high winds of the earth's surface will cause large amounts of dirt, dust, and other particles to be sucked up as the ball of fire rises."

It can be argued that the so-called "clean" bomb will reduce or eliminate radioactivity. It has, indeed, in certain circumstances already done so. But the big bombs are triggered by an initial fission reaction. The megaton-category weapons are three-stage devices. An atomic trigger explodes and provides the necessary heat to bring about the fusion (the second stage) of tritium. In turn, the fusion reaction releases neutrons which then cause the fission of the third stage, a casing of plutonium. The nuclear fission products are responsible for most of the dangerous radioactivity; if they could be eliminated, most of the long-lived global radioactivity could be eliminated and local fallout would be reduced.

The Effects of Nuclear Weapons gives some startling estimates. About one and three quarters ounces of fission products "are formed for each kiloton (110 pounds per megaton) of fission energy yield. At one minute after a nuclear explosion . . . the radioactivity from the one and three quarters ounces of fission products from a one-kiloton explosion is comparable with that of a hundred thousand tons of radium." This means that radiation—exclusive of that released at the instant of blast —for a megaton bomb is equivalent to that of about one million tons of radium. This radioactivity decays rapidly, but never-

theless some of the long-lived products could make an area uninhabitable for years.

Clean and Dirty Bombs

Actually, U.S. bombs have been made cleaner by reducing or eliminating the coating of uranium (the third-stage reaction) and by making the original fission trigger (the first stage) as small as possible. These steps must inevitably reduce the power of the so-called clean thermonuke, though it remains a city-busting weapon. But radioactivity has not been eliminated entirely. The fission trigger is still essential to produce the heat necessary to activate the fusion of the second stage. Someday, perhaps, other means of triggering a fusion reaction may be developed, and the 100 per cent clean bomb that Dr. Edward Teller and others have talked about may be possible.

Even so, this will not mean the complete elimination of radioactivity; no fission or fusion weapon can ever be clean in the sense that it will explode without any radioactivity. But the most dangerous radioactive by-products, the long-lived fission products, will be eliminated, and hence global fallout of strontium 90 and other dangerous elements will be largely eliminated and local fallout may be reduced. The burst of radiation incident to explosion will still occur, and if the fireball touches the earth man will still have to cope with local fallout incident to the impregnation of dust and dirt by radioactivity.

The problem of clean bombs is, in any case, a two-edged one. For the offensive side, if a ground army is to pass over an area which has been subject to atomic bombardment, a clean weapon would be tactically desirable. For the defense, a dirty weapon would increase the hazards of the enemy. For antiaircraft use or defense of one's own soil against enemy air attack, the clean bomb obviously offers a desirable safety factor. In all-out city-busting war, the side that used a clean bomb while an enemy used a dirty one might well be at a disadvantage. The clean-bomb problem, therefore, is far from simple; it has a Jekyll-Hyde aspect. The important point, however, is that no bomb now is completely clean; small clean

weapons may in time be developed, but only if testing is continued.

All this adds up to the fact that even the cleanest weapon is not subject to precise, pre-use prediction as to extent and lethality and area of fallout; these will depend upon the height of the burst over the earth, the speed and direction of the wind, the size and design of the bomb, the composition of the earth beneath the burst, and other factors. A metropolis-busting bomb might well be timed to detonate high above a city, to secure maximum blast effect over a maximum area; but, on the other hand, if an airfield or a missile emplacement were the target, ground or near-ground bursts, which would maximize local fallout, would be used.

Thus, it seems clear that, no matter what the target, the use of area-type nuclear weapons in war—huge thermonukes or powerful fission weapons—would present an incalculable problem which is not subject to prediction and which would produce incalculable effects, thus dangerously increasing the chance of spreading a limited war to an unlimited one.

There might be one exception to this. A single city-buster actually used against a single city might, in the case of war between two nations of greatly differing power, produce unlimited results with, in one sense, limited means. If Russia, for instance, destroyed Istanbul with a single megaton weapon, this limited use of force on Russia's part might bring about an unlimited result for Turkey: unconditional surrender (though Russia, of course, would face the danger of nuclear retaliation from the United States). But in the case of wars between great powers—specifically, war involving by proxy or subterfuge U.S. troops and Soviet followers—the use of megaton weapons would certainly imply unlimited war. Tremendous thermonukes, whether clean or not, almost certainly have no place in limited war.

Radioactivity and Small Weapons

What about the smaller atomic weapons, the so-called tactical or battlefield weapons?

Already there are some (many say not enough) of these

in the American[1] armory. Critics, including former Atomic Energy Commissioner Thomas Murray, point out, however, that the United States has no really small, "discriminating" tactical weapons today. Even a one-kiloton weapon (equivalent to one thousand tons of TNT) has almost one hundred times the explosive force of World War II's largest conventional bomb, which was used only *strategically* (against cities), not on the battlefield. There is an important, though so far minority, school of thought in the Pentagon which believes that atomic weapons with yields as low as ten tons of TNT equivalent must be produced. Their advantages, as compared with conventional explosives, would be lightness and small size and discrimination, or localization of the weapons' effects—the latter obviously important to the limitation of war.

In addition to weapons handled by ground troops, there are many different types of nuclear weapons for fighter-bomber use, for air-to-air missiles, and as warheads for anti-aircraft missiles like Nike-Hercules. The Navy has nuclear depth charges and warheads for missiles (replacing guns) and torpedoes.

These so-called battlefield weapons have one common characteristic: they are all fission weapons, except for the largest, which may be fission-fusion. Long-lived fission products are, therefore, an inevitable result, and clean small weapons are still some time in the future, if indeed they are ever developed.

Moreover, to destroy many so-called battlefield or tactical targets—airfields, fortifications, gun emplacements, hardened missile sites—ground bursts are required. Other targets, such as troop concentrations, can be eliminated by air bursts. Faulty fusing will, of course, detonate some weapons intended as air bursts at ground level. Furthermore, since many of these weapons are small and the atomic cloud does not rise to as high an altitude as the towering clouds produced by the bigger bombs, the fission particles are not carried upward into the stratosphere to be gradually precipitated after dissipation hundreds or thousands of miles away. Local fallout is therefore a danger.

---

[1] The Russians are known to have some tactical nuclear weapons, but details about types, yields, and numbers are, at best, "guesti-mates."

The point is that radioactivity presents much the same problem in miniature with small weapons that it presents with big ones; the danger on the battlefield is local, rather than global, fallout. The Army, indeed, has developed templates keyed to wind direction and intensity, size and height of burst, which, when laid down on a map and oriented to ground zero, indicate immediately to a commander the radioactive danger areas to the enemy or to his own troops. But radioactivity, in the case of the use of nuclear weapons against ground targets, tends to defy exact definition and limitation.

Target selection and elimination present another problem in the attempt to exercise restraint, to limit war, in a conflict in which tactical nuclear weapons are used.

Admiral Brown rightly observed that it is difficult to distinguish between so-called tactical and strategic targets. A 200-mile Redstone missile might be fired at some supply area, railroad junction, or communications bottleneck far behind the line of contact. Is this a tactical or a strategic target? This missile might well hit a city or damage it, with consequent danger—as in World War II, when area bombing by one side accelerated area bombing by the other—of spreading the war.

Nuclear War in Europe

Even if targets are restricted to troops and guns and tanks and to communications and supplies in the immediate battle zones, the problem of making this restriction stick presents appalling difficulties if two large armies, both equipped with all kinds of nuclear weapons, stand face to face. The temptation will still be to up the ante, and in closely knit, thickly settled areas like western Europe the radioactive debris spewed forth by even the smallest weapons is bound to extend far beyond the fighting zones. This is particularly true since the Army's concept of our nuclear-age tactics envisages a battle zone with units dispersed over very great frontages and vast depth. Modern ground battlefields may, in other words, literally extend across entire countries.

Thus, in considering the possibility of utilizing small nuclear weapons in limited war, one must take into account not only the power and type and number of the weapons used, not only the targets against which they are employed, but the geography of the battle area. For favorable geographic factors, it is clear, can help to keep a war limited; unfavorable ones mean its certain extension. Any consideration of geography—always a key factor in war—makes it apparent that generalization about the utilization of nuclear weapons in limited war is footless and futile. Each case differs; the risks in one theater are overwhelmingly apparent, in another, slight.

All of the foregoing discussion tends toward one conclusion as far as thickly settled, closely integrated, compact western Europe is concerned. Limitation in war must mean, if it is to mean anything, limitation of devastation. Yet, in Europe, target systems are too intermixed: civilian and military, area and point, tactical and strategic; the battlefield is too small and not sufficiently defined by natural barriers. A limited nuclear war in western Europe is impossible; the use of nuclear weapons in this area would invoke catastrophe. One bomb would lead to another.

Moreover, as far as western Europe's opposing ground forces (with their supporting tactical air and missile forces) are concerned, it is at best questionable whether nuclear weapons give any great advantage to the defense. Today, yes; tomorrow, no. Today, yes, because the West probably possesses a greater variety and number of tactical atomic arms; but tomorrow, when both sides have these arms in quantity, a "good big atomic army" with no major geographic barriers to curtail and choke its power will possess an advantage over a "good little atomic army." Some critics even foresee the possibility that Soviet Russia may soon surpass us in variety and number of small atomic weapons. As one authority puts it, "Barring changes in present concepts and conditions (budget limitations and lack of interest at the top level) it is not likely that smaller weapons will be stockpiled in significant quantities."

Quemoy and the Nuclear Threat

But there are other battlefields in the world where the nuclear stalemate has not inhibited action, cold or hot, and where geography does aid the defense. During the Quemoy crisis in 1958, United States Marines moved some eight-inch howitzers from Okinawa to Quemoy, emplaced them, and turned them over to the Chinese Nationalists. The significance of this move was lost upon much of the world but not upon Peiping and Moscow. These guns have the capability of firing nuclear shells. We did not give the Nationalists any nuclear shells. But the mere emplacement of eight-inch howitzers on Quemoy served as a dual warning. In the first place, their arrival broke the Communist blockade at one stroke as far as artillery ammunition was concerned. A few nuclear shells flown in by plane would equal the power of thousands of conventional rounds, which had to be brought in by sea. In the second place, eight-inch nuclear shells, if fired to detonate above an invading fleet of amphibious vessels and small craft, would doom the invasion. The eight-inch howitzers discouraged by their mere emplacement Communist ideas of conquest.

Thus, in Quemoy, for the first time in history, tactical nuclear weapons played the ancient role of the fleet in being. They were never used; the nuclear weapons were, indeed, never sent to Quemoy, but they could have been sent there; the means of delivery, the howitzer, was at hand, and this was one of the factors which induced Peiping to back away. The United States won a limited, incomplete victory in the Quemoy crisis in 1958; we closed one chapter in an unfinished book with the advantage on our side. An island position thus offers some natural advantages to the defense and, from the point of view of geography, an optimum environment for the utilization of certain types of nuclear weapons with minimum risk of spreading a war.

Shells or missiles or tactical nuclear bombs used against an invading fleet at sea (in the defense of Taiwan, for instance) or the Nike-Hercules nuclear missile employed against raiding bombers would represent a finite and limited, as well as a defensive, utilization of atomics. The sea and the sky are broad enough to absorb without serious danger the radioactive by-products, and a minimal number of weapons would be necessary to insure a defensive success. No great risk of spreading the war would be involved; the enemy's temptation to spread it, to use "nukes" against Taiwan, would be discouraged by the strategic threat of our massed bombing fleets and missiles.

If, on the other hand, the United States in the defense of Quemoy or Taiwan undertook to knock out the Chinese Communist airfields on the mainland, the possibility of limiting the war would be much reduced, particularly when the Chinese acquire nuclear weapons. Thus, there seem to be some grounds for believing that nuclear weapons could be used purely defensively to hold some positions that are sharply delimited and defined by terrain or other natural barriers, particularly island positions or peninsulas such as Korea.

Similarly, nuclear weapons might be used at sea in the form of nuclear depth charges against submarines or possibly in antiaircraft or air-to-air missiles without too great a risk of larger involvement. But again a *sine qua non* for keeping a limited war limited would imply their defensive use; if they were used offensively, by enemy planes or submarines against our shipping or by our planes or missiles against enemy land airfields or missile emplacements, there would be far less possibility of limitation.

Thus, it is clear that limited war of any kind, but particularly limited war fought with nuclear weapons, must imply sanctuaries for both sides immune either to attack of any kind or to certain forms of attack.

Nuclear Bombing and Asian Opinion

In weighing the desirability of utilizing nuclear weapons in limited war, the alternatives must be considered, and the effects of such use upon political sentiment and mass psychology.

The alternatives to the use of small nuclear weapons in the defense of Quemoy might be defeat for the Chinese Nationalists and for the United States, their ally, or the development, deployment, and maintenance in the Taiwan Strait of far larger conventional forces than the U. S. Seventh Fleet can now muster. If the U. S. Seventh Fleet were ordered today to "take out" all Chinese Communist mainland airfields from which fighter-bomber attacks could be staged against Quemoy and Taiwan, the numbers of sorties required would be approximately one thousand times greater if conventional weapons were used than if nuclear bombs were used. Instead of seven sorties against seven airfields, seven thousand might be required. The United States today does not maintain enough aircraft to mount such a large-scale conventional assault.

This narrowing of alternatives, therefore—defeat or a far larger conventional force—funnels our efforts more and more toward the utilization of nuclear weapons in limited wars, despite the risks involved. And this canalization is occurring despite the obvious negative political and psychological effects of the utilization of nuclear weapons—particularly if used against Asiatics.

The use of A-weapons in Asia or Africa by the United States or our allies against the colored races would be certain to raise more of a ruckus, even if they brought a quick and advantageous end to the conflict, than the use of A-weapons by Asiatics against Asiatics or by Americans against Russians. This may not be logical, but emotion even more than logic is a major factor in war. The Asiatics cannot forget that so far the A-weapon has been used only by a Western country against an Asiatic one. They associate nuclear power with materialism and colonialism, and the whole is molded by fairly effective Communist propaganda into an anti-Westernism which provides inflammatory tinder for a fission or fusion explosion.

And the utilization of nuclear weapons by the United States would also produce a great surge of public opinion among our allies—perhaps in the United Nations—which, depending upon the circumstances, might hamper or help us in achieving our political goals. Security in the atomic age is thus a complex equation.

It is clear that many factors govern the utilization of nuclear weapons in limited war: the objectives to be attained; the type, military utility, and manner of employment of the atomic weapons selected; the target system; the geography; the probable reactions of our friends, the enemy, and neutral nations; the political, economic, and military alternatives.

In some circumstances, under certain conditions, some types of nuclear weapons could be used without undue danger of making a big war out of a little one and probably should be used, all factors considered. Under other circumstances their use would be fatal. Our policy makers must make the weapon fit the battlefield and the enemy; the force used must be tailored to the objective desired.

Ability to Fight Is Our Best Defense

Thus our military policy today presents something of a paradox. For, between extensive global political commitments, some of them to dangerous salients like Quemoy, and an increasingly limited military budget, we are narrowing the alternatives available to us. We seem to be committing our armed forces more and more to the utilization of nuclear weapons in small wars as well as large, despite the risks.

Limited wars require conventional arms, not nuclear weapons. If an enemy is prepared to fight with both large and small nuclear weapons, we would be at a fatal disadvantage unless we were similarly prepared. Just as we must keep the right fist of strategic nuclear power ready in order to deter enemy nuclear attack upon our cities, so we must maintain highly efficient tactical nuclear capabilities to deter the battlefield use of A-weapons.

What general conclusions, then, can be drawn?

A limited war can be fought with weapons—depending upon geographic, political, economic, moral, and military circumstances—that range from atomic bombs to cloaks and daggers.

The larger and the more powerful the weapon, the less the limitation in selectivity, in destruction, and in particularization.

The right fist of all-out nuclear power must remain ready as a sanction to help insure limited war. But this right fist will not alone deter an enemy from embarking upon a limited war; nor can it win such a war without transforming a local conflict into a global one.

This establishes the requirement for a second capability, the capability of deterring and, if necessary, winning local and limited wars, with or without the use of nuclear weapons.

This may seem a large order. But it is not an impossible one. Such a deterrence implies, of course, more than a military capability: creeping communism cannot be stopped by the sword alone. It implies economic, moral, psychological, and political, as well as military, measures.

The problem, the great problem, of our military planners is to organize and maintain armed forces capable of fighting any kind of war anywhere. We cannot afford not to prepare to fight any kind of war anywhere. This does not, of course, mean that all kinds of forces—strategic air, defensive air, tactical air, conventional land power, nuclear land power, submarines, carriers, amphibious forces, air-borne forces—should be maintained at great strength, ready instantly for war. It means, rather, that we must keep alive the art of fighting any kind of war anywhere in the world, that we must have at least cadre forces of many different types keyed to different missions, capable of expansion in case of war. We must have fire-fighting forces, police forces capable of taking the first shock, and a mobilization potential to raise more of the same after war starts.

If we do not maintain these diverse capabilities we shall freeze, in a one-weapon, one-concept mold, not only tactics but strategy, and our foreign policy will be rigidly tied to an inflexible strategic concept that permits us no freedom of action. Yet the art of diplomacy, the art of politics, the art of strategy and war, is the art of choice. We risk defeat in peace or war if we limit our military capabilities to nukes and thermonukes.

In this time of troubles let us remember that if physical force has to be invoked it must be tailored, to accomplish its purposes, to reasonable and limited objectives and used always with moral restraint and a sense of decent respect for the opinions of mankind.

20.   Needed: A New NATO Shield

by Alvin J. Cottrell and Walter F. Hahn

The Soviet attitude toward NATO is conditioned by both emotional and realistic considerations. Emotionally, the Soviet leaders continue to regard the alliance as a "threat" to the security of the U.S.S.R. Realistically, they view NATO as a roadblock to the achievement of their global objectives. Their opposition to NATO, in any event, is irreconcilable.

Indeed, Soviet pressure upon western Europe is likely to increase during the 1960s. In the immediate future, this pressure will be a military-psychological one, aimed not so much at military objectives as at reducing Western diplomatic flexibility and driving a wedge between the United States and its NATO allies. The Soviets will seek to demonstrate, through a carefully calculated series of "crises," that the main element of American military power, nuclear retaliation, has been neutralized and that, thus, American power can no longer be counted upon. This they can accomplish by provoking, at an appropriate time, a showdown—one in which the United States will be forced to back down.

Russia's growing nuclear maturity will open to the Communist leadership an increasingly wide range of political and military options. The Soviets' capability for waging or supporting nonatomic, indirect aggression remains considerable. The Soviets, as they approach full nuclear maturity, may well conclude that limited wars, especially those initiated by satellites under ambiguous circumstances, may be "safe wars"— wars that will not trigger all-out nuclear conflict. The various instruments of indirect aggression, such as the deployment of "volunteers," which have proven so successful in other areas,

This selection is adapted from a report, Western Europe, *written for the Committee on Foreign Relations, U. S. Senate, by the Foreign Policy Research Institute, University of Pennsylvania. It was published by the U. S. Government Printing Office as Report No. 3, October 15, 1959.*

may soon be tested in Europe. This capability for limited conventional war and indirect aggression may not have to be exercised in actual combat. The implied threat of its use may be sufficient to gain limited objectives.

Given the West's present defense posture and strategy in Europe, the Soviets are likely to exploit a wide spectrum of conflict possibilities short of a pre-emptive strike against the West. Their choice of weapons at all times is determined by an assessment of the West's strengths and weaknesses. As the gap between the United States and Russia in strategic retaliatory capabilities is narrowing, the balance of power may increasingly shift to the side which holds superiority in the ability to wage conflict on levels below that of all-out nuclear war.

We are approaching a period when a strategic nuclear capability, although indispensable in the total posture of each side, will not be the criterion for success or failure in a given crisis. Such a capability could become decisive again only if one side achieves the ability to strike a mortal blow without incurring unacceptable damage in return. Therefore, during the next few years, the danger of a direct Soviet military thrust against western Europe would seem less likely than that of a Soviet crisis strategy designed to paralyze NATO—a strategy calculated to present challenges that fall below the "threshold" of an obvious issue of American survival. The Soviets will seek to raise this "threshold" through an incessant campaign of nuclear blackmail—to a point where a move now held to be a *"casus belli atomici"* may not be considered an issue of American survival next year or the year after.

The Strategic Requirements of the United States and Western Europe

Notwithstanding military technological changes, Europe remains a key prize of the protracted war. Western Europe is thus indispensable to any U.S. strategy designed to arrest a decisive shift in the balance of power to communism. Soviet control of Europe, while it might not bring about the immediate defeat of the United States, would turn the tide of conflict irreversibly against the Free World. The fall of Europe would mean ultimately and inevitably the loss of Africa, the Middle East, and the remaining free areas of Asia.

The United States and its NATO allies together must have military forces capable of discharging three fundamental tasks:

1. To convince the Soviets that resort to all-out war is a prohibitive course of action.

2. To convince the Soviets that resort to aggression short of all-out war would entail costs out of proportion to the objective sought and would, in any case, court the risk of total war.

3. To provide Western diplomacy with an adequate military backing.

The Soviet Union may be deterred from a massive assault against Europe—an attack featuring the use of thermonuclear weapons against the centers of European and U.S. power on the Continent—as long as she is deterred from an all-out attack against the United States. In any such massive assault, U.S. strategic power would be the Soviets' prime adversary. Thus, within the context of an all-out global nuclear war, U.S. strategic power remains essential to the defense of western Europe.

Yet the willingness by the United States to resort to all-out nuclear war in order to counter local Soviet encroachments in Europe, in the immediate future if not already today, is open to question—especially if such encroachments are so ambiguous as to fall below the "threshold" of a clear issue of American survival. Soviet nuclear developments permit Communist expansion to proceed with greater impunity and in the face of a diminishing risk of an American nuclear response against the Soviet homeland.

Moscow's transcendent objective in Europe is to gain domination. By the Kremlin's reasoning, the inhabitants of western Europe, bereft of their own means of defense, paralyzed by the specters of nuclear war and skeptical of America's protective guarantees, will eventually come to heel. The Soviets are striving, through diplomatic and psychological means, to convert western Europe into a military vacuum. This objective is implicit in the various Soviet-sponsored schemes for disengagements and denuclearization in central Europe. The Soviets want to see neither the growth of western Europe's local military capability nor a build-up of American nuclear power at the very borders of the cold war. The Soviets seem convinced that by alternately badgering and cajoling the NATO nations they can effect the withdrawal of the United States from western Europe. If nuclear power within NATO remains an American monopoly, then such a withdrawal would mean *de facto* the denuclearization of western Europe. This explains the vehemence with which the Soviet Union, in both public and diplomatic statements, has opposed the introduction of tactical weapons into NATO countries.

It is clearly in Russia's interest that our NATO allies remain dependent on a strategy based exclusively upon American strategic nuclear power poised outside the European continent. So long as western Europe remains locally weak, each Communist challenge will strengthen the forces of pacifism, defeatism, and appeasement, and each Soviet-manufactured crisis will loosen another strand in the fabric of the Atlantic alliance. The period when the United States and its NATO allies could rely primarily on a counter-city retaliatory strategy has passed. The problem for the United States is to develop a strategy which will raise the threshold of nuclear reaction so that the strategic choice of NATO, in any Soviet-manufactured crisis, is not limited to the extremes of all-out nuclear war or limited defeat. The time has come, in other words, to give to NATO the capability for local defense.

Only a comprehensive array of forces can provide an adequate military underpinning of Western policy in Europe. The ability to retaliate massively against the centers of Soviet power will continue to be indispensable to deter a general nuclear conflict. Beyond that, however, the Soviet Union must be convinced that we can bar it from obtaining a specific objective, even a limited one like Berlin, with means appropriate to the given circumstance. Such a strategy would be more rational—and therefore more credible to Russia as well as our allies—than the threat to destroy the Soviet Union in retaliation for any Soviet "pinprick" into Europe.

Yet forces currently available to NATO in western Europe do not provide the supreme commander at SHAPE with the needed flexibility. NATO is particularly weak in conventional forces—the very kind of forces which the Soviets possess in abundance.

It does not seem likely that any single strategy or static combination of forces will suffice to deal with the military tasks confronting the United States and its allies in western Europe. Different combinations will be needed for different time periods as well as for the varying conditions of general-war, cold-war, and political-crisis support. While the United States must continue to bear the primary burden with respect to some tasks and some forces, western Europe in time should accept a greater share in its own defense.

With respect to total war, Europe's geographic position will continue to be important in terms of bases and warning stations. In the future it can contribute to some extent to the nuclear deterrent and assist the United States in the technological race. The problem of building a NATO local-defense capability is more complex. To analyze this problem, it is well to review the principal alternatives open to the United States.

The Alternative of Reliance on Tactical Nuclear Weapons

One of the principal military arguments adduced in support of a strategy which places exclusive reliance on nuclear tactical weapons for the defense of Europe is that, because of excessive casualties, troop concentrations in an atomic conflict must be held to a minimum and that there is, therefore, an inherent upper limit to the size of forces which can be effectively deployed on a nuclear battlefield. It has been estimated, for example, that an armored or mechanized division, in order to proceed against a potential atomic defense, must disperse over an area of more than 500 square miles. If the Soviets were to invade, say, West Germany along a 650-mile front, the total area for deployment, based on a depth of 50 miles, would be only about 32,500 square miles. This area could accommodate safely a maximum of 63 divisions, a number considerably below the figure of 175 divisions which the Soviets presumably hold in readiness. The use of tactical nuclear weapons, it is contended, goes a long way toward solving the logistical problems of NATO and, at the same time, permits

NATO forces to disperse over the inherently narrow terrain of the western European peninsula. The use of nuclear weapons could also serve to deny the enemy territory which could not effectively be defended with conventional weapons.

These claims have much validity, yet they court the danger of oversimplification. There is no absolute evidence that, even in a conflict in which tactical nuclear weapons are employed, the size of forces used ceases to be a meaningful criterion for victory or defeat. A good big atomic army is likely to remain superior to a good small atomic army, this despite the fact that the defending side in such a conflict does hold some inherent advantages.

Moreover, the vulnerability of NATO logistical echelons to Soviet nuclear attack is such that tactical nuclear war may tend to aggravate, rather than solve, NATO's logistical problems. United States forces in Europe rely on a long and tenuous line of communications stretching back across France and upon vulnerable port and supply facilities en route. Logistical vulnerability would seem to be a major obstacle to the profitable use of nuclear weapons.

The main issue, however, is whether a strategy for limited nuclear war is feasible or desirable in terms of western Europe's demographical and psychological climate. In an area as densely populated as western and central Europe, can atomic weapons be used with any degree of safety to civilian populations? The proponents of a strategy which calls for immediate resort to tactical atomic weapons in the event of a Soviet attack argue that the distinction must be made between large and small nuclear arms. They contend that "clean" weapons in the low-kiloton range can keep the dangers to the local population to a minimum.

How high, however, is this minimum? Military and civilian targets in western Europe are virtually inseparable; even if megaton weapons were not used, the level of destruction would inevitably be high. The problem is primarily a psychological one. The opponents of the present NATO strategy, which calls for the immediate use of nuclear weapons, point to the growing fear psychosis in western Europe, which is being exacerbated skillfully by Soviet propaganda. What the Europeans fear most, these critics claim, is extinction in a

Soviet-American conflict which would be limited by the tacit understanding of the major antagonists to the in-between areas. From the European point of view, such a conflict would hardly be a limited one.

Even if tactical nuclear weapons could be refined in terms of yield and accuracy to the point where existing casualty estimates could be drastically scaled down, there still remains the problem of the spiraling effect of these weapons upon the intensity of the conflict. The proponents of a tactical atomic strategy argue that the level of the conflict, not the weapons used, will govern its scale and intensity. This assumption implies that the enemy will tacitly agree to certain nuclear ground rules. Since he presumes that the West is not anxious to start thermonuclear war and since he himself is reluctant to start one, he will surmise that a nuclear weapon dropped by the West is not intended to start all-out war.

This line of reasoning, to say the least, is fraught with considerable risk. An enemy, swayed by the emotions generated by conflict, may well mistake the opponent's intentions and refuse to abide by such vaguely adumbrated rules of nuclear war.

The Alternative of Disengagement

Ever since the Hungarian uprising in 1956, a growing body of opinion in the West has articulated the concept of a disengagement of East and West along the battle lines of the cold war. The proponents of this concept hold that the best hope for European security lies not in a build-up or modernization of Western forces but in a mutual Soviet-American withdrawal from central Europe.

The concept of disengagement, while it has broad political implications, invariably is defended on military grounds. Its adherents take their cue from what they consider to be the salient points of American strategy in Europe today. The United States, in their view, has abandoned all but the pretense of a conventional defense in western Europe. The main purpose of American forces in central Europe is to act as a trip wire against Soviet attack—a trip wire which, if crossed, would automatically activate the mechanism of strategic retaliation against the Soviet Union. This, they contend, can be the only logical function of the small array of ground forces which the Western powers now hold in being. Such a policy is held to be in accord with the emerging facts of the air-nuclear age, in which long-range missile power will become the ultimate arbiter of conflict. The trip wire, it is argued, can be effectively replaced with an American guarantee of western Europe against Soviet aggression.

A number of military-strategic benefits are claimed for such a strategy. A physical separation of East and West along the line of conflict would relax tensions. More important, it would reduce the danger of an "accident" which might spark thermonuclear conflict. The Soviets, by withdrawing their forces from eastern Europe, would forfeit political control over this area; they could not return in force without clearly violating the sovereignty of independent states. Western Europe, moreover, would find relief from the formidable psychological and military pressures which the Soviet Army, poised across the Elbe River, has exerted since World War II. The removal of Soviet forces several hundreds of miles eastward would give the West, in the event of a concerted Soviet threat, precious additional warning time. Such an attack could then be met in territory beyond the present confines of the Atlantic alliance. In other words, disengagement may make it possible to fight the major actions of a local war outside NATO territory.

These arguments are superficially attractive—and profoundly misleading. They proceed from a basic premise: that the "balance of terror" is a stable balance and, since NATO shield forces serve no other purpose than that of activating strategic retaliation, a large-scale mutual withdrawal of Soviet-American forces can be made the subject of diplomatic negotiations.

Yet "breakthroughs" of the first magnitude could still upset the nuclear balance. Even in the absence of such a breakthrough, however, it would not be certain that the United States will make good its guarantee to protect the exposed sector of Europe through strategic retaliation at the price of millions of American casualties. The removal of American ground forces from the center of Europe would remove the simplest and most forthright cause for American intervention.

The main political argument advanced by proponents of disengagement—that a withdrawal of Soviet forces automatically would bring about the liberation of eastern Europe—is contradicted by the hard facts of Communist political control. Force need not be physically present in order to insure that each satellite bows to the wishes of the Soviet Union. Whether the eastern Europeans will or will not remain subservient to Russia will depend in large part upon their estimate of the balance of power and of the determination of the United States to provide a counterweight to Soviet power in Europe. An American withdrawal to the fringes of the Continent, let alone from all of Europe, obviously would belie such resolution.

Historically, geographical position has been subject to some but, on balance, to less depreciation than other strategic factors. For the United States, and therefore for NATO, the abandonment of the present forward position at the narrow waist of Europe would constitute a virtually irreversible step. The European peninsula is not an advantageous theater for defensive operations, for it lacks geographical depth. The distance from the Baltic Sea in the North to the Adriatic in the South is less than 600 miles, and from the iron curtain to Brest is no more than 850. Disengagement, while it might bring about a desirable withdrawal of Soviet forces from eastern Europe, would at the same time constrict the NATO operational area in western Europe to a mere "beachhead." NATO —if indeed the Western alliance could be maintained following a disengagement—would retain precious little space in which to deploy its forces. Because of contiguity, the Soviets will always find it easier to reoccupy the territory which they would yield.

A major attraction of proposed disengagement arrangements is that they seem to reduce the possibility of an accidental clash between the United States and the Soviets, a clash with which the United States is unprepared to deal on a conventional basis. This argument, however, is countered by the lessons of postwar history. The major case of Communist direct military aggression occurred in Korea, an area from which the United States had disengaged. It is quite possible that, following disengagement, Europe, which has been a relatively stable area of the cold war, might become highly unstable and invite diverse forms of Communist intervention.

Basic to the debate over disengagement is the question of Europe's importance in the West's global objective of holding communism at bay. It is the burden of this analysis that Europe's full political, economic, and military participation is absolutely essential to the success of Western strategy. A comprehensive disengagement would mean *ipso facto* the dissolution of the Atlantic alliance as it is presently constituted. Once it has been dissolved, NATO—as a live military force composed of national contingents from both sides of the Atlantic—cannot be put together again.

This does not mean that some limited form of a mutual Soviet–United States withdrawal from the present line of scrimmage will never be feasible. However, mutual disengagement, whatever its forms, will satisfy Western security requirements only if adequate local strength compensates for a redeployment of U.S. units on the Continent.

The Alternative of "Nuclearizing" Our NATO Allies

Several European countries now seek to acquire independent nuclear power. The United Kingdom has developed advanced nuclear weapons; France has successfully tested an atomic device; and Sweden and Switzerland undoubtedly have the resources for the production of atomic power. Although France, not to speak of Sweden and Switzerland, are far from becoming full-fledged nuclear powers—and, indeed, will never be "full-fledged" in terms of parity with the United States and the Soviet Union—the trend toward increasing independent nuclear capacity is clear. It poses a key question for U.S. policy: Should we assist certain European powers in the development of such a capacity or should we continue to withhold our secrets and our active support?

From the American viewpoint, an independent nuclear strength in Europe would hold some advantages. Briefly, they are these:

1. The individual European members of NATO, if armed

with their own nuclear weapons, would have more flexibility of defense. Assuming that they continue to maintain conventional forces, they could meet a conventional attack with conventional weapons. An attack with tactical atomic weapons could be met at the same level at which it is mounted. This greater flexibility in defense would, in turn, increase their ability and willingness to stand firm in the face of Soviet-created crises and nuclear blackmail.

2. As both the United States and the Soviet Union develop a long-range missile capability, Europe fears increasingly that the United States will (a) not retaliate against limited Communist challenges in Europe or (b) retaliate so massively that Europe will be destroyed in a nuclear holocaust. It is these fears which help to spur the Europeans' desire to develop their own nuclear retaliatory power. The Europeans argue, and not without some justification, that Western nuclear deterrent capability would be greater, more credible, and hence more effective if it were distributed among those nations which man the front line.

3. The desire for an independent nuclear capability on the part of European nations is to a large extent a quest for the prestige which redounds to those who hold membership in the "nuclear club." These nations, possessed of nuclear power, would develop a true feeling of "partnership" within the Atlantic alliance. Thus, they would overcome the third-class-nation neurosis which has inhibited their wholehearted participation in the common effort.

4. Throughout the nineteenth and early twentieth centuries, a multiple balance of power preserved the peace of Europe. The psychological basis of security in this period was the very uncertainty of risk which the would-be aggressor had to fear. This multiple balance has been transformed in our generation into a scale, or bipolar, balance. Because power is bipolarized, so is the deterrent. Soviet strategists, in contemplating any potential aggrandizement at the expense of Europe, need to be concerned only with skirting the risk of a determined American response.

If the multiple balance could be restored in the new form of independent nuclear power centers, a new dimension of risk would be introduced into Soviet calculations. The Soviets, in planning their gambits, would be forced to calculate, with considerable accuracy, the threshold of survival not only of the United States but of the countries immediately involved. A crisis which the United States does not consider an issue of national survival may well be deemed precisely such an issue by a nuclear-armed West Germany, France, or Great Britain. The greater the uncertainty, the stronger the deterrent against ambiguous aggression and the smaller, perforce, the Soviets' margin of maneuverability in Europe.

5. The possession of nuclear weapons by individual NATO nations would profoundly change the power relationship between the western European and the contiguous Communist satellite countries. We could give nuclear arms to our allies because, presumably, we can trust them. For various political reasons, which were demonstrated dramatically by the Hungarian uprising, the Soviets cannot place equal trust in the reliability of their "allies." The confrontation of nuclear-armed western European nations and "non-nuclear" eastern European satellites would impale the Soviets on the horns of a dilemma. It would drastically reduce the chances for success of a Soviet proxy action against western Europe. More important, it would strengthen divisive trends within the Communist bloc. The Soviets would be hard put to resist, without further weakening their grip upon their empire, the demands of their "allies" —including Red China—for "nuclear parity" with their western European neighbors. The anxiety to head off such a crisis in the internal relationships of the Soviet bloc undoubtedly looms large in such Soviet-sponsored proposals for the creation of a nuclear-free zone in Europe as the Rapacki Plan.

Although the reasons for opening fully the gates of nuclear development and know-how to our allies are compelling, such a policy does entail considerable risks. They are the following:

1. The cement of any coalition is necessity. The Atlantic alliance was founded in the realization of its members that, left to their own devices, they could not counter the Soviet threat and that their survival depended upon the protection afforded by the United States. To the extent that the acquisition of an independent nuclear capability may once again encourage unilateral policies, the alliance will be weakened.

2. One of the principal objections by Europeans to the dis-

engagement concept is the fact that it would remove the American protective presence. The development of an independent nuclear capability in Europe would to some extent argue for the withdrawal of American forces from Europe.

3. A change in the nuclear-power relationships within the Atlantic alliance would alter the *de facto* decision-making power of the various members. Individual NATO countries might easily become infatuated with their new nuclear capabilities, inadvertently push the button of all-out war, and expect the automatic backing of their alliance partners. World War I was touched off when Germany allowed its weaker ally, the Hapsburg Empire, to "drag" her into conflict. It is a cardinal principle of diplomacy that a strong power must not permit its own policy to be made by a weaker ally.

4. An even greater risk inherent in the proliferation of nuclear power is the use of nuclear weapons in the pursuit of national objectives. The French Army, for example, in its desperate effort to end the Algerian War, conceivably might succumb to the temptation of employing nuclear weapons against rebel redoubts. In such an event, the United States, as the donor of these weapons, would bear the brunt of an enraged world opinion.

5. There is the danger, also, that European nations, once they obtain nuclear weapons with all their connotations of prestige and power, will be reluctant to accept less dramatic, but nevertheless necessary, military tasks. The resulting gaps in NATO's weapons systems could prove disastrous. Exclusive reliance on nuclear weapons would significantly enhance the danger of total nuclear war.

There is no minimizing the risks inherent in a policy of giving nuclear weapons to our NATO allies. Yet the debate over this issue has already become largely academic. Given the nuclear facts of life in the mid-twentieth century, there is little question that all of our principal allies will sooner or later acquire nuclear weapons. The question is simply whether we shall give them these weapons or whether we shall permit them to squander their own resources in the quest for nuclear power—to the detriment of the over-all NATO defenses. Moreover, no western European power will be able to develop those second-strike capabilities which are the *sine qua non* of all-out nuclear war. For a long time to come, only the two super-powers will be able to afford so complex a weapons system.

A Dual Capability

Thus far, this chapter has been concerned with three major alternatives to the present policy tacitly being pursued by the United States in Europe—namely, the use of NATO contingents as a "trip wire" which, if crossed by Soviet forces, would activate strategic retaliation. Each of these alternatives has certain merits. None of them, however, taken singly, brackets the entire spectrum of challenges which the West is likely to encounter in the next decade.

A segment in this spectrum is the possibility of nonatomic war. The West, if it is to gird against this possibility, must devise some means for complementing its nuclear capabilities with the capacity to engage Soviet ground forces without automatic resort to nuclear weapons.

The need for such a strategy flows from an objective appraisal of the emerging military-psychological balance in Europe. The Soviets continue to station massive ground forces in eastern Europe. These forces have been held in check since World War II by the strategic nuclear superiority of the United States. The significance of Soviet technological-military progress lies precisely in the fact that by appearing to neutralize America's strategic capabilities it has released Russian ground strength as a formidable instrument of military-psychological pressure against the West. The new Soviet "crisis strategy," which was unveiled in Nikita Khrushchev's ultimatum on Berlin, is designed fully to utilize this pressure. So long as the weaknesses of allied conventional forces in central Europe compel the Western powers to contemplate the ultimate choice between a nuclear holocaust and limited defeat, for just as long are the Soviets able to drive their psychological advantage home.

Therefore, an effective conventional capability—on a scale at least twice the force levels available to NATO today—is imperative if NATO is to be prepared to (1) wage limited nonatomic conflict and (2) cope with the new Soviet crisis strategy in Europe. The danger which confronts NATO is not so much a deliberate Soviet aggression against western Europe—although such a possibility cannot be discounted. Rather, the main threat is a conflict triggered through a Soviet miscalculation of the West's unwillingness to go to war over a given issue (for example, Berlin) or conflict by accident (for example, another satellite uprising). In either case, the choice of weapons in all likelihood would be ours. And the West, lacking a nonatomic capability, would have to choose nuclear war.

Is it theoretically possible for the West to muster forces capable of dealing with the Soviets in a conventional action in Europe? In seeking to answer this question, Western analysts have tended to be overly impressed by the supposedly crushing superiority of the Red Army. It is true that the Soviets have sizable ground forces deployed in central and eastern Europe. A major function of these forces, however, is imperial control. The number of Soviet divisions actually available as a potential invasion task force is substantially below the total numerical strength of Soviet force levels. In the light of the Hungarian uprising, it is doubtful, to say the least, that the Soviets could release many of their garrison forces for an attack on western Europe. Thus the eastern European satellites can be a deterrent to Soviet-initiated ground action in central and western Europe.

The problem confronting the West, therefore, is not quite as hopeless as has often been assumed. It appears even less hopeless when the manpower pools of East and West are compared. At present, the United States has 31 million fit males of military age; the Soviet Union has 41 million. By 1965, it has been estimated, the available manpower figure for the United States will have risen to 35.2 million as compared with the slight increase to 41.5 million for the Soviets. If NATO is included, the West's relative position is even better. The Soviet bloc (excluding China) has 58.4 million fit males; NATO has 85.4 million. By 1965, this ratio will be 59 million versus 95.4 million.

Perhaps it is illusory to expect NATO to avail itself of its superior manpower reservoir in order to match the Soviets man for man. Conventional parity, however, may not be necessary. Given the space limitations of central Europe and the need for dispersal in the face of a possible nuclear counter-attack, the Soviets cannot concentrate their much publicized 175 divisions at a single point. They could, of course, bring up reinforcements rather rapidly—but not without alerting the West to the scale of the attack and raising at least the danger of all-out war. It may be quite possible, therefore, for 30 properly armed and trained NATO divisions—the number called for by the supreme commander—to deal with much larger Soviet forces without immediate resort to tactical or strategic nuclear weapons. It should be borne in mind, however, that the force objective of 30 NATO ready divisions was agreed upon at a time when the United States still held decisive nuclear superiority. Obviously, 30 divisions could not cope with all the ground forces which the Soviets hold in readiness.

Thus, the creation of the kind of conventional NATO force which would at least block Soviet forces in East Germany from overrunning western Europe is theoretically within NATO's means. The principal function of such a force would be to deter forms of limited aggression which, under thermonuclear parity, strategic retaliation alone cannot deter. This can be done by raising the enemy's cost of entry to a point where to undertake any direct military action he must deliberately invite strategic retaliation. Indeed, the Soviets may be discouraged from "feeling their way" into conflict. If a nuclear war looms as the logical result of a probing operation, then the Soviets may well deem such an operation a needless and expensive preface to total war. The Soviets, moreover, would have to face the risk that a large-scale ground probe into western Europe might provoke the United States into striking the first nuclear blow, an advantage which is now conceded to the Soviet Union.

If a "dual capacity" by NATO is theoretically possible, is it feasible in practical terms? Opponents of the concept of "dual capacity" base their arguments on military, strategic, economic, and political considerations.

Militarily, they argue, no war in Europe can be fought without nuclear weapons. These weapons will be used if only because they are the most effective weapons available to both sides: the Soviets already are integrating tactical nuclear weapons into their ground units and into their over-all strategy. The characteristics of an increasing number of weapons which are required to deal with atomic war are becoming less and less compatible with the characteristics of those weapons systems needed effectively to prosecute a conventional conflict. In other words, there can be no effective "mix" of atomic and nonatomic weapons systems. A "dual capacity" would mean the maintenance of completely separate systems. If we undertook such a parallel build-up of separate systems, we might discover suddenly that the Soviets had completely abandoned the capability to wage nonatomic war, leaving us with an expensive and totally useless conventional establishment.

Strategically, the most profound objection to re-emphasizing a local-defense capability in Europe has been the argument that such a strategy will serve to weaken the large deterrent. The contention is that, if we enunciate a limited-war strategy for Europe, we will thereby demonstrate to the Communists our reluctance to retaliate with our strategic weapons. Hence, statements on limiting our response will simply have the effect of making war once again a paying proposition for the U.S.S.R. Some proponents of this viewpoint even argue that the more we reduce our forces in Europe the more credible becomes our intention to resort to strategic retaliation.

Economically, the objective of a "dual capacity" is held to be impractical unless we are prepared drastically to hike our expenditures in order to generate an adequate mobilization base for a modern, sophisticated weapons system and at the same time build up and maintain a substantial nonatomic arsenal.

Politically, it is argued, a return by NATO to a major conventional capability is against current trends. So long as political leaders in the West are dazzled by the new superweapons, they will not vote the necessary funds for less glamorous conventional arms.

These arguments cannot be dismissed lightly. Every policy has its imperfections and pitfalls. The problem, however, cannot be solved simply by dismissing it as impractical.

The fact that the Soviets are integrating atomic weapons into their strategy in Europe is by no means proof that they have abandoned, or are prepared to abandon, the capability to wage conventional war. Indeed, the Soviets cannot give up this capability so long as imperial control remains a primary function of the Red Army contingents stationed in eastern Europe. The Soviets did not use nuclear weapons to put down the Hungarian rising; instead, they crushed the rebellion with a full-scale conventional attack. The problem of effectively "mixing" conventional and atomic capabilities, while admittedly a difficult one, is essentially one of proper integration, organization, and training.

Conventional capabilities are an integral element of the Soviet "crisis strategy" in Europe. The forces which have the greatest maneuverability along the critical points of contact between the Communists and the Free World—and which vest the diplomacy of both sides with ready power—are nonatomic forces. Should the Soviets, in the face of a NATO build-up of nonatomic forces, decide to shift to an exclusive reliance on nuclear weapons, then they would forfeit to NATO the very advantages of diplomatic maneuverability which they now derive from conventional military power.

This is not to negate the importance of nuclear weapons in any future conflict: we cannot expose to Communist nuclear attack forces which are prepared to defend themselves only with conventional arms. The nuclear weapons with which NATO forces are equipped will serve the purpose of injecting uncertainties into Soviet calculations and cautioning them against using their nuclear weapons in a limited attack. Evidently they will be used whenever the "limits" of nonatomic war are pierced by Soviet action. The onus of initiating nuclear war must, however, be shifted from Western to Soviet decision makers.

The argument that an increase in the local deterrent will detract from the over-all strategic deterrent is superficially convincing. Yet, as pointed out above, Soviet nuclear progress puts in doubt the willingness of the United States to resort to massive nuclear retaliation in response to every intermediate-range Soviet challenge. The greatest danger of total war in the next decade is not a pre-emptive strike on the part of either side, but rather the "degeneration" of a local engagement into all-out war. The Soviets may well calculate that they can effect a smash-grab of weakly defended areas in western

Europe and thus confront the United States with a *fait ac-
compli* which we will be reluctant to reverse at the cost of
initiating nuclear war. The same estimate of U.S. intention,
however, would not necessarily apply to a large-scale and in-
tensively contested local conflict. In Soviet calculations, an
American nuclear riposte would be much more likely in the
heat of a protracted ground engagement. The ability of the
United States and its allies to meet a Soviet ground probe with
effective military force thus enhances, rather than diminishes,
the deterrent to general war.

Can NATO afford a "dual capability?" The Soviets, with a
gross national product considerably below that of the combined economies of North America and western Europe, are
maintaining such a capability. The question, therefore, is not
whether the West can afford such a capability but whether it
will recognize the full spectrum of dangers and take the
requisite measures to deal with them. While this change in
strategy will impose added burdens upon the economies of the
individual members of NATO, these burdens can be lightened
by an effective specialization and co-ordination of tasks within
NATO. The problem is one of effective leadership. The United
States, in order to encourage its NATO allies to make the
necessary effort, must demonstrate its determination to implement a plausible strategy for the defense of western Europe.

A strategy based on a "dual capability" is thus compatible
with the psychological climate of Europe and with the objective factors of the European situation. It is compatible, too,
with the requirements of a "win" strategy which will enable
the Western powers to shift the psychopolitical conflict onto
the Communists' terrain. We failed to exploit, in 1956, Communist difficulties in Hungary because, having geared out
NATO strategy exclusively to nuclear weapons, we feared that
any Western interference in Hungary (such as the shipment
of arms to the Hungarian insurgents or the recognition of the
Imre Nagy government) would lead to war with the Soviet
Union—a war which, given our strategy, could only have been
a nuclear conflict. A successful campaign of psychological warfare against communism's most vulnerable area, namely eastern Europe, requires a supporting military establishment which
is flexible enough to allow us to take calculated risks.

21.   Security through Sea Power

by Commander Ralph E. Williams, Jr., U.S.N.

A graduate of the University of Texas, Commander Williams entered the Navy as an ensign in 1941 and during World War II saw service at Pearl Harbor and Tarawa. He is regarded by many as one of the most accomplished writers in the armed services today. He has served on the staff of the Naval War College and in the Strategic Plans Division of the Office of the Chief of Naval Operations. He has also been a special assistant to both the Chief of Naval Operations and the Secretary of the Navy. In 1958, Commander Williams was appointed to the White House staff.

Every so often in its military experience, a nation arrives at one of those critical points beyond which it finds itself no longer able to continue doing the things it has been doing in the way it has been doing them.

To the relatively few who actually saw them and to the millions more who read and heard about them, the Soviet earth satellites which appeared in the skies above the United States in the fall of 1957 seemed to herald such an event. But the truth is simply that Sputniks I and II, for all their spine-chilling implications, were but two particular items in a long

This article appeared in the March 1958 issue of the United States Naval Institute Proceedings *and is reprinted by the kind permission of the publisher and author. The United States Naval Institute, a private organization not connected with the Navy Department, is the Navy's professional society and acts as a "university press" for the Navy. In addition to publishing the* Proceedings, *a leading professional journal of naval and maritime affairs, it also publishes some 100 books of professional, technical, and historical naval interest.*

procession of political, military, and technological events which had already determined that the United States would soon reach a crisis of the first magnitude in its national security policy.

This crisis compounds both a budgetary and a strategic dilemma. Our terms of reference for the present conflict require that we maintain forces and weapons suitable for use against the contingencies of both general war and limited war. These weapons and forces are frightfully expensive and becoming more so, and, as they are now organized, they are largely mutually exclusive in the nature of their prospective employment. The fiscal effect of our having to maintain this dual panoply of armaments is such that we cannot continue the force levels we now have under anything remotely approaching a balanced federal budget. At the same time, the range and destructive effect of modern weapons have increased enormously, and, as they have done so, they have swept away the spatial limitations which used to form such useful guides in assigning tasks and missions. Finally, the deep and troubled stirrings of the world beyond our shores now urgently demand a review of the assumptions upon which our military posture is based.

In the critical and deeply earnest re-examination that the nation will surely make of its military posture, the Navy will fare according to the contribution it is demonstrably ready to make to the security of the United States. The word "demonstrably" is vital, for unless the American people are presented with a clear picture of the opportunities of sea power within the context of the strategic situation confronting them, they will not only fail to realize these opportunities, they will dissipate and eventually lose the sea power they now have. The object of this chapter is to invite attention to these very great possibilities open to us as the world's premier sea power and to suggest ways in which the power of modern naval weapons may be used to advance the prospects of our nation.

Weapons' Cost

First, let us consider the cost of weapons. There was a time when the Navy could buy a destroyer for $6 million and a

submarine for something over $4 million. We paid less than
$30 million apiece for the aircraft carriers *Enterprise* and
Yorktown. The later cruisers built during World War II
priced out at $60 million, including ordnance, or approxi-
mately the cost of the *Nautilus*. Today we are converting those
cruisers to missile ships at $90 million each, and we shall have
to pay a minimum of $150 million for a new atomic-powered
missile ship. The estimated cost of the first atomic-powered
carrier is about $300 million, with an aircraft load of at least
$100 million more.

The experience of the other services follows the same pattern. The Army Nike I replaced a gun battalion that cost one
third as much and is due to be superseded by the Nike B,
which costs four times as much. The B-52 at $8 million is
twice the cost of a B-36 and nearly fifteen times the cost of a
B-29. To replace our B-47s with B-58s, together with the new
jet tankers required, the Air Force will need $24 billion. And
we shall be extraordinarily lucky if we are able to get our intercontinental ballistic missiles into operational units for anything less than a billion dollars a wing.

The strategic effects of the skyrocketing costs of weapons
are equally far-reaching. By and large they are rooted in the
fact that atomic weapons, alone out of all the important arms
we own, have become vastly cheaper and more plentiful as
they have become vastly more powerful and efficient. In all
other cases, cost has gone up in virtually geometrical ratio to
performance. Today's operational fighter flies twice as high
and three times as fast as its World War II predecessor—and
costs twenty times as much. In many other cases we have paid
exorbitant prices for what turned out to be marginal gains in
performance. To a large extent the heavy emphasis which our
strategy now places on atomic weapons is due to the simple
fact that we have priced ourselves out of any conventional
capability in many fields. We pay so much to get the weapon
on the target that nothing less than an atomic warhead makes
it worth the effort expended.

Supplemental appropriation or not, we are headed for eventually lower personnel levels. We are part of a mechanized,
automated economy, and the solutions to our cost-control
problems will reflect this fact. At the matériel level, this trend

finds its complement in bigger, more expensive, and hence fewer units. This means a smaller establishment, both in terms of numbers and units. And because there will be fewer units, there is a powerful incentive to build into each of them as much destructive capacity as possible.

These two trends, of rising costs and ever greater destructive power of weapons, combine to rob us of much of our former flexibility. The concept of "Bigger Bang for a Buck" is not merely a clever slogan; it expresses very well this translation of the economy of mass production into the economy of mass destruction. There is in each case an enormous investment in the physical agents of the process, and, to make these costly agents pay their way, there is a like demand for enormous output: production in the one case, destruction in the other.

We are thus reaching a point where, for the first time in military history, what has always been the very hardest thing to do has now become the very easiest to do: that is, to destroy an opponent utterly. And precisely for this reason such a capability has no positive value whatever to a nation whose opponent can do the same thing. What will in fact be the hardest thing for us to do is to restrain the use of force to the minimum necessary to attain our political objectives.

This loss of flexibility of our own forces, combined with the great growth in Soviet nuclear power in all categories, has produced a fundamental change in the character of our alliances and the function they were designed to perform.

Our immediate strategic problem since World War II has been how to prevent Soviet domination of the remaining portions of the world, particularly those parts of it in Europe and Asia which are immediately and directly menaced. The present focus of the conflict is thus in the peripheral lands of the Eurasian mass which lie between the ocean areas and what the famous British geopolitician Halford John Mackinder called the central "Heartland." To accomplish our objectives in this critical area, we have actively sought to consolidate and strengthen the resistance of these threatened nations to further encroachment. This has led to large economic grants-in-aid and substantial military contributions undertaken under several bilateral and regional security agreements intended to give these nations some promise of security against not only atomic attack but a variety of other physical threats to which they, but not we, were being subjected. The essential *quid pro quo*, where there was one, took the form of permission to base elements of our Strategic Air Command on territory owned or controlled by these allies. These advanced bases were, of course, fully as vital to our own security as they were to the security of the countries on whose territories they were built.

Strategy of the 1950s

These agreements were consummated several years ago, when we had what amounted to an operational monopoly on atomic weapons. The risks incident to the construction of our new air bases were of an order acceptable to our allies, particularly those in Europe, who had the rapidly growing NATO defense structure to undergird their hopes for an air-ground shield which would keep the Russians out. But the surprisingly rapid development of Soviet nuclear capabilities over the past decade has brought a completely new face to the problem these agreements were designed to deal with. Because of it, the risks arising out of the prospective employment of these air bases have now been transformed into the risks of all-out atomic war, and these are the ultimate risks assumed by a nation. They are risks to which no government permits another to commit it for any reason whatever. They are risks that will only be taken, at the time they are presented, by the nation whose survival is the stake in the game.

Put simply, any arrangement whereby the acts of one sovereign nation put at risk the very survival of another will operate only where there is absolute identity of interest, and these occasions represent only a narrow band on the total spectrum of possibilities confronting the partners to the alliance. The remaining eventualities will be met with vagueness, delay, and dangerous irresolution, at the very time when speed, preciseness, and decision are urgently needed.

This serves poorly the interests of all parties concerned. Through it our allies—small, crowded, and geographically much closer to Moscow than they are to us—are made liable not only for their own failures and indiscretions but for ours as well. In our turn we suffer a large and uncompensated loss in flexibility and freedom of action by having our feet quite literally in concrete around the Eurasian perimeter—concrete owned in the last analysis by the host countries and subject to their disposal in the event of a showdown.

This does not mean that we cannot have viable security agreements with these smaller, weaker, more exposed members of the non-Communist world. It means rather that we should recognize that there is one particular category of risk in which we cannot reasonably expect them to participate with us on a general-average basis: that of all-out war. It happens that this eventuality is the very one whose likelihood we are seeking by every means to reduce to zero. If we are successful in this undertaking, our allies can play a very meaningful role in the cold- and limited-war situations with which we shall still be confronted. And this is of prime importance to our strategy, because it is within the context of those less violent situations that we must look for the answers to the security problems which now beset us. If we cannot win here, we cannot win anywhere, in any terms meaningful to a free people. Whether the cold war goes on for ten years or for a hundred, we shall urgently need the environment we can only have within a large confederation of free peoples.

The years ahead will inevitably see a progressive dissociation of our overseas allies from any responsibility for the American strategic striking capability. Considering the large and perhaps fatal chance of misfire in our present arrangements, this development can only be a good thing. It should be noted, too, that during the same period there will be a further loss of European power and influence in the remaining portions of Asia and Africa as the breakup of the colonial empires continues. Whether this is, on balance, good or bad is debatable, but it is nonetheless inevitable. The newly ransomed states will in almost every instance tend to be neutral and to stand aside from the main issue between the Communist and anti-Communist blocs.

There will thus be a steady falling away of land areas about the Eurasian crescent which will be available to the United States for military purposes in its struggle with the Soviet Union. Modest concentrations of conventional and tactical atomic forces may still be acceptable to certain host nations, but we shall have to look elsewhere for sites on which to base our all-out deterrent capability.

The Danger of a Fortress America Strategy

This was the situation we faced before Sputnik put its own heavy stamp on our defense thinking. We were already headed for a fundamental revision of our strategy forced by the factors just discussed. The impact of the Soviet missile program will serve greatly to accelerate and intensify these changes which were already under way. Our reaction to the new conditions had been evidenced in our efforts to produce a truly modern intercontinental bomber and a 5000-mile missile, together with a much lesser degree of interest exhibited in sea-based deterrent systems. Until recently, however, there was a lack of the necessary sense of urgency required to insure full budgetary support of the programs established in these fields.

Now we appear to have a greater sense of urgency, and we may expect greater expenditures of effort and funds to be made on nuclear delivery systems which will be wholly and exclusively under U.S. control. This can either be a blessing or a curse of unprecedented magnitude, depending on the direction we go, because the actions we are now at last prepared to take are sufficient to commit us irrevocably either to a sound and balanced strategy, still at the service of the larger purposes of the Free World alliance, or to the discredited, outmoded, and self-defeating concept of a Fortress America. The danger is not that we shall at the outset choose the latter deliberately, with our eyes open, but that we shall be led up to it gradually by the unintended consequences of actions we undertook with quite different objectives in mind.

In view of the demonstrated Soviet competence in longrange missilery, it is altogether natural for us to press for an operational capability in this field with the utmost speed. In the interim it would seem logical for us to broaden by every feasible means the base of our own piloted striking force by increasing both the numbers of its planes and the bases from which they operate. And finally, there is a strong incentive to adjust our continental defense to the new operational requirements as ballistic rockets replace manned bombers as the major threat to our security.

These are objectives which no one could oppose. But the real problem is how to accomplish them and at the same time provide for the other necessary concomitants of a balanced defense—for, however great, these are not the only threats confronting us.

Two things deserve to be mentioned here. The first of these is that, to achieve its objective in general war, the Soviet Union must first disarm us, and it must do it conclusively and early. Our atomic delivery capability is thus the prime target system in the Soviet war plan, the one whose destruction must be assured before any weapons may be allocated to the destruction of our economic and population base. Second, because this is true, the location of any portion of our delivery forces in the continental United States will inevitably draw down counterbattery fire upon it. If all our delivery capability comes to be based at home, we shall have enormously increased the value of the United States as a general target for thermonuclear weapons. At the same time, we shall have greatly simplified the enemy delivery problem by providing him with fixed targets of known locations, and we shall have further presented him with an important bonus effect in the havoc wrought upon our cities and countryside by the blast and fallout from the warheads delivered on the primary targets. This in itself achieves the practical effect of having increased the enemy stockpile by several dozen weapons.

The notion that this basically unfavorable set of relationships can be remedied by dispersal and the multiplication of planes and bases within the same general three-million-square-mile target area has always been a snare and a delusion and will become more so as the Soviet missile capability increases, for the simple reason that it is infinitely cheaper, and easier, and quicker, for our enemy to build missiles than it is for us to build bases. This is a race we cannot possibly hope to win. Ironically, the addition to our offensive strength in this particular manner compounds our own defensive problem rather than the enemy's, since every one of the new locations requires an elaborate point defense and throws a further load on our

warning and control nets. We can easily spend ourselves into
bankruptcy and on balance come out with less security than
we had before, because each new base we create assures a
measurable increase in the number of weapons that will fall
on the United States in the event of Soviet attack, without
securing a compensating decrease in the likelihood that such
an attack will occur.

Indeed, there is every reason to believe that this kind of
action on our part might well serve to increase the chances
of attack. In the age of ballistic missiles, the great inherent
flaw of a fixed and immobile striking system is that it confers
an enormous, and quite conceivably decisive, advantage upon
the side which hits first. If our enemy achieves an operational
capability in intercontinental missiles before we do, there will
be the added temptation to strike while he still has this very
considerable advantage. The combination of these inviting circumstances may well prove irresistible.

Other thoughts present themselves. Since, once begun, the
requirements of a "crash" program in these kinds of armaments
are bottomless, our capabilities in other fields of military effort,
already squeezed and straitened by the heretofore "moderate"
demands of these larger competitive programs, would simply
disappear. Inevitably this would lead to the loss one way or
another of the remaining non-Communist portions of the Eastern Hemisphere and our unceremonious retreat three to five
thousand miles to our own shores. This forfeit of the seas and
the Eurasian littoral would vastly weaken our defense, no matter how much effort we poured into our three-dimensional
"Maginot Line." And, as the conviction of the utter hopelessness of our situation settled in upon us, our whole nation would
take on the form of an armed camp.

The Advantages of a Sea-Based Deterrent

This transformation may indeed happen. Arms races are
common enough in military history. But it need not happen.
We can do far better—and at far less cost and risk. There is a
real and promising alternative. Instead of confining our critical
military activities to the land, and deploying our forces so as

to insure that a thermonuclear war, if it comes, will be fought on and over the land (including our own), we can play for all it is worth the role of the very great sea power we are.

As was previously mentioned, the great, perhaps fatal, disability of a land-based nuclear delivery system is its lack of security, which richly rewards the aggressor's initial surprise strike and, for that reason, greatly increases the chances of such a course being undertaken. We have enjoyed a degree of stability so far because our enemy has not fully developed his long-range strike capabilities and because our warning net seriously degraded the prospects of genuine surprise by piloted aircraft. These factors which have aided us up to this point will vanish with the advent of a Soviet long-range missile capability, against which there will be neither defense nor warning.

Well before this point is reached we must have taken the action necessary not merely to destroy the advantage of the aggressor's initial strike but to attach a severe penalty to it. Only if we can accomplish this can we hope to break out of the pernicious grip of strategic instability, which will lead us not only to sap our strength in a futile arms race but will tend powerfully to promote the very attack which we went to such great lengths to forestall.

Yet it is extremely unlikely that we can restore this critical element of stability to our relationships with the Soviets as long as we continue to base the major part of our retaliatory capability on land. For on land there is not only no place to hide, there is no place to go. The all-important features of mobility and concealment are effectively denied any land installation the size of an airfield or missile launcher. Only in the vastness of the world's oceans can we hope to base a striking force which, through its inherent capabilities for movement, concealment, and dispersal, can be made virtually immune to surprise attack. And with this immunity assured us, the whole advantage of such an attack disappears. Since the enemy must, as a first requirement, eliminate our retaliatory capability, which he cannot even locate, he is left with nothing to shoot at. He would be effectively deterred from attacking other vital targets by the knowledge that such acts would bring down upon him the full force of our sea-mounted striking force, unreduced in any important way by his own strike. Moreover, it would descend upon him from all directions, rather than along a narrow band of polar trajectories. This is not the kind of considerations that encourage an enemy commander to bold action.

The security available to naval forces buys a second important effect. It establishes the governing relationship as being that between our offensive forces and the targets they are designed to destroy, rather than that between our own offensive forces and those of the enemy. The very name "retaliatory force" implies that our long-range aircraft bases and missile-launching installations will begin any engagement as potential targets of an enemy attack. This means they must be sufficient in number to endure such an attack and still retain the capability of destroying their preselected targets. In the absence of any real security, it follows that the size of our offensive base must be related, not to the targets it must hit, but to the prospective order of damage it may receive. But as we have already seen, the enemy can increase this order of damage far more readily than we can expand our offensive base. If, on the other hand, our retaliatory forces are secure, there is no measurable increase in order of damage to be received, no matter how greatly the enemy increases his offensive force, and therefore no requirement to increase our own on this account. The problem, once solved, tends to stay fairly well put, and we shall be left with adequate resources available to apply to lesser contingencies.

This means something very much more than the simple availability of dollars, materials, and manpower for translation into U.S. forces capable of dealing with limited-war situations. It means that we also have something left over for military aid and the build-up and support of allied forces. It means that we can do a whole spate of things in the political and economic fields necessary to promote the strength and solidarity of our Free World collective-security system. But most important of all, it means that our big-war deterrent, our limited-war forces, and the forces of our allies can all be worked together in harness toward the common objective of maximum security for the resources expended. Our allies, freed from the paralyzing fear of being made the targets of a surprise thermonuclear attack, can employ their forces boldly in the common defense, knowing that they have much more to gain than to lose by so doing. Moreover, they would be further encouraged to resist by the knowledge that we had the forces to back them up which met the tactical and political requirements of the situation—and that we ourselves had some place to stand between the extremes of retreat and total war.

A Comprehensive Military Posture

Thus, the outlines of our new military posture begin to emerge. We must continue to have an adequate general-war deterrent, and to make it truly effective we must base a significant part of it at sea. If this is done, the size of our deterrent forces can be substantially less than it is now, and very much less than it is likely to become if we attempt a target-building contest with the Soviet Union.

The sea-borne portion of this deterrent would have its major strength in a force of nuclear-powered missile-launching submarines, which combine maximum concealment, mobility, and dispersion in the same system. Long-range missile-carrying seaplanes, jet- and eventually nuclear-powered, and based upon ships operating in remote water, offer an additional system with many of the desired virtues. There is mobility, dispersal, some degree of concealment, and an ability to approach from many directions. Finally, there is the important capability represented by naval carrier forces, which can apply the full range of air power from conventional high explosives to thermonuclear bombs. Together, these systems offer the best hope for preventing general war that we have had since the atomic age began.

In regard to continental defense, we would do well to recognize that its chief value is that of a warning mechanism, and that this value will diminish to the vanishing point as missiles take the place of bombers. Since the purpose of such a warning is to deter enemy attack by making its results unpredictable, the loss of this capability will not be serious if we have established a sea-borne deterrent by the time it occurs. As for the "defense" aspect of the term, we might as well swallow the unpleasant fact that there is not going to be any—and proceed to apply our resources to more promising programs.

In the more active field of limited and brush-fire wars, it seems inevitable that all services must come to depend largely upon low-yield nuclear weapons—of an order of two kilotons and below—for the good reason that we shall often lack the necessary number of units to achieve the required fire effect with high-explosive weapons. This admittedly means the loss of some flexibility, but the alternatives—surrender or all-out war—represent the loss of flexibility altogether. Even so, there is adequate basis for mixing both atomic- and conventional-weapons capabilities in the same structure, and this we are doing.

The tactical problems of employing low-yield weapons will, of course, be easier to master than the political problems they create. But these problems are susceptible of solution provided our general-war deterrent is made secure. A nation enlarges a conflict to better its prospects, not to worsen them, as our enemy would surely do by attacking us directly before eliminating our nuclear strike capability. There is obviously much we have to learn about the nuances of applying power of this order, but it seems appropriate to start with the assumption that it can be done without its getting out of hand. Unless we do this, we shall have made the capital error of supposing that small nuclear war is necessarily equivalent to big nuclear war and is therefore to be risked only for the ultimate stakes.

Whether nuclear or conventional weapons are called for, the requirement for mobility, versatility, and discrimination will remain. Prompt and spirited action is the essence of controlling local conflicts, as we have seen time and again. The time in which a military objective can be attained is perhaps the decisive factor in an enemy's calculation of risk. Days, even hours, are of crucial importance.

These special demands for time and place in the exercise of our national power have particular application to naval forces. Since the site of the present phase of the conflict is in the peripheral lands of Eurasia, most outbreaks of aggression will occur in areas readily accessible to the seas. The mobility and sustained combat power of the Navy's carrier and amphibious forces remain continuously at the service of the Free World in these vital areas. These forces contain their own strong defenses. Their logistics are part of the ready package. They have their own versatile, precise tactical aircraft, able to deliver both conventional and nuclear weapons effectively. And the same forces can be used repeatedly in different parts of the world as the needs for their services develop. There is no problem of salvage or roll-up, no duplication of effort, no costly, unused facilities left behind in the backwash. On the basis of utilization of effective capacity, naval forces represent the best money the nation ever spent on its national-security program.

In summary, several things may properly be said about the requirements of our defense posture and programs. We need a secure, effective general-war deterrent, constituted so that it will penalize, rather than reward, a surprise enemy attack. This deterrent must be stabilized at some level within our capacity to support over the long term. We want forces adequate to achieve our military and political objectives in small wars, and this too must be supportable over the long term. We want loyal allies, with working arrangements between us of a nature to develop the greatest possible combined strength out of the assets each brings to the alliance. We must find a way to meet the new challenge of Soviet missile technology without getting involved in an arms race and without walling ourselves off from the rest of the world. To accomplish these things, we must effectively use whatever contributions the various services are capable of making to the national defense.

These are some of the aspects of our basic security problem which we must deal with, and we must continue to deal with them for the rest of our lives. It has been the object of this chapter to show that these conditions can be met by the proper application of sea power. Once we grasp this all-important fact we stand to win for our country and the world a larger measure of security than we have known in a quarter century of turmoil and strife.

22. Unconventional Warfare

by James D. Atkinson

Associate professor of government at George-town University, Dr. Atkinson was from 1950 to 1954 director of Georgetown's special course in psychological warfare. His articles have appeared in Army, the Marine Corps Gazette, *the* Military Gazette, *the* United States Naval Institute Proceedings, *and other professional and scholarly journals. An intelligence officer during World War II, he is to-day a colonel in the Army Reserves, a member of the Advisory Board of Directors of the Association of the United States Army, and president of the American Military Institute. He lectured at the first National Strategy Seminar for Reserve Officers.*

Most people in the Western democracies still tend to think in terms of the traditional distinctions between peace and war and hence do not readily accept the idea of the mixture of the two, which the late General William Donovan called "unconventional warfare." The Communists have, without specifically using the term, practiced unconventional warfare for more than four decades. Lenin enlarged Marx's theory of the class struggle into the concept of universal conflict. On this broad battlefield, according to Lenin, the techniques of cultural, psychological, political, conspiratorial, and economic warfare would not be used so much to *support* military operations as in the past; rather they would supplement and even supplant the orthodox use of armed force.

Unconventional warfare fits perfectly the precepts of a revolutionary strategy. Unlike orthodox warfare, it can be expanded and contracted at will. Its pitch can be raised to the threshold of military conflict—as was the case in the Soviet blockade of Berlin in 1948—or lowered to the less provocative levels of propaganda and intelligence operations.

Unconventional warfare, therefore, embraces a broad spectrum of conflict which includes such diverse activities as propaganda, economic warfare, sabotage, espionage, subversion, strikes, civil disturbances, terrorism, political warfare, and guerrilla war. These methods of conflict are used either singly or in concert, within the framework of an over-all grand strategy. Unconventional warfare employs both nonviolent and violent techniques; indeed, its most distinctive characteristic is that it blends violence and nonviolence into a new synthesis of warfare.

Unconventional Warfare as a Modern Phenomenon

The Communists did not originate unconventional warfare, which has been waged in one form or another since the dawn of history. The makers of the French Revolution, for example, experimented with many methods of unorthodox warfare. In the United States, Presidents Thomas Jefferson and James Madison pioneered in such economic-warfare devices as the embargo against Great Britain. Yet, not until the early twentieth century did this mode of conflict come into its own. It did so for three basic reasons. First, the revolution in the communication of ideas—radio transmission, wireless telegraphy, and photography—provided unconventional warriors with ready-made weapons. Second, a burgeoning "thinking elite" in modern mass society furnished cadres for, and lent continuity to, revolutionary movements and fifth columns. Finally, modern society has become at once more complex and more vulnerable to attack by unconventional methods. The paralysis which gripped Singapore in 1955 after a Communist-inspired general strike is but one illustration of the sensitivity of today's highly organized, closely interlocking society to unconventional warfare.[1]

The West's conspicuous lag behind the Communists in this important area of the conflict spectrum cannot be traced so much to a lack of understanding of the capabilities of unconventional warfare. The effectiveness of resistance movements in German-occupied countries during the Second World War demonstrated that the democracies possess both extensive assets and know-how for waging—and waging successfully—this highly specialized version of combat. Rather, the West's failure to keep pace with its adversaries stems from a contrasting view of conflict as such: the Communists, possessed of a guiding ideology and an operational doctrine, have recognized more quickly and discerningly than the peace-loving and legalistic-minded Western democracies that unconventional warfare can be waged more effectively under the cloak of formal "peace" than under conditions of open and declared war.

Communist Propaganda

Propaganda is one of the oldest and most important weapons in the Communist arsenal of unconventional warfare. Its importance derives from the fact that not only is it a technique in itself but it is used in support of other techniques, such as strikes, economic warfare, and especially political warfare.

Immediately after they came to power in Russia, the Communist leaders created the Agitation and Propaganda Section of the Central Committee of the Communist Party. Their early operations against Germany set the tone for a propaganda offensive which has been waged unremittingly, and with many refinements, down to the present day. The Soviet embassy in Berlin served as a center for propaganda dissemination, as did the consulates in Stettin and Hamburg. Couriers and trained agitators regularly commuted between these centers and Moscow. The Petrograd Telegraph Agency (later renamed TASS), created ostensibly for commercial activities, also was used as a propaganda medium in Germany, thus establishing a pattern which was to become world-wide.[2]

Another pattern set during this early period was the lavish expenditure of money for propaganda purposes. The Soviet ambassador and his staff in Germany in 1918 had a large sum of money at their disposal for bribing writers, covertly controlling newspapers, and overt propaganda. These massive outlays have continued down to the present time. By 1953, for example, it was estimated that Communist countries were spending over three billion dollars annually for internal and external propaganda. One authority has estimated that the Soviet Union alone spent one and one half billion dollars in 1951.[3] There is every indication that these sums have mounted steadily in the years since.

The magnitude of Communist propaganda operations comes into focus when we look at two widely separated parts of the globe. In France, during 1953, the French Communist Party published 15 daily newspapers, 51 weekly newspapers, and 56 reviews and magazines of various types—this in addition to the Party's "routine" propaganda activities, such as the distribution of leaflets and posters and the harangues of speakers and agitators. While the Communists have lost ground in France since 1953, their propaganda efforts remain both vigorous and extensive.

On the other side of the world, the Chinese Communists employ a number of effective propaganda organizations as spearheads in the psychological battle for Asia. The "Chungking Democratic League," formed in 1946 as a federation of leftist groups and now completely dominated by the Communists, wages propaganda through student societies, cultural groups, and business firms among the overseas Chinese. Its chief work is along the Hong Kong-Bangkok-Singapore-Jakarta line, which the Communists call the "Great Nerve of Asia." The "Federation of Democratically-Minded Chinese Youth Organizations"—in collaboration with the Soviet-dominated "World Federation of Democratic Youth"—spreads propaganda among young people both in China and abroad. The "Min-Seng-She" organization, either directly or through affiliated organizations, conducts propaganda through the medium of sports clubs, debating societies, and other recreational-cultural groups in the Far East.

These are but several examples of an unrelenting offensive which the Communists have pressed, with remarkable success, ever since Bolshevism's seizure of power. The basic themes in this offensive—"anticolonialism," "anti-imperialism," "peace," "peaceful coexistence," and disarmament—have remained essentially unchanged, but they have been adroitly varied to fit

specific circumstances. While Western propaganda efforts
have been desultory, un-co-ordinated, and—more often than
not—starved for funds, Communist propaganda warfare has
been a highly specialized and centrally planned operation,
carefully integrated into the over-all conflict pattern. Its major
objectives are to confuse and divide the Free World, to inculcate guilt feelings among the Western elites, to camouflage
the real nature of the Communist conflict machine, and to
magnify the impact of Soviet power—in short, to undermine
the psychological defenses on which purposeful resistance to
aggression can be based.

Espionage and Subversion

Communist espionage and subversion operations are carefully meshed with propaganda activities if only because they
are carried out by the same "army": communism's global network of official and semiofficial Soviet agencies, militant Party
formations, "fronts," and other auxiliary organizations. This
dual function is illustrated by the role of Soviet commercial
representatives in the United States, Great Britain, and elsewhere. In 1927, for example, British security personnel raided
the official Soviet trade organization and Arcos, Ltd., a British
"front" company, and uncovered evidence which showed that
the Soviets had been using their foreign trade posts as a cover
for propaganda, espionage, and subversive activities. Volumi-
nous evidence attests to the similar employment of AMTORG,
a Soviet trade agency in America.

The Soviet news agency TASS is a prime example of an
organization which carries out espionage missions under the
convenient cover of diplomatic immunity. A report of the
Canadian Royal Commission indicated that Nikolai Zheveinov,
TASS correspondent in Canada, was engaged in the direction
and supervision of a large number of persons who were col-
lecting highly secret information from Canadian Government
sources for transmission to Moscow. Similarly, in 1951–52,
Viktor Anisimov, chief of the Stockholm bureau of TASS, was
revealed to be the director of a spy network in Sweden.

Soviet propaganda, in the years following the death of Stalin, took pains to place the onus for terrorism, espionage, and similar activities upon the reign of the departed dictator. The implied suggestion was that the book had now been closed permanently upon these "ungentlemanly" activities. Behind the new façade, however, the old activities have been carried on as before, albeit with greater subtlety and circumspection. In March 1956, for example, the Iranian Government expelled the assistant military attaché of the Soviet embassy after he had been arrested while engaged in receiving secret documents from an officer of the Iranian Air Force. In 1960, a West German court trial brought out information that a former West German naval officer had, along with other Germans, both civilian and naval, been transmitting naval and military secrets to Soviet intelligence officials in East Berlin.

In the sinister game of espionage and subversion, the Communists hold some strong cards over the Western democracies. One is the international Communist movement, which provides the agents, the saboteurs, the infiltrators, and the agitators. More fundamental, however, is a basic contrast in systems. An open democratic society is just that—open to the discerning eyes of its enemies. In order to compile his intelligence reports, a trained enemy agent very often needs only to read our free newspapers or listen to the unfettered debates of our free political system.

Economic Warfare

The Russian economy since 1917 has been a closed economy, totally subservient to the will of the Central Committee of the Communist Party of the Soviet Union. In the Soviet economy, therefore, foreign trade has always played a secondary role and has been used primarily for purposes of propaganda, as a cover for espionage and subversion, and as a support for Soviet political warfare. The role of foreign trade in Communist conflict techniques was set down by Lenin in 1920. In explaining the question of granting concessions to capitalist business concerns, he pointed out that "our chief interest is political; the economic importance . . . is but secondary . . .

[while] we do not for a moment believe in lasting trade relations with the imperialist powers."

The Soviet economic offensive, which has been in full swing since Khrushchev's rise to leadership, has four principal targets:

1. The removal by the non-Communist world of all export controls on sensitive and strategic goods destined for the countries of the Soviet and Chinese Communist bloc.

2. Soviet-bloc penetration of the emerging nations of Africa, the Middle and Near East, southeastern Asia, and Latin America under the guise of economic or technical assistance. Undersecretary of State C. Douglas Dillon has stated that the Soviet Union has granted about two and one half billion dollars in military and economic credits to the new countries between 1954 and 1959 and that one billion of this has been in a one-year period, 1958–59. At the same time, the number of Soviet technical "representatives" in these nations has risen to four thousand.[4]

3. The beckoning of American business to Communist-bloc countries. The immediate objective is to secure technical know-how and industrial prototypes and processes—especially in chemicals, drugs, and light metals—from American industry. An additional aim is to soften up America's business and financial community in order to prepare the way for the extension of economic aid and long-term credits to the Communist bloc. Mr. O. V. Tracy, vice-president and director of Esso Standard Oil Company, has issued a warning concerning Soviet trade blandishments which should be required reading for every American businessman. He has said: "Both Khrushchev and Mikoyan have asked for technical knowledge and equipment. They want the latest models of our advanced machines and instruments—to serve as prototypes for their own production. . . . The Russians are buying machinery and specialized processes only to copy them—and I don't think too much 'repeat business' can be expected."[5]

4. Eventual grants of economic aid and long-term credits or loans to the Communist bloc by the United States and by other countries of the highly industrialized Western allied powers. The Communist leadership appears quite cognizant of the fact that the only sure way it can make good Khrushchev's boast to "catch up" with the United States is by the

massive transfusion of goods, credits, and processes from the
American and other economies (the booming West German
economy, for example) into the Communist bloc's economic
system.

Guerrilla Warfare

The degree of physical force used by the Communists in
their unconventional-warfare operations depends on the concrete situation. Guerrilla warfare represents the application of
a greater amount of physical force than most methods of unconventional warfare. Nevertheless, from the Communist viewpoint, guerrilla warfare must not be equated with physical
force alone. Rather, Communist guerrilla operations deftly
blend violent warfare with such nonviolent techniques as propaganda and political organization.

Mao Tse-tung, who has written about guerrilla warfare
more extensively than any other Communist leader, illustrated
the concept of guerrilla warfare as a mixture of violent and
nonviolent methods when he stated that "without a political
goal guerrilla warfare must fail, as it must if its political objectives do not coincide with the aspirations of the people and
if their sympathy, co-operation, and assistance cannot be
gained." Implicit in this assertion is an idea which permeates
all Communist unconventional warfare—namely, that guerrilla
warfare issues from the agitation and propagandizing of the
people, from economic bases, from political-organization activities, and, in many cases, from acts of sabotage and of
terrorism.

There is ample evidence that the Communists adhere to
this concept in concrete situations. Thus Tito, when he
launched his partisan warfare campaign in Yugoslavia, built
a powerful political machine well before his partisans engaged
the German forces or (later) the anti-German and non-
Communist Chetniks of General Mikhailovitch. A "People's
Committee" was set up to serve as a framework for a "shadow"
government in Serbia; a Communist guerrilla newspaper,
Borba (*Fight*), was printed; and a "People's Front" was established to attract Yugoslav nationalists along with Com-

munist sympathizers. All these steps were taken with the pre-meditated idea that they would form the basis for the new Communist regime which Tito and his associates hoped to forge from the fires of the guerrilla war. Similarly, in Greece the ELAS (Communist) partisan force, according to Field Marshal Papagos, "was developed not to help the Allies win the war but to help Moscow win the peace after the war—and with the ultimate, very long-range objective of placing the Soviet Union in a dominant position in the Mediterranean."

Terrorism has become a major stock in trade of the guerrilla fighter. During the Second World War, Khrushchev was the Soviet political commissar in charge of guerrilla warfare in one large sector of the Eastern Front. In order to gain more recruits for the guerrilla bands and to inflame the populace, he gave orders for the assassination of the milder local puppet rulers set up by the Germans, while the more cruel puppet leaders were to be spared. This was done with the calculated object of fanning hatred of the Germans among the occupied population.

Whether the methods used are "People's Fronts" for winning over segments of the population, the employment of clandestine newspapers and roving agitators to enlist sympathy, the use of terrorism, or extensive hit-and-run raiding (as in Laos and South Vietnam early in 1960), the object of Communist guerrilla warfare is to combine violent and nonviolent techniques into an integrated politico-military effort. It can be expected to play a continuing role in Communist-bloc strategy during the next decade.

Political Warfare

Political warfare is in many ways the synthesis of all unconventional-warfare techniques. Its distinguishing characteristic is that it is conducted not only against people, classes, institutions, or political parties but also on the broadest possible scale against governments themselves. It embraces the pressures and intimidation of diplomacy, cultural propaganda, the stirring up of class, religious, racial, and ethnic tensions and hatreds, the imposition of threats to governments and their citizens, and, above all, the sapping of the will of both governments and of the popular mass to resist.

While "peaceful coexistence" has by now become a standard theme of Communist political-warfare thrusts, a less obvious campaign has been also under way for some time. This is political warfare on the grand scale, in the gradual yet relentless process through which the Moscow-Peiping axis is encircling the United States with a ring of countries ranging from actively anti-Western to avowedly neutralist. A Peiping radio broadcast on December 26, 1959, underscored this Communist strategy when it pointed out: "The unprecedented upsurge of the fight against dictatorial rule and the brilliant victory of the Cuban people are the most outstanding events in Latin America this year. . . . The successful struggle of the Latin-American peoples has greatly shaken the dominant position of the United States in Central and South America." There is little question that Communist political warfare in Latin America as well as in the new nations of Africa and Asia will be accelerated in the coming years. It will be waged side by side with diplomatic, propaganda, and political pressures directed toward weakening and ultimately breaking up the North Atlantic Treaty Organization and the other mutual-security systems (such as SEATO and CENTO) which link the defenses of the Free World.

A new and frighteningly effective form of Communist political warfare has been that of nuclear-missile blackmail. Communist propaganda hammerings on the horrors of nuclear war, on the power and deadliness of Soviet missiles, and on the development of even newer and deadlier weapons have been a calculated counterpoint to the "peaceful coexistence" theme. The aim is to produce a somber climate of fear and futility, and hence a paralysis of the will, in the non-Communist countries. This was the obvious purpose of Soviet rocket firings into the Central Pacific in early 1960. The boast that a rocket "fell less than two kilometers away from the predetermined point" was intended to support the doubtful claim that any American city could be hit with pin-point accuracy by Soviet missiles.

These and similar threats are used to convey to Americans the false proposition that the United States faces only *two* alternatives: utter destruction or "accommodation"—a Communist euphemism for appeasement. Public opinion in both Europe and the United States is implicitly exhorted to pressure their respective governments to make concessions on a broad political and military front.

Important as is the scientific and technological race in the current conflict, it may well be overshadowed by the politico-psychological struggle. As both sides amass the means to annihilate each other, the conflict will be decided not so much by military capabilities as by the will and determination to use these capabilities. It is this "arsenal of intangibles" which is the principal target of Communist political-warfare thrusts.

Summary

The weapons of unconventional warfare forged by Lenin and Stalin have been used skillfully by their Russian and Chinese disciples. The world is witnessing a climactic period in the clash of techniques that are not so much unique in themselves but "new" in the way in which they are employed on a massive and co-ordinated scale. A Communist Party theoretician, writing in *Kommunist* in December 1953, stated that "Lenin and those who agreed with him fought for a Party functioning as the combat staff of the working class, an organizational whole, built as a united and centralized organization working under a single plan." The "single plan" continues to guide Communist efforts.

Thus far the great democracies have responded to the challenge of this new form of warfare only hesitantly and haphazardly. Notwithstanding the success of export controls and other economic-warfare devices directed against the Moscow-Peiping axis, the non-Communist nations have been reluctant to meet their adversaries in the arena of unconventional warfare. They have shied away from this engagement despite their huge stockpiles of potential weapons which could carry the struggle onto the Communist terrain.

The late Secretary of State Dulles suggested the most potent of these weapons in a speech in Cleveland, Ohio, on November 18, 1958, when he pledged the support of the United

States to "political independence for all peoples who desire it and are able to undertake its responsibilities." The hope of liberation continues to beckon powerfully to the captive nations of eastern Europe, the former states of Latvia, Lithuania, and Estonia, Tibet, and other nations and ethnic groups subjugated by the new colonialism of the Moscow-Peiping axis. Yet the West has failed to exploit the centrifugal forces which continue to tear at the Communist empire. In view of this sorry record, it may well be asked whether the Free World will ever tread purposefully on that vast and shifting battleground which is unconventional warfare.

Notes

1. See, for example, the New York *Times*, June 13, 1955.
2. Today TASS seems to concentrate more heavily on espionage than on propaganda. See, for example, the *Report of the Australian Royal Commission on Espionage*, Sydney, August 22, 1955.
3. Richard L. Brecker, "Truth as a Weapon of the Free World," *The Annals*, Vol. 278 (November 1951), p. 1; see also F. Bowen Evans (ed.), *Worldwide Communist Propaganda Activities* (New York: Macmillan, 1955), *passim*.
4. C. Douglas Dillon, "The Challenge of Soviet Russian Economic Expansion," *Free World Forum*, I, No. 5 (1959), 23.
5. O. V. Tracy, "Doing Business with the Russians," address before the Manufacturing Chemists' Association, June 11, 1959, pp. 10–12.

23. Disarmament: Illusion and Reality

by Henry A. Kissinger

Dr. Kissinger is recognized as one of the leading writers in the field of international relations. He received his A.B., M.A., and Ph.D. degrees from Harvard University and is now Director of Special Studies at Harvard's Center for International Affairs. He has written articles for numerous journals, including Foreign Affairs, *the* Yale Review, *the* Reporter, *and the* New Republic. *His book* Nuclear Weapons and Foreign Policy *was published for the Council on Foreign Relations by Harper in 1957 and later reissued as a Doubleday Anchor Book. Dr. Kissinger lectured at the first National Strategy Seminar for Reserve Officers.*

The notion that armaments are the cause rather than the reflection of conflict is not new. It has been the basis of schemes of disarmament throughout history; it was the rationale for all the disarmament conferences in the twenties and thirties. Nevertheless, it is open to serious doubt. Between the Congress of Vienna and the unification of Germany, the standing armies were very small because the outstanding disputes did not involve, or were not thought to involve, matters of life and death. After 1871 there started an armaments race which has not ended to this day. Between the unification of Germany and World War I, Europe was torn by two schisms which, to

Excerpted from Nuclear Weapons and Foreign Policy, *by Henry A. Kissinger (abridged edition; Garden City, N.Y.: Doubleday Anchor Books), Chapter 8. Copyright by Council on Foreign Relations, New York.*

the powers concerned, seemed to involve "vital" interests: that between France and Germany over Alsace-Lorraine and that between the Austro-Hungarian Empire and Russia over the fate of the Balkans. After the First World War the rebellion of Germany and the U.S.S.R. against the Treaty of Versailles and the rise of the dictatorships created a climate of insecurity which doomed all disarmament efforts to futility. And after the Second World War the intransigence of the Soviet bloc forced the Free World to restore a measure of its strength even after it had disarmed unilaterally almost to the point of impotence.

There is little indication that the level of armaments itself produces tension. Great Britain has a strategic air force and a nuclear stockpile capable of inflicting serious, although perhaps not fatal, damage on the United States. But this fact has caused no uneasiness in the United States and no increase in our defense effort. Conversely, Great Britain did not seek to forestall the development by the United States of a navy superior to its own—something it had fought innumerable wars to prevent in the case of other powers. This was because the "vital interests" of both powers are in sufficient harmony so that they can have a large measure of confidence in each other's intentions. Each can afford to permit the other to develop a weapons system capable of imperiling its security and perhaps even its survival because it knows that this capability will not be so used.

The Vicious Circle of Armaments

To be sure, the degree of confidence between the United States and Great Britain is exceptional. More usually, powers are conscious of some clashing "vital interests." As a result, a rise in the level of armaments of one major power may set in motion a vicious circle. Increased military preparedness serves as a warning of an increased willingness to run risks. The other powers can escape the pressure implicit in a stepped-up defense effort only by making concessions (a dangerous course, for it may whet appetites and establish a method for settling future disputes) or by entering the armaments race themselves. But while the vicious circle of an armaments race is plain, it is not nearly so obvious that it can be ended by an international convention. If disagreements on specific issues had been tractable, the armaments race would never have started. Since negotiations on outstanding disputes have proved unavailing, it is improbable that a disarmament scheme acceptable to all parties can be negotiated.

A general disarmament scheme, to be successful, must deprive each party of the ability to inflict a catastrophic blow on the other; at the very least, it must not give an advantage to either side. A meaningful agreement is, therefore, almost impossible under present circumstances. For the same mistrust which produced the armaments race will reduce confidence in any agreement that may be negotiated and it will color the proposals which may be advanced. Each side will seek to deprive the other of the capability it fears most as a *prelude* to negotiations, while keeping its most effective weapon under its control until the last moment. Thus, the phasing of disarmament has proved almost as difficult a matter to negotiate as the manner of it. During our atomic monopoly, the Soviet Union insisted that the outlawing of nuclear weapons precede any negotiations on disarmament, while we in turn refused to discuss surrendering our atomic stockpile until an airtight control machinery had first been put into operation. With the growth of the Soviet nuclear stockpile, both sides have continued to strive to neutralize the other's strongest weapon. The Soviet Union has attempted to expel our troops and particularly our air bases from Eurasia. We have striven for means to neutralize the Soviet ground strength. Each side wishes to protect itself against the consequences of the other's bad faith; each side, in short, brings to the disarmament negotiations the precise attitude which caused the armaments race in the first place.

The Technological Problems

A reduction of forces is all the more difficult to negotiate because it seeks to compare incommensurables. What is the relation between the Soviet ability to overrun Eurasia and American air and sea power? If the United States weakens its

Strategic Air Command, it would take years before it could be reconstituted. If the Soviet Union reduces its ground forces, the strategic impact would be much smaller, and, given the structure of Soviet society, the troops could be reassembled in a matter of weeks. A substantial reduction of Soviet forces would not deprive the Kremlin of its large reserves of trained and rapidly mobilizable manpower.

In such circumstances a reduction in forces would not contribute a great deal to a lessening of tensions. Even if a scale of comparison between different weapons systems could be agreed upon, it would still not remove the real security problem: the increasingly rapid rate of technological change.

Disarmament plans of the past were based on a reasonably stable weapons technology. Once the proposed reduction of forces was implemented, strategic relationships remained fairly constant. But under present conditions, the real armaments race is in the laboratories. No reduction of forces, however scrupulously carried out, could protect the powers against a technological breakthrough. Even were strategic striking forces kept at fixed levels and rigidly controlled, an advance in air defense sufficient to contain the opposing retaliatory force would upset the strategic balance completely. The knowledge by each side that the other is working on ever more fearful means of destruction or on means of attacking with impunity would cause current international relations to be carried on in an atmosphere of tenseness and imminent catastrophe, whatever agreements may be concluded about reduction of forces.

In addition to the technological problems, the structure of international relations will prevent a reduction of forces from going beyond a certain point. None of the major powers, certainly not the U.S.S.R., will accept a disarmament scheme which impairs its relative position vis-à-vis secondary states. Nothing is likely to induce the U.S.S.R. to accept a level of armaments which reduces its ability to control the satellites or to play a major role in contiguous areas such as the Middle East. But forces sufficient to accomplish this task are also sufficient to imperil all the peripheral powers of Eurasia. A reduction of forces which does not affect the relative Soviet position vis-à-vis the secondary powers will not diminish the basic security problem of the non-Soviet world.

Nor is it a foregone conclusion that a reduction of forces would inevitably be beneficial. A reduction of nuclear stockpiles might well increase the tenseness of international relationships. Given the diffusion of nuclear technology, a reduction of stockpiles would be almost impossible to verify. Thus, each power would probably seek to keep back part of its stockpile to protect itself against the possibility that its opponent might do so. An attempt to reduce nuclear stockpiles, far from removing existing insecurity, may merely serve to feed suspicions.

Moreover, to the extent that nuclear stockpiles are in fact reduced, any war that does break out is likely to assume the most catastrophic form. The technical possibility of limiting nuclear war resides in the plentifulness of nuclear materials. This makes it possible to conceive of a strategy which emphasizes a discriminating use of modern weapons and to utilize explosives of lesser power which, from a technical point of view, are really "inefficient" high-yield weapons. But if the quantity of weapons decreases, a premium will be placed on engineering them to achieve maximum destructiveness and to use them on the largest targets. The horrors of nuclear war are not likely to be avoided by a reduction of nuclear armaments.

Inspection and Control

Because a reduction of forces has proved so nearly impossible to negotiate and because its rewards would be so questionable even if achieved, the major emphasis of disarmament efforts has turned to the problems of inspection and control and to the prevention of surprise attack. However, for a variety of reasons, every inspection scheme that has proved acceptable to the Free World has been objectionable to the U.S.S.R. As a result, the negotiations about control and inspection have produced the same vicious circle as the efforts to bring about a reduction in armaments: were it possible to agree on an inspection-and-control machinery, it would also be possible to settle some of the disputes which have given rise to existing tensions. As long as specific issues prove obdurate, there is little hope in an over-all control plan.

In addition to the psychological and political problems, the technological race makes it difficult to negotiate a control plan. For the rate of change of technology has outstripped the pace of diplomatic negotiations, so that control plans change their meaning while they are being debated. The control scheme of the first United States disarmament proposal (the Baruch Plan) assumed that an international authority with powers of inspection and in control of mining, processing, and producing fissionable materials would be able to eliminate nuclear weapons from the arsenals of the powers. The United States contribution was to be the destruction of our nuclear stockpile as the last stage of the process of disarmament. Even this scheme would not have been "foolproof." Within the United States atomic energy program, with every incentive to achieve an accurate accounting and no motive for evasion, the normal "slippage" in the handling of fissionable materials due to error and mechanical problems of handling is several per cent. A nation determined on evasion could easily multiply this percentage without being in obvious violation of international agreements and utilize the "saved" slippage slowly to build up a nuclear stockpile of its own. Their awareness of this possibility would, in turn, give other powers a motive for evasion.

Nevertheless, at the early stages of the atomic energy program the stockpiles were still so small and the possibility of building them up to substantial proportions through evasions was so slight that an inspection program would have contributed materially to reducing the danger of nuclear war. Any power determined to produce nuclear weapons would have had to break existing agreements flagrantly and thereby bring down on itself either the international enforcement machinery or war with the United States. But in the age of nuclear plenty, the control machinery envisaged by the Baruch Plan would prove futile as a means to eliminate stockpiles. So many nuclear weapons of so many different sizes have been produced and they are so easy to conceal that not even the most elaborate inspection machinery could account for all of them. Control machinery cannot effectively prevent the accumulation of nuclear weapons at this stage of their development, even assuming the desirability of doing so.

And so it is with each new technological discovery. In the very early stages of development, a scrupulous control system may forestall its being added to the weapons arsenal. But by the time disarmament negotiations have run their tortuous course, the weapon will have become so sophisticated and the production of it will have reached such proportions that control machinery may magnify rather than reduce the existing insecurity: it may compound the fear of surprise attack with fear of the violation of the agreement by the other side.

The inconclusiveness of negotiations about inspection machinery reflects also the difficulty of controlling the development of new weapons. And without such control, disarmament schemes will be at the mercy of a technological breakthrough. Since each scientific discovery opens the way to innumerable other advances, it is next to impossible to define a meaningful point to "cut off" weapons development. At the beginning of the atomic age, a strict inspection system might have succeeded in stopping the elaboration of nuclear weapons. By 1952 it might still have been possible to "control" the development of thermonuclear weapons, albeit with great difficulty. For the hydrogen bomb developed so naturally out of research on nuclear weapons that the definition of a meaningful dividing line would have been exceedingly complicated. By 1957 the production of thermonuclear devices had so far outstripped any possible control machinery that the emphasis of disarmament negotiations turned from eliminating stockpiles to methods of restraining their use. And with the diffusion of nuclear technology among other powers, effective control of the development of nuclear weapons even by smaller states will be almost out of the question.

Moreover, once a weapon is developed, its applications are elaborated until ever wider realms of strategy become dependent on it. A nation may be willing to forego the offensive uses of nuclear weapons, but it will be most reluctant to give up its defensive applications in, for example, the form of antiaircraft or antimissile devices. But in advanced stages of their elaboration weapons find a dual purpose: the launching site for antiaircraft missiles can be used as well for attacking ground targets; a nuclear weapon launched from a plane against enemy bombers will be equally effective against enemy supply centers. Thus, weapons can be kept from being added to stockpiles only at their inception, when their implications are least understood. By the time their potential is realized, the possibility of preventing their addition to existing arsenals by means of inspection or control has usually disappeared. Hence it may already be too late to control missiles, many of which have entered production, with others soon to follow.

"Preventing" Surprise Attack

The difficulty of devising effective machinery to control the development of ever more destructive weapons has caused most disarmament negotiations since 1955 to concern themselves with means to prevent surprise attack. Since one of the causes for present tensions is the insecurity caused by the fear of imminent catastrophe, so the argument goes, an inspection system which would reduce the danger of surprise attack would also remove some of the urgency from international relationships. This reasoning produced President Eisenhower's proposal at the Geneva summit conference, in July 1955, to exchange military blueprints with the Soviet Union and to permit aerial reconnaissance of each other's territories.

It cannot be denied that the danger of surprise attack contributes to the tensions of the nuclear age even if it does not cause them. It is less clear, however, that inspection schemes so far proposed would add a great deal to existing warning methods and intelligence information or that they would significantly reduce the element of surprise.

The relative ineffectiveness of inspection in preventing surprise in an all-out war is due to the nature of strategic striking forces. Because it cannot afford to be caught on the ground, a strategic striking force must be prepared to attack from its training bases at a moment's notice. If properly prepared, it should require no noticeable mobilization to launch its blow. Since "normal" peacetime maneuvers of a strategic striking force should approximate as nearly as possible its behavior in case of emergency, an enemy should not be able to tell whether a given flight is a training mission or a surprise attack until his early-warning line is crossed. Unless most planes are grounded all the time, there is no guarantee that planes on so-called training missions will not be used for a surprise attack.

Even when all planes are grounded, the maximum warning achievable by inspection is the interval between the time when planes leave their bases and the time when they would have been detected by existing warning systems. With the present family of airplanes, an inspection system at best would add perhaps three hours' warning to the side which is being attacked. To be sure, three hours' additional warning is not negligible; it may indeed spell the difference between survival and catastrophe. But since the victim of aggression cannot be certain what the apparent violation of inspection signifies, he may have difficulty in utilizing the additional warning effectively. And if inspection is coupled with the grounding of the strategic striking force, the gain in warning time may be outweighed by the aggressor's knowledge of the opponent's deployment.

As the speed of planes is increased the warning time afforded by even a perfect inspection system, correctly interpreted, is progressively reduced. In the age of the intercontinental ballistic missile the maximum warning time, assuming perfect communication between the inspector and his government, would be thirty minutes, the period of time the missile would be in transit. In the age of the missile and the supersonic bomber, even a foolproof inspection system will tell the powers only what they already know: that the opponent possesses the capability of launching a devastating attack at a moment's notice and with a minimum of warning.

The proposals for inspection as a bar to surprise attack in fact reflect the thinking of a period when forces-in-being could not be decisive and when their power and speed were of a much lower order. As long as the forces-in-being were relatively cumbersome and had to be concentrated before an attack could be launched, the warning afforded by an inspection system might have been strategically significant. As late as 1946, had the Baruch Plan been accepted, a nation determined on nuclear war would have had to wait several months or even years after a violation until its stockpiles had been built up to respectable levels. The existence of a control system in such conditions afforded a breathing spell to all powers. With the power and speed of current weapons, however, even an airtight inspection system would not supply such guarantees. When wars can be fought by the forces-in-being and when striking forces are designed to be able to attack with no overt preparation, warning can be attained under optimum conditions only for the time the delivery vehicles, whether planes or missiles, are in transit.

It is, therefore, difficult to imagine that present vigilance could be reduced or that insecurity would be removed by any inspection system now in prospect. The machinery required would be so formidable and the benefits relatively so trivial that an inspection system may actually have pernicious consequences. It may give a misleading impression of security and, therefore, tempt us to relax our preparedness. More likely, given the prevailing distrust, it will induce both sides to place their striking forces in an even greater state of readiness in order to compensate for the loss of secrecy by a demonstration of power.

Indeed, unless designed with extraordinary care, a system of inspection may well make a tense situation even more explosive. The value of an inspection system depends not only on the collection but also on the interpretation of facts. But the information produced by inspection is of necessity fragmentary and it is likely to be most difficult to obtain when it is most needed, when international tensions are at their height. On the other hand, the only meaningful reaction to an apparent violation of the inspection system is to launch an immediate retaliatory attack, because negotiations or protests could not begin to be effective before the enemy force has reached its targets. The knowledge that all-out war is the sanction for seeming violations may well add to the tenseness of relationships. Instead of reducing the danger of all-out war, inspection systems may make more likely a showdown caused by a misunderstanding of the opponent's intentions.

The Chimera of an International Authority

The technical complexity of inspection and its futility in the present climate of distrust has induced some thoughtful individuals, appalled at the prospect of nuclear war, to advocate an international disarmament authority as the only solution. As long as both sides possess thermonuclear weapons and the means to deliver them, it is argued, a vicious spiral of constantly growing insecurity is inevitable. The only solution, this school of thought maintains, is the surrender of all strategic weapons to a world authority which would be the sole agency to possess heavy armaments and the means for delivering them. The disarmament executive should be composed of minor powers which are not part of the East-West struggle. With a preponderance of force, it could play the role of a world policeman and enforce peace if necessary. The United Nations Emergency Force for Egypt was greeted in some quarters as the forerunner of such an international agency.

The idea of escaping the tensions of international relations by an analogy to domestic police powers has come up repeatedly in the past and usually at periods when international schisms made it least realizable. It is true, as the advocates of the plan of world government contend, that the system of sovereign states produces international tensions because a sovereign will can be ultimately controlled only by superior force. But it is hardly realistic to expect sovereign nations, whose failure to agree on issues of much less importance has brought about the armaments race, to be able to agree on giving up their sovereignty. History offers few examples of sovereign states surrendering their sovereignty except to outside compulsion. To be sure, the lessons of history are no more conclusive than the unparalleled destructiveness of modern weapons; still, it is difficult to imagine any motive which could induce the Soviet Union to give up its thermonuclear stockpile to an international body. And the reaction of the United States Congress will hardly be more hospitable.

The various proposals for a world authority would, therefore, scarcely warrant extensive consideration were they not

such an excellent illustration of the prevailing notion that the
United Nations somehow has a reality beyond that of the
powers comprising it. It is a symptom of our legalistic bias that
so many consider a legal entity, the United Nations, as somehow transcending the collective will of its members. For as long
as the United Nations is composed of sovereign states it will
reflect the precise rivalries that animate these powers outside
that organization. To be sure, the United Nations offers a convenient forum for the settlement of disputes, and it can give
symbolic expression to world consensus on particular issues.
But the gap between the symbolic acts of the United Nations
and its willingness to run substantive risks is inherent in its
structure. The delegates represent not a popular constituency
but sovereign governments, and they vote not according to
their convictions but in pursuance of the instructions they receive. The effectiveness of the United Nations can be no
greater than the willingness of its component governments to
run risks. The United Nations Emergency Force would never
have entered Egypt had not both parties sought a device to
liquidate military operations. The United Nations Emergency
Force did not cause the cessation of the war; rather, it ratified
a decision already made. For this reason it does not offer a
particularly hopeful model for what will be the real security
problem of our period: the growing Soviet power coupled with
a refusal to yield to anything except superior force.

The argument that a supranational authority composed of
neutral minor powers will be able to resolve tensions which
have proved intractable to direct negotiations and that it can
be entrusted with the exclusive custody of weapons capable
of encompassing the destruction of humanity reflects two related beliefs: that the nature of aggression is always unambiguous and that weakness somehow guarantees responsibility
and perhaps even superior morality. But in the nuclear age,
recognizing aggression has proved as complicated as resisting
it. Were a supranational disarmament executive charged with
enforcing the peace, it is predictable that its major problem
would be to define a meaningful concept of aggression. It is
significant that in 1957 the United Nations had to give up a
prolonged effort to achieve such a definition.

Moreover, it would be difficult to find powers clearly recognized as neutral to act as custodians of the thermonuclear stockpile or with sufficient technical competence to administer it were they so recognized. And the very quality which would make powers acceptable as members of a disarmament authority—their neutrality—will reduce their willingness to run risks. In the face of a dispute between the United States and the U.S.S.R., these states will lack the power to impose their will or the will to use their power.

Nor is it clear why a monopoly of power in the hands of states dependent for equipment, training, and facilities on the two superpowers should bring about stability. It is not at all obvious that weakness guarantees responsibility or that powers which have difficulty playing a role in their own regions will be able to judge global problems with subtlety and discrimination. And this still overlooks the dilemmas of where to store the international stockpile of bombs, and where to locate the bases of the international air force—all of which will become matters of life and death to the nations of the world. In short, there is no escaping from the responsibilities of the thermonuclear age into a supranational authority, for, if all its complicated problems could be negotiated, the substantive issues now dividing the world would be soluble too.

24.   The Strategic Role of Civil Defense

by Rogers Cannell

A professional engineer, Mr. Cannell received his training in both mechanical and industrial engineering at Stanford University. During World War II he served as a captain of the Army Engineers in the Pacific. Since 1954 he has been a member of the Stanford Research Institute, where, as Manager of Industrial and Civil Defense Research, he has been most recently engaged in studies to develop nonmilitary-defense systems and programs for the survival and recovery of the nation following an attack.

Nonmilitary-defense programs have a key role in preventing a "cold war" from becoming a "hot war." The United States announced policy of nuclear retaliation in response to major aggression can hardly convince the Russians unless we are also capable of withstanding attack.

While deterrence can be the most desirable function of nonmilitary defense, an adequate program has other vital advantages even if the primary function fails and war does break out. Lifesaving protection is available to the bulk of the population, and a foundation for post-attack recovery is provided.

It is important to remember that nonmilitary actions may be defensive but they are not passive, not submissive. They can be a positive war-deterrent force, and they are a prerequisite to survival in any total-war situation.

This article was originally published in the Stanford Research Institute Journal, *Fourth Quarter 1959. Reprinted by permission.*

Nonmilitary Protection in Total War

Two of several possible situations illustrate the importance of nonmilitary defense in total war—one in which the United States is attacked first and the other in which we respond to an act of aggression with massive retaliation. The examples are chosen to show that even in the least destructive attack the nonmilitary-defense role is important.

Assume first that the Russians attack the United States but aim their weapons at our military bases and try to avoid our cities. With our present limited civil protection, we could lose about 25 per cent of our population just from fallout. On the other hand, should our damaged forces strike back, they would be assaulting an enemy whose population has been trained in civil defense and has adequate warning to evacuate and make fallout shelters.

A large portion (perhaps most) of the adult population of the Soviet Union participated not long ago in a compulsory nation-wide civil-defense course of twenty-two hours. It was to be followed by a fourteen-hour course. In addition, large civil-defense organizations are maintained on a local basis. These are trained in such activities as decontamination, shelter improvisation, and atomic-, biological-, and chemical-warfare protection. In 1958, Khrushchev claimed that 20 million people were trained in civil defense, a reference probably to the number in organized cadres. With Russian industry decentralized, with military targets empty of weapons and cities empty of people, we would have difficulty inflicting a serious blow with our second-strike forces.

Even if the Soviets purposely avoided wiping out our cities, our population losses would be greater than Russia's, principally because our population has virtually no protection. When metropolitan areas are targets, protection becomes even more of a necessity. In fact, it is the only way we can avoid giving enemy forces an insurmountable advantage if they strike first.

There is also the possibility that if Russia marched into western Europe and we followed our announced policy of mas-

sive retaliation, we would be the first to launch a nuclear attack. If our strategists thought we could achieve surprise, we
would probably aim at Soviet military bases. Russian civil defense could be effective against the fallout from such an attack, since their program emphasizes radiological protection.
In any event, the natural dispersion of Russian population centers and the fact that many of their military targets are far
from cities would keep Russian casualties to a smaller percentage. Any attack returned to the United States from Russia's damaged forces would probably be aimed at our cities
and industry, since our retaliatory bases would be empty. Under these circumstances, our chances of survival would depend
upon just how many of our people we could protect from the
attack by evacuation and hastily built fallout shelters. With
Americans inadequately informed or ill-prepared to react
properly in such a situation, it is questionable whether we
would dare to launch a massive retaliation considering the vulnerability of our people.

Shelter, then, is the central feature of nonmilitary protection, because it saves lives directly. Evacuation can also save
lives, but it is effective only with sufficient warning—and does
not eliminate the need for fallout shelter.

People have been led to believe that one nuclear weapon
could destroy an entire city, so they conclude that no type
of protection can be effective. Preoccupation with this notion
has obscured the truth: protective actions can be quite effective—not only at distances from a target city but also within it

The first need is protection from fallout. In many areas, existing structures would provide enough protection depending
on their construction and the radiation intensity. Fallout intensity is difficult to predict at any place; however, adequate
shelters should reduce exposure to radioactivity by a factor o
1000. This could be accomplished either by improving existing buildings or by building special shelters. Calculations fo
many possible attacks show that over one half of the United
States population would survive if they had fallout shelter
yet would die without it.

Fallout is not the only hazard, however. The immediat
weapon effects—heat, fire, blast force, and radiation from th
nuclear fireball itself—are the principal dangers in the area

near ground zero. Blast shelter would reduce the fatal areas of destruction for one weapon to one two-hundredth of the area that would be so affected if shelters were lacking. Studies of many possible attacks indicate that a program providing good blast shelters in urban areas plus fallout shelters in the rest of the nation could hold total casualties to less than 10 per cent of the population.

The Cost of Protection

The United States has the technical know-how to provide the protection needed to save 90 per cent of the population in nuclear war. In 1958 a report stated: "Postponement of basic shelter construction is not warranted in our judgment by any lack of essential technical knowledge."[1] It is significant that a government research program has carried us this far.

But authorities have expressed doubts about the economic feasibility of such a program. Studies at the Stanford Research Institute[2] have indicated that effective shelter systems can be designed for costs which are small in comparison with our present total defense budget.

This fact can be illustrated by three nonmilitary-defense programs. Each depends on a different shelter system: (1) maximum use of existing fallout shelter, (2) construction of special fallout shelters, and (3) construction of special blast shelters in metropolitan areas and fallout shelters in non-metropolitan areas. About one third of the cost of the first two programs and one half of the third is in shelter. The remainder is for warning, decontamination, monitoring, stockpiling of food and fuel, and so on. These programs cover the range between the lower and upper limits of complete programs for protection and recovery.

Program 1. Shelter in the first program fits the current government policy. The government is now urging the public to make maximum use of existing shelter—improving it where necessary—and to provide themselves with survival supplies. The average family investment would be about $200 and the cost to the government would be an additional $5.00 per family per year.

The government must act to make the individual's investment effective. For example, warning is essential, because
without it no one would enter a shelter. (We have warning
measures in most cities, but not in smaller communities, where
fallout shelters could be most effective.) Other neccessary activities include: survey and marking of existing shelter in large
buildings, monitoring of radiation hazards, public information,
and so on. The cost of these to the government would be about
a half billion dollars. If the program were completed in two
years, its annual cost to the government would be about $1.50
per person, contrasted with $230 per person for the present
military budget.

This program could—if there were substantial public response—add 20 to 30 million survivors over and above those
who would survive without it. For the next several years this
would be adequate effectiveness in an attack against military
targets—but not against major population centers. It would be
less than adequate in any attacks later on.

Program 2 would involve construction of special fallout shelters. In this case, the government would bear the cost of the
shelters and the emergency supplies in addition to the expense
of warning, monitoring, and the like. A program of this scope
would cost on the order of $5 billion per year if completed in
six years. This is equivalent to an annual cost of about $30 per
person.

This plan would not seriously compete with any military
program for manpower or resources. On the contrary, over
the past few years we have frequently had idle in the United
States sufficient plant and personnel to undertake it without
even pressing the economy (over 10 billion dollars' worth in
1958). This program could add 60 to 90 million survivors over
and above the number who would survive with no program.
It would provide adequate fallout protection in any attack on
the United States at least through the 1960s. However, in attacks against population centers this program could not prevent millions of blast casualties.

Program 3 would provide maximum shelter against immediate blast effects in metropolitan areas plus fallout shelter
elsewhere. If this program were to be completed in eight years
it would cost about $5 billion per year for the blast-shelter

portion of the program, but the fallout portion of the program would cost less because fallout shelters would no longer be needed in cities. The total annual cost would be $55 per person. This program would add approximately 80 million more survivors than would be saved by a fallout-shelter program in the case of a heavy attack against military and population targets.

The Objective of a Civil-Defense Program

The true value of any defense program lies in its contribution to national objectives. If total war should come, the survival of the people—and they are the nation—would be a primary objective. A program saving 20 million lives in target areas would be satisfactory if virtually the entire population survived. But even a program saving 20 million lives would not be satisfactory if virtually no one else survived. In the one case, the nation could achieve its objectives; in the other, it could not. What the nation is willing to spend on defense programs is an indication of how intent it is on achieving its objectives. At present, this nation is spending each year about 25 cents per person for nonmilitary defense—a rather low valuation of human life for a Western nation. Even a neutral country like Sweden spends about $4.00.

Civilization Can Recover

Many accept the idea that shelter can effectively reduce casualties but believe that survival in the post-attack environment would be impossible. They fear the invisible and mysterious atomic radiation and believe that recovery from the loss of a major portion of the nation would be impossible.

A radioactive environment will take its toll. This fact must not be minimized. But it is also important to know that its toll is not worse than a setback of only a few decades in medical history. Our lives would be as long as our grandfathers', and the proportion of stillborn children and child deformities should be no worse than thirty years ago. In fact, with our present state of medical knowledge the post-attack environment would be somewhat safer than the one most of us entered at birth.

History offers further evidence that a civilization can recover from a devastating war. Take, for example, the Thirty Years' War—an ideological conflict fought in central Europe in the first half of the seventeenth century. The loss of life due directly to the war has been placed by the lowest estimate at one third of the entire population of both Germany and Bohemia. Other estimates run as high as 80 per cent. The social effects were catastrophic—entire districts were turned into deserts, wolves ran in the streets of once populated cities, and cannibalism was widespread. Yet, in roughly fifty years, these areas had recovered in most respects. After a nuclear attack short in duration and starting from a much higher base of knowledge, recovery would be far easier for us. War must be prevented at any cost—and protection and preparation for recovery are part of that cost. But war is not the end of civilization. We must take every step we can now to accelerate the recovery process.

Recovery from Total War

The second task for nonmilitary defense in total war is recovery from attack—whether or not the war continues after bombs fall. The purposes of the recovery effort are to reestablish the nation's social structure and to get the economy back into business.

The first job would be to make available to the people the surviving resources—food, medical care, housing, and so forth —needed for their physical and mental well-being. Then, with the people cared for, the job is to control the investment of surplus manpower, materials, energy, and productive capability for repair and rebuilding. Effective central planning and control would be the key to the rate of recovery.

If attack is directed only against military bases, few cities are damaged and there is little permanent disruption of the social order or the economy. The net effect on the economy in nuclear war of this sort will be mainly a loss of production while fallout denies access to the facilities.

But if cities are targets, the post-attack situation will be vastly different. A segment of the social order will be destroyed, and a large percentage of the industrial plant will be lost. Such an attack would force the economy back to a more primitive form. In this case, the problem will be to redevelop a modern industrial society.

Historically, the growth of an industrial economy has depended on agriculture. Crops have fed more people than it took to raise them, leaving a manpower surplus for industry and services. Industrial recovery after any attack will depend first on adequate farm production. Analysis of the effects of many possible attacks has shown that the crop-producing facilities of this nation would survive well enough to permit a strong agriculture in the post-attack period. At least 30 per cent of our crop land should receive less than 100 roentgens per hour an hour after attack. This is sufficient land to meet our food requirements under any shelter program, and foods grown in soil with this level of contamination would be quite safe for human consumption. Enough farm machinery would be available to meet the need for ten to fifteen years after an attack, but the fuel for this equipment would be in question.

In addition, farm surpluses stored by the Commodity Credit Corporation and other food stockpiles would feed the population for at least two years. Even if petroleum to run farm machinery were in critically short supply after an attack, we would not need to take a crop from the land immediately.

A major obstacle in making use of the surpluses, however, would be their location. The stocks should be moved nearer population centers so they will not have to be hauled there in case of attack. This is just one of the many examples of the need for planning to speed recovery.

Besides agriculture, a strong economy would need transportation and power. Preliminary studies indicate that sufficient transportation equipment would survive to last many years. Dependent only on the availability of fuel, air transport could be back in operation immediately, railroads would be running within a few months, and trucks would operate in all local areas within six months after an attack. Electric-power-

generating plants should stand attack better than their consumers, and they are generally close to the demand. These
plants normally have on hand fuel for several months' operation. With a reduced load, these stocks should last many
months.

The immediate demand for fuel, then, would be for transportation. It could be provided by stockpiling of some fuel in
secure storage. Production could finally be resumed from continuing supplies of petroleum and by setting up distillation
units stockpiled before the attack.

Recovery also requires manpower—laborers as well as people with technical and managerial skills. With farming mechanized, a few people will still be able to produce food for
many. Accordingly, sufficient labor will be available to repair
and rebuild the country. A substantial number of technical
and managerial persons would also survive an attack on the
metropolitan areas of the country. They would provide a reservoir of leadership and know-how to rebuild a productive
society.

The people who would survive would have about a fourth
of the nation's industrial plant with which to start recovery;
that share is located in non-metropolitan areas and could be
recovered. In many instances the surviving plant would have
to convert to new products and use different materials, but
these changes are not impossible. Abandonment of "planned
obsolescence" and the use of salvaged materials would speed
the recovery process.

We have had examples of rapid recovery in the industrial
age. In World War II, the Soviet Union lost from its control
about 60 per cent of its coal, iron, steel, and aluminum production and up to 95 per cent of some key military production.
The problem was further complicated by the relocation of
much of the remaining plant. Yet, through all of this, Russia
was able to maintain some productivity and recover. With a
broader base of technical know-how, more plant intact, and
more material that could be saved, our problem would not
likely be as difficult as was Russia's.

The United States cannot be defended, much less be victorious against an attacker, with any strategy that does not include an effective nonmilitary program. Many so-called "im-

practical" protective measures do not become obsolete as quickly as complicated weapons systems. Furthermore, they *are* effective. Countless independently conducted studies, based on much more than mere arbitrary assumption, conclude that protective shelter can save many millions of American lives for a relatively low outlay of funds. Because it can, it should be an indispensable part of our country's policy of deterring an enemy attack.

Notes

1. *The Adequacy of Government Research Programs in Nonmilitary Defense*, by the Advisory Committee on Civil Defense of the National Academy of Sciences and the National Research Council.
2. For the Office of Civil and Defense Mobilization.

PART FIVE

PROBLEMS OF ECONOMIC STRATEGY

INTRODUCTION

The surge of science and technology confronts our generation with a vexing dilemma. Vast new wealth and resources have been unlocked, and powerful new forces have been harnessed. Yet, at the same time, the very burgeoning of this wealth across the globe and the changes which it has wrought in international society pose an ever increasing host of baffling questions.

What is the nature of the Soviet economic threat? What is the import of Soviet economic growth for United States policy? How are we to cope with this challenge, satisfy the rising demands of awaking peoples, shoulder the military burden, and preserve the health of our economy?

25. The Economic Threat of Soviet Imperialism

by Lieutenant General Arthur G. Trudeau, U.S.A.

General Trudeau graduated from the United States Military Academy in 1924, later receiving an M.S. in civil engineering from the University of California. His military career has marked him as a highly efficient combat commander, staff officer, and lecturer. He saw service in Europe and the Pacific in World War II and later in the Korean War. In 1958 he became Chief of Research and Development, Department of the Army. General Trudeau lectured at the first National Strategy Seminar for Reserve Officers.

It is a truism that the capacity of any nation to carry out its national objectives is based not only on its national will and military strength but on the strength, balance, and flexibility of its economy. The Soviets early recognized this principle. Lenin proclaimed it in his report to the Eighth Congress of the Soviets in 1919:

> *Communism is the Soviet power plus electrification of the whole country. . . . We are weaker than capitalism, not only in the world scene but within the country. . . . Only when the country has been electrified, when industry, agriculture, and transport have been placed on a technical basis of large-scale industry, only then shall we be finally victorious.*

When we look at the Soviet economy today, we see that Lenin's goal has been attained. The U.S.S.R. is the world's second-largest industrial power today. Its gross national product is over two fifths that of the United States and has been growing at a rate more than twice that of the United States. Undoubtedly this last statistic prompted Khrushchev to make the ominous statement: "We will bury you." When questioned about this remark during his 1959 visit to the United States, he blandly remarked that he did not mean burial by war but "only by economic competition." It will be shown later that "only by economic competition," in the Communist parlance, means that if the present rates of industrial growth remain unchanged, the U.S.S.R. will surpass the United States before the turn of the century. Khrushchev boasts of accomplishing this in a much shorter time.

A comparison of the two economies as they exist today is not reassuring. The U.S.S.R. and other Communist-bloc economies are expanding at a much faster rate than those of most of the Free World. Moreover, our potential enemy is devoting a substantially larger portion of his economy both to armament and to the rapid expansion of his industrial base. He is able to do this by denying consumer goods to his people and imposing upon them a spartan standard of living.

Steel and Petroleum Production

A comparison of the industrial strength of the U.S.S.R. and the United States might focus on two primary items: steel and petroleum.

American steel production during 1959 totaled over 100 million metric tons. During the same period, the steel production of the entire Soviet bloc amounted to almost 80 million metric tons. Of this, the U.S.S.R. accounted for 60 million tons, the eastern European satellites for 20 million. These figures do not include the small Chinese production, although recent reports indicate substantial increases in Communist China's output.

In 1940, before the U.S.S.R. entered the war, she was producing 18 million tons of steel. A large part of the steel capacity was lost as a result of the German invasion; only 9 million tons annually were produced in 1943 and 1944. Of this annual output, about 6 million tons were devoted to direct military production, including production of 30,000 tanks and

80,000 pieces of artillery per year. Of course, the United States was then pouring tremendous quantities of steel in the form of trucks and weapons into the U.S.S.R.; nevertheless, the above figures reflect the reasonably small amount of steel needed by the Soviets for military production. As a matter of comparison, the United States produced 20 million tons of ships during World War II, and in 1944 our military requirements for steel alone totaled 27 million tons.

The experience of Germany and Japan in World War II reveals that the steel production of these two countries, although low by U.S. standards, was not a limiting factor in their armament production. Germany fought the war with an average annual production of 20 million tons, and Japan with only 5 million tons. After all, one million tons of steel can turn out 25,000 tanks, or more than our entire Army and Marine Corps possess today. In terms of comparative military potential, therefore, the present disparity between American and Russian steel production is misleading.

If the Soviet military machine faces any shortage in the event of war, it is probably in petroleum, especially jet fuel. This is one of the factors impelling Soviet expansion into the Middle East. Nonetheless, the Soviet Union now has access to over 140 million tons of petroleum per year—a figure which includes eastern European satellite production. Significantly, this represents an increase of 80 per cent in the last four years, and current Soviet petroleum exports, while limited, indicate that the Soviets have largely solved this shortage.

At the start of World War II the Soviets were producing only 31 million tons of petroleum annually, or less than a third the present amount. Production fell to 17 million tons at the height of World War II, but even this amount almost sufficed to meet the wartime needs of the Soviets. Increased mechanization of the Army and more aircraft have stepped up current Soviet war requirements. Meanwhile, petroleum production is one of the fastest growing industries in the Soviet bloc, and oil production has more than kept pace with Soviet requirements.

The threat to the Western oil supply from the Middle East inherent in the unrest in the Arab world and the vulnerability of the Suez Canal and the pipelines traversing Syria is the most critical danger confronting the economy of the Free World today. It is still valid to assert that whoever controls the oil of the Middle East controls the economy and hence the industrial and political complex of western Europe. The flow of oil from Africa will materially change this situation by 1970. In the meantime, however, control of the area within a thousand-mile radius of Cairo will remain the key to control of most of the Eastern Hemisphere.

The Soviet Labor Force

Let us turn to another vital cog of the Soviet economy—its labor force. The total Soviet labor force numbers roughly 100 million, as compared with approximately 70 million for the United States. Yet, while our total labor force is much less than that of the Soviets, our industrial labor force is 20 per cent larger than theirs. The reason is that only 6 million Americans are employed in agriculture, whereas in the U.S.S.R. 48 million peasants till the soil. While one Russian peasant supports five persons with his produce, one farmer in the United States feeds twenty-eight Americans. By a similar comparison, it is apparent that American industry is still at least twice as efficient as Soviet industry today.

So far, the comparison between our economy and that of the Soviets appears extremely favorable to us. We produce more than they do, both on the farm and in the factory, with a smaller but more effective labor force. There are two danger signs, however. First, as has been noted, the economy of the U.S.S.R. is growing at a faster rate than ours. A major reason for this is that the Soviet Government channels an inordinately large portion of its production effort into capital goods at the expense of consumer goods. The Soviet and satellite peoples are denied food, clothing, and housing in order to produce more factory buildings and machine tools—the means of further industrial production.

A second danger sign is that the U.S.S.R. habitually devotes a greater percentage of its gross national product to both investment and armament than we do. In 1959, the Soviets devoted more than 15 per cent of their gross national produc to their military establishment while we spent less than 9 per cent of our GNP for this purpose. The Soviets invested about 25 per cent of their income in expansion while we invested less than 20 per cent. Consumer goods accounted for about 70 per cent of our GNP, but only somewhat more than 50 per cent of the Soviet GNP was allocated for this purpose. It is difficult to compare price structures, but a single illustration bears out the disproportionately meager emphasis given to consumer production in the Soviet Union. In Russia, a tank costs the equivalent of at least 2000 pairs of shoes; in the United States, by contrast, a tank costs at least 10,000 pairs of comparable quality.

The Soviet Industrial Surge

A comparison of Soviet and U.S. industrial production from 1895 to date brings to light some interesting facts. United States industry has grown at a rather steady rate, with short-term upward surges occasioned by war or booms and short-term depressions, which in the case of the 1929–32 crash was severe.

In Russia, substantial industrial progress was made in the period between 1890 and World War I. This period witnessed the emergence of the industrial proletariat—a class of workers which the Bolsheviks roused in revolt against the Czar. During the period of World War I through the Revolution, production dropped to a negligible amount. The period 1921–27 featured a high growth rate, which is deceptive in that the Bolsheviks started from "scratch" and simply put war-damaged plants back into operation. From 1928, when the first Five-Year Plan went into effect, real progress was made to the extent of an average annual growth rate of 11 per cent up until 1940. The German invasion in 1941 caused a setback, for much of Russia's main industrial centers were overrun by the Wehrmacht. The period 1944–45 shows an over-all dip due to the difficulties of reconverting and relocating industries, although steel and some other basic industries actually raised their production. From 1948 to 1955, however, production regained its high prewar average annual growth rate of 11 per cent, tapering off toward the end of the period. It is believed that this high growth rate will level off at 8 to 9 per cent annually during the coming years, but the rate of industrial growth will probably continue to be at least double that of the United States. Even in periods of high prosperity, our growth rate seldom approaches 5 per cent. Today, the rate is considerably slower.

At these comparative rates—say, 4 per cent compared with 8 per cent—the U.S.S.R. could match the United States in industrial production by 1990, or at least by the turn of the century. This is only thirty to forty years hence—a relatively brief span in the lifetime of a nation. It would be disastrous if we fail to plan ahead or if we lack the foresight and initiative to take dynamic measures to insure our security and the advancement of our way of life.

Comparative Trade Positions

A comparison of the Soviet economy with ours must take into account also a study of access to the world's markets and to the raw materials which feed production. Although the United States contains within its continental boundaries an abundance of certain natural resources, it lacks, either entirely or in part, sufficient quantities of more than fifty critical materials to satisfy our current industrial needs. Examples are manganese, tin, chromite, bauxite, mica, rubber, cobalt, and niobium. The Soviets, by contrast, are self-sufficient in most raw materials required by modern industry. Moreover, the Soviet bloc includes vast stretches of comparatively or completely unexplored territory which will undoubtedly yield untold wealth in coal, iron, oil, and other minerals yet untapped. The United States has been explored to a much greater extent, and it is doubtful that we possess natural resources in substantial excess of those already discovered.

An important underpinning of the Communist bloc's economy is intra-bloc trade. The percentages of trade conducted, during the period 1936–38, among the countries which constitute today the Communist bloc were small: 17 per cent for the satellites and only 5 per cent for China, the bulk of their commerce being conducted with the Western world. Today the picture has changed drastically. The satellites now carry on 75 per cent of their external trade with Communist-bloc members, and China conducts 80 per cent of its trade with Communist nations, with only a dribble to nations in the Free World.

The degree of actual Soviet control over China's economy —as well as Soviet political control of China—is a subject of much dispute among experts. However, the two nations can be expected for some time to provide as solid a front against the Free World in the economic arena as they do in the political and ideological fields. If further Communist intrusion into the Free World is prevented, however, the future fate of this alliance is highly problematical, to say the least.

The relationship between the U.S.S.R. and the satellites is clearer. The U.S.S.R. dominates her satellites economically as well as politically and has integrated their economies into its own. For this reason, the contribution made to the Soviet economy by the addition of the satellites is particularly pertinent to any analysis of U.S.S.R. economic strength.

It is estimated that the satellite economies combined equal about one third that of the Soviet Union and, by order, they are complementary to it. It is noteworthy, however, that the rate of growth of satellite production in coal, electric power, steel, petroleum, and aluminum during the last three years has been less than that in the U.S.S.R. itself. It is quite likely that this lag has been due to disruptions in satellite economies caused by resistance to intrinsically harmful Soviet economic policies.

Meanwhile, the U.S.S.R. steadily increases its efforts to woo the uncommitted and economically underdeveloped nations of the world with real or promised economic assistance. As of December 1959, the Soviet bloc had extended $3.2 billion worth of credit to these nations. Of this sum, about $800 million was for military equipment ($315 million for Egypt, $132 million for Syria, and the balance for Afghanistan, Indonesia, and Yemen). Trade between the Soviet bloc and the underdeveloped countries also has increased markedly. In 1957 this trade was more than 50 per cent greater than in 1955.

Economics as a Controlled Soviet Weapon

When we realize that slightly more than one third of the world lives under the hammer of communism, we begin to gain some appreciation of the Communist economic threat. Production and trade within the Communist bloc, unlike that within competitive Free World markets, is manipulated and controlled for political as well as economic purposes. No competition injurious to bloc objectives is permitted to exist. The Communists can destroy the Free World through military means; they can destroy it more slowly but no less surely by gradual seizure of world markets and the sources of raw materials. Unless the Free World rises to the challenge the time may come when the Communist businessman and banker may exert such control over international trade that they can, in effect, say to the still uncommitted nations of the world: "Comrades, you can either join us or be destroyed. The game is open, but the play for trade in our sphere of influence is now four dollars to the ruble and no longer four rubles to the dollar." Imagine the pressures on those nations of the world who are committed to freedom but must trade in order to survive. Imagine the dilemma faced by a nation like Japan if more of its natural markets and sources of raw materials should fall under the Communist sway.

Congressional testimony before the Joint Economic Committee has emphasized this point of control over a command economy. It was reported: "While there may be economic motivation underlying the expansion of Soviet trade, it is undoubtedly entwined with political considerations. Centralized control makes trade more readily subject to manipulation. Friends can be rewarded and enemies punished by shifts in the trade pattern. The Soviet Union has demonstrated that it can turn trade on (Iceland, Burma, Egypt) or off (Israel, Yugoslavia, Japan) at the spur of the moment. One can fear that this increase in the Soviet capabilities has created a greater capacity to disrupt world markets, as happened recently in the case of tin and a few other incidents."

If we acknowledge and understand the facts of economic

life today as they exist in our bipolar world, we can only sense that something must be done by the United States, and done soon. Over the next few decades, the economic race between the two opposing economies may prove to be more decisive than the armaments race. It is with these thoughts in mind that we must consider some of the requirements for a positive American economic policy that will insure dynamic growth.

The Gross-National-Product—Debt Ratio

The first area of interest in our own economy is the relationship between our gross national product and our national debt. One often hears the statement that we cannot afford the current expenditures to support both our national and international commitments when our national debt is so high. We hear the warning that we can spend ourselves into economic ruin. Certainly we are keenly conscious of the need to maintain a healthy national economy. We realize that more than the prosperity and happiness of our people are at stake. It is hardly necessary to explain that a strong American economy is *the* indispensable Free World bulwark against communism. But are we spending too much today in comparison with our income? And just what is the comparison between the gross national product and the national debt? This ratio is the most valid and meaningful measurement of the strength of our economy.

There are some interesting statistics on this matter. In 1940 the GNP was twice as great as the debt; in 1945 it was only eight tenths of the debt; in 1949 the GNP and the debt were about equal. Since then the GNP has increased, until in 1958 it was one and a half times the national debt. Although the national debt has risen since then by about 15 billion dollars, our GNP has increased by more than 40 billion dollars. President Truman's prediction, more than ten years ago, that the GNP would reach 500 billion dollars by 1960 will be realized.

An interesting historical parallel was the GNP-debt ratio in Great Britain in 1815. In that year, after the British had spent the preceding two decades fighting Napoleon and had been at war during most of the eighteenth century, the GNP was only six tenths of their national debt—an "imbalance" much worse than any we have ever known.

World leadership, then, may become as expensive today as it was in 1815. Yet we must be willing to spend whatever is necessary to insure our survival. And there are ways of doing this while still significantly increasing the value of the gross national product and without significantly increasing the national debt.

Increasing Our Growth Rate

The U.S.S.R. aims at an economic growth rate of about 8 per cent annually in its new Seven-Year Plan, and it has exceeded this pace for the last ten years. The most optimistic estimates call for an American growth rate of 5 per cent over the next few years; in recent years it has been less than 2 per cent. The Russians—and the Chinese Communists as well—are working harder and with a greater sense of direction than we are, and are devoting a far larger proportion of their output to national strength. It is indispensable to our economy that we increase our growth rate to upward of 5 per cent so that the needs of an increasing urbanized population are met and an adequate national defense can be provided.

One method to make possible a meaningful increase in the GNP would be to use existing American plants at full capacity, rather than at the three-fourths capacity at which they are generally operating today. This would permit an increase in the resources that we are using for national purposes and putting into competition in foreign trade without lowering our standard of living. Our economy has not yet begun to test its full strength. In order that it may do so, there must be a strong stimulus to expand the rate of growth—a stimulus in the form of expanding markets and lower unit prices.

Pressing Our Economic Advantages

One of the greatest possessions of America is its system of private capital and free competitive enterprise. The dynamic, kaleidoscopic nature of our kind of capitalism, if we are determined to preserve and extend it, cannot be matched in the long run by a system which delegates exclusive responsibility for creative, progressive thinking and execution to one management team for each product line. What is almost completely lacking in the Russian system is entrepreneurial opportunity and incentive. There being but one entrepreneur, the state, the urge and opportunity for the individual to venture, to invest, and to create new enterprises are almost entirely lacking. Therefore, we must maintain and strengthen the array of incentives—worker incentives, manager incentives, and entrepreneurial incentives—which has built and sustained our economy.

As our population grows and our natural resources become depleted, we are becoming increasingly dependent on foreign trade, including imports of raw materials. What is more, our continued growth may not be possible unless it is matched by similar advances in the remainder of the Free World.

Our general policy should seek to create the kind of healthy world economy into which the European Common Market and similar regional undertakings can fit and within which they can grow to full maturity. There should be enhanced opportunity for direct private investment to create, in time, increased demand for our goods and further outlets for capital investment. We should give needed assistance, accompanied by thoughtful counsel, to the underdeveloped countries and their two billion people. These peoples—diseased, undernourished, illiterate, impoverished, in many cases living in overpopulated areas—are caught in the sweep of a gigantic revolution. They share a common awareness of their problems and a passionate conviction that they can bridge the gap between their living standards and those of the West. In the interests of peace and stability, their transition must be a slow and gradual one.

If we accept assistance to the development of these areas as an enduring phase of our foreign policy, then certain decisions must be taken. First, we must encourage private investment and protect it with adequate guarantees against expropriation or war. Next, we must emphasize long-term commitments and, where feasible, liberal term loans rather than grants. Third, over-all economic planning for any country must be addressed to the objectives of progress and sta-

bility. Efforts must be concentrated initially on those undertakings where private investment is least likely to be attracted
or is unavailable.

Much of the answer to Russia's challenge is to be found in
bolstering our own economy and those of our allies by encouraging a high level of multilateral trade and Free World
co-operation. We must embrace an economic policy that is
fully integrated into our national strategy—one that serves our
over-all interests and objectives. It should support a free and
expanding world economy and not be encumbered by vested
interests, crash programs, and negative or impracticable solutions.

Whether we are formulating a policy toward Europe's Common Market, extending technical assistance to southeast Asia,
disposing of surplus wheat, or fixing the tariff on Japanese
textiles, our decisions should be aimed at promoting a broad
framework of multilateral co-operation. This implies a recognition on our part that we can continue to grow and prosper
and maintain our strength relative to the U.S.S.R. only if the
remainder of the Free World keeps pace.

26. Soviet Economic Growth and United States Policy

by Howard C. Petersen

President of the Fidelity-Philadelphia Trust Company, Mr. Petersen has served the nation in many capacities since the beginning of World War II. He received his B.A. degree from DePauw University and a law degree from the University of Michigan. In 1941 he became Assistant to the Undersecretary of War, then Special Assistant to the Secretary. From 1945 to 1947, as Assistant Secretary of War, he supervised the Army's military-government activities in Europe, Japan, and Korea, representing the Army in all foreign politico-military matters in the State Department. He has been a member of the Subcommittee on Economic Policies for National Security and of the Committee for Economic Development.

The following analysis of the size and growth of the Soviet economy in relation to our own is based on three major assumptions.

The first assumption is that at the start of the 1960s the total gross national product of Russia is at least two fifths that of the United States and its per capita output at least one third of ours, but not much more.

The second assumption is that the yearly percentage increase in Russian gross national product during the past decade has significantly exceeded that of the United States. In

This selection consists of excerpts from a report prepared by the Committee for Economic Development in 1959 for the Joint Economic Committee of Congress.

this period the Russian growth rate may have been 6 or 7 per cent a year. By contrast, our average long-term rate, in which there is no clear evidence of change, has been about 3 per cent. If that figure is used as measuring our current trend, the average absolute yearly increase in total Russian gross national product is less than that in ours but is approaching it and, if recent growth rates continue, may soon exceed it. On the basis of the same estimates, the absolute yearly increase in Russian per capita gross national product already is larger than ours.

The third assumption is that the difference between the growth rates of the two countries cannot be extrapolated into the distant future. It is easy enough to show arithmetically that if one country maintains a higher growth rate than another, eventually it will reach and surpass it. If the Soviet gross national product is now two fifths as large as ours, and if the Russians maintain a growth rate one percentage point above ours—say, 4 per cent as against 3—their gross national product will match ours in 93 years. If the difference is two percentage points, it will take 47 years; if three percentage points, 31 years; and if four percentage points, 24 years. Such calculations are startling but provide an inadequate basis for present policy. While economic growth results from a complex of influences, the exceptional height of the Soviet growth rate, if it really exists, is evidently made possible, in the main, by five forces. These are:

1. Russia has devoted a large proportion of her output to investment. On a comparable basis, gross investment in real assets, public and private, represents perhaps 25 per cent of gross national product in Russia and 20 per cent in the United States. The difference in net investment rates is larger.

2. The Soviet authorities have been able to control demand patterns in a way that has diverted production and supporting investment from activities where the value of output per employee is low, calculated on the basis of controlled internal relative prices, to activities where it is high.

3. The Russians have experienced a large expansion of the nonagricultural labor force, based on the shift of workers from agriculture.

4. Russia has experienced the large gains made possible by

the spread of a basic education among a previously largely illiterate population and the initial training of a quickly expanding industrial labor force.

5. Russia has had opportunities to increase productivity greatly by the introduction of techniques already prevalent in Western countries and, increasingly, in the technologically advanced sectors of the Soviet economy. This is probably the most important element of all in making possible her large output advances.

These advantages are not, of course, unique with Russia; they are at least potentially available in varying degrees to all but the most advanced countries. Unlike most other countries, however, Russia has had an all-powerful centralized authority with the drive to take full advantage of them to push growth regardless of the present sacrifice imposed upon her population.

Can Russia's high growth rate be maintained? Despite internal pressure for better living conditions, Russia may continue indefinitely to devote the present high proportion of gross national product to investment. This would permit consumption to expand in proportion to gross national product, which may be sufficient to satisfy her population. But the other four elements permitting exceptionally rapid growth are essentially transitional advantages which will become of decreasing importance as the stage of development of the Russian economy becomes more similar to ours. As the differential in the level of output is reduced, it is likely that the differential in growth rates will also narrow. The realistic expectation as of the present time is that our relative advantage over the Russians will continue to diminish, but at a slackening rate.

If we compare the output of the NATO alliance as a whole with that of the European Communist-bloc countries as a whole, the comparison with respect both to present level and to growth appears more favorable to us. Some of the western European countries have been growing about as fast as Russia, and the total economic potential of our NATO allies greatly exceeds that of the European satellites.

Ways in Which Soviet Economic Expansion
May Affect Us

The relative size and growth of the Soviet and American economies may affect the Soviet threat to us in a number of ways. Among the principal points of possible impact are: (1) the ability to bear the burden of military programs and to progress in military strength; (2) aid and trade with the underdeveloped world; (3) the Soviet ability to conduct an offensive economic policy against the United States and other industrial countries and our ability to withstand or retaliate; (4) the attitudes of the "neutrals," mainly underdeveloped countries; (5) the attitudes of the U.S. population and government; (6) the attitudes of our allies; (7) the attitudes of the Soviet satellites; and (8) the internal Russian political situation and the international objectives of Soviet policy.

The prospect of faster economic growth in the Soviet Union than in the United States probably is adverse to our position in almost all of these areas. Nonetheless, it does not seem likely to be the decisive factor in the outcome of the East-West struggle, provided that our own performance is at least as satisfactory as in the past.

Military Strength

The larger a country's national income, the smaller is the burden of financing military expenditures at any stated level. Economic growth clearly increases the size of the military program which a nation can support. Among countries with at all comparable resources, however, differences in actual military strength are much more closely related to their appraisals of need and willingness to sacrifice than to rates of economic growth or absolute limits imposed by the size of their economies. If we were devoting the same proportion of gross national product to national security as in fiscal year 1953, as we would be if defense expenditures had kept pace with economic growth over the intervening period, we would now be spending $66 billion a year for national defense instead of $46 billion. Were our government convinced that it was necessary, we could and would spend a good deal more than that.

Despite a much smaller economy and a larger population to support, the Soviet Union maintains a powerful and diversified military machine sufficient to provide approximate military parity with the United States. She does so by devoting a larger portion of her gross national product to this purpose than we do, by eliminating features that add more to the comfort and safety of her armed forces than to their striking power, and by paying her armed forces a great deal less than we do, as well as by less obvious means.

Clearly the size and rate of growth of the United States and Soviet economies, though important variables, are not the decisive ones in determining the relative military strength of the two countries.

Aid and Trade with Underdeveloped Countries

Soviet aid has very largely taken the form of loans at rather low interest rates. Whether, and under what conditions, Soviet loans to underdeveloped countries outside the bloc are adverse to our interests is itself a complicated question. If Soviet loans actually contribute to economic progress in these nations, which certainly is an objective of our own policy, they may even be in our long-term interest. In any case, even more than that of military programs, the scope and character of economic aid to underdeveloped free nations will be determined by considerations other than the capacity to provide aid. In neither Russia nor the United States does such assistance amount to more than a fraction of 1 per cent of gross national product or to any considerable proportion of defense spending. Heavy concentration on aid requiring use of a particular type of facility, such as the provision of steel mills, might well tax Russian capacity at present. But this is a matter of foresight in arranging for expansion of specialized capacity in such areas or in scheduling aid programs rather than of general economic growth.

Trade of most underdeveloped free countries with the Soviet

Union is presently trivial in comparison with their trade with the West. Russia accounts (based on 1956 data) for more than 10 per cent of imports only in Afghanistan and Yugoslavia, and of exports only in these two countries and Iran. Measurement by trade with the bloc as a whole would add only four other countries to such a list. Soviet trade is small primarily because Russia has followed a policy of extreme autarchy. The Russian policy of self-sufficiency has been relaxed in recent years, but only slightly insofar as countries outside the bloc are concerned. If Russian trade with most countries were doubled or tripled as a result of Soviet economic growth, it would still be tiny in comparison with their trade with the West. The volume of Russia's future trade, conducted for ordinary commercial purposes, will depend far more on her trade policy than on her rate of economic growth.

Most underdeveloped nations are greatly dependent on the export of one to three raw materials. A sharp drop in the volume or price of exports of these commodities has catastrophic consequences for these countries' balance of payments and hence for their development programs. In the past few years, Russia has stepped in with offers to buy whenever such situations have developed. In some well-publicized cases these commodities have reappeared in markets outside Russia to compete in the original exporter's usual markets, and the transaction has neither helped the underdeveloped nation nor earned good will for the Soviets. It is evident, however, that real opportunity exists for Russia to advance her influence by buying raw materials in depressed markets in good faith. Consumer commodities like coffee and fish can be offered to Russian consumers. Industrial raw materials can either be permitted to replace Russian production or, if she is unwilling to relax her policy of self-sufficiency, stockpiled or destroyed. Only in the last case is any real cost imposed upon the Russian economy by this type of purchasing; it then becomes, in effect, a form of aid.

Russian growth will contribute to Russia's ability to expand trade on a commercial basis. It may result in a wider variety and better quality of goods offered for export. It will increase her ability to absorb imports. It will increase her economic capacity to provide aid through purchase of unwanted commodities, just as in other forms. But the future course of all forms of Russian trade with underdeveloped countries will be determined much more by her policy decisions than by the rate of her economic growth.

The larger the Russian economy, the greater will be her ability to incur the costs of a policy of economic warfare against the United States and other industrial nations. This might involve dumping commodities to disrupt Western markets, preclusive buying of commodities in short supply, and possibly attempts at manipulation of foreign currencies. But there is little evidence of any deliberate Russian policy to engage in such activities. Such practices would necessarily involve costs to her. In fact, the aggressor in this type of warfare usually is not likely to inflict as much loss on an opponent as he himself incurs. Moreover, defensive steps are possible. This writer does not see strengthening of Russia's capacity to engage in this kind of activity as an important consequence of her higher growth rate.

Attitudes of Peoples Throughout the World

A situation in which the Soviet economy is generally recognized to be growing faster than ours, not only in percentages but also absolutely, not in spurts but steadily, and is approaching ours in total size, could, it may be supposed, greatly affect the attitudes of peoples throughout the world. It might greatly strengthen the confidence of the Russians in their own system, strengthen the dependence of their satellites upon them, increase the attraction of the Communist system for the independent, underdeveloped countries, make our allies apprehensive of their reliance upon us, and weaken our own morale. Yet, all of these things are either unlikely to occur as a result of comparative U.S.-Russian growth rates or unlikely to be important to our position.

Consider the underdeveloped nations of the Free World that are either emerging into a phase of sustained economic growth or hoping to do so. Their success is of the utmost importance to us. If they achieve vigorous growth and visibly rising living standards, they are not likely voluntarily to aban-

don freedom for communism; if they do so, it will be for other
reasons, such as the inability of the masses to eliminate by
other means an unacceptable distribution of income or system
of land tenure. If their plans for economic development are
badly disappointed, they will, indeed, consider the Communist
alternative. But they are more likely to compare their experiences with that of China, Mongolia, North Korea, or North
Vietnam than with that of Russia or the European satellites.
Insofar as third-party comparisons are made at all, a comparison of the growth rates of India and China, the largest underdeveloped countries of the Free and Communist worlds, is
likely to seem more relevant than that of Russia and the United
States.

It is the effect upon Russian attitudes that is most open to
question. Surely, the Russians may be expected to take pride
in their progress and to exult if they ever succeed in their goal
of overhauling us in what they view as an economic race. But
it is hard to see how the Soviet leaders could become more
implacable enemies of the Western democracies than they
have been in the past. And it is hard to see why their own
success should increase hostility toward us among the Russian
people.

On the other hand, there is at least reason to hope that rising living standards will lead to humanizing political and economic changes within the Soviet society, the emergence of a
different type of leadership, and a less truculent attitude toward the outside world. This must, indeed, be our principal
hope for a more assured peace in some future period. But this
hopeful prospect is far too hypothetical to permit us to rest
policy upon it now.

Implication for U.S. Policy

The rise of Russian economic power is one of the great developments of world history. It was probably inevitable regardless of the form of Russian government. It is important
that we understand it and that the peoples of the world understand it and place it in its proper perspective.

Our reaction should not be one of amazement or despair.

What Russia is doing other nations have done, though other nations have done it with less feverish haste and far less human cost. Our reaction should not be to attempt to match the present Russian growth rate simply because the Russian rate is higher than ours.

In general, there are four broad types of action we might consider to accelerate our own rate of growth.

First, we can try to reduce involuntary unemployment of resources, especially to minimize the depth and duration of recessions.

Second, we can try to make our economic system work more smoothly so as to get more real product from the resources now going into production. We can try to make our system more competitive and remove public and private impediments to the mobility of resources and to the introduction of improved techniques. We can reduce barriers to trade. We can re-examine our tax structure with a view to improving incentives and reconsider various governmental subsidies and price supports.

These are desirable things to do. In our own interest we should try to reduce unemployment and increase the efficiency with which we use resources regardless of the Russian threat. But the reduction of unemployment and elimination of most of the barriers to efficiency we can readily think of would mainly provide one-time gains. They would yield a limited nonrecurrent increase in output but not an increase in the rate of growth. Nonrecurrent gains, though well worth while, will not go far toward matching the Russian growth rate.

The third possibility, then, is to increase the amount of work done in our society. In the past, average annual hours of work have declined about one half per cent a year. If we stopped this reduction now, we might thereby hope to add to our past growth rate about one half per cent a year, on the very favorable assumption that none of the past increase in output per man-hour was the result of shortening hours. The other possibility of increasing total man-hours is through faster expansion of the labor force, but the possibilities for cumulative effects here, except by affecting the size of the total population, appear much smaller.

Fourth, we can increase the rate of economic growth by devoting more of our output to uses that promote growth.

More investment, more research, more education, are needed for growth, but they are needed just to sustain the rate of growth we have been getting. We have achieved an average growth rate of 3 per cent per annum over the past fifty or seventy-five years by increasing our annual devotion of resources to investment, research, and education. In order to increase the rate of growth, it is not sufficient just to increase these things; it is necessary to increase the rate of increase.

The amounts of increase in the rates of savings, investment, education, and research needed to get any given increase in the rate of growth are literally unknown. There is great need for much more information before we can talk sense about this subject. Some crude calculations of what might be necessary give staggering results. They suggest that we have to find out not whether it would take $3 billion or $5 billion or even $10 billion more a year of investment, research, and education to get our growth rate up from 3 per cent to 5 per cent, but whether it would not take something like $75 billion a year.

Suppose the 3 per cent growth rate results from an annual increase in the labor force of 1 per cent a year and an annual increase in output per worker of 2 per cent a year. Unless we speed up the increase in the labor force, to raise the 3 per cent growth rate to 5 per cent would require the annual increase in output per worker to be raised from 2 to 4 per cent —that is, to be doubled.

To obtain the present increase in productivity, we are spending something like $75 billion a year, or 15 per cent of our total output at high employment, on net investment in productive assets, public and private, on education, and on relevant research. The simplest estimate is that to double the increase in output per worker we would have to double these expenditures to $150 billion a year, or 30 per cent of our output. An increase of $75 billion in these private and public outlays implies, of course, a corresponding increase of $75 billion a year in the sum of the nation's savings and tax payments. To get a simultaneous increase in taxes and savings on such a scale without seriously impairing incentives important to growth would clearly be extremely difficult.

These figures may be debatable, but the main point is that the requirements for an increase in the rate of economic growth, say from 3 per cent to 5 per cent—which still would not equal the present Russian rate—may be very large, much larger than seems to be contemplated in current discussion.

There is no reason to think that the United States is exempt from the law that we are preaching to underdeveloped countries all over the world—that more growth in per capita income requires more savings and more investment in productive facilities, education, and research. And there is no reason to presume that the proportionate increase required is smaller than the proportionate increase in the growth rate desired. In fact, this assumption is in all probability overoptimistic, since it is not likely that an increase in growth-supporting expenditures will yield a fully proportionate return.

To increase the long-term growth rate by one or two percentage points is a formidable undertaking, requiring some really basic changes. It probably can be done, if this is accepted as a sufficiently urgent objective of national policy to give it an overriding priority.

A Competition of Systems, Not of Growth Rates

The United States should promote its own growth by reasonable means, not by all means. Our past performance has given us an economy that has long been the envy of the world and that has given us the highest living standard ever known. Surely we wish to progress as rapidly as in the past and to do better if we can—but not at any cost. There is no necessity for us to match the present Russian growth rate.

We are engaged in a competition of systems, not a competition of growth rates. Our strategy in this competition should be to make our own system work as well as we can, in terms of its own values. The values that our system serves are the values that men everywhere would choose if given the chance. Men want freedom, security, rising living standards for themselves and their families, relief from the burdens of toil, fair treatment, and personal dignity. If they did not, we would be faced with an awful dilemma. But we are justified in believing that people everywhere want the basic things that we want, and that the attractiveness of our system is enhanced by its demonstrated success in achieving these goals.

More rapid growth contributes to the success of the system, but it is not identical with success or the sufficient means to its achievement. For us to seek to force our rate of economic growth by a great expansion of the role of government, and by curtailing the freedom of families to choose between consumption and saving and between work and leisure, would be inconsistent with our own values. And it would not make our system more appealing to others.

The Russian threat is grave. It demands from us a strong and varied response. The response should not be imitative. Our danger is not that our total economic resources are, or will be in the foreseeable future, too small for the promotion of U.S. policy. Our great need is not for larger resources but for the best use of the resources we have. We should use the resources we have—which are superior to those of the Russians now and will be at least equal to them for the foreseeable future—to promote U.S. policy better.

Our Untapped Economic Resource

If larger defense expenditures will add to our security, they should be made. Our greater economic strength gives us the ability, if we wish to use it, to seize the initiative in the development of large and varied military forces and in the deliberate obsolescing of equipment and to place pressure on the Russians to maintain equality with us. Whether we should do so is a political question, not a matter of economic potential.

We should be providing much more economic development assistance to the underdeveloped countries of the world than we are doing now. Their success is vital to us, and our assistance to them may be critical to their success.

In neither of these fields should we hold back because of vaguely felt fears that we cannot afford to do what is necessary, that financing adequate defense and assistance programs will somehow damage our economy or impair our growth. Any additional public expenditures for these purposes must be matched by higher taxes to avoid feeding inflationary pressures. Stability of the value of the dollar is properly an important objective of our economic policy. Attention must be given to the way in which taxes are raised so as to minimize any curtailment of private saving or incentives to work. Given the exercise of a reasonable degree of common sense and responsibility in these matters, however, such fears have little foundation.

We should be acting vigorously to counter the Soviet drive for foreign expansion in all its aspects—not only the Soviet use of, or threat to use, force but their propaganda, their use of foreign trade as a political weapon, their support of subversion of government, and their meddling in domestic politics everywhere, often combined with the supplying of money and arms. Wherever possible we should be seizing the initiative.

We should be moving vigorously to reduce international trade barriers. We should utilize fully the powers granted by the Trade Agreements Act to achieve gradual and selective reductions in our own tariffs and, by negotiation with other countries, to secure reductions in their barriers to international trade. Aside from the direct advantage of such a policy to us and to other advanced countries, we must insure a structure of international markets that will provide newly developing nations opportunity to participate fully and fairly in international exchange. Our new addiction to the imposition of quotas when foreign countries successfully penetrate our markets is the worst possible course for us to follow, one that is especially well designed to harm our friends and to create opportunities for the politically inspired Russian trade offensive.

At home, we and other advanced Western nations should adhere to our own values of what is good and desirable and manage our domestic affairs in the light of our own criteria of success, not by the criteria of Soviet communism, if we wish to maintain vigorous and self-confident societies. Of course, economic growth decidedly continues to be one of the central objectives of domestic policy in our own interest. Public policies must be reviewed from the standpoint of their effect upon growth. It is the source of our ability to provide better living standards, more freedom of choice, more leisure, and better educational opportunities and to protect the less fortunate against the hazards of life. We are far from having reached the state where additional income is of little interest to us. But economic growth is not an overriding objective that calls for drastic changes in the way we organize our society and allocate our resources.

Our success in the continuing struggle against Communist imperialism will be determined by our faith, determination, willingness to sacrifice, intelligence, and ingenuity. If we fail, it will not be the result of an inadequate economic base, unless future changes in relative economic growth are much different from what we can now foresee.

27. The Stages of Economic Growth

by Walt W. Rostow

Professor Walt W. Rostow is director of the Center of International Studies, Massachusetts Institute of Technology. A Yale graduate and former Rhodes Scholar, he has written a number of books on Soviet society, American foreign policy, and economic assistance. The following is a condensation of a lecture delivered by Professor Rostow in Moscow in the spring of 1959.

All societies, past and present, may be usefully designated as falling within one of the five following categories: (1) the traditional society, (2) the preconditions for take-off, (3) the take-off, (4) the drive to maturity, and (5) the age of high mass consumption. Beyond the age of high mass consumption lie the problems and possibilities which are beginning to arise in a few societies when the burdens of scarcity gradually retreat and what Karl Marx called communism is approached.

These five stages of growth are based on a dynamic theory of production. Out of this theory comes one key proposition: At any period of time the momentum of an economy is maintained by the rapid rate of growth in a relatively few key leading sectors. In some periods, cotton textiles have been a key leading sector; in others, railways, chemicals, electricity, and the automobile have served this function. Specifically, key sectors have two effects: their rapid growth sets up a direct demand for new inputs; second, the development of these new

In its original form, this selection was published in the December 1959 issue of Fortune. *Copyright 1959, Time, Inc. All rights reserved.*

primary and secondary sectors induces new developments in-directly, elsewhere in the economy.

Each stage of growth is associated with certain ranges of income and types of demand. But we must go beyond mere technical economic analysis. For at each stage of growth so-cieties have been confronted with choices—basic choices of pol-icy and of value—which transcend economic analysis.

How should the traditional society react to the intrusion of a more advanced power? When modern nationhood is achieved, how—in what proportions—should the national ener-gies be disposed: in external aggression, to right old wrongs or to exploit newly created or perceived possibilities for enlarged national power; in completing the political victory of the new national government over old regional interests; or in modern-izing the economy?

Once growth is under way with the take-off, to what extent should the requirements of increasing the rate of growth be moderated by the desire to increase consumption per capita and to increase welfare?

When technological maturity is reached—and the nation commands a modernized and differentiated industrial machine —to what ends should it be put, and in what proportions: to increase social and human security, including leisure; to ex-pand consumption into the range of durable consumers' goods and services; or to increase the nation's stature and power on the world scene?

The stages of growth are, then, not a set of rigid, inevitable, predetermined phases of history. The process of growth does pose for men and societies certain concrete problems and pos-sibilities from which they must choose, and these problems and possibilities may be observed at similar stages in each so-ciety—including contemporary societies.

The Stages in History

I define the traditional society as one which has not learned to make invention and technological innovation a regular flow. The traditional society is not static; but its growth is con-strained by a productivity ceiling beyond which it cannot penetrate. This ceiling decrees that something like 75 per cent of the labor force will be in agriculture; that its income above minimum consumption levels is likely to be dissipated in high living for those who command land rents (or otherwise dissipated); and that its social values will be geared to relatively limited fatalistic horizons.

Historically, the traditional societies of western Europe were stirred into what I call the preconditions for take-off by the expansion of trade from, let us say, the sixteenth century forward. The rise of trade interacted with the development of modern science, invention, and innovation to produce an interlocking series of developments in transport, industry, and agriculture, as well as a rise in population. Britain was the first to move from the preconditions period into take-off.

Once the British take-off—or Industrial Revolution—was under way from, say, 1783, it set in motion a series of what might be called positive and negative demonstration effects. These profound demonstration effects, still operating actively in the world, will bring industrialization to virtually the whole of the planet. The last major take-off may well begin before two centuries have passed since the British showed the way.

Technically, there are three leading sectors in the preconditions period whose transformation is a necessary condition for sustained industrial growth. First, agriculture: a productivity revolution in agriculture is required to feed the expanding population of the preconditions period and to feed the cities likely to be expanding at even higher rates than the average. Second, the export sector: industrialization in its earliest stages is likely to create an expanded bill for imports, which can be met only by quickly applying modern techniques to the extraction and higher processing of some natural resource. Third, social overhead capital: the technical transformation of a traditional society into a position where growth becomes relatively automatic requires large outlays on transport, education, sources of power, and so on.

The development of these sectors is not an antiseptic technical process; it requires profound social, psychological, and political change—from the attitudes of peasants to those of civil servants and politicians. Much analysis—both Marxist and non-Marxist—has emphasized the role of the new commercial and industrial middle class in bringing about this transformation. But the role of the middle class and the profit motive is only a part of the story. Both in the contemporary world and in the more distant past it is perfectly clear that another factor was the repeated demonstration that more advanced societies could impose their will on the less advanced. This demonstration of the national and human costs of backwardness has accelerated the preconditions process in many lands. A reactive nationalism has been a major factor in leading men to take the steps necessary to permit growth to become a society's normal condition. This was so for the transitional periods of Germany, Japan, and Russia in the nineteenth century; and, earlier, it played a crucial role in the formation of the United States under the Federalists. And it is perfectly evident that in the contemporary world the most powerful motive for modernization in the underdeveloped areas is not the profit motive of the middle class but the widespread desire to increase human and national dignity.

Nationalism may be diverted to external goals or ambitions or it may be channeled at home into the economic and social modernization of the society. It is, therefore, one of the technical preconditions for take-off that the governments which come to power in the transitional areas be prepared to channel a high proportion of their peoples' energies, talents, and resources into the tasks of economic growth rather than other possible objectives. For the leading sectors of the preconditions—a productivity revolution in agriculture, the generation of increased foreign exchange, and the build-up of social overhead capital—all require a significant degree of governmental leadership and programing—phrases not to be confused with total government ownership and total planning, which are *not* necessary conditions for the preconditions period.

In essence, the take-off consists of the achievement of rapid growth in a limited group of leading sectors: textiles for Great Britain; railroads for the United States, France, Germany, Canada, and Russia; modern timber cutting and railroads in Sweden. The take-off is distinguished from earlier industrial surges by the fact that growth becomes self-sustained. Investment rises and remains over 10 per cent net, sufficient to outstrip population growth and to make an increase in output per capita a regular condition.

After take-off there follows what I call the drive to maturity, defined as the period when a society has effectively applied the range of (then) modern technology to the bulk of its resources. During the drive to maturity new leading sectors gather momentum to supplant the older leading sectors of the take-off. After the railway take-offs of the nineteenth century —with coal, iron, and heavy engineering at the center of the growth process—it is steel, the new ships, chemicals, electricity, and the products of the modern machine tool that dominate the economy and sustain the over-all rate of growth.

As societies move toward technological maturity, a number of economic and noneconomic changes occur: the working force not only becomes more urban but the category of semi-skilled and white-collar workers expands; real incomes and standards of consumption rise; the professional managers begin to take over from the original buccaneers who launched the take-off and dominate the early stages of the drive to maturity.

But there is a deeper change as well, reflected in literature, social and popular thought, and in politics. What is that change? Men react against the harshness of the drive to maturity; they begin to take growth and the spread of technology for granted; they cease to regard the further spread of modern technology as a sufficient human and social objective; and they ask this question: How shall this mature, industrial machine, with compound interest built firmly into its structure— how shall it be used? As suggested earlier, there are essentially three directions in which the mature nation can go: toward social security and leisure; toward the expansion of power on the world scene; or toward what I call the age of high mass consumption—the diffusion of the mass automobile, improved housing, and the electric-powered household gadgetry, from iceboxes to TV, that an industrial civilization can offer to make life easier, more pleasant, and more interesting in the home.

American history in the twentieth century reflects, at different times, elements of each choice. There was the brief American flirtation with world power at the turn of the century. Then there was a phase of social reform in the Progressive era, followed by the plunge in the 1920s into the age of high mass consumption, with its new leading sectors: automobiles, rubber, oil, roads, suburban housing, and the familiar gadgetry. As for the Germans, at maturity they were terribly tempted and twice succumbed to the temptation of pressing for world power; and as Japan came to technological maturity in the 1930s, it did the same. In the past decade western Europe has made that transition and is now experiencing a version of the American 1920s. And in Japan (at lower levels) something of the same sort is happening. This new phase of growth has given these economies a momentum beyond that predicted by the greatest optimists just after World War II.

As for the Soviet Union, in the 1920s it reorganized the society which had experienced a take-off between 1890 and 1914 but had broken down under the terrible pressures of the First World War. Then, in 1929, the drive to maturity began, and it was resumed with great energy after reconstruction of the damage of the Second World War. This sequence then, since the 1890s, brings the Soviet Union to the point where the three-way choice of the technologically mature society now confronts its political life. That is, in what proportions shall the resources of the society be used for leisure or for mass consumption or for increased power on the world scene.

The Stages Today

While the stages of growth have been moving forward since the end of the Second World War in reasonable order and briskness in the northwestern part of the world, elsewhere a great historical drama has been unfolding; these vast societies, embracing the bulk of the world's population, have been accelerating the preconditions for take-off or actually moving into take-off. Mexico, Argentina, Brazil, Venezuela, and—notably—China and India are actually in the take-off. These societies face many vicissitudes; but the bases have been laid for sustained growth. The commitment to carry forward goes very deep. In China and India, for example—looking ahead over the next decade—none of us can be confident of the political form those societies will assume; but they will, on the average, maintain investment rates that substantially outstrip current rates of population increase. South of the Sahara are societies in the traditional stage, which will need a longer preconditioning process.

The question now arises: Is it scientifically correct to use the concept of the stages of growth derived from a generalization of the historical past to analyze the contemporary problems of the underdeveloped areas? There is much that is familiar to the historian in the current scene. The technical problems of the preconditions still center about the three leading sectors of that stage: social overhead capital, the generation of increased exports, and a technological revolution in agriculture. The social and psychological transformations that must occur are, again, broadly familiar from the past: the siphoning off of land rents into the modern sector, the changing of peasant attitudes, the training of a new leadership—public, private, or both in various combinations—capable of bringing modern techniques to bear in the various sectors of the economy. And, above all, we can again see, as in the past, that a reactive nationalism, tempted to move in directions other than economic growth, lies close to the heart of the political process in many of these regions.

But there is a major technical difference; the pool of technology available to these underdeveloped nations is greater than ever before. At periods in the past, other late-comers—Germany, Russia, Japan—have been able to benefit somewhat by learning from the leading nations. But in degree we must admit that there is a substantial difference between the present and the past, stemming from the size of the pool of available technology.

This difference, however, cuts two ways: it both complicates the problem of growth and offers the possibility of accelerating growth. It complicates growth because the availability of modern techniques of medicine and public health leads to a radical fall in death rates, which yields much higher rates on population increase than those in most societies in the past. Excepting the United States and Russia, which had reserves of good land, population increase in the preconditions and take-off were under 1.5 per cent—generally about 1 per cent. Today the newer nations without reserves of good land are trying to move forward with population-increase rates of 2 per cent and more. This means that higher rates of investment must be generated to achieve sustained growth; more precisely, it means that the revolution in agricultural technique must be pressed forward with great vigor if the whole development process is not to be throttled for lack of food.

The Conditions of Aid

Now, what about peaceful coexistence in the face of this problem? If the only objective in the world of the Soviet Union and the United States were to assist these new nations into sustained growth, technically the more advanced countries should execute a joint program in three parts. First, offer the underdeveloped areas ample supplies of capital—to ease the general problem of capital formation under regimes with high rates of population increase. Second, offer these nations special assistance—to achieve prompt and radical increases in agricultural output. Third, conduct them toward policies which would encourage local politicians to concentrate their hopes and energies on the task of economic development; and avoid policies which would divert them from these objectives.

The United States, for its part, would have to do these four specific things: First, accept the idea that its major objective in these areas was to create independent, modern, growing states, whether or not they were prepared to join in military alliance with the United States.

Second, the United States would have to accept each nation's right to choose its own balance between private and public enterprise; and so long as the growth process was seriously pursued, it would have to refrain from imposing as a condition for loans the acceptance by other societies of American patterns of organization.

Third, the United States would have to accept the fact that the democratic process is a matter of degree and direction and not expect these transitional societies to blossom forth promptly with forms of political organization similar to those of the United States and western Europe.

Fourth, with these objectives and self-denying ordinances,

it would have to offer substantial, long-term loans and technical assistance which the local politicians and planners could count on over, say, a five-year interval.

These are precisely the directions in which American policy has been moving in recent years. This trend lies behind the creation in 1957 of the Development Loan Fund and the recent initiatives in the U. S. Senate to enlarge that fund and put it on a long-term basis. Many in the United States—including this writer—believe this trend has not gone far enough; and, as citizens, we are pressing to see it further developed. But an objective assessment will support the judgment that this is the trend in American policy.

Many Roads to Growth

Now, what about Soviet policy? Leaving China and eastern Europe apart, what is required from Moscow is a parallel set of shifts in policy. The bulk of Soviet lending outside the Communist bloc has been localized in a few areas: Egypt, Syria, and Iraq; Afghanistan, Yugoslavia, and India. It is clear that in each of these areas, excepting India, the Soviet Union has had clear, short-run strategic objectives—objectives other than increasing the rate of growth. The Soviet economic-assistance program would have to be substantially modified if it were to offer a basis for a serious collaborative effort with the United States in the underdeveloped areas.

We all know, however, that the problem of coexistence is not merely a technical matter of collaboration in accelerating the process of economic growth. The presently underdeveloped areas are moving through the preconditions or into take-off in a world setting of cold war—of intense ideological and military competition.

It is the general theme of much Communist thought in the underdeveloped areas that only a Communist dictatorship is capable of overcoming the social and psychological resistances to modernization and of pressing forward into sustained economic growth. We in the West, on the contrary, believe—as a matter of history and faith—that the problems of the preconditions and of the take-off can be overcome without the surrender of human liberty which the Communist formula requires.

I would not wish to enter into the discussion going forward in Communist countries as to whether there is one or whether there are many roads to socialism. But I would assert categorically that there are many roads to economic growth. Coexistence demands that we leave the outcome of the ideological debate to the processes of history within each of these societies; and if we are anxious in our concern for their fate, that they proceed to solve their problems in a setting where capital and technical assistance is made available to them, without strings concerning their political and military orientation.

One may recall the famous phrase of Mao Tse-tung, shortly after the Communist victory in China in 1949. He announced his intention to pursue a lean-to-one-side policy. The condition of competitive coexistence in the underdeveloped areas is that we both pursue policies—both the United States and the Soviet Union—which encourage stand-up-straight policies.

28. Military or Economic Aid: Questions of Priority

by Arnold Wolfers

Born in Switzerland and an American citizen since 1939, Dr. Wolfers' attention has long been directed toward the study and interpretation of U.S. foreign policy. He is Sterling Professor Emeritus of International Relations, Yale University, has been a member of the resident faculty of the National War College, and since 1957 has been director of the Washington Center of Foreign Policy Research, Johns Hopkins University.

In recent years, serious pressures have been exerted upon the Administration for a shift from the prevailing emphasis on military assistance (including defense support) to a greater emphasis on economic aid. These pressures are generated by at least three distinct motivations, which raise different sets of questions:

1. Many people, both inside and outside of the United States, are disturbed that so much expenditure goes into building up defenses against the Soviet or Communist threat when millions of men and women are living in a state of dire poverty. In terms of American values, or human values generally, they would naturally prefer to see their country engage in economic rather than in military aid—as they would prefer a national budget devoted to social welfare instead of military preparedness. Perhaps the late John Foster Dulles had this in mind when, on November 26, 1958, he said that "as an abstract proposition, too much throughout the world is being spent on military and not enough on economic."

This selection consists of excerpts from the Report of the President's Committee to Study the Military Assistance Program, July 1959.

However, whether the United States can afford to engage in costly humanitarian tasks abroad, given the limited funds likely to be available for foreign aid even under the best circumstances, depends obviously on the requirements for pressing nonhumanitarian tasks and on the priorities to be allotted to the various tasks falling under foreign aid.

2. A second motivation behind the demand for a shift to economic aid is less clearly or not exclusively humanitarian. The Millikan-Rostow school of thought[1] argues forcefully in favor of an aid program designed to assist all countries "in achieving a steady, self-sustaining rate of growth" irrespective of the "short-run political interests of this country."

The assumption here is that "self-sustaining growth," once attained, will not merely relieve human poverty but "resolve the cold war," "render military deterrence superfluous," "convince the Kremlin that the game for Eurasian power hegemony is hopeless," and thus, in the long run, accomplish more effectively the defense task that is presently being assigned to military aid and short-run economic aid.

It is necessary to determine whether the assumptions on which the M.I.T. study rests are valid if a decision is to be reached on the relative emphasis to be placed on short-range military and economic aid, on the one hand, and on long-range economic-development aid on the other.

3. Pressure comes from a third source: Eight senators, in a letter to the President on August 25, 1958, criticized the "serious distortion in the present relative importance which is attached to military and related aid, on the one hand, and technical assistance and self-liquidating economic-development assistance on the other." These senators may have been motivated in part by the humanitarian and M.I.T. arguments mentioned above, but they stated a different reason to justify a shift to economic aid.

The primary task of the aid program in their view consisted in "strengthening the resistance of the other nations to totalitarianism." They see the danger now faced by the United

---

[1] See the study "The Objectives of United States Economic Assistance Programs," presented to a special committee of the Senate in July 1957 by the Center of International Studies, Massachusetts Institute of Technology.

States and the Free World as a Sino-Soviet threat to individual freedom and civil liberties, rather than as a threat to the independence of nations from Sino-Soviet control. As a consequence, they fear that military assistance may increase what they regard as the chief danger, by contributing to the maintenance in power of "regimes which have lacked broad support within the countries we have assisted," by creating "a militaristic image of the United States," and by "creating in them perpetuating military hierarchies . . . which . . . may endanger the very value of individual freedom which we seek to safeguard."

Here the question must be answered whether, in the light of the threat of further Sino-Soviet expansion, the United States can afford to give priority to the promotion of American democratic ideals and to the defense of individual freedom against autocratic government, Communist or other, even where such defense would tend to increase the Sino-Soviet military menace. In any case, it should be asked: (1) whether defense aid against Sino-Soviet expansion cannot be administered in a way that will minimize the danger of promoting the type of autocratic or militaristic rule that runs counter to American values, and (2) whether it would be wise, anyway, to interfere with the internal development of other countries or to try to insist on democratic institutions where the preconditions for their effectiveness are absent.

The problem here is not whether the development of democracy in other countries is desirable when the necessary preconditions exist—which nobody would deny—but whether in the face of the Sino-Soviet threat the United States can afford to combat non-Communist autocratic government in situations where the short-run result would be to weaken the military defenses against the Sino-Soviet threat.

Labels versus Purpose

It clarifies the issues if one distinguishes the actual purposes for which aid is intended from the labels under which it is presented to the public at home and abroad. At times, it is expedient to speak of military assistance, although the recipi-

ent country is actually in need of aid to bolster its economy
or to balance its payments; in other instances, it is politic to
label the aid as economic although the aim is to strengthen the
military establishment of the recipient. Usually the terms are
almost interchangeable, since almost all military aid, whether
in dollars or hardware, will relieve the economic strain on the
recipient country and allow it to divert more of its own fund
from armaments to other uses. Conversely, almost any type c
economic assistance gives the recipient country new opportu
nities to spend more of its own funds on military preparedness
if it so desires.

What needs to be decided, therefore, is not under wha
name to accord aid but to what uses the United States wishe
such aid to be put, whether to military use, to economic
emergency purposes, or, finally, to the end of long-term economic growth and industrialization.

A division into the two categories of military assistance and
economic assistance is not particularly enlightening and may,
in fact, be confusing. The chief distinction is between short-
run aid, military or economic, both being in the field of defense broadly conceived, on the one hand, and, on the other,
economic-development aid that will bear material fruit at best
after two or three decades. It should be noted that some
sound long-run economic-development programs have favorable short-run psychological and political effects that place
them in the first, or defense, category.

The demands for a shift in the U.S. aid program raise two
different questions:

1. Has the present struggle between East and West changed
in such a way that the short-run task of defense of the West
has come to require more emphasis on economic and less,
therefore, on military aid?

2. Has the present danger of the East-West struggle re-
ceded to a point where short-run defense efforts, whether military or economic, should give way to long-run efforts at economic development?

Short-Run Defense Needs

The dangers of the cold war are present dangers. To meet them, efforts of the most exacting kind are needed that can be expected to produce results immediately, or within a brief period of time. Only if and after they have been met can there be room for efforts that will bear fruit at best in two or more decades hence.

Concerning the short-run efforts, controversy has arisen as to whether changes in the circumstances characterizing the East-West struggle have not made military assistance less valuable than it was some years ago, and economic assistance more urgent than before. Several arguments have been put forth sustaining this thesis.

1. It is said that the Soviet bloc has practically given up the idea of expansion through military conquest, which it tried in Korea, and is now concentrating on gaining control over other nations through economic penetration and particularly through economic aid. The United States must, it is said, be prepared therefore to meet competition in this new field rather than to emphasize the race for adequate military defenses.

Undoubtedly, East-West competition in economic aid has become a fact, but it may be asked whether it constitutes a substitute for the earlier military competition or has merely added a new dimension to the struggle. It is worth remembering (a) that in the case of all of the recent serious cold-war crises—Quemoy, Iraq and Lebanon, Berlin—the character of the challenge was military rather than economic, and (b) that the Soviet and Red Chinese governments can return to the method of military expansion at any time, since they have not reduced but continue to increase their military striking power.

2. According to another argument, American strategic doctrine places chief reliance on long-range strategic nuclear striking power rather than on local forces of countries receiving military assistance. Moreover, since allied local military power is alleged to have lost much of its former value, it therefore becomes more important to supply friends and allies with economic staying power that will help them resist indirect con-

quest by infiltration and subversion than to assist in building up local forces.

If we leave aside for the moment the question of whether economic aid is regularly a better means of warding off the dangers of indirect conquest, it should be noted that the strategy of deterrence and defense through strategic nuclear power is meeting mounting criticism, with many experts arguing that, in the light of the high degree of nuclear stalemate, the possibility of limited military engagements that require on-the-spot local forces should in the future be given more attention.

3. The argument of the eight senators is also relevant to this point. As mentioned above, they assume that the issue today is a struggle between totalitarianism or autocracy, on the one hand, and individual freedom or democracy, as we understand it, on the other, rather than a struggle between two antagonistic blocs, one of which is seeking to upset the present world balance of power in its favor. If this assumption were correct, only such aid would be justified as promised to promote democracy and freedom, and it is more likely that economic rather than military aid would serve this purpose, although neither may be able to stem the tide of autocracy in underdeveloped countries.

Against this argument it should be said that if the struggle in fact were essentially concerned with autocracy in all of its forms, and not with Sino-Soviet expansion and control, the United States and its Western allies would have lost the battle for the time being. The West today is a democratic island in a sea of autocracy, though autocracy varying widely in degree and character, Communist here, Fascist or military elsewhere.

The struggle has not been lost for good, however, as long as the Sino-Soviet bloc remains contained within its present borders. In time, many of the autocracies may become liberalized. Meanwhile, although foreign aid should be administered in a way that will promote rather than hinder a process of liberalization, democratic values would not be served if the means of containment were neglected and these countries were allowed to fall into the arms of Soviet totalitarianism, thereby becoming the enemies of the West and losing most of their chance of future liberalization.

External versus Internal Defense

In the defense field it makes sense to distinguish between aid intended to help countries protect themselves against *external* Sino-Soviet military attack and aid intended to help them withstand *internal* events and pressures that would draw them into the Soviet orbit even in the absence of any external attack. The first, which covers both military deterrence and defense, might be called aid in the context of "hot-war strategy," the latter, aid in the context of "cold-war strategy."

1. In terms of *hot-war strategy*, there can be no substitute for military aid (including defense support) if the aim is to improve the abilities of the indigenous forces of the recipient country to stand up against an external military attack. This is not to say that it would be wise for the United States to try to bolster the military capabilities of all members of the non-Communist world. Military assistance to the countries that are exposed to Sino-Soviet military attack must be looked at with a critical eye and with regard to a number of considerations. The area of the recipient country may not be worth the costs of its defense; or no amount of aid within reason could build up local forces to a level at which they would be both able and willing to take up arms against a Sino-Soviet attacker; or better military results, dollar by dollar, may come from expenditures on the American defense establishment; or the effort required to build up indigenous forces adequate for external defense may wreck the recipient country by destroying its internal political, social, or economic balance. However, where the conditions are favorable, military assistance adds to the defensive power of the anti-Soviet coalition and thus to the security of the United States.

(It might be worth mentioning that on occasion it makes sense to give external-military-defense assistance to countries that are in no danger from the Sino-Soviet bloc at all but whose survival is necessary to the stability of a regional power balance. Military assistance to Israel or Jordan falls under this heading since it serves the purpose of balancing the military power of non-Communist countries and, by making them capable of mutual deterrence, of pacifying the non-Communist world.)

2. In respect to *cold-war strategy*, where the issue is internal rather than external defense, the relative merits of military aid and economic aid, and the character to give to either, raise difficult and controversial questions. Unless they are answered, no decision can be reached for or against a shift to more economic aid, or from short-range economic aid to more long-range economic-development assistance.

There would seem to be three distinct ways in which countries might fall under Soviet control by events short of war, or at least refuse to be aligned with the West:

(*a*) The government in power may decide to shift the allegiance of its country to the side of the Soviet bloc, or to choose a course of "positive neutrality" favorable to the Soviets, or, finally, to give up ties with the West based on collective-defense agreements in favor of genuine neutrality.

(*b*) Opposition parties may come into power and replace a pro-Western or neutral government with a pro-Soviet government.

(*c*) Communist forces within the country may arise to power, presumably on the basis of considerable revolutionary public support, and turn the country into a Soviet or Red Chinese satellite and people's democracy.

Not all of these dangers are present in each of the countries that are presently or potentially recipients of U.S. aid. The government of Chiang Kai-shek will not, and in fact cannot, swing to the Soviet side or turn neutral. In Europe, the only conceivable danger would be a shift of a NATO country from alliance to genuine neutrality, which would raise the question of the price it would be worth paying to prevent such a shift.

Almost everywhere, there are opposition forces with more or less anti-Western sentiments but whose ascendancy to power would not everywhere be sufficiently detrimental to Free World defenses for the United States to let itself be blackmailed into giving unlimited support to the "friendly" in group.

The danger of a rise of indigenous communism, supported by the Sino-Soviet bloc, differs greatly from country to country. It, too, is frequently exaggerated by a government in power as a means of obtaining whatever aid it wants. It is also doubtful in many instances whether such aid will stem the Communist tide. Some aid, in fact, tends instead to increase Communist strength in the recipient country, because it bolsters an unpopular regime.

Stability Aid: Military and Economic

It is often argued that the economic poverty of the mass of the population is the source of the major internal threat to Western interests. The conclusion is that economic aid is the logical answer, whereas military assistance tends to burden the recipient country with a military establishment that will reduce the living standards of most of the civilian population and thus, in fact, enhance the internal danger.

However, of the three types of internal threats to the West listed above, none can be definitely and universally traced to the misery or aspirations of the mass of the people, though a dissatisfied and rebellious populace may be a factor behind any one of the three threats. As a rule, the most effective type of aid will be aid that promises to give the greatest satisfaction to those elite groups who are eager to keep the country out of Communist or Soviet control.

1. In many instances military assistance may be the best means of bringing about such stability and satisfaction. A strong military establishment can be an element of order; it gives the government authority and prestige; it offers to many a chance of social and technical advancement. However, not all demands for military assistance or for "internal order and immunity against communism through military strength" are justified in terms of the American interest. Military autocracies are not always stable; they may provoke rebellion led by the Communists. They are not always reliable; there have been cases where the leaders of the armed forces or influential junior officers have gone over to the Soviet camp (Syria? Iraq?). Excessive militarization may break the economies of weak countries, or it may arouse fears in neighboring non-Communist countries, or split the international non-Communist camp (Pakistan-India). Military assistance as a means of stemming the internal dangers should be scrutinized carefully, therefore,

country by country, with an eye to any adverse effects it may have in particular instances.

2. Short-run economic aid, or what can be called either economic-emergency aid or economic-defense aid, has a vital part to play in the defense against the internal dangers mentioned earlier. Here Soviet competition in economic aid becomes a major factor, though it is not the only justification for such aid.

Soviet economic competition or no competition, there is reason to fear that governments in grave financial, monetary, or commercial difficulties may be overthrown, or may look elsewhere for support, and that economic crises may lead to the kinds of dangerous unrest on which the Communists can capitalize. Therefore, economic-emergency aid—short-run assistance to help countries overcome monetary, fiscal, or balance-of-payment troubles—is an important defense tool. Its significance has increased since the Soviet Union entered the economic field and now stands ready to offer emergency aid if help from the West is not forthcoming, or is not adequate.

One should not conclude that the U.S. aid program should provide funds sufficient to meet every emergency. In many instances, reliance on U.S. aid tends to perpetuate the emergency or increase the probability of its repetition—governments that can count on being bailed out have no incentive to raise taxes, reduce spending, or do any of the other painful things that would remedy the situation. As a consequence, the dollar gap, the inflationary pressures, the budgetary deficits, may continue unabated. In the case of all countries receiving or demanding economic-emergency aid, it must be asked, therefore, whether the risks of their alienation or of their acceptance of Soviet aid are great enough to justify an assistance intended to remedy deficiencies caused by their own unsound fiscal or economic policies.

Long-run economic aid, properly called economic-development aid, must be treated separately, both because of the large investment of funds it requires and because of its peculiar relationship to the defense tasks of the United States and its allies.

Economic-Development Aid

The idea of long-run economic-development aid to underdeveloped countries is extremely appealing, not only because it suggests help to the underprivileged and represents a constructive effort but also because it conforms with long-run American interests. It promises advantages to the "haves," the countries of high living standards, similar to those that slum clearance offers to the privileged parts of an urban community. However, the benefits that flow from the actual completion and successful operation of economic-development schemes, for which the Aswan Dam can serve as a symbol, are likely to translate themselves into benefits for the mass of the impoverished sections of a people only after decades, as the M.I.T. report emphasizes. Therefore, even if all the assumptions of the M.I.T. report were accepted—that the recipient country will, in fact, devote the development aid to development and not to current uses, that it has and employs the necessary skills to bring the projects to fruition, that it will survive the long interim period as a free country—the material benefits of industrialization which lie in a more or less remote future cannot in themselves remove or lessen the present dangers of the cold war.

In order to serve as an instrument of cold-war strategy, here and now, economic-development aid must be of a kind that has psychological results favorable to the West long before it produces any material results. Some development aid has this effect, and the Soviets have not been slow to realize it. In the competition for the allegiance of governments and for the preferences of elites and peoples, particularly of the uncommitted nations, the winner may well be the country that can best demonstrate its concern for an underdeveloped country's industrialization and future economic well-being, no matter how remote and uncertain these may be. (Victory in this competition may come long before the long-run projects are completed, and in fact independently of whether they ever are completed or ever prove economically sound.)

Here one runs into a serious dilemma. From the point of

view of cold-war strategy, a relatively phony "economic-development" project, such as the paving of the streets of Kabul by the Soviets, may be more successful than a very costly but in the long run sound irrigation project. Yet it would be tragic if large funds had to be wasted on the type of phony aid for which the Soviet Union shows a marked preference. Probably it will be found that the competitive value of the phony aid is short-lived and that sound projects, if properly publicized and attractive to the elites of a country, will pay higher dividends even in the cold war.

What needs to be stressed, however, is the fallacy of thinking that the time has come to shift from "unconstructive" defense aid (military aid and short-term economic-emergency aid) to "constructive" sound long-term economic-development aid. The latter can at best have a psychological side effect that will be valuable to the present and exacting defense effort imposed by the cold war. It is also likely to have unfavorable effects, such as creating social dislocation, increasing a restless industrial proletariat, or undermining an established cultural and religious order. The M.I.T. report takes lightly the probability that the transition period of several decades preceding self-sustaining growth will witness "an increase in the appetites for improvement surpassing the resources for their satisfaction and cause unrest." The authors of the report must assume that the Free World can afford to create additional dangers for itself while waiting for the happy outcome of its long-range efforts. If this assumption is not justified, economic-development aid must be judged in each instance on the basis of shorter-range calculations, which weigh the favorable psychological effects of "holding out the prospect of economic betterment" against whatever unfavorable effects—social disruption or increased political instability—may materialize during the transition period. Only so can the expected net benefit be compared with the advantages that would flow from using the funds for economic-emergency aid, military assistance, or additional American national armaments.

It may seem out of place to raise doubts about the value of underwriting the economic development of friendly but underdeveloped countries or to suggest limiting such aid, as a rule, to the amounts either needed to meet Soviet competition in development aid or likely to produce short-range psychological capital for the donor. Particularly with respect to India, it is argued that unless India, through our assistance, can match Red China's economic development, the cause of the Free World and its way of life will be damaged beyond repair throughout the underdeveloped parts of the world. To this it can be answered that unfortunately no amount of economic aid will be able to supply India with the equivalent in capital and working hours that the Communist regime can extort from its people. It can also be suggested that if external economic aid by the United States helps India over its short-run emergencies, gives her technical and educational assistance, and meets Soviet psychological competition by some striking demonstrations of Western skill, the United States may be doing as much as it can to meet the dangers flowing from a Red Chinese victory in the productivity race. Similar considerations would apply to other countries in which the government, like that of India, is genuinely concerned with economic development. Where it is not—and cannot be induced to be so concerned—favorable psychological side effects are the only worthwhile results to be anticipated from economic-development aid anyway; here, even the resort to "phonies" may be expedient.

29. Private Enterprise: America's Best Export

by Robert L. Garner

Mr. Garner, president of the International Finance Corporation, has since 1917 been active in the banking field. A native of Mississippi, he received his B.S. degree from Vanderbilt University and did graduate work at the School of Journalism, Columbia University. During World War I he served as a captain with the 77th Infantry Division in France. From 1947 to 1956 he was vice-president of the International Bank for Reconstruction and Development. Since it was formed, in 1956, he has been president of the International Finance Corporation, an affiliate of the World Bank. Mr. Garner lectured at the first National Strategy Seminar for Reserve Officers.

The Communist objective to bring all the world under its domination, frankly proclaimed by its leaders, is steadfast; the strategy and tactics of communism are most flexible. Having emphasized various combinations of violence, military threats and action, subversion and propaganda, the Communists' most recent strategy gambit is economic penetration.

The play now seems to be centered on the underdeveloped world, principally the Middle and Far East and Africa but also, to an increasing extent, Latin America. If Communists can gain control of the manpower and natural resources in

This chapter is based on an address made by the author to the fourth annual National Military-Industrial Conference in Chicago, February 18, 1958. Printed by the kind permission of the author and the International Finance Corporation.

such areas, they might well hope gradually to isolate and strangle the United States and Europe.

The Stakes in the Underdeveloped World

In these less-developed areas, the revolution of communism encounters another revolution in process—an economic and social revolution. Whole peoples are learning for the first time of ways of life different from their ancestral status. This awakening, in certain areas, coincides with the decline of colonialism and other forms of control or supervision on the part of the more highly developed countries. It is not surprising that the impact of new economic, social, and political factors, even in those less-developed countries which have long been politically independent, have produced great stresses and strains.

A great part of the world is now catching a glimpse of the industrial progress which transformed the United States and Europe during the past centuries. The peoples of the emerging nations face new and difficult conditions and problems, a fact which we need to keep in mind when we meet with their sensitivities, their sometimes extreme nationalism, and their suspicions. Since the past with which they are breaking was related to the West, their suspicions and fears are directed principally in that direction, not toward Russia, from which they have heretofore been largely isolated. All of this affords a happy hunting ground for the Communists.

The above outline of Communist strategy is obviously oversimplified. It requires two additional comments. First, only at our peril do we fail to realize that the Communists will quickly use any possible weapon or device whenever the changing scene, or any misstep or weakness of the Free World, provides them with an opening. Second, in working toward their objective, the Communists take the long-range view. They will not be discouraged if they cannot dominate the world in this decade; there still lies before them the next century.

We, too, need to plan for the long pull. Economically, we have a vital stake in what happens in the non-Communist world outside our borders. Increasingly our growing industry feeds upon imported raw materials—iron ore, copper, manganese, and innumerable other essentials which we either lack or of which we have insufficient quantities. Industry, as well as agriculture, is geared to produce in excess of our consumption, and our needs for foreign markets are growing. Access both to raw materials and to the markets will depend upon the political, social, and economic direction taken by the countries concerned. This applies particularly to those countries which are in the early stages of economic development. They are going to develop—the question is whether they will develop along the lines of economic and political freedom or in ways which incline them towards communism.

The Fallacy of Rapid and Massive Development Schemes

A substantial number of informed Americans basically agree that the course of the economic development of emerging nations will have a significant bearing on our security and prosperity. However, there is a wide range of opinion regarding the pace at which progress in the less-developed countries can be made. A considerable school of thought takes the line that, to meet the rising expectations of these countries, we must somehow speed the pace of development so that living standards of their peoples will be greatly improved within a few years. These advocates feel the hot breath of communism on our collective necks and stress that, unless we muster an extra burst of speed, much of the world will go Communist by default. And, believing that money makes the mare go, they hold that the speed of development depends largely upon the amount of funds the United States provides. They contend that any possible expense to us for such development is small compared with the cost of war.

The motives behind these exhortations are beyond reproach. But will the methods suggested be effective?

The greatest experiment in intergovernmental aid was the Marshall Plan for Europe. On balance, the plan was successful: it assisted western Europe to get back on its feet and perhaps saved it from communism. But the Marshall Plan was a reconstruction project in an area long developed industrially, politically, and socially. Experienced leaders, competent administrators, and skilled workmen were available. The Europeans knew how to use the tools we supplied.

While U.S. aid has not widely won the gratitude of Europe (which we should never have wished or expected) or, more important, won general agreement with, and support of, our policies, the Marshall Plan was justified in our own self-interest. Whether or not European countries like us, Europe has today a relatively strong and stable economy, with many basic interests similar to ours.

It seems wise to consider some lessons learned from this experience.

First, it gives strong support to the view that government-to-government aid does not win friends. Second, it shows that economic aid, as all other aspects of foreign policy, should be based on national self-interest. And finally, the experience of the Marshall Plan indicates that economic progress is not chiefly a matter of capital, but of men competent to apply capital to natural and human resources under conditions of relative political and social stability. And the scarcity of such men and of such conditions on the economic frontiers of the world today is holding back development much more than is lack of capital.

The Characteristics of Underdeveloped Areas

In varying degree and with exceptions which do not alter the general pattern, it is accurate to outline the prevailing characteristics in underdeveloped areas somewhat as follows:

1. A considerable degree of political and financial instability, particularly among the newly independent countries, but not uncommon even among those with a century or more of political independence behind them, as in Latin America.

2. Economic systems largely agricultural—much of it merely subsistence farming—with wealth in the hands of a few and little in the way of a stabilizing middle class in between.

3. A shortage of people trained and experienced in management and administration, public or private; at the same time,

many with good academic or professional education find no
suitable jobs.

4. Unsure and erratic financial administration, accompanied by inflation, which induces flight of local capital, quick-
turn speculation, and investment largely in such things as real
estate.

5. Traditions and habits which frequently run counter to
economic development.

These are some of the handicaps. On the credit side of these
new frontiers are substantial natural resources—some of them
exceedingly great—waiting to be put to use. There is an
abundance of people who, with sound leadership, training,
and the prudent application of capital, could produce much
more and live much better. Almost everywhere these people
are in the throes of economic development. The question is
how development can be achieved, and what manner of effective assistance the United States can give.

The objective of United States policy should be to encourage and aid orderly and continuous progress toward the development of the natural and human resources of these countries,
along lines which give promise of their achieving the habits
of free and stable institutions and a decent living for their people, and in the hope that this will block the encroachments of
communism.

However attractive another objective might appear—namely,
to bind recipients to us as firm allies in our defense against
communism—we must regretfully conclude that our aid program has had only limited success in this area and seems unlikely to have greater success in the future. Countries are anti-
Communist or neutral or inclined toward the Communists
because of their own interpretation of their self-interests, and
seldom, if ever, because of our financial assistance. Only as
they achieve conditions which bring them to identify their interests as being in accord with the way of life which we represent will they act on our side.

The Shortcomings of Government Assistance

Now let us consider some of the means by which we might obtain the objective. This writer's observation leads him to question the merit of large amounts of loans and grants from the U. S. Government, whether their purpose is primarily to promote development in the recipient countries or to facilitate certain special classes of U.S. exports. This does not mean, of course, that in certain special cases U. S. Government aid cannot be justified on grounds of important national interests of the United States and where there is not a basis for the recipients to borrow on the test of capacity to repay.

Financial assistance to underdeveloped areas should largely be to improve basic human and physical facilities as a necessary foundation for future economic progress. Such assistance would be more realistic if given largely in the form of grants and not of loans, which may well be beyond their capacity to repay and may prevent them from becoming credit-worthy for a long time in the future. This is quite different from a program of our government's financing economic development everywhere. It is not so much that the amount of money involved might not be worth the gamble, but such a program is not likely to achieve the objective of soundly building the economies of the recipients or of reducing the blandishments of communism. It is doubtful that in the long run it helps either them or us.

Experience in international lending seems to indicate that only a limited amount of funds can effectively be invested by most of these countries in any given time. They need outside planning and supervision of expenditures, but their national sensitivity makes it difficult for the United States to set effective economic limitations and conditions. Political considerations inevitably play a large part in such transactions—a fact which is realized and resented by the recipients. Short-range programs, inherent in our legislative process, change constantly and thus reduce the effectiveness of the aid. There are inevitable contradictions between financial aid on the one hand and tariff and other policies on the other, which retard the progress that our funds seek to promote. Aid to one country spurs pressure from others, and the attitude has been built up among some undeveloped countries that they have a vested right to financial assistance from the United States, irrespective of what they do to help themselves.

Furthermore, the U. S. Government is frequently induced to finance industrial projects owned and managed by governments, sometimes in the absence of all efforts by these governments to raise all or part of their capital from private sources and in the absence of any provision for adequate management. Not only are the governments generally ill-equipped to provide efficient management, with the result that not infrequently these projects are liabilities to economic development, but their control by government encourages a trend to the collective state, which is certainly more in accord with Communist objectives than with ours.

The Merits of Private Investment

The question may well be raised as to where, if the U. S. Government is not to provide the funds, reasonable credits may be available to governments for those appropriate enterprises necessary to economic development. The answer is that the World Bank was created for such purpose and that it is continuing to provide loans to credit-worthy countries under conditions not only to insure sound selection and execution of projects but to influence the adoption by the borrowing countries of economic policies and practices which promote solid development. More than $3 billion of such loans have been extended (helping to finance projects having a total cost of some $6 to $7 billion). The record will confirm that they have been handled on a sound business basis without political considerations and have made a notable contribution to economic progress.

There are several reasons why the encouragement of private industrial development in the less-developed countries, particularly through the establishment and expansion of private American business operations in them, can best promote development. Our private-enterprise system is an intrinsic part of our way of life—it is what we do best and what, therefore, we can demonstrate most effectively. And free enterprise is an integral component of man's whole free way of life.

The most dynamic force in producing a better life, and a more worthy life, comes from the initiative of the individual— the opportunity to create, to produce, to achieve for himself and his family—each to the best of his individual talents. This is the essence of the system of competitive private enterprise— twentieth-century model—as it has been developed by enlightened and successful business concerns.

Since this system has produced its benefits for us, why should we not promote most vigorously its spread among those we wish to aid in their development? American business is now increasingly inclined to look abroad. It is aware of the profitable record which companies operating abroad have achieved in the past. It feels the need for developing new resources overseas and the opportunities for profitable markets.

There are tangible results when U.S. business (and this can apply to European business as well) extends its operations abroad. Among them can be listed the following:

It provides foreign capital and management, so that unused local resources can be profitably utilized.

It creates new jobs and teaches new skills. Usually these jobs pay better than the local prevailing wages.

It offers opportunities to local people to learn the elements of modern management and business, now so often lacking even among men of education and ability.

It introduces new concepts of production and marketing, labor relations and financing, and other progressive business practices. It plants the seeds of initiative, ingenuity, change, and growth.

It provides better and cheaper products to local consumers, and in certain cases develops new export products.

In a number of cases, and the trend seems to be in this direction, foreign enterprise attracts local capital, thus stimulating the investment climate and laying the basis for development of local capital markets.

And finally, by demonstrating the widespread advantages of sound free enterprise, not only to local entrepreneurs but also to employees, to consumers, and to the community at large, it helps to remove misconceptions that private enterprise benefits only the few. All of this tends to relieve pressures on governments to extend their activities into business.

American business, in looking for opportunities abroad, is naturally selective, being wary of those countries where political or financial instability or hostility to foreign enterprise presents acute risks. It is properly cautious of the risks of rampant inflation and of such ill-advised actions by local governments as burdensome controls and restrictions, expropriations, and violation of contracts. Yet one can confidently say that there has been, over the past several years, a general improvement in the investment climate in the undeveloped countries. If American enterprise extends its operations where conditions are reasonably favorable, the benefits of American investment will become quickly apparent to other countries.

Some Concrete Measures

The following steps are suggested as part of a definite program for the encouragement of the export of American private enterprise:

First, our government must support more positively expansion of private business abroad. Too frequently officials take a negative attitude toward free enterprise and neither defend nor promote it. We must enlarge existing information programs for foreign students, journalists, and businessmen in order to explain and demonstrate our system. Perhaps we might say less about our comforts and gadgets and more about how, setting foot on a hostile and unexplored continent, we have by hard work and initiative created a better life for all our people in freedom.

Second, use should be made of every legitimate inducement to stimulate foreign investment. The most practical would be positive tax incentives.

Third, there must be firm support by our government of the rights of U.S. business which invests abroad, including vigorous stands against discrimination or against violation of contractual rights by foreign governments.

Fourth, our government agencies should exercise restraint

in financing foreign governments in enterprises suitable for private capital. Exception should be made only in cases of absolute urgency where every effort to develop private interest has failed.

There is frequently an alternative to government investment if sufficient effort is made. The World Bank has proved this in more than one instance. The Communists preach their doctrine of absolute state control of all economic activities. We should counter their offensive by promoting our incomparably superior system.

In assisting economic development we should take care to assure recipients that our help will strengthen the values in which we believe. Modern machines and money alone will not win the minds of men to our side. We need to demonstrate faith in our way of life. Let us not merely defend against the Communist Manifesto, but let us attack their brutal system with our own Manifesto of Free Enterprise.

30.   The Defense We Can Afford

by James F. Brownlee

A trustee of the Committee for Economic Development since 1946, Mr. Brownlee brought to the organization wide experience and knowledge acquired in business and in government service. He served as a member of the Business Advisory Council and the War Production Board; was director of the Transportation War Food Administration, deputy administrator in the Office of Price Administration, and deputy director in the Office of Economic Stabilization. He served as chairman of the CED Subcommittee on Economic Policies for National Security, which in 1958 issued the policy statement "The Problem of National Security." He is chairman of the board of Minute Maid Corporation and a director of the American Sugar Refining Company, R. H. Macy & Company, the Chase Manhattan Bank, and the Gillette Safety Razor Company.

How much should the American people be willing to spend for security against their foes?

This is a question that has no easy answer. But the American people, determined that their national defense be assured

This selection is based on the article prepared by the author to present in brief form the substance of the "Statement on National Policy" issued by the Research and Policy Committee of the Committee for Economic Development. It was originally published in booklet form by the CED in August 1958 and is reprinted by permission of the CED and the author.

and hoping to avoid war, cannot afford the luxury of not paying the bill.

Periodically the timid suggestion comes from many quarters that high expenditures for national defense might lead the country to economic stagnation or collapse. A realistic appraisal of the situation shows that this fear has been greatly exaggerated. The truth of the matter is that the American people will have to decide for themselves what they think security is worth. But *they can afford whatever has to be spent in the cause of national defense.*

We live today in a situation of constant danger, a danger we are likely to be living with for years to come. Since there seems to be no foreseeable future without danger to peace, no probability of a return to normalcy, we must not hobble ourselves with the notion that there is some arbitrary limit on what we can spend for defense or a limit that we can exceed only with disastrous consequences.

Threats We Face

Today we are in a position of great uncertainty. We cannot select one most probable form that the threat to our security may take and prepare for that in the hope of thus avoiding the costs of preparing for alternative threats.

We do know that we will *not* be the aggressor in any possible war. We do know that we have no ambitions of world conquest. At the same time there is great uncertainty as to both present and future Communist capabilities and intentions. We must prepare for many contingencies. The Soviets maintain and utilize a wide variety of capabilities. Their policies will be adapted to exploit our weaknesses. The consequences of putting all our eggs in one basket would be terrible to contemplate. We must accept the circumstances that any "hot" war, total or peripheral, would come at·a time and, initially, at a place chosen by our adversaries. We will not get in the first blow, and we must be prepared to react to military aggression whenever and wherever it may come.

With the advent of thermonuclear air power and ballistic missiles, the swiftness with which the Soviet Union has de-

veloped its atomic and missile capabilities, and the decisive
superiority of offensive over defensive weapons, the United
States now lives under the threat of instantaneous and immeasurable destruction. To deter such an attack, and meet it
should it come, even the largest war potential is of no avail.
In the United States as well as in allied countries, what is
needed for this purpose is military forces-in-being and the capacity quickly to restore a broken economy. Previous preparations, not reserves or potential reserves, will be crucial in such
a war.

But it is not only the military threat we must face. The
Soviet bloc employs economic blandishment on a wide scale,
uses foreign trade as a political weapon, combines subversion
with supplying arms and money, and capitalizes upon the economic and political instability of the underdeveloped countries
in its unceasing struggle to control the world.

Meeting this threat is costly. From 1955 to 1957 expenditures for provisions for national security averaged 11 per cent
of our gross national product, as compared with only a little
over 1 per cent back in the 1930s. We are not sure even these
sums have been adequate.

The Soviet Union has developed with great speed in the last
few years a series of operational modern weapons systems. We
have no reason to think she will not continue to advance in
this field. Her rapid growth in science and industry and her
leaders' determination to assign the best of Russia's human and
material resources to the increase of its military power only
prove to us that the Communists can, and probably will, increase their pressures upon us.

At no time in history has our survival depended not so much
upon the state of combat readiness as upon "the battle of the
laboratories." It is for this reason that Soviet leaders have invested much more than we in training manpower for research
and development. They know that, like saving and investing,
research and innovation are keys to growing productive and
military power. They firmly believe we are living in a scientific
age. Their educational system has become permeated with this
view.

We should meet the challenge. By accelerated research and
rapid technological advance in our own weapons and those of

our allies, we might well render obsolete the military equipment of our opponents and thus put a great and even crippling strain upon the Communist economies.]Indeed, whether the point of cold-war competition is scientific leadership, international trade, economic development of the underdeveloped countries, propaganda, or whatever, our larger economic base is an advantage upon which we should capitalize far more than we have done up to this time.

It would be a delusion to believe that the Soviet threat will let us continue with "government and business as usual." We do not live any more in a "usual" world.

The Problem of Choice

We face a seemingly endless list of choices. Should we concentrate upon delivering hydrogen bombs to the homeland of the potential aggressor, thus running the risk of a full-fledged, universal nuclear war? If we follow this course, should we use more of our resources for building up civil defense and our capacity to recuperate from disastrous retaliatory blows? Or should we support a military organization geared to react to local and limited aggression by use of conventional forces and nuclear weapons adapted to the attainment of strictly limited objectives?

How much should we spend on increasing the mobility of ground forces? How much on guided and ballistic missiles and their supporting installations? How much for basic research? How much to the improvement of weapons likely to be out of date two or three years from now? How much on submarines? How much on the conquest of outer space?

The implications of these questions are apparent, and many of the choices may have awful consequences. They may seriously affect our future survival. If we shift too large a proportion of our funds from planes to research and development, we may find ourselves at a critical moment without sufficient retaliatory striking power. Prototypes and missiles on the drawing board cannot fight. If we economize excessively on research and development, including basic research, we may discover that the Soviet Union has achieved a technological breakthrough in a weapons system which renders our forces-in-being obsolete. If we are parsimonious about active and civilian air defense, and the "big deterrent" fails to deter, we may have caused the death of millions who might have survived. If we spend so much on air defense or on large conventional surface forces that we cannot provide enough for retaliation, we may have blunted our crucial power of deterrence. If we economize excessively on mobile ground forces and tactical air forces that are able to engage in local wars, we may see Communist rule expand by means of military blackmail or local warfare because we hesitate to unleash an unlimited nuclear war of mutual destruction.

These choices, once made, cannot be quickly changed. They will determine our state of readiness for many years into the future. Throughout the military establishment there is a lead time, often stretching over several years, before decisions on the development of weapons or new fighting units yield new military power ready for immediate use.

It took six years for the B-52 to move from the drawing-board stage to that of combat readiness. It takes a long time, from the initial decision, to man, equip, and train an air-borne division. This lengthy cycle in the production of modern military forces means that many errors in deciding on the size, composition, and equipment of the armed services cannot be quickly retrieved. This holds equally true of measures designed to prepare the United States for withstanding and recovering from unlimited thermonuclear attack.

In making important decisions on defense, errors are likely to be frequent, fateful, and, except over long time spans, irrecoverable. This calls for prudence. We cannot afford to gamble for the sake of economy.

Thus, it can be seen that the making of choices on the division of our national-security dollars are many and hard. That we will err in some of our decisions is obvious. Even with reasonable intelligence in making the decisions, the less we spend on defense the harder will be our choices, the more we will have to rely on our frail capacity to foresee the future. And the fewer will be the contingencies against which we can defend ourselves.

The Health of Our Economy

The United States need not turn itself into a garrison state. But it may have to spend more of its output in order to save itself from disaster in this frighteningly changing world. Since this is unfortunately, but overwhelmingly, the case, we are faced with a serious problem. And this is the main theme of this chapter: How much are we willing to spend for national defense? To this should be added another question: How much can we *afford* to spend?

In determining the size of our defense effort, we will have to distinguish clearly and sharply between the limitations imposed by the amount of our total production that we are *willing* to devote to this purpose and the limitation imposed by the consideration that too heavy a defense burden will weaken our economy—and with it our ability to maintain our security for the long run.

In recent years there have been periods of contraction in defense spending of some magnitude, based primarily on the widely held belief that the so-called "American way of life" has been threatened by economic deterioration within, as well as by aggression from without, and by the belief that a "sound economy" is the first mainstay of defense.

This sharply felt, but vaguely understood, fear may well have acted as a hindrance to making rational decisions by our people and their national leaders. What it has most effectively done is to make apparent the need for a new look at both defense and nondefense programs to see whether we should spend more on the military aspects. As the Research and Policy Committee of the Committee for Economic Development has stated:

> *Preconceptions about the expenditures we can afford, the taxes we can stand, or the debt we can bear should not be allowed to interfere with informed and rational balancing of the gains and losses of enlarged national security programs.*

This raises two important questions: (1) Should we accept a high rate of defense expenditures (and the taxes that go with it), even if this leaves the nation's economy fully intact? (2) Will this high spending (and taxing) undermine the soundness of the economy, even if as patriotic individuals we are willing to assume the tax burden?

If high defense expenditures threaten to sap the strength of the economy, we must take heed; a healthy economy is the major base not only of our defense effort but of the entire American way of life. By a healthy economy is meant one in which saving, investment, and innovation are sufficient to keep up productive growth, with the GNP rising by an annual average of from 3 to 4 per cent. It means, too, generally high employment, without inflation or deflation. And finally, it means the maintenance of an acceptable balance between private and public economic decisions, without unwarranted governmental controls.

If we can finance defense without inflationary methods, we need not—in the absence of war—impose direct governmental controls over the economy to stabilize prices. Such controls are in conflict with our private-enterprise system's major economic objectives of growth and stability. The Committee for Economic Development is convinced that the necessity to choose between defense-occasioned inflation and governmental controls can be avoided by sufficient taxation.

We see no need to be apprehensive about whether or not the American economy can stand the strain of the present budget or even a considerably larger one. The risk that defense spending of from 10 to 15 per cent of the gross national product, or if necessary even more, will ruin the American way of life is slight indeed. It is even less likely that there is some magic number for defense expenditures that, if exceeded, would bring economic disaster; rather, the impairment of growth caused by increasing taxes is a gradually rising one. We have not reached a point at which anxiety over the healthy functioning of the economy demands that defense expenditures be slashed regardless of the dictates of military prudence. *We can afford what we have to afford.*

We will not soon be able to reduce defense expenditures. But, while acknowledging this, we should also realize that if changes in the world situation should make it possible, we should *not* fear that contraction of defense markets inevitably means a depression.

This would mean an increase in private disposable income, and a consequent expansion of private purchasing to offset the decline in defense spending. There is, in fact, no end of desirable private and public uses to which the resources freed by a reduced armament burden could be applied. For example, there is the apparent need and value of expenditures for urban redevelopment and roads, to say nothing of the possibilities for additional investment in education and developmental assistance abroad.

Such an adjustment cannot be carried out without some temporary unemployment and disruption of production. But twice within the past fifteen years—after World War II and after the Korean armistice—it has been shown that the readjustment period need not be long. Such transitional difficulties would be a small price to pay for the permanent increase in living standards that a substantial reduction in the defense burden would make possible.

PART SIX

RESPONSES
TO THE CHALLENGE

INTRODUCTION

However we may assess the march of history in the past decades—whether the yardstick is strategic real estate, technological prowess, or economic preponderance—the verdict is
clear: we have been losing the struggle at an accelerating rate.
Our losses have been all the more tragic because, buoyed by
comforting notions regarding the innate superiority of our
spiritual and material wares, we have failed to appreciate the
full extent of our retreat.

Our wares *are* superior. Once before we tested them on the
battlefield against those of a totalitarian opponent and emerged
victorious. But we confront today an enemy who has mastered
the refinements of the indirect approach and the flanking maneuver. Until he is assured of victory, he is not likely to present
us with the kind of forthright challenge which galvanized us
into action in the past.

What we lack is a national policy which brackets the full
spectrum of challenges and synthesizes the means and weapons
at our command. The following proposals are not offered as
panacea: there is no magic solution to the nettlesome problems
which we face. They are presented here simply to stimulate
thought and generate the kind of discussion on which purposeful policy can be based.

31.   The Premises of American Policy

by Dean G. Acheson

Mr. Acheson served as Secretary of State under President Truman from 1949 to 1953. He has been Undersecretary of the Treasury and Assistant Secretary and Undersecretary of State. Much of his life has been devoted to the service of his country in the military, economic, legal, and diplomatic fields. He received his A.B. from Yale University and his LL.D. from Harvard University.

At the root of many of our difficulties today is our failure to see what is around us. We fail to see the world in perspective because we regard it through eyes which we have inherited from our grandparents and great-grandparents.

Our conceptions are essentially nineteenth-century conceptions. We do not see the world in which we live. The nineteenth century represents normalcy to us. We live almost in a way which proves Bishop Berkeley's theory that reality is subjective, that there is no oak which crashes unheard in a forest to which man has not come.

Yet, the nineteenth century, instead of being normal, was perhaps the most abnormal period through which man has ever lived. It was an unusual century. No century in the annals of human history knew fewer international wars. There was greater freedom of movement, thought, goods, and capital than in all the previous ages of the history of man put together. The world, in a curious way, partly by domination, partly by other means, seemed to be one world. This unity was brought

This selection, which originally appeared in the Fall 1959 issue of Orbis, is based on an address the author gave at the first National Strategy Seminar for Reserve Officers. Reprinted by permission.

about through the Concert of Europe and through the six great empires, European empires, whose dominion stretched over almost the entire globe. Not that these empires controlled every part of the world, but their influence did.

Because we have accepted these unique conditions as norms of international life and because we are really nineteenth-century people, we speak of world organization and absence of conflict as though they were the normal state of international society. We aspire to a state of equilibrium because the nineteenth century had reached such a balance.

The fact is, however, that all of the great empires of the nineteenth century are no more. Some have disappeared altogether. Others are greatly weakened. Others have completely changed their character, as, for example, the Russian Empire. The Austro-Hungarian Empire has disintegrated; Germany as an empire has disappeared; the Ottoman Empire has been erased from the map; Italy has lost her overseas possessions; the French retain only scattered imperial outposts; and the British Empire has transformed itself into a Commonwealth.

Two world wars were conspicuous in this transition from empire. They were not its cause but, rather, its manifestation. A marked trend during the nineteenth century was the steady movement of power eastward—from the time when it took all of Europe to contain France, to a period when it took more than all of Europe twice to contain Germany, and to the present period, when it is at least open to doubt whether all the rest of the world will contain the Sino-Soviet combination. The great problem of the twentieth century is whether a new equilibrium can be brought into being; whether the expansion of the Sino-Soviet bloc can be checked; whether there can be a balance of power.

One of the great questions of our time is the destiny of what we call the uncommitted people—largely the masses of Asia and Africa but also, to a lesser extent, the nations of South America. What will happen to this vast mass of people will strongly determine whether or not there will be an international equilibrium.

Another phenomenon which we fail to see and understand clearly is not merely the industrial revolution through which we have lived but the scientific revolution in which we find ourselves today. We cannot accept the fact that there is nothing superior, nothing very complex, about an industrial civilization. We think that it implies some mystical processes which other people cannot master. This is nonsense. The Russian people, starting with very little, have succeeded in coming, not abreast of the United States, but certainly more than halfway toward matching us in production—and they are bridging the gap rapidly. As a matter of fact, the period of Soviet construction spans only twenty years. The other two decades since the Bolshevik take-over—the ten years after the Revolution and the ten years of World War II and its aftermath—were years of conflict and reconstruction. Twenty years is a very short time in the life of a people. This progress can be achieved by other peoples. It can be accomplished by the Chinese. It can be done by the Africans. It can be done, in short, by all peoples who are capable of learning. Surely it is important whether a country has resources. But the idea that there is in industrial progress something mystical and difficult which only white people can master is an illusion. Thus, there will perforce be ever more profound changes in the world in which we live.

The Requirement of Western Unity

What are the policies which will direct those changes and will direct the efforts of the Free World to maintain an equilibrium to hold in check the movement toward unchallenged power by the Soviet Union and China?

It is quite apparent that the United States alone cannot bring about this equilibrium. In the first place, America does not control enough territory. There must be spaciousness in the environment in which free peoples live. Therefore, it is not enough that the United States be free from domination. There must be no further diminishment of that part of the world which now lies outside the dominion of Russian or Chinese communism.

How is this "spaciousness of freedom" to be guaranteed? Basic to the problem is the will of independent peoples to remain independent. Second, they must have the ability, and therefore the opportunity, to develop in their own way. And, finally, there must be the military strength to protect them and ourselves in this effort.

Effective military strength means inevitably a coalition, or a number of coalitions—a combining of national efforts into greater efforts, directed by a central leadership. No one except the United States is strong enough to exercise this leadership, and sometimes the United States shows neither the desire nor the understanding for this task. Indeed, a key question of the twentieth century is whether the United States can develop this desire and this understanding. If she cannot, then the Sino-Soviet drive for global hegemony will remain unchallenged.

Yet, when we engage in coalitions, we must do so with clearly defined objectives. The most important objective today —indeed the *sine qua non* of Free World survival—is to hold together those sources of strength which we possess. These sources are North America and western Europe—highly industrialized areas capable of a productive output which can be three times that of the Soviet Union and its satellites; of a military effort which can be as great if the will exists; and of effective manpower three times that of the Soviet Union. This equation excludes Chinese manpower. A billion people are not a power factor if they are merely a mass. Only when they become organized and possess the tools of power do they become formidable, and Communist China has not yet reached this level of development.

The Free World, in short, possesses the capacity for bringing about a new equilibrium—provided that its core, western Europe and North America, is maintained intact, that it follows harmonious policies, and that it directs its great capacities toward effecting this equilibrium.

This assertion immediately draws the usual objections: "But you will throw in your lot with the colonial empires. Great new movements are afoot in the world. Don't you see how important it is to sustain American principles in Asia, in Africa, and in South America?"

If we would approach life from the point of view of formal moralistic rules, this caveat may be interesting. But if we approach our problem from the point of view of solving it, then these considerations are not at all important. It is not that we consider the French, or the Germans, or the British more desirable people than the Indians, the Burmese, or the Vietnamese; it is simply that, at the present time, the center of power in the non-Communist world is in North America and western Europe. Once this center is dissolved or fragmented, then the problems of the world, from our point of view, become unmanageable. We may enjoy the most intimate relations with South America and other areas. But these relations will not solve the problem of the balance of power at the present time.

The unity of the Atlantic world has been undermined in recent years by imprudent policies on both sides of the Atlantic. One of these led to the Suez crisis of 1956. Suez was a disaster from every point of view. This was virtually the lowest point in the history of American diplomacy, for we maneuvered ourselves into a position in which we ultimately took the side of our enemies against our friends. This shortsighted policy destroyed Europe's confidence in American leadership, and the healing process has, to date, been far from complete. One of the prescriptions of leadership is that those who are led must believe that the leader has their interests, and not only his own interests, at heart. After the Suez debacle, the belief was widespread in western Europe that American leaders had placed purely American interests above the wider interests of the Atlantic alliance.

But if American policy has, at times, created difficult problems for NATO, its principal allies, France and Great Britain, have also been responsible, on more than one occasion, for cracks in the alliance. They have tended to give priority to national, rather than community, interests.

The United States must meet with her European allies to discuss thoroughly and candidly the problems which are driving all of us apart, with a view to determining whether we cannot modify those divisive policies in the general interest. If the United States will take the lead in this direction, then we can revive in Europe the will to make greater sacrifices for NATO and cement the unity of the Atlantic nations.

Therefore, the first political principle on which we must operate is that the unity of western Europe and of North America is the single most essential factor in the policy of both of those areas.

Many considerations follow from this premise. It follows, for example, that one does not become stronger by becoming weaker—a principle which seems to have been embraced by the advocates of disengagement. Under present circumstances, there can be no effective unity between western Europe and North America if the very military pillar of this relationship, namely NATO's forward position in Europe, is removed. Therefore, if Germany should be neutralized, disarmed, and wrested from the Western alliance, then the dissolution of the alliance is only a question of time, leaving us no place to make our stand except in the United States. And we cannot solve the problems of the world from Fortress America.

Selectivity in Assistance Programs

So much for the basic premise of Free World security. In addition to maintaining the Atlantic alliance, we confront another task: namely, to create an environment in which people who wish to develop will have the opportunity to do so. We must make it possible for them to develop—if for no other reason than they will and must develop in one way or another.

Many of us seem to approach this problem within the conceptual framework of the nineteenth century. They suggest that if uncommitted peoples threaten to go Communist unless given American aid, we should simply tell them: "Go!" This is like a child throwing its toy onto the floor and breaking it because it is told to go to bed.

Uncommitted peoples will not go Communist out of pique; they may go Communist because they choose what seems to them the shortest road to modernization. No longer do they live in the darkness which in the past benevolently shielded from them the magnitude of their plight. They are aware of the outside world.

They know that they no longer must live like Neanderthal man. They know, in short, that progress can be made. There is nothing mystical about development: people can learn—they can learn within a generation. What they need besides learning is capital, and the capital can be obtained either from the West or from the Soviet Union.

The Soviet Union will not strain its economy in order to meet the demands of underdeveloped peoples everywhere. In the foreseeable future she will not enter into a competition with the United States over which side can give the most assistance. But she will put capital into areas the development of which is likely to cause the most trouble in the Free World.

The Communists are pursuing this strategy in Asia today. The economic development of Communist China confronts all of Asia, including India, with a formidable dilemma. If Peiping's "forward leap" should prove successful—and there is no reason to believe that it will not—then India will be under tremendous pressure to achieve a comparable level of development. And, indeed, there is no reason for Indians to believe that in deference to something called democracy they must live on a standard below that of their Chinese neighbors.

People, in short, will turn anywhere, and to any system, for a solution to their economic problems. It is of overriding importance that we be the ones to extend to them this opportunity. We have it in our power to give them the needed help. If, then, the Russians also offer assistance, all to the good. That the Russians are building steel mills in India is not a misfortune. It will be a misfortune, however, if they build all the steel mills in India as well as all the other plants of India's industry.

But the burden of development is too great to be shouldered by the United States, or even by the United States and western Europe. We cannot give assistance "across the board." What we should endeavor to do is to help people who are willing and able to help themselves.

This means selectivity in our assistance programs. We cannot, and should not, for example, try to assist development in countries torn by revolution. One cannot move forward in the midst of an upheaval. We should be understanding of, and sympathetic with, the efforts of troubled countries. But, in extending aid, we should select areas in which it is possible to do something.

It is possible to do something in India, in Brazil, and in other parts of the Western Hemisphere. Let us show that it can be done. Let us create an environment in the Free World in which people can say: "Look, if we just once stop fighting among ourselves, we can raise our standard of living, of health, of food, and of education." This incentive is essential to the growth and vitality of the Free World.

The Requirements of Military Security

The problem of a military forward strategy for the Free World is a more vexing one. How can we, at the present time, design and implement a strategy which can provide the Free World with a sense of security?

At the end of the war, we had the only atomic weapons in the world. We were preoccupied with the comforting thought that possession of these weapons represented the key to security. This concept never was wholly correct. Most of the "facts" upon which the public based its belief in the efficacy of nuclear deterrence were not facts. But the concept had an element of truth which formed the basis of the initial strategy of NATO—namely, a strategy based on the possession of an atomic striking force which can inflict massive damage upon the Soviet Union in the event of a Communist invasion in western Europe and on sufficient forces in Europe to prevent a Communist *coup d'état* or a probing thrust by Soviet or satellite forces.

It was a sensible theory, which contained but one flaw: it could not, and did not, last. As military men in our government had pointed out for a long time, nations of comparable power and techniques will, given equality of will, eventually achieve equality of power. Thus, the Soviet Union put its scientists and espionage agents to work and became a nuclear power.

We waited until the Soviet Union possessed nuclear weapons and then announced the doctrine of complete reliance on them. This decision was the triumph not of intelligence, nor of any military group, nor of any foreign-policy concept, but of the Treasury Department, which does not always represent the highest form of human thought. In 1954, we announced a strategy of massive retaliation, at a time when it was becoming impossible to carry it out. Since that time we have placed more and more reliance on atomic striking power, and weakened more and more the conventional branches of our defense. The result is that we are rapidly getting into the position

where we have not the requisite power to sustain our
positions.

We need not have strayed into our present quandary.
pose, for instance, that instead of the scattered and w
ground forces which NATO holds in being on the central front
western Europe were guarded by the well-equipped and well-
trained army of 30 divisions called for by General Lauris
Norstad. The situation would be entirely different. It is perfectly clear that Mr. Khrushchev has no more desire to provoke
war over Berlin or any other issue than we have. But he will
make every effort to drive us from Europe short of provoking
war.

By making it clear to him that all the available means for
defending ourselves by force will not, or cannot, be used, we
can hardly expect to deter him in this objective. Given the
present inadequacies in our military posture, Khrushchev's
only problem is time, and he is a master of time. Yet we can
upset his timetable if we take the requisite measures.

What are these measures? In the first place, we should continue to look to our atomic strength. It is rather shocking, to
say the least, when our Secretary of Defense tells us that within
three years the Soviet Union will achieve a three-to-one superiority over us in long-range missiles. He seems to derive
comfort from the possibility that our intermediate-range missiles and manned bombers will bridge the power gap. None of
these hopes are comforting, however, if one looks at the situation several years hence. If, by that time, the Russians will
have conquered—as it appears that they will—the problem of
putting missiles on target through intercontinental space and
will have ICBMs in quantity, then a new strategic situation
will have arisen.

This new strategic situation will either be one of Soviet nuclear superiority or, if we put forth all possible efforts under
the very best of circumstances, one of nuclear parity. The implications of a Russian nuclear superiority are clear: the Soviets would gain the power at any time to disarm the United
States and, once the United States is eliminated as a con-
tender, to dictate the terms by which the rest of the world
must live. A Soviet nuclear superiority, in other words, would
be the death knell of the Free World.

et us suppose that we reach a state of nuclear parity.
lear "parity" is not meant nuclear "equality." Equality
mbers is not necessary to parity. Nuclear equality con-
s a condition which is highly unstable—one in which the
ower of destruction lies with the side which strikes the first
blow. Parity, by contrast, describes a situation in which the
nation which strikes first cannot so wipe out the nuclear capacity of the other that it will not receive a blow greater than it
wishes to receive.

Such a situation, once it is reached, will have somber implications for American strategy. All other factors of power remaining the same, we will confront vastly superior Russian
conventional forces. And in the long run, power casts its
shadow before it. In the long run, the Soviets will be able to
impose their will upon all areas within physical reach of the
Red Army.

There is still time to redress this imbalance in East-West
ground forces. Modern science and technology have given us
the means whereby we need not match the 175 ground divisions which the Soviets presumably hold in readiness. It is
quite conceivable that 30 NATO divisions, equipped with
modern weapons, can contain a much larger Soviet invasion
force. They can do this by achieving tactical mobility, by preventing the enemy by scientifically designed obstacles from
striking along a broad front, and by using new weapons to
brake the thrust of a Soviet ground offensive—just as the English archers at Agincourt prevented the French knights from
gaining the momentum which would have enabled them to
break the line of English foot soldiers.

The problem, in short, is not hopeless. The West has it
within its means to muster the forces called for by General
Norstad and to deploy them in such a way as to confront any
Soviet ground probe with the very danger which the Kremlin
wants to avoid—namely, the risk of a nuclear holocaust. If the
West achieves the capacity to contain an invading army with
a smaller and modernly equipped force for a period of, say,
six months, then the Soviets, in contemplating such an attack,
must calculate that tensions will mount to the point where
they cannot be sure that the United States will not strike the

thermonuclear blow. In other words, a situation will be created in which predictability will be impossible.

An effective and credible defense of Europe is not only a military necessity but the *sine qua non* of any prospective settlement of the political problems of the Continent. The transcendent Soviet objective is to drive us from Europe. So long as the Soviet leaders believe that this objective lies within their grasp, for just so long will a conclusive settlement—in Berlin and elsewhere—be impossible. If, on the other hand, the Soviets are brought to realize that in the foreseeable future their aims will be blocked by a comprehensive and flexible defense of western Europe, then the psychological groundwork will be laid for a reduction of armaments and the possible solution of outstanding political problems.

The Chimera of a "Moral" Solution

This, then, is the general picture of the world as it is unfolding in the last half of the twentieth century. It is a disturbing picture. There is a strong tendency to escape from it —to believe that this can somehow be avoided through the United Nations. This is impossible.

When the late Senator Arthur Vandenberg called the General Assembly of the United Nations "the town meeting of the world," he was being poetic. It had none of the qualities of the town meeting. The town meeting was the whole, the entirety of government in New England. The town meeting was to New England what the Curia Regis was to England under the Plantagenet kings. It was all things: legislative, executive, judicial. It was the government. The United Nations has no power, and it will not acquire any power.

The United Nations is as excellent as its Secretary-General, a very wise and sensible man, has said it is, when it acts as an aid to diplomacy. The United Nations, insofar as it believes that by its votes and by its debates it is accomplishing anything, could not be more mistaken. In fact, it can be harmful. Therefore, we cannot look to that organization by itself for a solution to problems. We must look to our own understanding of the problems and to our own will and the will of others to solve them. This is the nature of things.

Another escape from our problems is to call for a new revolution. I remember some earnest people who once came to me, asking me what I thought of a scheme by which one of the great foundations would finance a vast campaign to carry the doctrine of disarmament to the general public. I said: "You need not carry the doctrine of disarmament to the American public. Everybody in the United States is desperately eager to get rid of the burden of armaments. You need to carry this message to the very places which are closed to you, namely, the Soviet Union. If you can enlist people with that same sense of devotion which sustained the Jesuits in Canada in the early days when they carried the Gospel to the Indians risking torture and death, then by all means send them out. But you will not find many graduates of American colleges enrolling in such a crusade."

A realistic vision of what lies ahead can easily be mistaken for cynicism. Yet to look at things as they are is neither cynical nor amoral.

For example, in 1862 President Lincoln received a letter from Horace Greeley in which Greeley queried the President on his attitude toward slavery. President Lincoln replied that he was concerned with the preservation of the Union. If he could preserve the Union by freeing all the slaves, he would free all the slaves. If he could maintain the Union by freeing none of the slaves, he would accept that alternative. And if he could do it by freeing some slaves and leaving others in bondage, he would take that course. In short, his attitude toward slavery would be governed by the exigencies of preserving the Union.

To be sure, there is a moral content in man's action in the international sphere. Yet moral teachings and moral doctrines can be of little guidance, if any, in assessing the substance of international problems. Moral concepts are important insofar as they determine the actions of men. Telling the truth, being loyal to one's friends, being courageous at the risk of suffering harm—these doctrines should govern one's conduct. If they do, not only will one not deceive one's enemies and one's friends but one also will not deceive oneself. This is what matters most in a democracy.

Self-deception is very easy in a democracy. Leaders are tempted to deceive the people because the people themselves want to believe, despite some concrete evidence to the contrary, that this is a good world inhabited by none but men of good will. Such illusion should not be mistaken for morality.

The armed forces have a perfectly clear idea when they speak of the conduct becoming an officer and a gentleman. A gentleman is he whose code of conduct prevails even when common sense urges an easier course. Why do people stand up when it would be easier to give in? Because, as the British say: "It simply is not done." When this axiom guides the conduct of nations, then diplomacy and politics are made of sterner stuff. Then there is hope that democratic peoples, knowing the truth and willing to face it, can solve the problems of the next half century.

32. A Political Offensive against Communism

by David Sarnoff

Brigadier General David Sarnoff, chairman of the board of the Radio Corporation of America, is recognized throughout the world as a pioneer and leading force in the development of radio, television, and electronics. Born in Russia, he was brought to this country when he was nine and shortly thereafter began his business career by selling newspapers. The innumerable awards, service medals, presidential citations, and honorary degrees he has received have been given in recognition of the service he has rendered to the nation in the communications field. General Sarnoff lectured at the first National Strategy Seminar for Reserve Officers.

Political-psychological offensives are not new. They have frequently been employed in wartime to supplement ordinary military action. The United States used them in both world wars. Their purpose has been to soften the enemy's will to resist, to win friends and allies in hostile areas, to drive wedges between belligerent governments and their citizenry.

The democracies are familiar with warmaking in the normal military sense and hence do not hesitate to make huge investments and sacrifices in its name. They do not shrink from the prospect of casualties. All of that seems "natural." But they are startled by proposals for effort and risk of such

This selection consists of excerpts from "Program for a Political Offensive against Communism," a memorandum prepared by the author for President Eisenhower in April 1955. Reprinted by the kind permission of the author.

dimensions in the life-and-death struggle with nonmilitary means. Under these circumstances it has become incumbent upon our leadership to make the country aware that nonmilitary war, or cold war, is also terribly "real"—that the penalty for losing it will be enslavement.

Hot war is always a possibility. It may come through force of circumstances even if no one wants it. Limited, localized wars are also a continuing threat. Indeed, superior physical force-in-being is the indispensable guarantee for effective nonmilitary procedures.

But short of a blunder that ignites the Third World War which nobody wants, the immediate danger is the debilitating, costly, tense war of nerves that is part of the cold war. Because there is no immediate sense of overwhelming menace, no thunder of falling bombs and daily casualty figures, we are apt to think of this period as "peace." But it is nothing of the sort.

The primary threat today is political and psychological. That is the active front on which we are losing and on which, unless we reverse the trend, we shall be defeated. Its effects are spelled out in civil wars in parts of Asia, legal Communist parties of colossal size in some European countries, "nationalist" movements under Communist auspices, "neutralism" and rabid anti-Americanism in many parts of the world—in pressures, that is to say, of every dimension and intensity short of a global shooting war.

Unless we meet this cumulative Communist threat with all the brains and weapons we can mobilize for the purpose, the United States at some point in the future will face the terrifying implications of cold-war defeat. It will be cornered, isolated, subjected to the kind of paralyzing fears that have already weakened the fiber of some technically free nations. We will have bypassed a nuclear war—but at the price of our freedom and independence. We can freeze to death as well as burn to death.

Our Counterstrategy

Logically we have no true alternative but to acknowledge the reality of the cold war and proceed to turn Moscow's favor-

ite weapons against world communism. We have only a choice
between fighting the cold war with maximum concentration
of energy or waiting supinely until we are overwhelmed. Our
political counterstrategy has to be as massive, as intensive, as
flexible as the enemy's. We must meet the cold-war challenge
in our own household and in the rest of the world and carry
the contest behind the iron and bamboo curtains. We must seek
out and exploit the weak spots in the enemy's armor, just as
the Kremlin has been doing to us these thirty-odd years. We
must make our truth as effective as and more productive than
Moscow's lie.

Our political strategy and tactics should be in terms of a
major enterprise, on a scale for victory, with all the inherent
risks and costs. We cannot fight this fight with our left hand,
on the margin of our energies. We have to bring to it resources, personnel, and determination to match the enemy's.
This is a case where, as in a military conflict, insufficient force
may be as fatal as none at all.

If obliged to make tactical retreats, moreover, we must not
bemuse ourselves that they are enduring solutions. To do so
would be to disarm ourselves and open ourselves to new and
bigger blows. This is a principle of particular importance during intervals when negotiations with Moscow or Peiping are
being discussed or are in progress.

The question, in truth, is no longer *whether* we should engage in the cold war. The Soviet drive is forcing us to take
countermeasures in any case. The question, rather, is whether
we should undertake it with a clearheaded determination to
use all means deemed essential, by governments and by private
groups—to win the contest. Our countermeasures and methods
must be novel, unconventional, daring, and flexible. They
must, moreover, be released from the inhibitions of peacetime,
since it is peace only in outer forms.

Almost against our will, in point of fact, we have launched
more and more cold-war activities. But they have been piecemeal, on an inadequate scale, and often without the all-
important continuity of action. Worst of all, they have not been
geared for total victory, being treated as extras, as harassment
operations, while hoping against hope that there will be no

outbreak of war or that there will be a miraculous outbreak of genuine peace.

Our current posture shares the weakness inherent in all defensive strategy. The hope of a real compromise is a dangerous self-delusion. It assumes that Soviet Russia is a conventional country interested in stabilizing the world, when in fact it is the powerhouse of a dynamic world movement which thrives on instability and chaos. Our duty and our best chance for salvation, in the final analysis, is to prosecute the cold war—to the point of victory. To survive in freedom we must win.

The Enemy Is Vulnerable

The Free World, under the impact of Moscow's cold-war victories, has tended to fix attention on Soviet strengths while overlooking or discounting Soviet weaknesses.

The Communists expertly exploit all our internal tensions, injustices, and discontents. Yet within the Soviet empire the tensions are incomparably greater, the injustices and discontents more vast. Our opportunity, which we have failed to use so far, is to exploit these in order to undermine the Kremlin, exacerbate its domestic problems, weaken its sense of destiny.

The nature of a malady can be deduced from the medicine applied. In its fifth decade of absolute power, the Soviet regime is obliged to devote a major portion of its energies, manpower, and resources to keep its own subjects and captive countries under control, through ever larger doses of terror. There we have the proof that the Communists have failed to "sell" their system to their victims. After all discounts are made for wishful thinking and error, ample evidence remains that in the Soviet sphere the West has millions of allies, tens of millions of potential allies.

Whether the potential can be turned into actuality, whether the will to resist can be kept alive and inflamed to explosive intensity, depends in the first place on the policies of the non-Soviet world. Our potential fifth columns are greater by millions than the enemy's. But they have yet to be given cohesion, direction, and the inner motive power of hope and expectation of victory.

Guidelines for Political Offensive

Our guiding objectives in an all-out political offensive are fairly obvious. They must include the following:

1. To keep alive throughout the Soviet empire the spirit of resistance and the hope of eventual freedom and sovereignty. If we allow that hope to expire, the Kremlin will have perpetuated its dominion over its victims.

2. To break the awful sense of isolation in which the internal enemies of the Kremlin live—by making them aware that, like the revolutionists in Czarist times, they have devoted friends and powerful allies beyond their frontiers.

3. To sharpen, by every device we can develop, the fear of their own people that is already chronic in the Kremlin. The less certain the Soviets are of the allegiance of their people, the more they will hesitate to provoke adventures involving the risks of a major showdown.

4. To provide moral and material aid, including trained leadership, to oppositions, undergrounds, resistance movements in satellite nations and China and Russia proper.

5. To make maximum use of the fugitives from the Soviet sphere, millions in the aggregate, now living in free parts of the world.

6. To appeal to the simple personal yearnings of those under the Communist yoke: release from police terror, ownership of small farms and homes, free trade-unions to defend their rights at the job, the right to worship as they please, the right to change residence and to travel, and so forth.

7. To shatter the "wave of the future" aura around communism, displacing the assumption that "communism is inevitable" with a deepening certainty that "the end of communism is inevitable."

8. To inspire millions in the free countries with a feeling of moral dedication to the enlargement of the area of freedom, based on repugnance to slave labor, coerced atheism, purges, and the rest of the Soviet horrors.

This inventory of objectives is necessarily sketchy and incomplete. But it indicates the indispensable direction of the cold-war effort.

The Message of Freedom

We must be quite certain of our destination before we can begin to figure out means of transportation. There is little point in discussing the *how* of it until a firm decision for an all-out political-psychological counteroffensive is reached. In hot war, you need a weapon and means of delivering it to the target. The same is true in cold war. The weapon is the message; after it has been worked out, we can develop the facilities for delivering it to the world at large and to the Communist captive nations in particular. The essence of that message (and its formulation is the critical first step) is that America has decided, irrevocably, to win the cold war; that its ultimate aim is, in concert with all peoples, to cancel out the destructive power of Soviet-based communism.

Once that decision is made, some of the means for implementing it will become self-evident; others will be explored and developed under the impetus of the clear-cut goal. Agreement on the problem must come before agreement on the solution. Adjustment of our thinking in accord with such a decision to win the cold war demands clarity on at least the following points:

1. The struggle by means short of general war is not a preliminary bout but the decisive contest, in which the loser may not have a second chance.

2. It must therefore be carried on with the same focused effort, the same resolute spirit, the same willingness to accept costs and casualties, that a hot war would involve.

3. In order to establish credence and inspire confidence, our conduct must be consistent. Our philosophy of freedom must embrace the whole of mankind; it must not stop short at the frontiers of the Soviet sphere. Only this can give our side a moral grandeur, a revolutionary *élan*, a crusading spirit not only equal to but superior to the other side's.

4. We must learn to regard the Soviet countries as enemy-occupied territory, with the lifting of the occupation as the

over-all purpose of freedom-loving men everywhere. This not only applies to areas captured since the war, but includes Russia itself. Any other policy would turn what should be an anti-Communist alliance into an anti-Russian alliance, forcing the Russians (as Hitler forced them during World War II) to rally around the regime they hate.

5. The fact that the challenge is global must be kept clearly in view. Red guerrillas in Burma, Communists in France or the United States, Red agents in Central America—these are as much "the enemy" as the Kremlin itself.

6. We must realize that world communism is not a tool in the hands of Russia—Russia is a tool in the hands of world communism. Repeatedly Moscow has sacrificed national interests in deference to world-revolutionary needs. This provides opportunities for appeals to Russian patriotism.

7. Though the Soviets want a nuclear war no more than we do, they accept the risk of it in pushing their political offensive. We, too, cannot avoid risks. The greatest risk of all, for us, is to do less than is needed to win the cold war. At worst that would mean defeat by default; and at best, a situation so menacing to the survival of freedom that a hot war may become inevitable.

Toward Cold-War Victory: Organization

An organizational framework for fighting the cold war already exists. It needs to be adjusted and strengthened in line with the expanded scale and intensity of operations.

A Strategy Board for Political Defense, the cold-war equivalent of the Joint Chiefs of Staff on the military side, is suggested. It should function directly under the President, with cabinet status for its head. Top representatives of the State Department, the Defense Department, the Central Intelligence Agency, the U. S. Information Agency, should sit on this board. Liaison on a continuous basis should be maintained with all other agencies which can play a role in the over-all effort.

There will be various operations which the Board would undertake in its own name, with its own facilities. But its primary function should not be operational. It should be to plan, initiate, finance, advise, co-ordinate, and check on operations by other groups and agencies, whether already in existence or created by the Board for specific undertakings.

Financing

On the matter of funds one cannot at this stage offer specific estimates. As a working hypothesis, it is suggested that a specific and more realistic ratio between military and nonmilitary appropriations be worked out: say, an amount equivalent to 5 or 7½ per cent of military-defense appropriations to be granted to the Strategy Board for Political Defense—this, of course, without reducing the military budget and not counting foreign military aid and Point Four types of expenditure.

If the American people and their Congress are made fully aware of the menace we face, of the urgent need for meeting it, and the possibility of doing so by means short of war, they will respond willingly, as they have always done in times of national crisis. They will realize that no investment to win the cold war is exorbitant when measured against the stakes involved and against the costs of the bombing war we seek to head off.

Implementing the Counteroffensive

We must go from defense to attack in meeting the political, ideological, subversive challenge. The implementation of the attack would devolve upon specialists and technicians. In gearing to fight a hot war, we call in military strategists and tacticians. Likewise, we must have specialists to fight a cold war.

This implies, in the first place, the mobilization of hard, knowledgeable anti-Communists who understand the issues and for whom it is not merely a job but a dedication. The specialist in communications is important; but the message to be communicated is even more important.

The main weakness of our efforts to date to talk to the masses —and even more so to the elite groups (Army, intelligentsia, and others)—in the Soviet camp is that we have not always been consistent in what we had to say to them. Our message has been vague and subject to change without notice. As long as we regard Communist rule as permanent, we can have no strong psychological bridges to those who are under its yoke. The only Free World goal that is relevant to them is one that envisages their eventual emancipation.

With the formulation of a message, we will at last have something to say that interests them, not only us, and can devote ourselves to perfecting the means of delivering the message.

Before essaying a breakdown of cold-war methods and techniques, we should recognize that many of them are already being used, and often effectively. Nothing now under way needs to be abandoned. The problem is one of attaining the requisite magnitude, financing, co-ordination, and continuity —all geared to the long-range objectives of the undertaking. The expanded offensive with nonmilitary weapons must be imbued with a new awareness of the great goal and a robust will to reach it.

In all categories the arena of action is the whole globe. Our cold-war targets are not only behind the iron and bamboo curtains but in every nation, the United States included. In the battle for the minds of men, we must reach the Soviet peoples, our allies, and the uncommitted peoples.

The agencies involved will be both official and private. The objectives must aim to achieve dramatic victories as swiftly as possible, as a token of the changed state of affairs. While the Kremlin has suffered some setbacks and defeats, its record in the cold war has been strikingly one of success piled on success. This trend must be reversed, to hearten our friends, dismay the enemy, and confirm the fact that Communist power is a transient and declining phenomenon.

Propaganda

If the weapon is our message, one of its basic elements is propaganda. It is the most familiar element, but we should not underestimate its inherent difficulties. Hot war is destructive: the killing of people, the annihilation of material things. Cold war must be constructive: it must build views, attitudes, loyalties, hopes, ideals, and readiness for sacrifice. In the final check-up it calls for greater skills to affect minds than to destroy bodies.

Propaganda, for maximum effect, must not be an end in itself. It is a preparation for action. Words that are not backed up by deeds, that do not generate deeds, lose their impact. The test is whether they build the morale of friends and undermine the morale of foes.

No means of communication should be ignored: the spoken word and the written word; radio and television; films; balloons and missiles to distribute leaflets; secret printing and mimeographing presses on Soviet-controlled soil; scrawls on walls to give isolated friends a sense of community.

Communist Targets

The Communist sphere must be ringed with both fixed and mobile broadcasting facilities, of a massiveness to overcome jamming. The Voice of America will acquire larger audiences and more concentrated impact under the new approach. Its name, it is suggested, should be expanded to "Voice of America—for Freedom and Peace." This slogan added to the name will, through constant repetition, impress the truth upon receptive ears.

Besides the official voice, we have other voices, such as Radio Free Europe and Radio Liberation. There are other popular democratic voices that should make themselves heard: those of our free labor movement, American war veterans, the churches, youth and women's organizations.

Already there is a minor flow of printed matter across the iron curtain, especially aimed at the Soviet occupation forces. The volume and effectiveness of this effort can be enormously enlarged. Magazines and newspapers which outwardly look like standard Communist matter, but actually are filled with anti-Communist propaganda, have brought results.

A greater hunger for spiritual comfort, for religion, is reported from Soviet Russia and its satellites. Programs of a spiritual and religious character are indicated. They should preach faith in the Divine, abhorrence of Communist godlessness, and resistance to atheism. But in addition they can offer practical advice to the spiritually stranded—for instance, how to observe religious occasions where there are no ordained ministers or priests to officiate.

The enslaved peoples do not have to be sold the idea of freedom; they are already sold on it. The propaganda should wherever possible get down to specifics. It should expose the weaknesses, failures, follies, hypocrisies, and internal tensions of the Red masters; provide proof of the existence of friends and allies both at home and abroad; offer guidance on types of resistance open even to the individual. It should appeal to universal emotions, to love of family, of country, of God, of humanity.

Free World Targets

The fighting front is everywhere. The program of the U. S. Information Agency should be reappraised with a view to improvement and expansion. "The Voice of America—for Freedom and Peace" has tasks to perform in many nations of the Free World second in importance only to those in the unfree world.

Merely to point up the inadequacy of our present effort, consider Finland—a country on the very edge of the Red empire and under the most concentrated Soviet propaganda barrage. Soviet broadcasts beamed to Finland total over forty-three hours weekly. A television station is now being built in Soviet Estonia which will be directed to a million potential viewers in nearby Finland. To maintain their morale under this pressure, the Finnish people, still overwhelmingly pro-West and pro-American, have desperate need of our encouragement. Yet the Voice of America in 1953 was compelled to discontinue its daily half-hour broadcast to Finland to save $50,000 annually.

We need, in every country, newspapers, magazines, radio and TV stations, consciously and effectively supporting our side. Those that exist should be aided materially to increase their range and vitality; others should be started with our help. The strongest individual anti-Communist voices must be provided with better facilities for making themselves heard in their own countries.

Mobile film units are already penetrating backward areas. The operation should be enlarged, its message and appeal perfected. In addition, mobile big-screen television units in black and white and in color can carry our message. Their very novelty will guarantee large and attentive audiences. Vast regions in Asia and elsewhere, where illiteracy bars the written word and lack of radios bars the spoken word, could thus be reached. To quote the Chinese saying: "One picture is worth ten thousand words."

The so-called backward parts of the world, particularly Asia, are under the most concentrated Communist psychological attacks. Of necessity the counteroffensive must take this into account and develop special techniques for reaching both the masses and the elite of those areas.

Use of Facilities in Friendly Countries

Nearly all European and many Asian countries possess broadcasting facilities. We should seek to enlist their use to supplement and intensify American broadcasting on a worldwide scale.

In some cases this could be negotiated on a *quid pro quo* basis where we are providing military or economic aid; in other cases we may have to buy the necessary time for transmitting our message. Our friendly allies, such as Great Britain, have vast short-wave facilities of world-wide scope and range and have the same reasons as we have for seeking to win the cold war. We need their help in this field. We are fully justified in asking for such help and ought to receive it.

Propaganda is a large concept. In a sense it includes and exploits all other activities. Its successful use calls for imagination, ingenuity, continual technical research, and, of course, effective co-ordination with all other operations that bear on the problems of the cold war.

Passive Resistance

Pending the critical periods when active resistance in one or another Soviet country is possible and desirable, full encouragement and support must be given to passive resistance. This refers to the things the individual can do, with minimum risk, to create doubt and confusion in the ranks of the dictatorship, to gum up the machinery of dictatorship government.

The worker in the mine and factory, the farmer, the soldier in the barracks, the office worker, are able to do little things that in their million-fold totality will affect the national economy and the self-confidence of the rulers. It is the method that comes naturally to captive peoples, especially in countries with a long historical experience in opposing tyrants.

Our opportunity is to give the process purposeful direction. In this concept the individual opponent of the regime becomes a "resistance group of one." He receives, by radio and other channels, specific suggestions and instructions. The tiny drops of resistance will not be haphazard, but calculated to achieve planned results.

Special action programs of the type that do not require large organization—or, at most, units of two or three—would be worked out and transmitted. Our sympathizers in the Soviet orbit would feel themselves part of an invisible but huge army of crusaders. Symbols of protest would appear on a million walls. The rulers' morale would be deliberately sapped by a multitude of actions too small, too widespread, to be readily dealt with.

The special value of passive resistance, aside from its direct effects, is that it nurtures the necessary feeling of power and readiness for risk and sacrifice that will be invaluable when the passive stage is transformed into more open opposition.

Organized Resistance

Pockets of guerrilla forces remain in Poland, Hungary, the Baltic States, China, Albania, and other areas. There is always the danger of activating them prematurely. But their existence must be taken into the calculations and, in concert with exiles who know the facts, they must be kept supplied with information, slogans, and new leadership where needed and prudent.

Many of these resistance groups are so isolated that they do not know of each other's existence. The simple realization that they are not alone but part of a scattered network will be invaluable; methods for establishing liaison, for conveying directions, can be developed.

The uprisings in East Germany and Hungary, the strikes and riots in Pilsen, Czechoslovakia, and Poznan, Poland, the dramatic mutinies inside the concentration camps of Vorkuta in the Soviet Arctic, are examples of revolutionary actions that failed. But they attest that insurrection is possible.

We must seek out the weakest links in the Kremlin's chain of power. The country adjudged ripe for a breakaway should receive concentrated study and planning. East Germany is among the weakest links. Its revolt would ignite neighboring Czechoslovakia and Poland. The time to prepare for such actions is now—whether the time to carry them out be in the near or distant future. Meanwhile we must not allow the Soviet propaganda to make unification appear as the Communist's gift to the Germans. It is a natural asset that belongs to West Germany and her allies.

Collaboration with Emigrés and Escapees

Tens of thousands of self-exiled fugitives from Communist oppression emerge eager to plunge into movements for the freeing of their homelands. When they fail to find outlets for their zeal, disillusionment and defeatism set in.

Maximum exploitation of this manpower and moral passion is indicated. They must be drawn into specific, well-organized, well-financed anti-Communist organizations and activities; utilized for propaganda and other operations; enabled, in some cases, to return to their native lands as "sleeper" leaders for future crises.

Officers' corps of émigrés can be formed: perhaps groups of only a score to a hundred, but available for emergency and opportunity occasions. The existence of such nuclei of military power—a fact that will be widely known—should help generate hope and faith among their countrymen back home.

Planned Defection

Escapees have come, and will continue to come, spontaneously, now in trickles, other times in rivers. Beyond that the need is to stimulate defection on a selective basis. Individual "prospects" in Soviet missions and legations, in Red cultural and sports delegations, can be carefully contacted and developed. Types of individuals needed to man cold-war undertakings will be invited to escape, assured of important work. Special approaches can be worked out to encourage defection of border guards, army officers, secret-police personnel disgusted by their bloody chores, scientists, important writers, and others.

Escapees today are often disheartened by their initial experience. They are taken into custody by some foreign intelligence service, pumped for information, and sometimes then left to shift for themselves. Their honest patriotism is offended by the need to co-operate with foreigners before they are psychologically ready for it.

It is suggested that émigré commissions be set up, composed of trusted nationals of the various countries. The fugitive would first be received by the commission of his own countrymen. Only when found desirable and prepared for the step would he be brought into contact with American or British agencies.

Training of Cadres

The immediate and prospective activities of the cold-war offensive will require ever larger contingents of specialized personnel for the many tasks; to provide leadership for resistance operations; to engage in propaganda, subversion, infiltration of the enemy; even to carry on administrative and civic work

desire to belong, to be respectable, is by no means alien to Red officialdom.

3. Economic leverages, too, must be applied. Trade can be turned into a powerful political weapon. The stakes are too high to permit business-as-usual concepts to outweigh the imperatives of the cold war. Where acute distress develops in a Communist country, our readiness to help must be brought to the attention of the people as well as their bosses. If and when food and other relief is offered, it must be under conditions consistent with our objectives—to help the victims, not their rulers.

4. In virtually all countries outside the Communist sphere there are large or small organizations devoted to combating communism, at home or abroad or both. There is little or no contact among such groups—no common currency of basic ideas and slogans, no exchange of experience. Without at this stage attempting to set up a world-wide anti-Communist coalition, or "Freedom International," we should at least facilitate closer liaison and mutual support among anti-Soviet groupings already in existence.

33.   What Is to Be Done?

by Frank Rockwell Barnett

*Mr. Barnett's intense concern with the pres-
ervation of freedom and his abilities as a
speaker have earned him the applause of
military and civilian organizations both here
and abroad. A native of Illinois, he studied
at Wabash College and the universities of
Syracuse, California, Zurich, and—as a
Rhodes Scholar—Oxford. His proposal to re-
cruit a "Legion of Liberation," printed in the
Congressional Record in 1951, induced Congress to appropriate $100,000,000 to form
iron-curtain refugees into military units for
the defense of the Free World. Mr. Barnett
is director of research of the Richardson
Foundation, Inc., and an officer of the Institute for American Strategy. He lectured at
the first National Strategy Seminar for Reserve Officers. It was due largely to his efforts that the seminar was organized and
convened.*

A half century ago, an unemployed lawyer wrote an obscure
little book. It had a limited—almost private—circulation. Its title
had no sex appeal. It was called, very simply, *What Is to Be
Done?*

When the book was published, in 1902, its author was in
exile, living in a dingy boardinghouse. Living frugally on small
subsidies from the political underworld and scorning all the

*This selection is based on the article "Disengagement or Commit-
ment," which appeared in the Winter 1959 issue of* Orbis. *Reprinted
by permission.*

values of his middle-class heritage, this bald, squat lawyer was the self-appointed leader of a handful of other outcasts from society.

To the property owners, statesmen, and generals of the Victorian world, this man and his circle of impractical agitators were "rabble." The power elite of that day ignored his pamphlets and did not read his book. Nor, for the most part, have the property owners, statesmen, and generals of mid-century America.

Yet the man who wrote it and his disciples—exploiting the practical, concrete ideas set forth in *What Is to Be Done?*— have seized two continents and set fire to the others. Today, whole libraries, as well as the graves of twenty nations and 40 million people, bear witness to the deadly political science of a movement whose cumulative conquests now exceed the combined empires of Alexander, Hitler, and Tamerlane—and whose accelerating capability to lay waste the great globe itself must be the touchstone for determining our national and even our private objectives. The lawyer's name, of course, was Lenin.

Nearly six decades removed from the publication of *What Is to Be Done?* Americans who never heard of Vladimir Ulyanov confront the consequences of his mind, will, and fearful talent. Until Lenin, various forms of socialism were quack experiments or futile terrorism in the night. But to Lenin, communism was not simply an idea; it was a power technique. Communism, after Lenin, was more than a philosophy. It was a triumph of organization. Under his tutelage, Communists became "managers"—*conflict managers*. They learned how to integrate and co-ordinate almost every form of human activity to achieve the goals of a heartless Policy Committee.

The position of America in 1960 is, of course, not nearly so hopeless as the plight of Lenin in 1902 or of General Washington in the winter of Valley Forge. But the odds against this republic are far heavier than some may suppose. Because no exploding bombs illuminate the "precinct politics" of Communists in Afro-Asia, too many imagine there is still time to refer the conduct of the battle to another research committee. Because our defeats have been chiefly in the twilight, undeclared war of nerves, propaganda, and trading, no dramatic scoreboard signals the loss of a Free World bishop or the enemy's ambiguous gambit to advance the red queen, fifteen moves hence, to check and mate. Indeed, for amateurs at chess or geopolitics, each move of an opponent seems to present an isolated challenge; the pattern is concealed; the savage end game not even imagined.

The Lead Time of Survival

A struggle for markets, a clash between armies, competition in research and development—these are not static affairs. To the untrained eye, the contest is evenly matched at a particular time and place; yet triumph and disaster have been foreordained by "lead time" in logistics and the laboratory. Although Nazi Germany and Japan seemed to sweep the board in 1942, their fate had been unobtrusively influenced in a laboratory in Chicago and on the production lines of Detroit.

The Chinese Communist fighter pilots who died not long ago, in sky battles over Quemoy, were doubtless brave and skilled airmen. But they were dead airmen when Sidewinder missiles uncoiled from American jets. Technically, those pilots were still "alive" until the missile actually struck; but were they not dead when the release button was pushed, since no courage or wishful thinking on their part could thereafter avert the predetermined end? Were they not, in a sense, already doomed when the blueprints for the Sidewinder were approved for production?

Whole civilizations, as well as a single aircraft, have a point of no return if they permit an opposing society to gain too much lead time in the science of conflict—whether the "war" is hot, cold, economic, political, limited, or all-out. The conflict managers and chess players of Russia have planned on a century of conflict if need be—though they are now arrogantly confident we will not last that long. They do not need to debate their one clear-cut objective; their tactics, rather than their policies, are flexible; and their economy is geared to the cost accounting of the battlefield. And they have gained a "lead time" of more than forty years in the arts of nonmilitary warfare, deception, and the training of professional cadres for ideological combat and subversion.

Our democracy, sensitive to the variable breezes of public opinion and the random tides of pressure groups, improvises "strategy" from one election to another. As free men, we would not dispense with elections or limit debate. But surely, for all our individualism, we can achieve a working consensus on the need to survive—on the obligation to preserve intact, and with its charter of incorporation unchanged in principle, this unique *laboratory* called America—a co-operative research institute where, on a *voluntary* basis, men from all lands join together to conduct experiments in liberty and opportunity. When more Americans become serious students of strategy, there is little doubt that our response will be adequate to the enemy's challenge. But first we must place the problem on the agenda of business groups, universities, and professional societies as well as government.

Students of Strategy

"Strategy" connotes perspective, the selection of the right priorities, relating the parts to the whole. The student of strategy is never so hypnotized by science and sputniks that he ignores the other battle fronts of foreign-language training, propaganda analysis, international trade, and our domestic economic growth. While he evaluates the challenge of Soviet trade, aid, patronage, and manipulation of the markets, he will not, however, ignore the clenching of the Soviet mailed fist —or the jostling of Moscow's political elbow.

If it is true that the U. S. Strategic Air Command cannot— with massive retaliation—prevent Moscow's subtle penetration of Latin-American markets, it is equally true that economic aid to India cannot avert a *coup d'état* and assassination in Iraq. Expanding technical assistance and U.S. business investment in Africa may be vital to our security; it will not, however, avert butchery in Hungary or Tibet. It will not carry the cold war, by nonmilitary means, into the restless, vulnerable empire of the enemy, where the people of eastern Europe and Asia groan under Russian conquistadores and Peiping's cruel dogma of the yellow man's burden.

Economic aid to emerging new nations is important to our

own future as a free people; but, by itself, this assistance will
not blunt the danger of communism. One does not win a nonmilitary war—whose victories thus far have gone to the enemy
—by simply denying that enemy a further series of advances
on Free World soil.

American aid, whether private or governmental, will not offset the Soviet economic thrust unless the managers of U.S.
economic activities are themselves sensitive to ideological, political, and strategic nuances. Random largesse, with no regard
to specific goals or national priorities, may be "humanitarian." It has nothing to do with "strategy" and the science of
conflict management. The best-selling book *The Ugly American* amply illustrates how the Communists have applied
Gresham's Law to international politics—that is, bad propaganda drives out good deeds. To be specific, $1 million worth
of Communist agitation, covert activity, and blackmail can
sometimes offset $100 million worth of American economic aid,
distributed with "no strings attached"—indeed, not even the
strings of requiring prudent management and accounting. Of
course, we need to do more in the economic sphere, both
through government and the private sector; but we need
"strategists" and "conflict managers" of our own to disburse
and co-ordinate those sums to insure better returns for Free
World survival.

Finally, in any discussion of strategy, it is imperative to keep
science and military readiness on the agenda. A nuclear war
over Berlin may be "improbable." But we dare not delude ourselves with the wishful cliché that hydrogen bombs have made
general war "unthinkable." The categories of thought employed by the heirs of Ivan the Terrible and Lenin are not
necessarily the same as those which prevail in the peace-loving
democracies of the West. Stalin cheerfully scorched the Russian earth and sacrificed 25 million countrymen to stop the
Nazis. Hitler was prepared to let all Germany burn in some
mad Wagnerian sacrifice to Thor and Woden. Mao and Chou
En-lai will not blink at the loss of 100 million Chinese, upon
whose broken bodies, in the next decade, they intend to rear
the heavy industry and nuclear armaments of the anthill state.

Khrushchev, who stood at Stalin's side while 3 million
Ukrainians were deliberately starved to death, is not likely to

be more squeamish about liquidating Americans en masse, if he ever has the chance. Let the Russians spend more for basic research; let them shorten the lead time between invention and production. Let Moscow develop some as yet unknown electronic defense against our aircraft and missiles. Let Soviet engineers erect that defense system only six weeks before we have a similar capacity to ward off their rocket-launching submarines and ICBMs. In short, let the Kremlin but once enjoy over us the weapons advantage we once held over them (but did not use) and the world is likely to have another demonstration of how Khrushchev defines "peaceful coexistence." In this country, not even our military leaders talk of preventive war; but Soviet military journals are full of the doctrine of strategic surprise, the use of deception in the nuclear age, and the case for the pre-emptive blow.

Where Our Opportunities Lie

What is to be done? Lenin's question challenges us not only to think but to implement. Some responses to the question can only be made by government. For example, $20 million could be allocated for a special political-warfare fund to organize intensive, persistent propaganda throughout all Afro-Asia against Chinese machine guns in the monasteries of Tibet; or $500 million, if necessary, to form a NATO Board of Economic Warfare to make "flooding the market" bad business for the Kremlin; or $5 billion, if needed, to keep SAC in the air, to give the Army an airlift for limited war, to put missiles on merchant ships or "obsolete" destroyers as a temporary makeshift while the Navy perfects Polaris and builds an invisible armada of nuclear submarines.

But it is in the field of nonmilitary warfare that our greatest opportunities may lie today. Russia is now the last of the great colonial powers. Russian *colons* exploit the people of Soviet Central Asia. Russian colonialists govern the Ukraine, Georgia, the Baltic Republics, and Armenia; their confreres manipulate power in the captive nations of eastern Europe and are active in Korea and China. In all the forums of world opinion—relentlessly and without cessation—Russian colonialism must be exposed, condemned, and used as a psychological-warfare weapon against communism.

Nor should we forget that, conceivably, the Russian power elite itself is divided. We know now that the supposedly monolithic Nazi state was in reality a caldron of intrigue. The SS, Gestapo, Nazi bureaucracy, and German General Staff were at one another's throats. From time to time, we glimpse signs that the same laws of internal contradiction may plague the Sino-Soviet empire. In World War II, Lieutenant General Andrei Vlassov led a Free Russian Army against Moscow. More than 300,000 Ukrainians fought with the Germans. More recently, Beria has been executed, Zhukov demoted, Molotov, Malenkov, and Kaganovich dispatched to the provinces, Bulganin "retired," and General Serov purged. Others may be next. Will Gomulka remain? How does the Red Army really feel about the Secret Police and the Communist Party?

We know now, in the light of history, that Germany had an underground—that members of the German General Staff were in touch with the British Foreign Office prior to World War II. Some of these proud Junker generals would have liked to move against the Nazi upstarts before Munich. But when Mr. Chamberlain went hat in hand to Munich, he served unwittingly to defeat the one compelling argument of the anti-Hitler conspirators—that Hitler's designs on Czechoslovakia would lead the nation into a disastrous war. From the moment Chamberlain bowed to Hitler, the dissident elements in the General Staff were helpless: the Führer was demonstrating to the German people that his policy of bluff was paying dividends. The majority of the Germans were convinced that German hegemony in Europe could be bought without payment of blood or treasure.

The Fourth Weapon: Psychopolitical Forces

The lessons of the past suggest that America must learn the arts of four-dimensional warfare—of conflict by communications and of psychological combat. Subversion might be a hundred times more dangerous to Moscow and Peiping than to Washington and London. But subversion and political warfare require as much professional competence as commanding an aircraft carrier or an infantry division—and, as yet, while we have splendid academies to train young people how to use firepower, there are no training schools in this country which equip Americans to compete with the graduates of Soviet institutes of irregular warfare.

One operational objective might be, therefore, the creation of an American *fourth weapon*, coequal with the Army, Navy, and Air Force. Its purpose would be to offset the current Soviet advantage in nonmilitary weapons systems, which may enable them—under the umbrella of nuclear terror—to seize Asia, the Middle East, and Africa piecemeal by *coups d'état*, precinct politics, fifth columns, and popular fronts. Obviously, in order to wage psychopolitical warfare, we must have an impenetrable shield of science and military power. We must match the Soviets in missiles and air power, in submarines, in capacity to wage limited wars—including guerrilla wars through our own proxies—and finally, in psychosocial combat.

An American "fourth weapon" might consist of the following components and activities:

1. A separate cabinet office with at least the status and budget of the Department of Health, Education, and Welfare. (If we are driven into a thermonuclear corner, where we can only choose either to surrender or to cremate the earth, there will be no health, education, or welfare.)

2. A joint congressional committee on cold-war strategy—to take advantage of the fact that our own practicing, professional politicians have skills which may profitably be employed in the arena of political warfare.

3. An Assistant Secretary for Nonmilitary Defense in the Pentagon.

4. A career service for officers who elect to become specialists in the propaganda and psychological-warfare fields. Too often, the intelligence function in this country has been regarded as "the shelf" by able officers who feel that, in order to win promotion, they must get back to troops and military hardware.

5. The creation of foreign legions composed of Russians, Poles, Hungarians, Koreans, Chinese, Ukrainians, and others who have fled from behind the Iron Curtain. If the Soviets

threaten to send "volunteers" to the Middle East or Indonesia, the Free World should have another string to its bow: namely, the possibility of sending free Russians against Soviet volunteers. This international "captive nations' brigade" would be trained in all the arts and sciences of propaganda and conflict through communications. Part of its mission would be what the mission *might* have been in Korea—if we had used defecting Chinese and North Koreans to promote defections from the enemy on the field of battle.

6. The establishment of what Brigadier General David Sarnoff, in his memorandum of April 1955 to President Eisenhower, called a "West Point of political warfare."

Citizen Experts in Political Warfare

Another operational objective to be achieved, if we are to survive the contest of the next two decades, is the voluntary commitment of private resources to certain aspects of national defense. The Communist Party manifestly can mobilize the total resources of the Soviet empire for the cause of conflict —because the Communist Party has the machinery of *total* government. By definition, our *limited* government cannot, and should not, compete with Moscow in kind. This means, however, that unless trade associations, educational institutions, private foundations, labor unions, and opinion leaders commit a portion of their energies to ideological, economic, and political defense, the Kremlin's total thrust will continue to be unopposed in many vital sectors of nonmilitary and ideological combat. What we need to achieve, therefore, is a new kind of informal partnership in defense between civilian and governmental sectors.

In World War II, the American military developed new forms of teamwork and learned to work successfully in combined operations. Air power, naval gunfire, frogmen, and infantry assault troops all worked together on the beachheads in splendid co-ordination. The combined operations of the cold war require even broader teamwork. They require that diplomats, military attachés, college professors, American businessmen overseas, foreign correspondents, and technicians—to name just a few—all work together informally to undergird national strategy.

In this new kind of war, radio commentators, teachers, and investment bankers are on the front line just as surely as the men who man the missiles and guard our positions overseas. Unfortunately, too few leaders in the private sectors of American life as yet realize that we are at war—and that the survival of Western civilization is at stake. Americans do not like to do their homework in world politics, economics, geography, or history. We refused to read *Mein Kampf;* today we refuse, with equal indifference, to read and study the strategy of Lenin, Stalin, and Khrushchev.

If strategy is now the business of private citizens, as well as government, what is to be done by voluntary action? The ideas which follow are samples of the literally dozens of projects that could be translated into action once private funds and staff were allocated to the prosecution of nonmilitary strategy.

Proposal: A Dynamic History of the American Experiment

There are missionaries for Communist dogma. There are high priests of socialism. Fascism had its philosophers and publicists. There are exponents of "classical economics," disciples of Adam Smith and followers of Lord Keynes. But there are almost no articulate spokesmen for the constantly evolving, dynamic system that is twentieth-century America. Modern capitalism is as different from the monopoly capitalism assailed by Karl Marx as it is from Chinese communism. But American business has no party theoreticians; hence, the enemies of the system monopolize the international networks of communication.

Some American union leaders talk the language of the Fabian Society's discredited efforts to achieve Utopia through nationalization of industry. Some American business leaders— who are learning how to integrate automation, atomic energy, and the behavioral sciences—nevertheless prefer to think in the cherished symbols of nineteenth-century capitalism.

What few have realized is that communism—which is

really a new and brutal form of state capitalism—is obsolete. Socialism has been tried and found wanting in western Europe, Britain, and Australia. Cartel capitalism, which fed the maw of empire, is rightly on its way out. American-style capitalism—which might be called the "private, voluntary welfare state"—could be the wave of the future. It is incredibly productive. It is consumer-oriented rather than government-directed. It concentrates on products that bring an easier life to the masses, rather than on luxury items for the few. And, increasingly, American-style capitalism is not only efficient; it is attentive to social, ethical, and cultural values.

Socialists argue that America is a *political* not an *economic* democracy owing to private ownership and the profit system. Quite to the contrary! America is more of an economic democracy than socialist Sweden or Britain under the Labour Party. In a socialist system, voters cannot appeal the day-to-day decisions of administrators and politicians who make economic decisions. Short of turning the government out at the polls, they must live with arbitrary policies for years on end. In America, every citizen casts economic votes every day—by the choice he makes when he buys one product and declines another, purchases one stock and sells another, changes his occupation, agitates for an increased pension plan, lobbies for or against a tariff, quits his job to start a new business for himself, goes on strike or votes not to go on strike.

Some socialists have represented their model to the world's uncommitted nations as the "moderate third force" which stands midway between reactionary capitalism and the police terror of the Communist empire. This argument will not bear scrutiny. American-style capitalism is itself an *effective* "third force" in the world, but we have not been able to project that image forcefully either to foreign nationals or to some of our own intellectuals and new generations of students.

No one has adequately described the American phenomenon—an ever flexible and self-renewing pattern of self-government characterized by diffusion of power, partnership between Washington and the private sector, voluntary welfare, creative altruism, citizen action, checks and balances, and idealism mixed with practical business and material benefits for almost everyone. Where but in America are there more than 4000 private organizations which labor to solve social, economic, health, and education problems by nongovernmental action? Where do men more earnestly seek to accomplish objectives by persuasion, co-operation, and good will?

What is to be done? Books, unpublished manuscripts, speeches, and journals should be examined to see if a "capitalist manifesto" is already in being—although scattered about in bits and pieces. If so, random articles should be edited into a coherent whole. If not, a scholar—with a flair for popular writing—should be commissioned to do the job. Liaison should be established with college and public school authorities to insure that the finished product will be used in our own educational system. The U. S. Information Agency might be contacted with a view toward giving an inexpensive edition of the book widespread distribution all over the world. Conceivably, new material for this book could be elicited from a number of scholars by offering a sizable prize, similar to the *Atlantic* prize-novel contest.

Proposal: A Propaganda-Analysis Newsletter

There is nowhere any persistent, sophisticated daily effort to analyze Communist propaganda for American audiences and reveal it for what it really is. Owing to the structure of our mass media, statements by Communist political leaders are reported as "news" on the front page. Thus—in a sense— the press, radio, and TV of America give millions of dollars' worth of publicity to Communist propaganda themes.

American leadership must expend half of its energies in debating spurious and irrelevant themes which the Communists put before the courts of world opinion. This is one of the reasons why we seem always to *react* to Communist initiative.

What is to be done? We must see if a group of editors, publishers, columnists, and editorial writers would volunteer to form a committee to refute Communist propaganda. Scholars associated with research groups could prepare a series of papers analyzing persistent Soviet themes and setting forth— in historical perspective—the facts. These scholarly materials could be reduced to a newsletter and mailed out to, say, a

thousand editors and editorial writers. Perhaps some newspapers would even agree to print a brief front-page box en-
titled "The Current Party Line." This could serve as a touchstone for the reader who is bewildered by the gyrations and
seeming "concessions" of Khrushchev and his associates.

Proposal: Business Training for Overseas Community Relations

The Communists have trained, literally, tens of thousands
of professional propagandists and agitators. These cadres are
saturating the Afro-Asian world, the Middle East, and Latin
America. Their job is to create a climate of opinion hostile to
American diplomacy, to American military bases, to American
investments and business opportunities.

American business trains executives for labor relations, industrial relations, and public relations here at home. There is
very little training as yet, however, for the delicate job of
"community relations" in an overseas area that is threatened
by Communist penetration, insurrection, economic pressure,
and *coup d'état*.

What is to be done? In co-operation with a business school,
research institute, or management association, a special seminar should be set up to concentrate on over-all problems of
management in a specific *target area*, including political,
strategic, and community-relations factors that bear both on
national and investment security.

To that seminar would be invited representatives of all corporations and banks with present investments and business in
—or future plans for—Area X (let us say one of the new nations
in Africa, or southeast Asia).

The seminar would include such "normal" components of
a management course as: economic-feasibility reports on Area
X; market-research data; currency-exchange problems; and
training and personnel matters. However, in addition to this,
there would be discussion of: (*a*) Communist objectives,
strategy, and tactics in that part of the world; (*b*) analysis of
leading Soviet propaganda themes and how to refute them;
(*c*) the social responsibilities of modern capitalism—in other

words, practical case studies in how American corporations can be good citizens of a foreign community; and (d) an inventory of Free World institutions that might be helpful in promoting stability in Area X—including: universities which sponsor private technical-assistance programs; private foundations, welfare agencies, church groups, youth clubs, and labor unions with contacts in that area; and trade associations and international professional societies.

Conceivably, this seminar for businessmen might be attended also by a few officials from the Department of State and USIA, plus two or three officers about to be assigned as military attachés in the given area. The object of including some government personnel would be informally to "build a team" —through personal contacts and joint training—that would be better able to cope with the integrated, disciplined cadres dispatched by the Communists to various parts of the world. Joint training at the National War College and the Industrial College of the Armed Forces is building understanding and respect among officers of all the rival services. That principle can be extended to improve co-operation between American businessmen overseas and U. S. Government personnel.

Freedom, in short, rests on economic know-how and political skill as well as military power. The American businessman overseas, the foreign service officer, and the military attaché each have a vital role to play—and, if possible, they should play it more in harmony with one another. The expansion of the private sector overseas and the growth of foreign middle classes can greatly strengthen our diplomatic and military alliances.

An excellent report, "Expanding Private Investment for Free World Economic Growth," prepared in April 1959 under the direction of Ralph I. Straus, has pointed to perhaps the central reason for the success of our private system of enterprise— namely, its adaptability. Throughout the West's economic development from the dawn of the Industrial Revolution, private enterprise has had to adjust to almost every conceivable economic and political situation. In the tremendous diversity which is the so-called underdeveloped world, no single blueprint of central planning can accommodate the gamut of problems which beset societies ranging from the nearly destitute to the nearly developed. Private enterprise can do the job, and do it effectively and dynamically.

But selling this, what Robert L. Garner calls "America's best export," is the responsibility not only of American business. Our government should key its economic-assistance policies to the objective of creating the kind of climate abroad in which free enterprise can take root. Specifically, our policy makers might heed the Straus Report's recommendation that U.S. aid programs increasingly emphasize:

1. Training of foreign teachers and students at American business schools;

2. University contracts whereby American business schools establish programs and assist local institutions abroad to train businessmen;

3. Analogous arrangements for training in public administration, law, and economics bearing on the institutional framework for effective business activity;

4. Programs for establishing local trade, manufacturing, and business-management associations;

5. Practical on-the-job training in industrial plants.

The "Ultimate Weapon"

The rather passive business of conducting seminars, studying strategy, and steeping the mind in the operational techniques of communism may strike some practical men of affairs as a waste of time. Yet effective action does flow from doctrine, doctrine so thoroughly absorbed that it guides the intuition and governs the reflex of statecraft.

The "ultimate weapon," of course, is neither science nor politics nor psychological warfare. The "ultimate weapon" is human courage based on faith in certain unalterable moral laws. Unfortunately, some in our midst have forgotten the true meaning of America. We are already half afraid of the honorable word "revolution," although we are the true revolutionaries. It was an American Revolution that gave the world its finest revolutionary ideal—the notion that government is the servant, not the master, of the people. The Communists—who call us "reactionary"—have turned society back to the days of